THE DICTIONARY OF
FINANCIAL RISK
MANAGEMENT

Gary L. Gastineau

Senior Vice President
American Stock Exchange

and

Mark P. Kritzman

Partner
Windham Capital Management

PUBLISHED BY FRANK J. FABOZZI ASSOCIATES

Gary L. Gastineau
American Stock Exchange
86 Trinity Place
New York, NY 10006-1881
ggastine@amex.com

ISBN: 1-883249-14-7

Printed in the United States of America
1 2 3 4 5 6 7 8 9 0

TABLE OF CONTENTS

PREFACE

Financial risk management is the measurement and the attempt to control trade-offs between risks and rewards in both profit-motivated enterprises and non-profit organizations. The vocabulary of financial risk management is the heart of the language of finance. Financial activities have grown more complex in recent years, and the terminology used by financial managers reflects that complexity.

This dictionary is designed for professional financial analysts and managers. It does not attempt to compete with such general reference works as the *Barron's Dictionary of Finance and Investment Terms* or *The Encyclopedia of Banking and Finance*. The present volume defines and describes many financial terms and concepts that these reference works do not attempt to cover, but it does not list many of the basic terms and concepts a financial analyst learns in introductory courses in finance or in daily experience in financial markets. The principal criterion for inclusion in this volume is that a word or phrase be something that a working finance professional might want to look up.

We list the vocabulary a sophisticated reader might encounter for the first time in an article in an academic finance journal. We include terms an analyst might encounter when reading the work of a fellow analyst who uses a different set of quantitative tools. We include extensive listings and profit/loss diagrams of new (or newly named) financial instruments. Common acronyms are enclosed in parentheses and printed in a bold font with each definition. We *do not* include the specialized terminology a securities analyst will encounter in covering companies in a specific industry.

There is heavy coverage of derivatives, new products, and quantitative techniques that a finance professional might not have come across in his or her formal education, or in a CFA or CPA review course. The listing cannot be complete even within these boundaries; for, as Samuel Johnson said in the preface to his own dictionary, "...no dictionary of a living tongue ever can be perfect, since while it is hastening to publication, some words are budding, and some falling away."

Our purpose was not to produce the world's most comprehensive dictionary, but one that will be particularly useful to the working financial analyst and financial manager. Like Dr. Johnson, we have no illusions: "Every author may aspire to praise; the lexicographer can only hope to escape reproach, and even this negative recompense has been granted to very few."

We encourage users of this dictionary to reproach us freely if they feel a definition is inadequate, inaccurate, or absent. We want to make any future versions more useful.

Gary L. Gastineau
Mark P. Kritzman

ACKNOWLEDGMENTS

I n the spring of 1992—shortly after I joined Swiss Bank Corporation to prepare financial risk management research material for customers—the great Chicago flood shut down Swiss Bank's offices in the Board of Trade building, forcing me to work at a trading desk in New York.

While there are advantages to an active trading environment, maintaining a high degree of concentration on analysis and writing is not one of them. I had planned to assemble a dictionary of financial risk management terminology eventually, but my limited attention span on the trading floor was more compatible with writing definitions one paragraph at a time than with more complex research projects.

Once the first draft of the dictionary was completed, my colleagues at Swiss Bank were helpful and supportive in checking definitions for accuracy, suggesting additional terms and, in some cases, mentioning new topics that should be examined. I received extensive help and support from Perry Beaumont, Prescott Beighley, David Dubendorfer, Arash Farmanfarmaian, Gerald Herman, Phillip Nehro, David Purcell, Glenn Satty, Sebastian Steib, Joseph Troccolo, and Eric Weinstein.

Additional suggestions and criticisms from Charles Baubonis, Rolf Böni, Edward Chambliss, Thomas Curran, Steven Depp, Jeffrey Diehl, Keith Fishe, Michael Gorham, Thomas Hickey, Gordon Holterman, Claire Leaman, Suzanne Martin-Reay, Satish Nandapurkar, Michael Reveley, Barry Seeman, Sam Serisier, Jim Singh, Christophe Trefalt, and David Weiner are also gratefully acknowledged.

On the production side, Albert Gerra and Masatsugu Takahashi were helpful in establishing the basis for the first edition's graphics. Elizabeth Thompson prepared and edited the text and the graphs for the first edition with extraordinary skill and patience.

As holder of the copyright on the first edition, Swiss Bank has granted permission to incorporate the original definitions in new hard copy and electronic editions—in recognition of the fact that the vocabulary of financial risk management continues to grow.

There are three major new contributors to this edition. Coauthor Mark Kritzman's definitions of terms used on the quantitative side of finance help round out the lexicon. Many readers will find his additions to the breadth of coverage extremely useful. Don Rich contributed an unusually large number of new terms and helped Mark and me define them. His insights into the mathematical tools of finance have been invaluable. My associate, Margaret Shergalis, has taken on the production and graphics responsibilities with skill and enthusiasm. She has taken full advantage of the advances in desktop graphics technology and has helped knit together the numerous cross references. Others who have checked part or all of the revised manuscript for accuracy, contributed new terminology, or provided other assistance include James Angel, Michael Bickford, Don Chance, George Chow, David DeRosa, Ognian Enchev, Frank Fabozzi, Stephen Figlewski, Jack Clark Francis, David Helson, Ira Kawaller, Robert Kopprasch, Sandra Lee Kurecki, Robert Loffredo, Richard Mikaliunas, Philip Nekro, Phil Rivett, Charles Smithson, and Joseph Stefanelli.

I would also like to acknowledge the kind and useful comments of many reviewers and readers who have called to suggest additional terms for inclusion and to point out the inevitable errors that creep into any work of this nature. Particular thanks are due to John F. Marshall, Executive Director, International Association of Financial Engineers and Professor of Financial Engineering, Polytechnic University for his support and encouragement.

Gary L. Gastineau

THE ESSENTIALS OF FINANCIAL RISK MANAGEMENT[1]

"New financial instruments are not created simply because someone on Wall Street believes that it would be "fun" to introduce an instrument with more "bells and whistles" than existing instruments. The demand for new instruments is driven by the needs of borrowers and investors based on their asset/liability management situation, regulatory constraints (if any), financial accounting considerations, and tax considerations."[2]

— Frank J. Fabozzi and Franco Modigliani

Many of the derivatives disaster news stories of 1994 and 1995 seem to take issue with Fabozzi and Modigliani's comments. Some financial instruments may have been bought and sold for "fun" (or profit) and with limited regard for the sensible reasons advanced in the quotation.

Criticisms of financial markets and instruments may include complaints about sales practices, accusations of speculation by managers whose mandate is to reduce risk, predictions of systemic meltdown of markets, and laments over the complexity of many new instruments and techniques. Some of these criticisms are justified, but correctable. Others, specifically the forecasts of market meltdown and complaints over complexity, are generally off the mark.

We leave the sales practice and speculation issues to others. The facts of each case of inappropriate use or inappropriate instruments will be decided by negotiation between the parties, by regulators, or by the courts. While we avoid comment on the highly specific problems encountered by a handful of financial market participants, we can provide plenty of comfort in these introductory comments that the financial system is not at risk. Furthermore, one of the primary purposes of this volume is to take some of the mystery and complexity out of financial markets and instruments. On both these points, much confusion clears when an observer remembers that the principal applications of most financial instruments are the funding and risk management of an enterprise.

We attempt to distinguish among various kinds of risk and discuss how they affect the soundness of the financial system. We also explain how financial intermediaries provide financial risk management products and services to a variety of institutional investors, corporations, and governments around the world—without necessarily taking on risk themselves.

The risk transfer process is far simpler than much recent commentary suggests. The market risks that financial intermediaries exchange can be broken into basic components, which are readily understandable and manageable. Some non-market risks are more difficult to manage. The lat-

---

[1] An earlier version of this essay introduced the first edition of the *Dictionary of Financial Risk Management*. Variations have appeared in many publications, including the *Financial Analysts Journal*, September/October 1993. The present version was updated for this new edition.

[2] F.J. Fabozzi and F. Modigliani, *Capital Markets—Institutions and Instruments* (Englewood Cliffs, NJ: Prentice-Hall, 1992), p. xxi.

ter are an appropriate topic for public policy debate and political or regulatory resolution. The policy issues are clear, and, given appropriate political will, can be resolved—with an attendant improvement in public confidence in financial markets and institutions.

Shifting Price or Rate Risk

The market risks that financial intermediaries reallocate are price, interest rate, and currency exchange rate risks. Price and rate risks come in a variety of flavors, but all markets share two features:

1. Any movement in a price or rate will be undesirable to some market participants. The popular name for exposure to an undesirable market movement is *market risk*.
2. One person's risk is usually someone else's potential reward. By exchanging packages of risks and rewards, both parties to a risk management transaction can be better off.

To draw an illustration from a prototypical price risk environment, consider a new issue of common stock from the viewpoints of three key market participants:

- the corporate *issuer* that sells the new stock into the marketplace,
- the asset manager or *investor* who buys the stock on the initial offering or in the secondary market, and
- the *market maker* who trades the stock in the secondary market as the needs of asset managers and investors change over time.

The figure illustrates each market participant's notion of risk. Each is exposed to financial loss—accounting loss or opportunity loss—but each views the possibility of loss from a different perspective.

Starting our examination of risk with the market maker, we find a classic risk position. He is exposed to any large price change. Nothing could make him happier than a regular alternation of buyers who take his offer and sellers who hit his bid. However, by posting a continuous bid and offer, the market maker exposes himself to potential loss if the stock

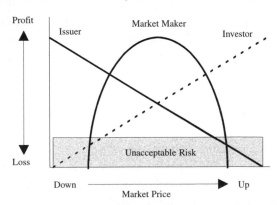

Market Risk—The Viewpoints of Three Participants

price moves very far in either direction. If the market falls, the market maker will be called upon to buy more stock, and his inventory will decline in value. If the price of the stock rises, the market maker will be called upon to deplete his inventory of stock. With a reduced inventory, the market maker's participation in the rally will be limited. He might even sell stock short to meet market demand. As a short-seller, the market maker will face out-of-pocket losses in a market advance. The market maker's position is disadvantageous—risky—if prices fall or rise sharply.

The stock's issuer and the investors who hold the stock in portfolios view risk from very different perspectives. Each views risk from only one side of the market. The issuing corporation views risk as exposure to a rising market. If the corporation had waited to issue the stock until after the market rise, it could have obtained the same amount of cash for fewer shares. For the issuer, risk is a stock price that rises after it sells stock. If the stock price falls tomorrow, the issuer's sale of the stock today will appear fortuitous.

The asset manager or investor who buys stock as a portfolio investment sees risk as the possibility of a stock price decline. If prices drop tomorrow, the investor will wish she had waited to buy. Of course, a stock price that rises after purchase is a favorable development for the investor.

In this simplified picture of the stock market, participants have no obvious way to trade some return potential for a reduction in risk. In the real world, risk management products and services provided by options and futures exchanges and by financial intermediaries can help to reduce risks.

Many market participants are willing to trade some of their opportunity to profit from favorable price behavior for protection against an adverse price move. The essential role of options and futures markets and financial intermediaries is to help asset and liability managers—investors and issuers—modify risks and rewards so that some or all of the effects of price movements are transferred to others. Actual or opportunity losses often cause more pain than an equivalent profit causes pleasure. Consequently, many market participants are willing to give up sizable profit opportunities in exchange for protection from risk. This normal, human aversion to risk creates the market for financial risk management products and services.

In the stock market or in virtually any other price or rate risk situation, combinations of swaps, options, forward or futures contracts, and traditional financial instruments can reallocate participation in price or rate movements in a variety of ways. When a single market or market sector is integrated with financial instruments and markets around the world, the opportunities for risk and return reallocation become extremely complex. However, the basic principle behind all financial risk management is the exchange of one set of risks and rewards for another set that fits a market participant's utility preferences more closely.

The essential characteristic of all financial management is the modification of the natural risk/reward position of an issuer, an investor, a market maker, a bank, a public treasury, or a nonfinancial corporation. The manager evaluates instruments and measures their ability to neutralize unwanted risks or enhance returns. The outcome of this process should be a financial structure that reflects the preferences of the organization's constituents.

The Risk Management Process

The most complicated risk management structure can be broken down into components that any high school graduate should be able to understand thoroughly. Ph.D.s with various specialties—the "rocket scientists" described in the press—play an important role in financial risk management. Nonetheless, a Ph.D. is not necessary to understand any single aspect of financial risk or to evaluate the overall effectiveness of risk control.

In our simplified stock market example, options can help the issuer trade some of the possible opportunity gain from a falling stock price for protection from the opportunity loss associated with a rising stock price. Correspondingly, the investor can use options to exchange some of her upside potential for downside protection. Convertible bonds and some equity offerings like preference equity redemption cumulative stock (PERCS) have risk-reallocating option provisions embedded in the security itself. The market maker can buy options for protection from large price movements in either direction.

If price or rate risk were the only kind of risk, there would be no controversy over the market in risk management agreements of any kind. After all, consenting adults are simply exchanging cash flows, and they expect these exchanges to improve or protect their financial well-being.

When customized risk management contracts transfer financial risks from one party to another, the process often leads to the mistaken view that these instruments are used exclusively to reduce some specific risk element, and that the financial intermediary who creates the product or facilitates the risk exchange is acting as a reservoir for risk absorption. Actually, the creator of the product is primarily a provider of liquidity. The financial intermediary typically disaggregates, repackages, and redistributes risks and their corresponding rewards to other market participants.

For example, one contract may insulate a pension or profit-sharing plan from a downside stock market move. Another contract may transfer equivalent stock market exposure to an investor who expects substantial cash inflows in the near future, and who wants immediate participation in stock prices. The intermediary who handles the transfer is not taking *any* increased stock price risk.

The financial intermediary who sells risk management products is the ultimate risk manager, but not the ultimate risk-taker. In addition to managing risk balanced "books" in one or a variety of markets, the financial intermediary is sharply attuned to the credit of counterparties (in cases where credit is a significant issue). Cash securities markets and exchange-traded option and futures contracts are used extensively by the providers of liquidity to manage the risks of their customer positions. The financial intermediary—by linking specific customer needs through cash markets and exchange-traded and OTC derivatives—provides liquidity to international capital markets.

Liquidity Risks

Our stock market example assumes that the market maker was prepared to make a market, and our discussion of risk management has implicitly assumed that appropriate financial instruments can be traded. In reality, not all packages of risks and rewards are freely or actively traded. Many financial markets are characterized by extreme illiquidity. Examples of illiquid markets include real estate, small-capitalization stocks, and a variety of debt contracts between financial institutions and consumers (including accounts receivable, credit card debt, and auto loans).

Financial market innovations have sharply reduced many liquidity risks in recent years. Real estate investment trusts, publicly traded limited partnerships, and several other vehicles have made modest steps toward improving liquidity in real estate markets. Small-capitalization stocks have some way to go before acceptable liquidity is achieved, but exchange-traded contracts like the S&P midcap SPDRs, options, and futures are a small step in the right direction.

Probably the greatest achievement in improving the liquidity of financial instruments has come in the area of securitization. Credit card debt, automobile paper, and consumer loans have joined mortgages as prime candidates for securitization. A bank or other loan originator is no longer committed to holding these instruments for the life of the loan. They can be traded in securitized form as easily as any traditional security. Government affiliates such as Ginnie Mae, Fannie Mae, and Freddie Mac have played essential roles in mortgage securitization, but most of the steps taken to improve liquidity have occurred at the initiation of private market practitioners searching for liquidity or trying to earn a profit by providing it. Fortunately, most market structures and regulations have been sufficiently flexible to permit the introduction of new securitized instruments.

The phenomenon of securitization illustrates what market forces can accomplish in an environment that permits innovation. However, innovation has not yet eliminated market price discontinuities, a particularly severe liquidity problem.

Market Price Discontinuities

The classic market of economic theory is a call auction market where all market participants meet in one place at one time to arrive at a market clearing price through open outcry of bids and offers. In agricultural societies, these markets were often held annually, at harvest time, but the development of futures contracts has spread commodities trading over the year. Financial markets have traditionally been open each business day. As volume in many markets has grown, efficient continuous markets—some operating on a twenty-four-hour basis— have become the norm in currencies and in a few widely held securities.

Implicit in many naive risk management calculations is the doubtful assumption that most markets are continuous from one trade to the next, with only gradual price changes. The October 1987 stock market break was a dramatic challenge to the assumption of market continuity.

In general, market forces have dealt effectively with the reallocation of price and rate risk and have provided liquidity through securitization and the allocation of capital to market making. Market forces have not yet dealt adequately with the risk of market discontinuities. Ironically, the mechanism for dealing with this problem is in place—the option market.

Anyone willing to accept downside discontinuity risk can sell a put option. Unfortunately, regulation of securities option position limits often restricts the number of exchange-traded option contracts any market participant can buy or sell. As a result, large investors who want to buy or sell protection against market discontinuities are denied meaningful access to the exchange-traded option markets. Listed option markets, in turn, often lack depth because of the virtual absence of large investors. The thinness of the option market denies all investors opportunities to use options to build automatic risk adjustments into their portfolios at a reasonable cost.

Financial intermediaries have provided some help in bringing the providers of this specialized form of liquidity to buyers who value it highly, but an intermediary's role is limited if both sides of the discontinuity risk exchange are not accessible. Financial intermediaries are not in the business of betting their companies on the proposition that October '87 will never happen again. So-called dynamic hedging, or replication of option risk and return patterns with futures and cash market trades, may occur on the margin, but major financial intermediaries serve by redistributing financial risk, not by absorbing it. Until position limits and other restrictions on the widespread use of option markets are eliminated, market discontinuities will be an unnecessarily large short-term risk to the stability of the financial system.

Credit or Counterparty Risk

Some of the concern regulators and the financial press have expressed over the state of the market in risk management instruments has centered on the issue of credit or counterparty risk. Credit evaluation will never be an exact science. However, appropriate price or rate discounts and premiums that reflect differences in credit quality can adjust for reasonable differences in credit risk exposure.

Financial intermediaries closely scrutinize the credit risk element in a risk management agreement, because most intermediaries have experienced sizable credit losses in recent years. The credit exposure of a risk management agreement depends on the type of contract and on the underlying markets, as well as on the credit status of the counterparty. In most instances, credit issues are manageable if both parties are imaginative and the incentive for undertaking the risk management agreement is strong enough.

To encourage financial and non-financial parties to enter into risk transfer agreements that improve market liquidity, public policy often helps counterparties to reduce unnecessary credit risks. Netting arrangements and collateralization agreements made in good faith are often protected in the event of a counterparty's subsequent financial distress. One justification for this policy is that an appropriate risk transfer agreement can alleviate or even prevent distress. The growth of netting and collateralization have combined to reduce concern over credit issues to a manageable level.

Some regulations applied to hybrid derivatives contracts and some bankruptcy policies create credit and counterparty problems where none need exist. Clearing up confusion and eliminating inappropriate regulation will require an internationally coordinated effort. As an example of movement in the right direction, U.S. bankruptcy law reform has sharply reduced many credit and counterparty risks when U.S. law applies. The U.S. example and competition from the U.S. has pushed the U.K. government in a similar direction.

Legal and Regulatory Risk

Legal and regulatory risk is one of the greatest obstacles to effective functioning of the market in risk management instruments. In the notorious case of *Hazell v. The Council of the London Borough of Hammersmith and Fulham and Others*, the House of Lords held that, as a matter of public law, entering into swap transactions was beyond the legal capacity of the local government counterparty. This case is the kind of financial land mine that reduces the efficiency of the market in risk management products, and endangers the financial structure. The solution is to clarify the legal and regulatory framework so that parties to risk management agreements need not fear similar events in the future.

Such events impose a "tax" on the financial system, which is reflected in wider trading spreads and in a reluctance to trade with some parties that need to transfer risks. Financial intermediaries can manage market risks, but they cannot protect themselves from legal and regulatory risks except by declining to trade.

Another extremely important legal and regulatory "tax" is the cost of keeping the financial system afloat. Major financial firms rarely create public distress when they fail. Their problem positions arc transferred to a stronger competitor or divided among several firms. The cost of their breakup and absorption is spread among former competitors and major creditors. Often, customers outside the financial industry are protected at the expense of the financial industry's survivors.

The demise of much of the savings and loan industry in the U.S. is an example of a problem too large to be absorbed by the remaining companies in the financial industry. The S&L crisis was essentially caused by a regulatory and incentive structure that created a moral hazard: The system rewarded management handsomely if it took huge risks that paid off, and protected depositors from loss if management's high-risk business strategies failed. Depositors had no incentive to limit management's risk-taking. Some simple changes in the regulatory structure could have prevented a large part of this fiasco. Unfortunately, the legal and regulatory framework changes slowly.

Partly in response to the S&L example and partly in response to widely expressed concerns, risk management transactions have become a popular subject for study. A sound financial intermediary should not be reluctant to meet with groups studying markets or to face any other open-minded inquiry. Broad and deep knowledge of these markets is the world financial structure's best protection from groups that articulate their conclusions before they ask questions.

Suitability Risk

In the aftermath of the derivatives disaster stories of 1994 and 1995, a corollary to legal and regulatory risk—suitability risk—has been an item of some concern. The key issue is what responsibility, if any, a dealer in financial instruments has for the decision of a customer to take positions that expose the customer to inappropriate risks. Brokers and dealers have long had responsibility in many markets for the suitability of what they sell to individual investors, but there have been few special rules other than obvious (but important) prohibitions against fraud to protect institutional investors. Any rule that goes beyond a reiteration of the law on fraud will probably increase a dealer's costs and reduce market efficiency. The customer will ultimately pay for any suitability protection imposed from outside the market itself.

Tax Risk

The S&L situation is not the only case where risk reduction and effective risk management have been discouraged by government policy. In the *Arkansas Best* case, the U.S. Supreme Court affirmed an Internal Revenue Service position that certain losses on risk-reducing (hedging) positions were capital losses, and hence could not be offset against ordinary income. This ruling generated very little incremental tax revenue, but it encouraged corporations to retain risks they would lay off in a tax-neutral environment. A Fannie Mae tax court decision eliminated some of the tax problems caused by *Arkansas Best*, but other tax issues remain in the U.S. and elsewhere. Recent tax policy proposals from the Clinton administration to eliminate use of short-against-the-box hedging techniques and to increase taxes on certain intercorporate dividend payments serve to increase tax uncertainty and risk management complexity.

Accounting Risk

The Securities and Exchange Commission's opposition to matching unrealized or partially realized risk management gains and losses for accounting purposes creates uncertainty about the financial reporting impact of risk management solutions that make economic sense. In the U.S., and to a lesser extent in other countries, sensible risk management policies often conflict with results reported on a corporation's tax return, income statement, or balance sheet. No simple solution to this problem is imminent. Tentative proposals from the Financial Accounting Standards Board (FASB) that would essentially eliminate traditional hedge accounting without a reasonable replacement or an effective mark-to-market alternative will increase apparent earnings instability with little relationship to any change in real economic performance. The FASB continues to wrestle with this issue.

A variant of accounting risk is disclosure risk. While disclosure is generally desirable, U.S.

companies are under pressure to disclose many details of their risk positions and risk management activities. Too much disclosure of specific risk management positions that must be rolled forward can encourage other market participants to trade against a company's disclosed position. SEC derivatives disclosure proposals place too much emphasis on the structure of a position and too little emphasis on its function. In their search for a workable solution, the FASB and the SEC need to revisit the thorny issue of marking liabilities as well as assets to market. Some of the most important developments in risk management in the late 1990s will come in accounting and disclosure.

Improving Settlements

The most important improvements in systemic risk reduction since the 1992 edition of this book have been enhanced credit risk management through improved collateralization and netting and the reduction of settlement risk. Securities and futures clearing houses and central banks have been the leading proponents of shorter settlement periods and new systems to reduce settlement exposure, particularly in stock and currency markets.

The greatest systemic risk in the 1987 market crash in the U.S. was not the direct impact of market losses, it was the risk that trades made before and during the decline would not settle five business days later and that funds transfers (which took an additional day) would not occur. In 1995, following the recommendation of a G-30 study that predated the crash, the settlement interval for stock transactions was reduced to three business days. The adoption of same day funds settlement (SDFS) in early 1996 eliminated the extra day for funds transfers. SEC Chairman Arthur Levitt now advocates same day settlement for stock transactions by the end of the century.

Cross-border fund transfers (currency settlements) have been the object of many efforts to streamline procedures and reduce credit exposures. Two major multilateral currency payment netting and settlement systems are in advanced planning/start-up stages. The level of attention given to currency settlement risks suggests that the remaining problems will be solved. Within a few years, settlement risk should cease to be an issue in mature financial markets.

Conclusion

The central bankers' and clearing houses' efforts on settlements—and progress on payment netting and collateralization—must extend to securities regulation, accounting rules, and tax policy. The SEC, the CFTC, the IRS, and their counterparts in other countries often send conflicting signals. The SEC has played a major role in shortening the stock settlement period from a week to three business days, but its accounting and option policies are far from progressive. The IRS ruling that excluded swaps and other notional principal contracts used by tax-exempt institutions from the unrelated business income tax removed an important obstacle to effective financial risk management by pension funds and endowments. At the same time, the Fannie Mae decision does not eliminate all tax obstacles to effective risk management by taxable entities.

It is unfair and unnecessary to assign blame for weaknesses in the global financial structure to the regulatory agencies, the legislature, or the executive branch of any government. It is both fair and reasonable to expect their help in making improvements. The world's central bankers are moving toward system risk reduction with settlement procedure improvements that risk managers and financial intermediaries cannot achieve on their own initiative. The central bankers' example is a model for others.

It is common to address concerns for the stability of the financial system by emphasizing strict capital requirements and increased capital charges for certain banking and securities transactions. Capital adequacy is certainly important, but no amount of capital can substitute for intelligent management of a firm's business risks in a legal and regulatory framework free of unnecessary hazards. Even the best capital rules create inappropriate behavioral incentives as they oversimplify risk analysis to standardize capital charges. Capital rules are no substitute for a thorough understanding—by both managements and regulators— of the risk characteristics of diverse transactions.

The only viable legal and regulatory framework for financial markets is a system that rewards intelligent decisions with profit, encourages constructive innovation, and discourages risk-taking for its own sake. Capital requirements play a role in ensuring the integrity of the market, but rigid proscriptions stifle innovation. Improving the clarity and rationality of commercial, bankruptcy, and tax codes to give the parties to financial contracts a clear picture of their non-market risks will do more than stricter capital rules to remove unnecessary risks from the global financial structure.

THE DICTIONARY OF FINANCIAL RISK MANAGEMENT

A/B Structure: A two-tranche liability position consisting of senior (A) and subordinated (B) securitized loans. *Also called Junior/Senior Structure.*

À la Criée: *Fr., Swiss.* Open outcry.

Abandonment: (1) *Swiss.* Withdrawal from a cancellable forward contract to purchase securities. *See Premium Business.* (2) Used infrequently as a reference to letting an option expire unexercised.

Abschlay: *Ger.* Discount.

Absolute Call Privilege: The right of an issuer to redeem a bond at any time without any preconditions.

Absolute Market Risk: *See Market Risk.*

Absolute Priority Rule (APR): A provision of many bankruptcy systems that senior creditors are fully compensated before junior creditors receive anything, and that junior creditors are fully compensated before sharcholders receive anything. In practice, lower-ranking creditors and shareholders often receive something as compensation for expediting the settlement process. *See Cram-Down Rules.*

Absolute Rate: The fixed interest rate of a swap expressed as a percentage return rather than as a premium or discount to a reference rate such as LIBOR. *Also called Absolute Swap Yield.*

Absolute Risk: (1) A measure of interest rate risk usually expressed as the loss associated with a 100 basis point (1.0%) parallel shift in the yield curve. *See Curve Risk, Spread Risk, Loss Limit.* (2) The volatility of an asset's absolute return as opposed to its return relative to a benchmark. *See also Relative Risk.*

Absolute Swap Yield: The fixed rate in an interest rate swap expressed as a percentage rate. *Also called Absolute Rate.*

Accelerated Cost Recovery System (ACRS): A reference to tax provisions governing the rate of depreciation of assets. Essentially a 150% or 200% declining balance system, depending on the expected useful life of various categories of assets. Modified ACRS (MACRS) is the current version in use in the U.S. *Also called Accelerated Depreciation.*

Accelerated Depreciation: *See Accelerated Cost Recovery System (ACRS).*

Acceleration Covenant: A provision of a debt instrument or swap agreement that requires early payment and termination in the event of default or credit downgrade.

Accounting Risk: Potential for loss or for stimulation of pathological management actions resulting from inappropriate signals given by an accounting or financial reporting requirement. *See Accounting Risk discussion, pp. 7-8.*

Accounting Standards Board (ASB): The (separate) organizations with the primary responsibility for setting accounting standards in the United Kingdom and Canada. Each organization is analogous to the Financial Accounting Standards Board (FASB) in the U.S.

Accounts Payable Turnover Ratio: Cost of goods sold divided by accounts payable.

Accounts Receivable Turnover Ratio: Sales divided by accounts receivable.

Accredited Investor: An individual or institutional investor who meets the requirements under the Securities Act of 1933 for purchase of securities in a private placement transaction.

Accreting Principal Swap (APS): In contrast to a traditional swap, where the notional principal amount is fixed for the life of the swap, and an amortizing swap, where the notional principal declines as a mortgage or other loan is repaid, an accreting swap has a growing notional principal amount. Applications might include a situation in which a fixed-rate payer has growing working capital requirements. *Also called Accumulation Swap, Appreciating Swap, Construction Loan Swap, Drawdown Swap, Escalating Swap or Escalating Principal Swap, Staged Drawdown Swap, Step-Up Swap (2), Tailored Swap and, occasionally, Accrual Swap (2). See also Swap.*

Accretion Bond Index Range Note: *See Index Range Note.*

Accretion-Directed (AD) Bond: A collateralized mortgage obligation that pays principal from specified accretions of accrual or Z bonds. An AD bond may, in addition, receive principal from the collateral paydowns.

Accrual Bond: *See Z Bond.*

Accrual Note: *See Index Range Note.*

Accrual Swap: (1) A swap in which interest is earned and paid on one side under circumstances determined by the level or range of some index rate. The payment might be comparable to the coupon on an index range note. (2) An accreting principal or accumulation swap (increasing principal). *See Accreting Principal Swap (APS).* (3) A zero-coupon swap.

Accrued Interest: The current value of the earned portion of the next coupon payment due on a bond or note.

Accumulated Benefit Obligation (ABO): An actuarial estimate of the aggregate amount to be paid to retirees and present employees assuming immediate termination of a pension plan. *See also Projected Benefit Obligation (PBO).*

Accumulation Swap: *See Accreting Principal Swap (APS).*

Acid Test Ratio: (Current assets minus inventories) divided by current liabilities. *Also called Quick Ratio.*

Act of God Bond: Any of several types of bonds issued by an insurance company with principal, interest or both linked to the company's losses from disasters. Losses exceeding a designated size would change interest payments, delay principal repayments or otherwise change the debtor/creditor relationship.

Action: *Fr.* A share of stock.

Active Manager: A portfolio manager who takes an active role in security selection and risk management in an attempt to improve a portfolio's risk-adjusted return or reduce an issuer's cost of capital. *Contrast with Passive Manager.*

Actual Rate Swap: *See Zero Basis Risk (Zebra) Swap.*

Actuals: Physical commodities, typically those underlying agricultural and industrial commodity futures contracts. The comparable expression and concept in financial markets is the underlying cash market instrument, rate, or index.

Actuarial Rate: The rate of return assumed by a pension plan actuary in calculating liability coverage and coverage gaps. *Also called Assumed Rate of Return.*

Actuary: A certified professional who applies probability and statistics to the calculation of insurance premiums, pension fund contributions, and insurance and pension plan liabilities.

Add-On: A percentage of the notional value of a loan, a security, an OTC derivative contract, or some other position charged to a financial institution's regulatory capital. The procedure called for under the Basle Accord is to multiply the notional value of the contract by a factor for interest rate contracts with a remaining life of more than one year, and add that amount to the current credit exposure. The add-ons for foreign exchange contracts, equities, and commodities are much larger than the add-ons for interest rate contracts. The Basle procedures are a very crude approximation of potential credit exposure. Many sophisticated risk management systems use considerably more complex methods to estimate potential credit exposure. A popular approach in these systems is to measure credit exposure two or three standard deviation intervals away from the mean interest rate or currency exchange rate. *See also Basle Convergence Agreement, Value At Risk (VAR) (2).*

Add-On Yield: Standard yield calculation for Eurodollars and many other money market instruments: annualized interest divided by original principal and expressed as a percent. *See also Discount Yield.*

Adjustable Long-Term Puttable Securities (ALPS): *See Dual Currency Bond.*

Adjustable-Rate Convertible Debt: (1) A convertible bond with no conversion premium and a coupon equivalent to or linked to the dividend on the underlying common stock. This structure is designed to make dividend equivalents deductible by the issuer. The Internal Revenue Service has held that the coupon on such instruments is paid from after-tax income. (2) A convertible bond or note with a variable (floating-rate) coupon set by reference to a standard index rate (e.g., LIBOR).

Adjustable-Rate Instrument: Any of a wide variety of fixed principal obligations whose periodic payout is set relative to a reference index rate (such as LIBOR) to create a longer-term fixed principal obligation with a floating-rate interim cost. *Also called Adjustable-Rate Note. See, for example, Adjustable-Rate Preferred Stock (ARPS), Floating-Rate Note (FRN).*

Adjustable-Rate Mortgage (ARM): A mortgage agreement with interest costs tied to a short- or intermediate-term interest rate index such as rates on U.S. Treasury bills or notes. Rate adjustments are made at intervals and the premium over the index rate may vary over the term of the mortgage. *Also called Variable-Rate Mortgage, Floating-Rate Mortgage.*

Adjustable-Rate Note: *See Floating-Rate Note (FRN), Adjustable-Rate Instrument.*

Adjustable-Rate Preferred Stock (ARPS): Floating-rate preferred stock with a dividend rate reset based, for example, on the maximum of a series of short- and long-term rates plus or minus a designated spread. Designed to permit U.S. corporate investors to take advantage of the 70% intercorporate dividend exclusion. *Also called Cumulative Auction Market Preferred Stock (CAMPS), Dutch Auction Rate Transferable Securities (DARTS) Preferred Stock. See Adjustable-Rate Instrument, Auction Rate Preferred Stock (ARPS), Remarketed Preferred Stock, Single Point Adjustable-Rate Stock (SPARS), Variable Cumulative Preferred Stock.*

Adjustable Tender Securities: *See Puttable Notes.*

Adjusted Duration: *See Modified Duration. See also Option-Adjusted Duration.*

Adjusted Futures Price: The equivalent of the underlying cash market instrument price that is reflected in the current futures price. The-adjusted futures price calculation should also take into account any net cost or benefit of carry and any conversion factor for the specific underlying financial instrument to be delivered.

Adjusted Strike Price or Adjusted Exercise Price: When any capital change affects the shares subject to a stock option, the strike price and the number of shares subject to option are adjusted to reflect the change. For example, if a stock is split 3 for 2, and the original strike price of an option is $60, the adjusted strike price is $40, and the option becomes an option on 150 shares of the split stock. Strike price adjustments are uncommon in interest rate and currency option markets. *See Strike.*

Adjustment Swap: *See Off-Market Coupon Swap.*

Administrative Law: Regulatory decisions that take place outside the judicial process—under the aegis of regulatory agencies as opposed to formal court proceedings. Administrative law is subject to modification or reversal in the judicial system.

Admitted Assets: The assets of an insurance company stated as the values recognized and permitted by insurance regulators.

Advance Contract: A forward contract.

Advance Corporation Tax (ACT): A tax paid by U.K. companies on the dividends they pay. The ACT is subject to recapture by certain shareholders. It complicates the withholding tax picture in the U.K. and provides a modest additional incentive for some cross-border traders in U.K. equity securities and indexes to use derivatives.

Advance Decline Ratio: The number of issues in a market or index that has risen in price divided by the number of issues suffering price declines. Measured for a single market session or cumulatively for a fixed number of sessions. Often cited as a measure of market sentiment or tone.

Advance Guarantee: A call option.

Advance Pricing Agreement: A private tax ruling from two countries' tax agencies on how the earnings from a financial transaction or series of transactions will be allocated between the countries for tax purposes. *See Transfer Pricing.*

Advance Refunding: (1) Sale of new bonds in advance of the maturity or call of an old issue to assure continuous funding. (2) Offering of new bonds to holders of maturing bonds in advance of the maturity of the old bonds.

Adverse Selection: An unfavorable change in the composition of a group, usually in response to an economic incentive. For example, the withdrawal of healthy individuals from a group life or health insurance risk pool to buy cheaper individual policies. The reduced group is adversely selected, and will pay higher premiums if the insurer is alert to the problem. If the insurer is not aware of the adverse selection, the policy will be sold on the basis of false signals from the buyer(s). Similar adverse selections occur in credit risk management.

Adverse Selection Premium: The increased charge for an insurance policy or similar contract resulting from adverse selection in the risk pool. If the insurer is unsure of the presence of adverse selection and suspects the quality of the information it receives, it may increase the premium as a protective measure.

After-Acquired Clause: A provision of a mortgage bond indenture that permits issuance of additional bonds subject to the same mortgage. Limitations usually include a maximum additional issuance equal to a specific percentage of the value of assets acquired after the original issue.

After-Market: The market for a security after an initial public offering. The after-market or secondary market may be over-the-counter or on an exchange. *See also Secondary Market.*

Against Actuals (AA): *See Exchange of Futures for Physicals (EFP).*

Agency Costs: In a corporate context, the tendency for managers to make decisions that may be in their own interest but not in the interest of shareholders or consistent with the risks bondholders accepted when they purchased their stake in the company. A corporate aircraft or resort property might be useful to management, but not in shareholders' interest. A risky "bet-the-company" business strategy might be appropriate for managers and shareholders if it is the only chance to save their jobs and investments, but its failure will be borne by bondholders. *See also Moral Hazard.*

Agency Relationship: In securities markets, a broker may act as an agent and charge a commission for finding a trading counterparty. In contrast to dealer or principal relationships, an agent does not trade with a customer for the agent's own account.

Aggregate Exercise Price: The exercise or strike price of an option contract multiplied by the number of units of the underlying security or instrument covered by the option contract. For example, a bond option with a strike price of 101 ($1,010 per bond) covering 1,000 bonds would have an aggregate exercise price of 1,010 times 1,000, or $1,010,000.

Aggregation: *See Netting Agreement.*

Agio: *Swiss, Fr.* A bond's market value premium over par, expressed as a percent. For example, if the bond is at 101, its agio is 1%. Agio reflects market price increases after the offering. *See also Disagio.*

Agioteur: *Fr.* Speculator.

Agreement Corporation: *See Edge Act Corporation.*

Agreement Value: The market value of a swap, based on the cost to reestablish the swap position in the current market environment. The market value is determined by reference to previously agreed sources of price or swap rate quotations.

Algorithm: A formula or set of rules used to solve a problem. The algorithm usually simplifies a real world relationship. Dividend discount models are common algorithms for the valuation of common stock. The Black-Scholes and binomial option models and the cost-of-carry model for pricing forward and futures contracts are algorithms widely used to price derivatives contracts.

All-In Cost: (1) The total implementation cost of a transaction or instrument, including interest, spreads, commissions, fees, etc. Often expressed as a percentage of face or as an annual percentage rate. (2) In an interest rate swap, the all-in cost is expressed as the value of a single period fixed-rate payment as a percent of the notional principal amount.

All-In Premium: *Brit.* The warrant premium expressed as a percentage of the current price of the underlying. *See Premium (2).*

All-Ordinaries Share Price Riskless Index Notes (ASPRINs): Low- or zero-coupon equity index-linked notes with a specified percentage participation in the Australian All-Ordinaries stock index and minimum redemption at par. *See Equity-Linked Note (ELN) (diagrams).*

All-Or-Nothing Option: *See Binary Option.*

Alligator Spread: Another name for a butterfly spread. This name suggests that the commissions and bid-ask spreads associated with the position will eat you alive. *Also called Sandwich Spread. See Butterfly Spread (diagram).*

Allotment: In a securities offering, the quantity of securities allocated to a syndicate member or selling group dealer—or to the ultimate investor.

Alpha (α): (1) The net risk-adjusted premium return from a position or a portfolio. Calculated by subtracting (a) the risk-adjusted return consistent with the position or portfolio's place on the capital asset pricing model (CAPM) security market line from (b) the actual return. Alpha can also be negative if the position falls below the security market line. (2) The average non-systematic deviation from any performance benchmark. *Also called Jensen Measure.* (3) The intercept of a regression line. (4) The largest, most active stocks traded on the London Stock Exchange. The other tiers are beta (β), gamma (γ), and delta (δ). *See also beta (β), gamma (γ), delta (Δ).*

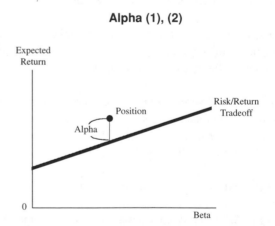

Alpha (1), (2)

Alphabet Stock: *See Target Stock.*

Alternative Currency Option: A currency option that, if exercised, settles in any one of two or more currencies at the election of the optionholder. Each currency has its own strike rate and the holder chooses the currency with the greatest option value at the time of exercise. *See also Alternative Option (diagram), Dual Currency Bond, Dual Currency Option. Compare to Outperformance Option (diagram).*

Alternative Minimum Tax (AMT): A tax calculation made as a supplement to the standard income tax calculation for individuals and corporations in the U.S. It is designed to insure that wealthy individuals and successful corporations pay a minimum percentage of their income in taxes in spite of any tax shelters or tax-exempt investments they may have.

Alternative Option: A put or call option on the best or worst return of two or more securities or indexes during a designated measurement period. *Compare to Outperformance Option (diagram). Also called Best-Of Option, Worst-Of Option, Better-Of-Two-Assets Option, Worst-Of-Two-Assets Option, Either-Or Option, Specialty Option, Min Max Option, Multi-Asset Option, Multifactor Option. See Rainbow Option. See also Alternative Currency Option.*

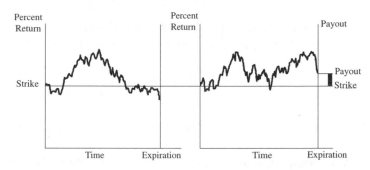

The Payout Pattern of an "A" versus "B" Alternative or Best-Of Option

American Depositary Receipts (ADRs): Certificates traded in U.S. markets representing an interest in shares of a foreign company. ADRs were created to make it possible for foreign issuers to meet U.S. security registration requirements, and to facilitate dividend collection by dollar-based investors. Some ADRs sold in the U.S. under Section 144a exemptions are not readily resellable to all U.S. investors; but most ADRs are nearly as freely traded in the U.S. as domestic issues. *See also Depositary Receipt, Global Depositary Receipts (GDRs).*

American Exchange Rate Quotation Convention: In currency markets, the practice of quoting exchange relationships in terms of the number of dollars per unit of the foreign currency—as in dollars per deutschemark, dollars per pound sterling, etc. *See also European Exchange Rate Quotation Convention.*

American Option: A put or call that can be exercised at any time prior to expiration. Most listed stock options, including those on European exchanges, are American-style options. Important exceptions are certain low strike price options and/or options on shares with restricted transferability. Most listed options on other instruments are also American-style options, but a number of European-style options have been introduced in recent years, particularly on stock indexes and currencies. The labels, European and American, come from a 1965 warrant article by Nobel Laureate Paul Samuelson. *See also Modified American Option, European Option, Japanese Option, Bermuda Option, Quasi-American Option, Deferred Payment American Option.*

American Window: A modified American-style option with an exercise interval at the end of the option's life that permits exercise at any time within that exercise period or "window." One of many variants that falls between European- and American-style exercise. *See Bermuda Option.*

Americus Trust: Sponsor of a technique to separate certain common stocks into a five-year warrant and a five-year covered call warrant writer's position at relatively low cost. No Americus Trust instruments have been created since 1987, largely because of an adverse change in a tax ruling. Although the last Americus Trust instruments terminated in 1992, the Americus Trust principle of decomposing a stream of returns has been widely incorporated in other derivative instruments. *See Buy-Write Option UNitary DerivativeS (BOUNDS), Preference Equity Redemption Cumulative Stock (PERCS), Prescribed Right to Income and Maximum Equity (PRIME) (diagram), Special Claim on Residual Equity (SCORE) (diagram), Termination Claim.*

Amortization: (1) A broad term incorporating any non-cash charge to earnings and/or asset values, such as depreciation, depletion, write-offs of intangibles, prepaid expenses, and deferred charges. (2) A decline in a number such as the notional or face value of a contract or, less frequently, a rate. *See, for example, Index Amortizing Note.*

Amortizing Cap: An interest rate cap with individual caplets covering declining notional principal amounts. This structure usually reflects repayment of principal on an underlying instrument.

Amortizing Collar: An interest rate collar that covers declining notional principal amounts. This structure usually reflects repayment of principal on an underlying instrument.

Amortizing Instrument: Any financial instrument with a declining notional principal or with repayments of principal on a predetermined or contingent schedule prior to ultimate maturity.

Amortizing Interest Rate Swap: *See Index Amortizing Swap.*

Amortizing Option: An interest rate or swap option (swaption) that covers declining notional principal amounts. This structure usually reflects repayment of principal on an underlying instrument.

Amortizing Swap: An interest rate swap with a declining notional principal amount reflecting the principal amortization of an underlying fixed- or floating-rate instrument. If the actual amortization schedules of the swap and the underlying are not set at identical levels in advance (as in a mortgage obligation), the fixed-rate receiver faces significant prepayment or extension risk. *See Index Amortizing Swap, Indexed Principal Swap (IPS), Interest Rate Swap, Tailored Swap.*

Amount at Risk: (1) In a swap agreement, the present value of a replacement swap. (2) Some risk management techniques, such as value at risk, adopt a convention that the amount at risk is the 95% or 99% probable loss limit for a fixed time period.

Analytic: (1) An equation, or set of equations, usually embodied in a computer program, that performs specific calculations too complicated to perform routinely by hand or with a pocket calculator. (2) A problem-solving approach that relies on equations rather than trial and error.

Analytic Model: A model whose solution can be determined by solving an equation or set of equations, as opposed to the use of numeric methods.

Anchoring: Use of irrelevant information as a reference point when estimating some unknown value.

Annualization: Translation or conversion of data or a rate calculation for part of a year or more than a year into an annual equivalent amount or rate.

Annuity: A periodic payment of a fixed or variable amount arising from a contractual obligation. The number of payments or the time over which payments extend may be fixed or contingent on an event (e.g., a human life, in the case of an insurance annuity).

Annuity Bond or Note: A fixed-rate instrument that pays the investor an equal amount of cash each year over the life of the issue. Individual payments contain increasing amounts of principal, and, correspondingly, declining amounts of interest.

Annuity Swap: (1) A currency swap with an exchange of coupons or interest payments only. (2) A variety of amortizing swap.

Anomaly: An unexplained or unexpected price or rate relationship that seems to offer an opportunity for an arbitrage-type profit, although not typically without risk. Examples include the tendency of small stocks to outperform large stocks, of stocks with low price-to-book value ratios to outperform stocks with high price-to-book value ratios, and of discount currency forward contracts to outperform premium currency forward contracts.

Anti-Crash Warrant: Call-type index warrant with a strike price equal to the lower of the index level at issuance or the index level at a predetermined future date, typically a few months into the life of the warrant. *Also called Partial Lookback Warrant or Option, Step-Down Option or Warrant. See Reset Option or Warrant (diagram).*

Anticipatory Hedge: (1) A long hedging position taken to provide participation in a market before an investor is ready to take a position in the related cash instruments or actuals. *Also called Long Hedge.* (2) A short equivalent position taken to protect against a decline when tax or other considerations force a delay in the sale of the related long position.

Antidilution Clause: A provision of a convertible security that provides for adjustment of the conversion ratio in the event of stock dividends or stock splits, and sometimes in the event of a sale of stock below market value.

Antithetic Variate Technique: A variance reduction technique used in conjunction with a numeric method such as a Monte Carlo simulation to improve an estimate of a derivative's price when a limited number of sample paths are estimated. This procedure estimates two values for the price of a derivative instrument, one thought to exceed the true value and one thought to fall below the true value. The two estimates are averaged to arrive at a final estimate of the price.

Application: *Fr.* A prearranged block trade within the current bid-asked range on the Paris Bourse.

Appraisal: Formal act of evaluation of an asset.

Appraisal Ratio: A measure of portfolio management skill that is computed as (1) a portfolio's incremental return relative to a benchmark, divided by its incremental risk, or (2) alpha divided by non-systematic risk.

Appreciating Swap: *See Accreting Principal Swap (APS).*

Appropriate Person: *See Eligible Swap Participant.*

Arbitrage: (1) Technically, the action of purchasing a commodity or security in one market for immediate sale in another market (deterministic arbitrage). (2) Popular usage has expanded the meaning to include any attempt to buy a relatively underpriced item and sell a similar, relatively overpriced item, expecting to profit when the prices resume a more appropriate theoretical or historical relationship (statistical arbitrage). (3) In trading options, convertible securities, and futures, arbitrage techniques can be applied whenever a strategy involves buying and selling packages of related instruments. (4) Risk arbitrage applies the principles of risk offset to mergers and other major corporate developments. The risk offsetting position(s) do not insulate the investor from certain event risks (such as termination of a merger agreement or the risk of delay in the completion of a transaction), so the arbitrage is incomplete. (5) Tax arbitrage transactions are undertaken to share the benefit of differential tax rates or circumstances of two or more parties to a transaction. (6) Regulatory arbitrage transactions are designed to provide indirect access to a market where one party is denied direct access by law or regulation. (7) Swap-driven arbitrage transactions are motivated by the comparative advantages that swap counterparties enjoy in different debt and currency markets. For example, one counterparty may borrow relatively cheaper in the intermediate- or long-term U.S. dollar market, while the other may have a comparative advantage in floating-rate sterling. A cross-currency swap can improve both of their positions. *See also Covered Interest Arbitrage, Index Arbitrage, Event Arbitrage.*

Arbitrage Bond: Usually a municipal bond that, by design or as a result of project delay or cancellation, faces loss of its tax-exempt status because too much of its proceeds are invested in U.S. Treasuries or other taxable debt instruments. *See also Zero Basis Risk (ZEBRA) Swap.*

Arbitrage Free: No arbitrage opportunities exist. An arbitrage-free environment requires complete markets. *See Complete Market.*

Arbitrage Pricing Theory (APT): A model of financial instrument and portfolio behavior based on the proposition that if the returns of a portfolio of assets can be described by a factor structure or model, then the expected return of each asset in the portfolio can be described by a linear combination of the factors. The factors can be statistical artifacts; market or industry related; or macroeconomic variables such as interest rates, inflation, industrial production, etc. The resulting factor model can be used to create portfolios that track a market index, to estimate and monitor the risk of an asset allocation strategy, or to estimate the likely response of a portfolio to economic developments. Starting from an initial model proposed by Stephen Ross, APT models have been created for applications in most cash and derivatives markets. *See Multifactor Model.*

Arithmetic Average: The probability-weighted sum of a set of values. For example, the arithmetic average of a 10% rate of return that has a 60% chance of occurring, and a 20% rate of return that has a 40% chance of occurring, is 14%. *Also called Mean. See also Expected Return.*

Arithmetic Brownian Motion (ABM): The stochastic process that results from continuous compounding of the return of a random variable that follows geometric Brownian motion. *See also Brownian Motion, Geometric Brownian Motion.*

Arizona Stock Exchange: An electronic call market for common stocks used primarily by institutional investors.

***Arkansas Best v. Commission*, 485 U.S. 212 (1988):** A tax case where the U.S. Supreme Court upheld an IRS position that some types of hedging transactions result in capital rather than ordinary losses. This decision complicated many taxable entities' risk management procedures, because capital losses are not fully deductible against ordinary income for U.S. taxpayers. A later case involving the Federal National Mortgage Association (Fannie Mae) largely offset the adverse impact of the *Arkansas Best* precedent.

Arrangement Fee: A commission-like charge paid to a brokerage firm or other intermediary for its role in initiating or implementing a transaction.

Arrearage: (1) Unpaid dividends that must be paid to holders of cumulative preferred stock before common stock dividends can be paid. (2) Any other past due obligation.

Arrears Swap: *See In-Arrears Swap (diagram), Reset Swap.*

Arrow-Debreu Security: An instrument with a fixed payout of one unit in a specified state and no payout in other states. *Also called State Contingent Claim, Supershare Option. See also Span.*

Artificial Neural Network: A simplified model of the human nervous system, exhibiting abilities such as learning, generalization, and abstraction. An analyst who is familiar with a problem selects inputs and outputs. The artificial neural network assigns weights to the inputs and the functional form of the relationships between the inputs and outputs. A genetic algorithm is then applied to screen for success, allowing the best weighting schemes to survive to subsequent generations.

As-You-Like Warrant: A warrant with a provision permitting the purchaser to designate it as either a call warrant or a put warrant for a limited period after the offering date. In general, the option to treat the instrument as a put warrant is of relatively little value. The underlying must decline substantially before a put will be worth more than the initial value of the call. *Also called Call Or Put (COP), Chooser Option, You Choose Warrant.*

Asian Option: *See Average Price or Rate Option (APO, ARO) (diagrams).*

Asked Price: Price at which an instrument is offered for sale.

Asset Allocation: (1) Dividing investment funds among markets to achieve diversification or a combination of expected return and risk consistent with the investor's objectives. (2) A value-oriented investment strategy that attempts to take long positions in markets or market sectors where prices appear to be low and to reduce positions, or take short positions in markets or market sectors where prices appear to be high. Tactical (TAA) or strategic (SAA) asset allocation advocates and value-seeking portfolio managers often use similar techniques and policies. In contrast to momentum investors who accentuate market trends, most asset allocators' trades tend to offset destabilizing market movements and counteract price and rate fluctuations. The asset allocator tends to buy when prices decline and sell when prices rise. *For contrast see Momentum Investor. See also Dynamic Asset Allocation, Tactical Asset Allocation (TAA), Strategic Asset Allocation (SAA).*

Asset-Backed Commercial Paper (ABCP): A technique for securitizing receivables and similar assets that might have served as collateral for a bank loan or been sold to a factor in an earlier generation. Now banks earn fees for monitoring the collateral and packaging the commercial paper program. *See also Loan Participation.*

Asset-Backed Security (ABS): A financial instrument collateralized by one or more types of assets, including real property, mortgages, receivables, etc. No connection with flat tummies. *For example, see Certificate of Amortizing Revolving Debts (CARDs), Certificate of Automobile Receivables (CARs).*

Asset-Based Swap: Usually refers to an interest rate swap agreement where the fixed-rate payer holds a bond whose coupon rate is reflected in the swap terms. The expression may also describe any swap initiated by the holder of an asset that generates the payment stream on one side of the swap. If the fixed rate reflects the coupon on a specific bond, there may be a one-time principal payment at the beginning of the swap to show that the coupon on the designated asset is different from the swap rate for the term of the swap. Depending on the swap terms, the credit risk of the underlying asset can be

Asset-Based Swap

Underlying Fixed-Rate Asset

(basic instrument underlying the asset swap)

Coupon or return stream from the underlying asset

Fixed Rate

Payer/Investor

(payer of fixed rate)

The fixed-rate payment is usually based closely on the coupon or (occasionally) return of the underlying asset

Receiver

(receiver of fixed rate)

Floating Rate

LIBOR or another reference index rate plus or minus a spread the responsibility of either party. *See Asset Swap.*

Asset Class: An investment grouping or type of instrument with a positive expected return that is not conditional on the return of another grouping or type of instrument. More precisely, an investment grouping with risk and return characteristics that cannot be dynamically replicated in a continuous market with positions in another asset class and the risk-free asset. Recently, there has been a tendency to divide the world of investments into more asset classes than are warranted or useful.

Asset/Liability Gap: Any projected shortfall in the ability of a financial institution to meet its contractual obligations from current holdings. Many institutions receive regular funding from outside sources, e.g., corporate contributions to a pension plan, so an asset/liability gap calculation that neglects expected contributions may cause unnecessary concern.

Asset/Liability Management: Any of a variety of techniques designed to coordinate the management of an entity's assets with the management of its liabilities. A simple example is a financial institution's management of the duration of its fixed-income assets to match the duration of its payment liabilities.

Asset/Liability Management Committees (ALCOs): Risk management organizations at banks and other financial institutions with broad responsibility to manage interest rate and other market risks, as well as credit exposure and operating risk in some cases. The focus at this management level is asset/liability matching.

Asset Manager: A portfolio manager, corporate treasurer, or other individual responsible for management of the risks and returns associated with a portfolio of securities or other instruments. *See also Liability Manager.*

Asset-Or-Nothing Option: A non-standard option with a payout equal to the value of the underlying asset if the price of the asset exceeds the strike at expiration. If the value of the asset falls below the strike, the holder of the option receives nothing. Although the optionholder pays a premium when the trade is initiated, there is no payment of an exercise price at maturity.

Asset Risk Management: Techniques and procedures used by a holder of securities, commodities, or related instruments to offset or counteract possible adverse changes in the value of part or all of a portfolio.

Asset Swap: Another name for a fixed-for-floating interest rate swap. *See also Asset-Based Swap (diagram), Interest Rate Swap (diagram), Fixed-Floating Swap, Swap.*

Asset Turnover Ratio: Total sales divided by total assets.

Assign: *See Assignment (5).*

Assignment: (1) Notice to an option seller that an option has been exercised by the optionholder. (2) Process by which exercise notices or decisions are allocated among the sellers (shorts) in a derivatives contract market. (3) Transfer of rights in settlement of an obligation. (4) Transfer of a swap obligation to a replacement counterparty, usually with the consent of the opposite counterparty, but occasionally as a result of legal processes. (5) Transfer of ownership in a structured product or other private placement with the consent of the issuer. A limited right of assignment is a common feature of many risk management instruments, but legal restrictions or credit issues may prevent totally free assignment.

Assumed Rate of Return: *See Actuarial Rate.*

Asymmetric Payoff: An irregular, even discontinuous, pattern of changes in settlement valuation that does not translate all linear changes in the value of the underlying instrument, index, or rate into a continuous linear settlement value. Asymmetric payoff patterns are characteristic of traditional securities with embedded options and of option contracts themselves. *See also Symmetric Payoff.*

Asymmetrical Margining Agreement: A collateralization agreement between the counterparties to a swap or other contract that requires more stringent margin coverage from one counterparty, usually because of a difference in credit rating. *See also Bilateral Margining Agreement.*

At-Market Swap: A swap without upfront payments by either party.

At the Money: The market price or rate of the underlying and the strike price or rate of an at-the-money option are equal. If the current market price of the stock is $80, an option to buy a stock at a strike price of $80 is at the money. Increasingly, particularly in currency markets, the phrase refers to the forward price associated with the current spot price, as in "at-the-money forward." *See also In the Money, Out of the Money.*

Atlantic Option: *See Bermuda Option.*

Auction Market Preferred Stock (AMPS): *See Auction Rate Preferred Stock (ARPS).*

Auction Rate Note: A type of floating-rate note with an interest rate that is reset on the basis of bids received at a Dutch auction conducted near the end of each rate period. *See also Dutch Auction, Dutch Auction Interest and Dividend Reset, Periodic Auction Reset Securities (PARS), Dynamic Asset Allocation.*

Auction Rate Preferred Stock (ARPS): A floating-rate preferred with the dividend date reset by Dutch auction, typically every forty-nine days. The interest rate is usually subject to a maximum, and the issue is puttable at each auction. *Also designated by the following names and acronyms: Auction Market Preferred Stock (AMPS), Adjustable-Rate Preferred Stock (ARPS), Dutch Auction Rate Transferable Securities (DARTS) Preferred Stock, Market Auction Preferred Stock (MAPS), Money Market Preferred Stock (MMPS), Remarketed Preferred Stock, Short-Term Auction Rate (STAR).* Other versions fix the coupon rate for a longer period. *Examples include Flexible Auction Rate Preferred Stock (FLEX) and similar products with diverse acronyms. See also Dutch Auction, STated Rate Auction Preferred Stock (STRAPS).*

Audit: The systematic examination and evaluation of a company's financial statements and control practices by a firm of accountants and auditors for the purpose of confirming the accuracy of published financial statements. Other published financial statements, such as investment performance reports, are also subject to audit. Internal audits that take place between full corporate audits are also common.

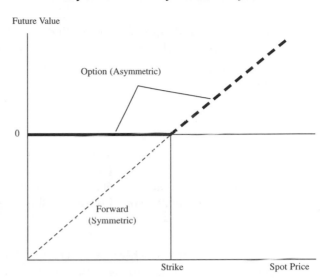

Asymmetric and Symmetric Payouts

Future Value

Option (Asymmetric)

0

Forward (Symmetric)

Strike   Spot Price

Aufgeld: *Ger.* Premium.

Authorized Futures and Option Funds (AFOFs): Publicly offered derivatives funds regulated by the Securities & Investment Board in the U.K. The funds invest in derivatives and interest-bearing deposits. Geared AFOFs offer leveraged market exposure through derivatives. *See Futures and Options Funds (FOFs).*

Authorized Unit Trust: *See Unit Trust.*

Auto-Quote System: A computer-based algorithm that automatically generates quotes for exchange-traded or frequently traded over-the-counter derivatives instruments based on input from a market data feed. The most common auto-quote systems price exchange-traded options off a market feed for the underlying based on specific implied volatility relationships. Advanced models use a term structure or skew volatility matrix.

Autocorrelation: A condition where the observations in a series are not independent of each other. The significance of autocorrelation for securities markets is that, if today's price change is independent of tomorrow's price change in direction and magnitude, a variety of statistical techniques can be used to value securities and measure risk—but technical analysis would be demonstrably worthless. If the direction and magnitude of today's price change has implications for tomorrow's, the statistician must exercise more care in making inferences from the data—and the technician cannot be discredited. *See Markov Process.*

Automated Pit Trading (APT): A screen-based after-hours trading system on the London International Financial Futures Exchange.

Automatic Cash-Out Call: An exploding call option. *See Capped Index Options (CAPS) (diagrams).*

Automatic Exercise: A procedure used by many option clearing organizations whereby expiring options that are in the money by a specified amount, or that are cash settled, are exercised without specific instructions from the optionholder.

Automatically Convertible Enhanced Security (ACES): *See Debt Exchangeable for Common Stock (DECS) (diagrams), Dividend Enhanced Convertible Stock (DECS).*

AutoRegressive Conditional Heteroskedasticity (ARCH) Model: A statistical procedure where the dependent variable in a regression equation is modeled as a function of the time-varying properties of the error term. *See Generalized Autoregressive Conditional Heteroskedasticity (GARCH) Model.*

AutoRegressive Moving Average (ARMA) Models: A family of time series forecasting models that rely on a tendency of the next item in some series to relate not just to prior values (autoregressive), but to a moving average of prior values. *See also Mean Reversion, Volatility Autoregressive Integrated Moving Average (VARIMA) Model.*

Average Downside Magnitude: An estimate of the average shortfall on occasions when an investor's target (minimum) return is not achieved. *See Target Return, Downside Probability.*

Average Price of an Option: *See Normal Price of an Option.*

Average Price or Rate Option (APO, ARO): An option whose settlement value is based on the difference between the strike and the average price (rate) of the underlying on selected dates over the life of the option, or over a period beginning on some start date and ending at expiration. The theoretical value of an average price or rate call is usually less than the value of an otherwise identical standard option, because the average price option acts like an option with a shorter expected life. The premium on an average price or rate option also tends to be less than the combined premiums of a strip of options expiring on each measurement date, because prices or rates on the wrong side of the strike reduce the average price or rate and, hence, the expected settlement value of the option. With a strip, observations on the wrong side of the strike would make one piece of the strip worthless but would not drag down the value of the others. *Also called Asian Option, Currency Average Rate Option. See also Average Strike Rate Option (ASRO), Average Rate Cap, Compound Average Rate Option, Exotic Options, Path-Dependent Option, Strip, Weighted Average Rate/Price Option (WARO).*

Average Price System (APS): A service available from many securities and futures exchanges that gives institutional money managers a single, average price for their transactions and instruments. The average price permits the managers to treat all accounts equally in their distribution of positions to separate accounts.

Average Rate Cap: A cap on the average interest rate over a period of time rather than on a single date. *See also Average Price or Rate Option (APO, ARO) (diagrams).*

Average Strike Rate Option (ASRO): An option whose settlement value is based on the difference between the spot price or rate at expiration and an average strike price or rate determined over the life of the option. These options are often embedded in employee stock purchase plans and pension plans. *Also called Floating Strike Option. See Average Price or Rate Option (APO, ARO) (diagrams), Floating Strike Asian Option.*

Avoir Fiscal: *Fr.* A dividend tax credit allowed to certain holders of French equity securities.

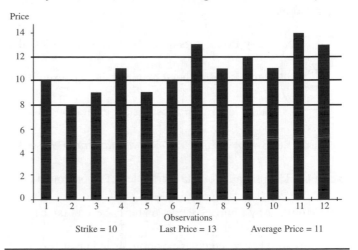

Monthly Observations for an Average Price or Asian Option

Strike = 10   Last Price = 13   Average Price = 11

Typical Premium Comparisons: Standard Option, Strip of Standard Options, Average Rate Option

Spot Strike Swiss Franc Call on Japanese Yen
(all figures in millions of Swiss francs or Japanese yen)

Term (months)	Standard Call Face (SF)	Standard Call Premium (JY)	Strip of Calls Face (SF)	Strip of Calls Premium (JY)	Average Rate Call Face (SF)	Average Rate Call Premium (JY)
12	120.0	428.4	10.0	35.8	120.0	264
11			10.0	34.4		
10			10.0	33.5		
9			10.0	31.9		
8			10.0	30.4		
7			10.0	28.6		
6			10.0	26.7		
5			10.0	24.9		
4			10.0	22.5		
3			10.0	19.7		
2			10.0	16.2		
1			10.0	11.7		
Total	120.0	428.4	120.0	316.3	120.0	264.0

Axe: A trader's preference, based on existing book positions, for a specific trade to reduce risk and/or help lock in a profit.

B

Baby Bond: A bond with a face value of less than $1,000—usually $100.

Back Bond: A bond obtained through exercise of an option or a warrant.

Back Contracts: Most distant expiration futures contracts currently trading.

Back End Set Swap: *See In-Arrears Swap (diagram), Reset Swap.*

Back Fee: The premium on the second leg of a compound option. *See also Compound Option, Front Fee.*

Back Month: Any futures contract maturity beyond the nearest expiration month.

Back Spread: (1) Any complex position, including at least one separate or embedded net long option position, that causes the entire position to increase in value in response to a significant price or rate move up or down. (2) A vertical or diagonal option spread with net premium received, usually because the short option is further in the money or less out of the money than the long option. *Also called Credit Spread (2).* (3) A reverse option hedge or any variable or ratio spread where more option contracts are purchased than sold. (4) An arbitrage-type relationship where the spread between the two prices or rates is less than the normal spread.

Back Stub Period: The last interim period in the life of a swap or other periodic reset agreement if that period is different (usually shorter) than preceding periods. *See Stub (2); also Front Stub Period.*

Back Testing: The practice of applying a valuation or forecasting model to historical data to help appraise the model's possible usefulness when current and future data are used.

Back-to-Back Loan: Originally designed to overcome currency restrictions, the initial back-to-back borrowing and lending arrangements were offsetting loans between two parties in two different currencies. For example, a U.S. firm might make a dollar loan to a U.K. company in the U.S., and the U.K. company would make an equal value loan (at spot exchange rates) in sterling to the U.S. firm in the U.K. Each party gets the currency it needs without going through the exchange rate mechanism. This structure has been replaced by currency swaps in major markets, but it is still used where exchange restrictions apply. Back-to-back loans are also used in credit enhancement, with or without the dual currency feature.

Back-to-Back Swap: A swap agreement that reverses the cash flow pattern of a simple swap, modifying the net paying or receiving position of the back-to-back counterparties. Back-to-back swaps have been used to extend the effective maturity of an issuer's fixed-rate debt or to enhance the credit of a financial intermediary's derivatives products subsidiary.

Back Up: When a market makes a bearish move it is said to back up.

Back-Up Facility: A stand-by underwriting or lending agreement that will provide the necessary financing if an issuer is unable to obtain prompt financing on reasonable terms in its traditional borrowing markets.

Backward Induction: The process of starting with the known terminal values of a binomial tree and using simultaneous equations to derive values of prior nodes until the value of the initial node is finally determined.

Backwardation: (1) A futures/spot market relationship in which the futures price is lower than the spot price. Agricultural commodity markets with a harvest due before the settlement date of the futures contract and energy markets during winter months are often characterized by backwardation. In periods of backwardation, the owners of the underlying forego a riskless profit in exchange for the surety of having the commodity on hand to meet demand. John Maynard Keynes argued that backwardation was normal in speculative markets, but this position has few adherents today. *See also Carrying Charge Market, Contango, Convenience Yield.* (2) Crossed or inverted market: a market with the posted bid price higher than the offer. *Also called Déport, Inverted Market, Locked Market. See Crossed Market.*

Balance of Payments: A summary of a country's international transactions for goods and services, financial instruments, and investments. In theory, this balance should be zero, because obligations or assets held abroad will increase or decrease to achieve a balance. An important subcategory of the balance of payments is the balance of trade, which is the net difference between the value of merchandise exports and imports. A more comprehensive trade balance is the current account balance, which includes services as well as merchandise. The state of a nation's balance of payments, balance of trade, or current account balance may provide an indication of the likely strength or weakness of its currency and the degree of flexibility the central bank has in conducting monetary policy. A capital account measures a country's borrowing and lending.

Balloon: (1) The final payment on a bond or note that is substantially larger than preceding amortization payments. Balloon instruments feature an amortization schedule intermediate between a level payment amortized loan and a bullet loan, in which the entire principal is paid at maturity. (2) A reference to an overvalued financial instrument or other asset.

Band: (1) The range of acceptable exchange rates between two currencies, as in exchange rate bands under the exchange rate mechanism (ERM). (2) *See Range (1), Wedding Band Swap (2).*

Bank Basis: *See Money Market Basis.*

Bank Capital Adequacy Requirements: An international set of risk-weighted capital charges and capital minimums for banks. *See Basle Convergence Agreement, Bank for International Settlements (BIS).*

Bank Deposit Agreement (BDA): *Same as Bank Investment Contract (BIC). See Guaranteed Investment Contract (GIC), Participating Account.*

Bank for International Settlements (BIS): An organization dominated by central banks, the BIS is concerned with international payments. *See also Bank Capital Adequacy Requirements, Basle Convergence Agreement.*

Bank Guarantee: A form of credit enhancement where a bank lends its own credit to assure timely payment of another party's obligation(s).

Bank Investment Contract (BIC): *Same as Bank Deposit Agreement (BDA). See Guaranteed Investment Contract (GIC), Participating Account.*

Banker's Acceptance: A negotiable time draft drawn to finance imports, exports, or other transactions in goods.

Banker's Acceptance Swap: An interest rate swap with a banker's acceptance rate as the floating rate. Banker's acceptances are the most common base for floating-rate swaps in Canada.

Banking On Overall STability (BOOST): *See Range Accumulation Option or Warrant.*

Bankruptcy Remote Entity: A subsidiary or affiliate corporation whose asset/liability structure and legal status makes its obligations secure even in the event of the bankruptcy of its parent or guarantor. *Also called Special Purpose Vehicle (SPV), Derivatives Product Company (DPC).*

Barbell Strategy: A duration management technique where debt instruments are concentrated at short and long durations with few or no intermediate-term holdings.

Bargain: *Brit.* An agreement to trade.

Barings Collapse: The failure of Barings, a major U.K. investment bank, has been attributed to inadequately controlled speculation in Japanese stock index futures by a Singapore-based trader. Barings was rescued by ING, a major financial institution headquartered in The Netherlands. *See also Windsor Declaration.*

Barone-Adesi-Whaley (BAW) Model: A method for valuing an option that uses quadratic approximation to solve the differential equation.

Barrier Discontinuity: Barrier options have an "in" or "out" condition triggered by touching or trading through an instrike or outstrike price. If the barrier condition can be satisfied only at certain times (e.g., the market close), or on certain dates, there is a barrier discontinuity, and evaluation of the option is more difficult.

Barrier Option: Path-dependent option with both its payoff pattern and its survival to the nominal expiration date dependent not only on the final price of the underlying, but on whether the underlying sells at or through a barrier (instrike, outstrike) price during the life of the option. Examples of barrier options include down-and-out and up-and-in puts and calls, early exercise trigger CAPS options, and a variety of similar instruments. *Related terms include Exotic Options, Stoption, Trigger Option. Also called Special Expiration Price Option, Limit Option. See also Exploding Option, In Option, Lookback Option, Out Option, Reset Option or Warrant (diagram), Deferred Start Option, Double Barrier Option, Down-and-In Call (diagram), Down-and-Out Call (diagram), Up-and-In Option, Strike-Step Option (diagram), Down-and-Out Put, Down-and-In Put.*

Barrier Price: The instrike or outstrike price that activates or deactivates a barrier option. The barrier price need only be touched under the provisions of some contracts, while others require it to be touched or breached at a market close (CAPS), or several times (baseball option).

Base Currency: The currency in which an investor or issuer maintains its books of account.

Baseball Option: A barrier option knocked out after the outstrike boundary has been touched for the third time. The name comes from the baseball phrase "three strikes and you're out." *See also Touch Option.*

Basis: (1) The difference between the forward price or yield and the spot price or yield of an instrument such as a futures contract, or the forward component implicit in an options contract. Alternately expressed as the cost minus the benefits of holding the hedged spot underlying until the forward or

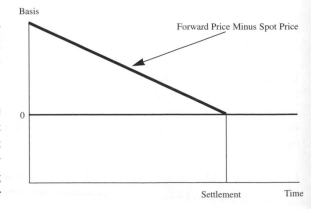

Basis of a Forward or Futures Contract

Basis

Forward Price Minus Spot Price

0

Settlement   Time

futures settlement date. *See Fair Value Basis, Carrying Charge Market, Hedge (1), Intrinsic Value of an Option, Call Option (diagrams). See also Long the Basis, Premium (7), Forward Intrinsic Value.* (2) The uncertain relationship between price or rate in two or more related but not identical markets. In a cross hedge, this uncertain relationship creates basis risk. *See Basis Risk (3).* (3) A convention for interest rate calculation. *See Bond Basis, Money Market Basis.* (4) A bond investor's yield to maturity. (5) The cost used to determine taxable capital gain or loss on an investment.

Basis Point (BP, BIP): 1/100 of a percentage point, also expressed as 0.01%. The difference between a yield of 7.90% and 8% is 10 basis points. When applied to a price rather than a rate, the term is often expressed as annualized basis points.

Basis Price: A reference or benchmark price or rate.

Basis Rate Swap: A swap in which counterparties calculate swap payments relative to different floating rates. One rate may be a very short-term rate, the other an intermediate rate. Differences in credit quality, duration, exchange rates, etc., may be reflected in a premium or discount on one side of the swap. A Treasury/EuroDollar (TED) swap illustrates a credit quality basis rate swap. *Also called Basis Swap, Floating-Floating Swap. See Treasury/EuroDollar (TED) Spread.*

Basis Risk: (1) The possibility of loss from imperfectly matched risk offsetting positions in two related but not identical markets. Examples include the risk of loss from using a deutschemark position to offset Swiss franc exposure, or using an intermediate instrument to hedge long-term interest rate exposures. (2) Exposure to loss from a maturity mismatch caused, for example, by a shift or change in the shape of the yield curve. (3) The variability of return stemming from possible changes in the price basis, or spread between two rates or indexes. *Also called Tracking Error, Correlation Risk in some applications. See Basis (2).*

Basis Swap: *See Basis Rate Swap.*

Basis Trade: (1) A portfolio or basket trade in which the price for the position is determined by a spread against the price of an exchange-traded derivative, usually a futures contract. *See Exchange of Futures for Physicals (EFP).* (2) An arbitrage-type transaction that attempts to profit from changes in the relative prices of derivative and underlying instruments. *Also called Relationship Trade.* (3) A cash and carry trade or its reverse. *See Cash-and-Carry Trade.*

Basket: A set of related instruments whose prices or rates are used to create a synthetic composite instrument that trades as a unit or serves as the underlying for a derivative instrument. *See also Composite Index, Equity Basket Option (diagram).*

Basket Hedging: The use of a basket of currencies to offset the risk of the non-base currencies in a portfolio. Typically, the basket has fewer currencies than the portfolio; but, because of close correlations among many of the currencies, the basket should provide a close, low-cost (and usually more liquid) hedge of the currency risk.

Basket Option or Warrant: (1) A third-party option or covered warrant on a basket of underlying stocks chosen because they represent an industry, economic sector, or other group designed to appeal to option or warrant buyers. Some basket contracts are settled by physical delivery and some are settled for cash. (2) A kind of average return or average change option on any group of interest rates, exchange rates, or indexes. The appeal of basket options is that imperfect correlations between the items in the basket often make the basket option premium lower than premiums on separate options on each item.

Basket Provision: A feature of many insurance company investment regulatory regimes that permits an insurer to invest a small percentage of its assets in a basket of instruments that do not qualify for purchase under general investment guidelines.

Basket Swap Rate: A composite interest rate equal to a weighted average of swap rates with a common term, but denominated in different currencies.

Basket Trade: A portfolio trade. *See Portfolio Trade, Program Trading.*

Basle Convergence Agreement: An international compact to establish and implement common standards for bank capital adequacy. These and similar capital adequacy rules have encouraged banks to embrace disintermediation with the object of cleaning up their balance sheets. In addition, banks have tried to replace interest rate spreads with trading spreads and fees. There has been an overall tendency to transfer credit risk from banks to other financial market participants. *See Bank Capital Adequacy Requirements, Capital Adequacy Directive. See also Add-On, Bank for International Settlements (BIS).*

Basle Standards for Market Risk: A set of bank capital requirements to cover financial market risk. These standards are complementary to capital requirements designed to meet credit risk. The Basle Committee permits a bank to use its own internal risk models once they have been thoroughly tested, provided they do not call for a lower capital standard. The Committee's version of a value at risk (VAR) capital requirement offers no credit for lack of correlation among markets, and requires a multiple of 3 times the 99th percentile VAR figure as minimum capital. The relationship of the Basle requirements to the EU Capital Adequacy Directive is not yet clear.

Bayes Stein Adjustment: An adjustment by which the sample means of several variables are compressed toward the grand mean of those variables. For example, if two variables have sample means of 10% and 20%, they can be compressed toward the grand mean of 15% by weighting the sample means by 70% and the grand mean by 30%. In this example, the adjusted means would equal 11.5% and 18.5%, respectively. The optimal weighting scheme is a function of the size of the samples used to derive the original estimates. The Bayes Stein procedure is often used in optimization applications to reduce the sensitivity of the results to errors in the parameter estimates.

Bayes' Theorem: A technique for estimating the conditional probability of a cause, given that a particular event has occurred. The theorem states that the probability of cause B_j, given the observation of event A, is equal to the joint probability of A and B_j, divided by the sum of the joint probabilities of A with B_1 through B_n. The theorem is named after Thomas Bayes, an 18th century English clergyman who was interested in mathematics.

Bayesian Adjustment: *See Bayes Stein Adjustment, Bayes' Theorem.*

Bear Floater: A floating-rate note that resets at a multiple of the floating reference index rate minus a fixed rate.

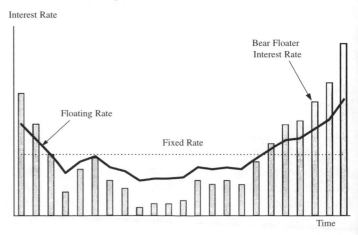

Anatomy of a Five-Year Bear Floater

Interest Rate

Bear Floater
Interest Rate

Floating Rate

Fixed Rate

Time

The floating rate increases or decreases by a multiple of the actual change in the floating-rate index, but the multiplication of the floating rate and the subtraction of the fixed rate cause the rate on the note to multiply changes in the reference index rate. The figure illustrates a bear floater that calls for a variable-rate payment of twice LIBOR minus the fixed rate. If floating rates rise, the floating-rate receiver will obtain a leveraged benefit. *Compare with Reverse Floating Rate Note (diagram).*

Bear Hug: A takeover bid so attractive that the takeover target's directors have little choice but to approve it.

Bear or Bearish: (1) A person who expects a market to decline. (2) A position that will increase in value if the market declines.

Bear Spread: A combination of options whose value increases (within limits) when the value of the underlying declines, and declines when the underlying advances. *See Bull Spread (diagram), Call Spread, Calendar Spread, Reverse Equity Risk Reversal (diagram).*

Bear Swap: (1) An interest rate swap agreement that amortizes more rapidly as interest rates rise, allowing the fixed-rate receiver to "reinvest" at higher rates. These instruments are used primarily in conjunction with mortgage derivatives to balance the extension risk of many mortgage instruments in a period of rising rates. (2) A basis swap with both swap streams based on index rates characterized by different credit qualities; for example, a TED spread swap or a Treasury/junk bond index swap. Typically, the lower-quality rate will rise most rapidly as all rates rise.

Profit/Loss Pattern of a Bear Spread at Expiration

Bearer Instrument: The physical proof of ownership of a bond or stock. A bearer certificate provides the only evidence necessary (or possible) to prove that the holder is entitled to the benefits of ownership. The instrument, or a coupon detached from it, must be presented to collect any cash due to the owner. In contrast to registered instruments, the issuer does not maintain a record of ownership of bearer instruments.

Bearer (Participation) Certificate: *See Participation Certificate.*

Bed and Breakfast: The functional (but not necessarily the economic) equivalent of an overnight repurchase agreement (repo). A security or a portfolio is sold to register a tax gain or loss, and repurchased the following day (or when the thirty-day wash sale period is over in the U.S.). A bed and breakfast trade might also be used to avoid showing a position at the end of a reporting period. *See also Repurchase Agreement (Repo), (RP), Wash Sale.*

Behavioral Finance: The study and development of descriptive models of behavior in markets and organizations. These models set aside the traditional assumption of rationality, emphasizing the observed psychological factors that influence decision-making under uncertainty. *See also Prospect Theory.*

Belgian Option: An option originally struck slightly out of the money that pays off like a standard option if the underlying is in the money at expiration, and pays off on a variable but growing fraction of the notional value of the underlying as the underlying moves from the initial spot price to the strike.

Bells and Whistles: Unusual or unique features of a financial instrument designed to appeal to a specific issuer or investor. Often used as a pejorative reference to features of an offering that seem to be added solely to attract attention.

Benchmark: (1) A reference index or rate that serves as a basis for performance comparison or return calculation. (2) A standard specification for a physical commodity or financial instrument underlying a derivative. (3) A standard of best practice or typical practice in finance, accounting, management, etc.

Benefit of Carry: A negative cost of carry. A benefit of carry occurs when the income (typically coupon interest or dividends) exceeds the short-term borrowing cost plus any storage charge. *See also Cost of Carry (2).*

Bermuda Option: Like the location of Bermuda, this option is located somewhere between a European-style option that can be exercised only at maturity, and an American-style option that can be exercised at the choice of the optionholder. The Bermuda option can typically be exercised on a number of predetermined occasions as stated in the option contract. *Also called Atlantic Option, Limited Exercise Option, Modified American Option, Quasi-American Option, Semi-American Option. See also American Option, American Window, Deferred Payment American Option, European Option, Japanese Option.*

Bernoulli Trial: A random event with three properties: (a) its result must be characterized by a success or a failure; (b) the probability of a success must be the same for all trials; and (c) the outcome of each trial must be independent of the outcomes of the other trials. The toss of a fair coin satisfies the conditions of a Bernoulli trial.

Best Bond to Deliver: *See Cheapest to Deliver (CTD).*

Best Buy Option: A partial or full lookback strike call option. *See Lookback Option, Lookback Currency Option (diagram).*

Best Execution: In the United States, investment advisors have a fiduciary obligation to obtain the best possible net execution for the accounts they manage. In the United Kingdom, a similar obligation falls on a broker acting as the investment manager's agent. Determining what constitutes the best execution is often difficult.

Best-Of Option: *See Alternative Option (diagram).*

Best Practice: This term has specific meanings in many financial fields, but one of its most frequent applications is in risk management, where the use of certain techniques, such as value at risk, stress testing (perhaps with a Monte Carlo simulation), and frequent—preferably daily—pricing of positions are important elements of what is currently considered best practice.

Best Price Option: *See Lookback Option.*

Best Strike Option: *See Lookback Option.*

Bet Option: *See Binary Option.*

Beta (β): (1) A measurement of stock price volatility relative to a broad market index. If a stock moves up and down twice as much as the market, it has a beta of 2. If it moves one-half as much as the market, its beta is 0.5. Because beta assumes a linear relationship, it can be seriously misleading if used in stock option evaluation or comparison. (2) The slope of a regression line. (3) The second tier of stocks listed on the London Stock Exchange. The other tiers are alpha (α) (4), delta (δ), and gamma (γ). *See alpha (α), delta (δ), and gamma (γ).*

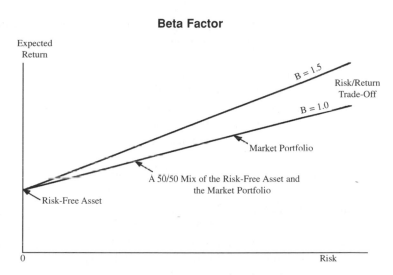

Beta Factor

Better-Of-Two-Assets Option: *See Alternative Option (diagram), Worst-Of-Two-Assets Option.*

Bid: The price at which a trader is willing to buy a security.

Bid-Asked Spread: The difference between the bid and offer price or rate. The most widely used comparative measure of market quality.

Bid-to-Cover Ratio: The ratio of the number of bids in a U.S. Treasury securities auction to the number of successful bids. Used as a rough measure of the success of the auction.

Bifurcation: Division of a financial instrument into two pieces. The term sometimes refers to a division for analytical or evaluation purposes, but it more commonly suggests a more complex approach to financial instrument taxation.

Big Bang: The name given to the events surrounding October 27, 1986, when fixed commissions were eliminated in most London markets. Analogous to May Day (1975) in U.S. securities markets.

Big Figure: *See Handle.*

Biger and Hull Model: *See Garman-Kohlhagen Model.*

Bilateral Margining Agreement: A collateralization arrangement to assure both parties' performance on a swap or other OTC risk management contract. The agreement requires each counterparty to deposit margin with the other counterparty or a third party depending on the value of its net obligations. *See also Asymmetrical Margining Agreement.*

Bilateral Netting: An arrangement between two parties where they exchange only the net difference in their obligations to each other. The primary purpose of netting is to reduce exposure to credit/settlement risk. *See Netting Agreement, Netting by Novation.*

Bill: A debt instrument with an original life of less than one year. Usually issued at a discount to face value (e.g., U.S. Treasury bills) and redeemed at par.

Bill Over Bond (BOB) Spread: The yield differential between a specific maturity Treasury bill and a designated bond. The inverse of a Bond Over Bill (BOB) Spread.

Bimodal Distribution: A relative frequency or probability distribution characterized by two peaks or humps rather than the more common single peak which characterizes the normal distribution and most other standardized distributions.

Bin: Another name for Bucket. *See Bucketizing.*

Binary LIBOR Note: A floating-rate note paying LIBOR plus a premium if LIBOR is, for example, above a designated strike rate on the reset date and no coupon if LIBOR is below the strike rate. *Compare with Range Accumulation Option or Warrant. See also Binary Swap.*

Binary LIBOR Swap: *See Binary Swap.*

Binary Option: An option with a fixed, predetermined payoff if the underlying instrument or index is at or beyond the strike at expiration. The value of the payoff is not affected by the magnitude of the difference between the underlying and the strike price. *Also called All-or-Nothing Option, Bet Option, Digital Option, Lottery Option. See also Binary Swap, Lock-Out Option, Lock-In Option.*

Binary Swap: A fixed- for floating-rate swap with the floating rate set at a spread over the reference index rate, if the reference rate is in a designated range on the reset date, and with no floating-rate payment if the reference rate is outside the range. A binary swap is usually embedded in a note. *Also called Binary LIBOR Swap. See also Binary LIBOR Note, Index Range Note, Binary Option, Range Accumulation Option or Warrant.*

Binary Variable: *See Dichotomous Variable.*

Binomial Model: A model of the form suggested by Cox, Ross, and Rubinstein and Sharpe, which is based on the tendency of a binomial distribution to approach normality as a limit. The structure of the model is a branch network where the underlying price or rate can rise or fall by a limited amount at each node. The weighted present values of the terminal node values

Bimodal Distribution

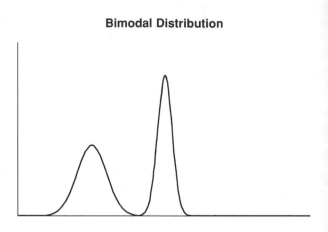

Payout Comparison of Binary and Standard Call Options

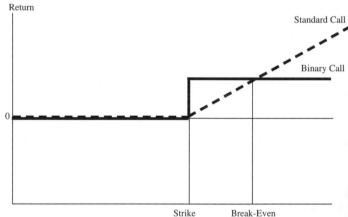

Binomial Model Lattice

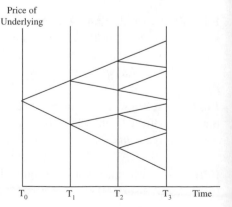

are summed to determine option value. Alternatively, the option value can be derived by backward induction. The binomial model is useful when the underlying distribution is normal or lognormal, yet adjustments for cash flows and early exercise are necessary, and when option payoffs are path dependent. Efforts to use a binomial model to approximate results of non-normal distributions should be viewed with suspicion. By the central limit theorem, a binomial distribution will converge to the normal distribution despite efforts to delay convergence by varying up and down probabilities. *See also Backward Induction, Central Limit Theorem, Implied Binomial Tree, Lattice.*

BIP, BP: *See Basis Point (BP, BIP).*

Bisection Method: A numeric method for finding the root of an equation. An analyst starts with two values that bound the interval certain to include the correct answer. The analyst divides the interval in half and tries the indicated value. If that value yields an answer that is too high, the analyst tries the midpoint of its value and the lower bound. If it yields an answer that is too low, the analyst tries the midpoint of its value and the upper bound, proceeding in this fashion until a solution is found.

Black Box: (1) A valuation or pricing formula for financial instruments that is not explained to users of the computer system that incorporates the formula. Users are expected to accept the output of the computer "box" on faith. (2) Any computer system, portfolio, balance sheet, or income statement that is not transparent to its users, and which consequently demands a high degree of trust in its creators.

Black-Derman-Toy (BDT) Model: An analytic model used to value interest rate dependent claims that incorporates the entire term structure of interest rates. The BDT model is a no-arbitrage, calibrated model that permits independent and time-varying spot rate volatilities. An important limitation is that its parameter specifications, assumed constant for the life of the instrument, must be updated as prices change.

Black-Karasinski Model: A single factor, analytic model used to value interest rate dependent claims. The single factor is the lognormally distributed short rate. This model is often used to value swaptions.

Black-Scholes Equation: The solution to the partial differential equation used to determine the appropriate price or theoretical value of an option on the basis of a neutral hedge created with risk-offsetting positions in the option and the underlying. Parameters or inputs to the equation are limited to: spot price of the underlying, strike price of the option, interest rate, time until option expiration, and volatility of the underlying. The elegance and simplicity of the Black-Scholes model, and its consistency with the capital asset pricing model of portfolio theory, are responsible for its widespread adoption. The model's weaknesses are its restrictive assumptions. It requires modification or the use of alternative formulations in many real world circumstances. The Black-Scholes equation for the fair value of a European call option on a non-dividend-paying stock is:

$$C = SN(d_1) - Xe^{-rt} N(d_2)$$

where

C	=	call option price
S	=	current stock price
X	=	exercise price
r	=	natural logarithm of the quantity 1 plus the discrete annualized rate of interest on a nominal riskless pure discount instrument maturing t years in the future
e	=	2.718

ln	=	natural logarithm
t	=	time remaining to the expiration date (as a fraction of a year)
s	=	standard deviation of the stock price
N (.)	=	the cumulative normal probability

$$d_1 = \frac{\ln(S/X) + (r + 0.5s^2)t}{s\sqrt{t}}$$

$$d_2 = d_1 - s\sqrt{t}$$

See also Delta (1) (diagrams), Fair Value of an Option.

Blended Index: A weighted average of two or more indexes, often used as the underlying for a financial instrument.

Blended Interest Rate Swap: A combination of two or more interest rate swaps, usually one with a spot start and one with a forward start. The result is that payments are calculated on a weighted average of rates.

Block Trade: A transaction involving a large number of shares of one or a small number of stocks or a large number of similar bonds. A block trade in stock is usually defined by the NYSE as a trade involving 10,000 shares or more, or as having a market value of $200,000 or more.

Blowout Bid: A large premium over previous prices, offered to shareholders of an acquisition target with the expectation that other bidders will be reluctant to engage in a bidding war starting at such a high price.

Blue Noise: A mean averting stochastic process. *Compare to Red Noise.*

Blue-Sky Laws: The securities laws of individual states in the U.S. that regulate new securities issues and many secondary market transactions. The name comes from unrealistic promises made by some promoters of new securities.

Board of Trade: A commodity or futures exchange. The term is sometimes used in Europe to refer to a chamber of commerce type of organization.

BOAT Spread: The yield difference between German Bunds and French OATs. *Also called Maginot Spread.*

BOATs: Yield differential warrants with a payout tied to the yield spread between the German Bunds and the French OATs, a relationship occasionally called the Maginot spread. *See International Spread Option, Warrant, or Note, Yield Differential Warrant.*

Bobl Over Bund (BOB) Spread: An interest rate spread transaction based on the relative yields on the five-year Bundes Obligations (Bobl) or Bobl future and the ten-year Bundes or Bundes future—a deutschemark yield curve transaction.

Boil Spread: The return difference between an investment in a bond and an oil contract.

Boiler Room: A crowded, high-pressure securities or commodities sales operation often characterized by a high noise level designed to communicate excitement and urgency to customers at the other end of a telephone line.

Boilerplate: Standard, non-controversial legal clauses often required by regulatory agencies or state or federal law. While boilerplate language usually appears in fine or small print, the phrase "fine print" typically refers to a non-standard provision in a financial instrument or contract that can create problems if one or both parties to the contract are not alert to it. In contrast, boilerplate clauses are unlikely to cause problems as long as they are present as required. *See also Fine Print.*

Bond: Traditionally, a written unconditional promise to pay a specific principal sum at a determined future date, and interest at a fixed or determinable rate on fixed dates. Increasingly, the promise to pay has become conditional, and the principal, interest, and payment dates have become contingent in real world instruments. *See also Note.*

Bond Basis: A method of interest calculation using a day count fraction equal to actual days divided by actual days in a year (usually 365). *Also called Day Count Basis. See also Basis (3), Money Market Basis.*

Bond Equivalent Yield (BEY): A bond or Treasury bill or other discount instrument's yield over its life, assuming it is purchased at the asked price and the return is annualized using a simple interest approach. Bond equivalent yield is equal to a bill's discount, expressed as a fraction of the purchase price multiplied by 365 divided by the number of days to maturity.

$$BEY = (discount/purchase\ price) \times (365/days\ to\ maturity)$$

Bond-Over-Bill (BOB) Spread: The yield differential between a specific bond and a given maturity Treasury bill. The inverse of a Bill-Over-Bond (BOB) Spread.

Bond-Over-Stock (BOS) Warrant: Outperformance warrant with a payout based on the performance of a bond index less the return on a stock index. These instruments are issued on a variety of fixed-income and equity indexes. *Compare Stock-Over-Bond (SOB) Warrant.*

Bond Value: The estimated market value of the fixed-income element of a convertible bond. Bond value excludes the value of the convertible's equity option component, but usually reflects any bond call privilege the issuer retains. *Also called Investment Value.*

Bond Warrant: *See Contingent Takedown Option.*

Bond With Attached Warrant: A combination of a traditional bond or note and a call warrant on shares of the issuing firm. The warrant can usually be traded separately after the underwriting period. The structure differs from the traditional convertible bond because the life of the warrant continues if the bond is called. Usually, the valuation of the bond with attached warrant is slightly different from that of a convertible bond, because the issuer's bond call provision would be used on the straight bond under different circumstances than it would be used to call a convertible bond. The interest rate on the bond is below straight bond market rates at issuance because of the value of the warrant, making an early bond call unlikely.

Bond Yield Warrant: A warrant, often exchange-traded, with a payout dependent upon a specific bond yield or bond yield index.

Book Entry Securities: Instruments represented in computer records rather than by traditional engraved certificates.

Bookout: Cancellation of a swap or other OTC derivatives contract prior to maturity.

Boot: Money or non-participating equity securities received in an exchange of securities or property, designed to be non-taxable. The boot receives special tax treatment under the U.S. tax code.

Bootstrapping: An iterative calculation technique often used in the construction of specialized time series. For example, the calculation of forward rates from traditional yield curves uses an iterative process to extract the implied rate for each forward period.

Borrower Option: A cap on a forward rate agreement.

Borrower's Option—Lender's Option (BO-LO): A debt instrument with embedded options giving the issuer (borrower) the right to change the coupon and the investor (lender) the right to put the instrument to the issuer if the new rate is not acceptable. *Compare to Retractable Note.*

Börse, Borsa, or Bourse: The most common name for a stock exchange in Europe, alternately said to come from "bourse," the French word for purse, or from Van der Buerse, a family who owned a house in Amsterdam near the site of early currency exchange transactions.

Boston Option: (1) *Another name for Break Forward. Also called Cancellable Option, Forward Break, Forward with Optional Exit (FOX).* (2) Less frequently used to name a deferred premium option where the premium is paid at expiration whether the option is exercised or not. *Contrast with Contingent Premium Option (diagram). See also Deferred Premium Option.*

Bottom Fisher: An investor who looks for bargains in the securities of troubled companies. *Also called Grave Dancer.*

Bought Deal: (1) A securities underwriting characterized by a firm price or rate guaranteed by the underwriting firm(s). This British term describes a procedure relatively new in the U.K., but long standard in the U.S. *See Underwriter (1).* (2) The term is also used in the U.K. to describe secondary market transactions called block trades in the U.S.

Boundary Conditions: In the valuation of financial instruments, boundary conditions are limitations on the value of an option or any other instrument determined by the provisions of the instrument and by the structure and value of any underlying instrument. Relevant boundaries for an option contract include relationships among the underlying price, the intrinsic value or forward intrinsic value of the option, and the stock price. Boundary conditions are usually expressed as equations that describe minimum and maximum values of the instrument under all possible circumstances. If boundary conditions are violated in the market, a risk-free arbitrage opportunity is created. *See also Put/Call Parity.*

Boundary Value Problem: A condition in the valuation of a contingent claim in which the path of the underlying asset price or rate is relevant to the solution of a partial differential equation. *See Path Dependency.*

Bounded Rationality: Recognition that real world solutions often cannot be based on complete information, and that reaching a satisfactory solution with incomplete information is usually better than making no decision.

Box Spread: (1) A combination of a long synthetic stock or index position (long call plus short put), and a short synthetic stock position (long put plus short call), that expire simultaneously and have different strike prices. An alternate view of a box spread might combine put and call spreads. Box spreads were once used almost exclusively to transfer gains from one tax year to the next. With changes in the tax code they are now used primarily to "borrow" or "lend" money. A lender is said to "buy" the box and a borrower is said to "sell" the box. Boxes are evaluated essentially on the basis of returns on the cash they tie up or free up. Index options with European-style exercise provisions are used most frequently, because early exercise of American-style options destroys the box. (2) Offsetting long and short synthetic stock positions with different expirations. Often used to roll a position to a more distant expiration. If all the transactions opened new positions, the

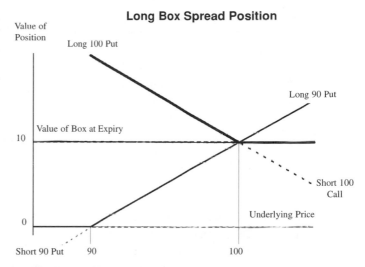

Long Box Spread Position

result would be a box spread. If one synthetic opened a distant position and the other closed a near position, it would be a jellyroll. *See Jellyroll, Synthetic Stock (2), Time Box.* (3) An over-the-counter interest rate spread contract.

Boxplot: A graph that shows the median, the interquartile range, 5th and 95th percentiles, and the outliers of a distribution. It is more descriptive than a histogram because it shows the skewness of a distribution. *See also Interquartile Range.*

Brady Bond: A consolidated restructured debt obligation of a less developed country (LDC). Brady Bonds are sponsored by the U.S. and at least partially collateralized by U.S. Treasury obligations.

Break-Even Point: (1) The sales volume where total revenue equals total cost, and an enterprise experiences neither profit nor loss. (2) A price at which a transaction produces neither a gain nor a loss. (3) A price on the underlying instrument at

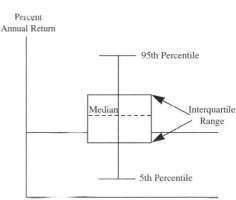

Boxplot of Annual Returns

which two derivatives strategies or a cash and a derivatives strategy produce comparable gains or losses. *Also called Pay Back. See Call (diagram).*

Break-Even Time: A technique used to appraise the relative attractiveness of a convertible security and its underlying. Break-even time is calculated by dividing the premium over conversion value by a convertible's current yield advantage over the underlying, giving the time needed for the convertible's yield advantage to "cover" the premium. This calculation rarely gives an unequivocal indication of the relative attractiveness of a convertible and the underlying stock because it neglects the effects of so many variables. *Also called Payback Period.*

Break Forward: An option-like mechanism used primarily in the currency markets to obtain full participation in a move in the underlying beyond a specified level without payment of an explicit option premium. The party long the break forward contract typically agrees to sell the underlying forward at a discount, or load, below the prevailing forward rate. The expected present value of this load pays for an option to cancel the forward agreement should the underlying rise above a predetermined level. The greater the load, the lower the price at which the holder of the option can cancel the forward agreement. *Also called Boston Option (1), Cancellable Forward Exchange Con-tract, Cancellable Option, Forward Break, Conditional Forward Purchase Contract, Forward with Optional Exit (FOX), GUAranteed Rate on Delivery (GUARD), Knock-Out Forward, Trigger Forward, Forward Reserve Option. See also Load (3), Participating Forward Contract (diagram).*

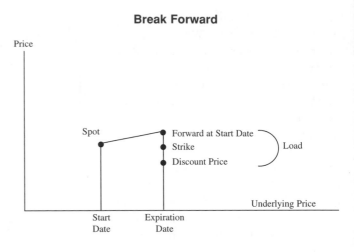

Break Forward

Break Out: The process of undoing a conversion or a reversal, reestablishing the option buyer's original position. For example, an investor who sells stock short to convert a long call into a synthetic long put may cover the short stock position to "break out" the call. *See also Conversion (1).*

Brennan-Schwartz Model: A two-factor analytic model used to value interest rate dependent claims. The two factors are the short-term interest rate and the yield on a perpetual bond.

Bretton Woods Agreement of 1944: A currency agreement that set fixed exchange rates for major currencies, provided for central bank intervention in currency markets, and set the price of gold at U.S. $35 per ounce. The agreement controlled currency relationships for nearly thirty years.

Bridge Loan: An interim financing arrangement provided by a bank, investment bank, or a special purpose investment fund to allow a corporation to make an acquisition before arranging permanent financing to carry the acquisition.

British Bankers Association Interest Rate Swap (BBAIRS) Terms: A set of standardized terms for interest rate swaps, largely supplanted by the International Swap and Derivatives Association (ISDA) documentation.

Broken Dates: Settlement terms for forward currency contracts that are not written for standard contract periods.

Broker: A financial market intermediary who acts as an agent for one or both parties to a transaction. It is important to understand the difference between a broker who does not commit capital to a transaction and a dealer who may take one side of a trade for his firm's account. The broker receives a commission for service, while the dealer hopes to find the other side of the transaction and earn a spread by closing out the position at a profit in a subsequent trade with another party. *See Brokerage, Commission, Courtage, Dealer.*

Brokerage: Commissions. This usage is most common in Europe. *See Courtage, Broker.*

Brownian Motion: A variable subject to geometric Brownian motion has a lognormal probability distribution and will always have a positive mean. A variable with arithmetic Brownian motion has a normal distribution. Arithmetic Brownian motion also refers to the irregular movement of pollen grains suspended in water. The phenomenon was allegedly observed by a botanist, Robert Brown, in 1828. This prototypical random movement was attributed to the effect of water molecules striking the pollen, and dispersing it throughout the water. Although more recent work has suggested that Brown's optical equipment was not up to the observations he reported, the hypothesized random process is still the basis of many security price models. *Also called Wiener or Wiener/Bachelier Process,* Brownian motion is a type of Markov process. *Also called Diffusion Process, Markov Process. See Arithmetric Brownian Motion, Geometric Brownian Motion, Lognormal Distribution, Martingale, Stochastic Process. See also Ito's Lemma.*

Bucket Shop: Prior to passage of securities legislation in the U.S. in the 1930s, many securities firms sold one-day or other short-term, over-the-counter, down-and-out calls or up-and-out puts. This practice was called bucketing, and the firms were called bucket shops. The term, which apparently originated in the practice of carrying beer into brothels in buckets, now characterizes any disreputable securities firm. Many states in the U.S. have bucket shop laws that impinge on the ability of financial intermediaries to create and trade certain types of over-the-counter instruments.

Bucketing: *See Bucket Shop.*

Bucketizing: The process of dividing contractual or expected cash flows from diverse financial instruments into categories, or "buckets," for the analysis and measurement of risk.

Building-Block Approach: A generic term for a variety of risk management techniques that separate a financial instrument into simpler components, reaggregate the components into portfolios, and manage specific types of risk in the separate portfolios.

Bull and Bear Notes: Terms used loosely to describe various tranches of interest rate or equity-linked instruments issued at the same time. A bear note can be a more "conservative" unit providing a higher minimum return and a lower ceiling than a bull note (which provides a wider range of returns). Alternately, the bull and bear notes can be direct offsets of one another, where the return to the bear note is essentially the mirror image of the return to the bull note. Thus, the bear note benefits from a decline in the underlying or an increase in the rate structure over a range of underlying values, while the bull note benefits from rising prices and/or falling rates. The issuer takes no market risk if the complementary tranches are arranged so that the bull note holder's gain is the bear note holder's loss, and vice versa. *Compare Residual Interest Bonds (RIBs) and Select Auction Variable-Rate Securities (SAVRs) for a similar structure. The diagram under Reverse Floating-Rate Note may be helpful in visualizing how a fixed-rate payout can be divided to create a floater and a reverse floater.*

Bull-cum-Bear Options: A zero-coupon note made up of a deep in-the-money call and a deep in-the-money put, either of which can be closed out prior to maturity to convert the overall position into a call or a put. Because both options are deeply in the money, the structure can be viewed as a bond attached to offsetting long and short forward contracts, either of which can be terminated early to provide desired market exposure.

Bull Floater: *See Reverse Floating-Rate Note (diagram).*

Bull Floating-Rate Note: *See Reverse Floating-Rate Note (diagram).*

Bull or Bullish: (1) An individual who expects a market to rise. (2) A position that benefits from a rising market.

Bull Spread: A partially risk-offsetting option spread position that will be profitable if the underlying instrument rises in price. In one-for-one spread positions, the profit is limited on the upside, and the downside risk is limited to the net premium paid. *See also Bear Spread (diagram), Call Spread, Calendar Spread, Capped Call.*

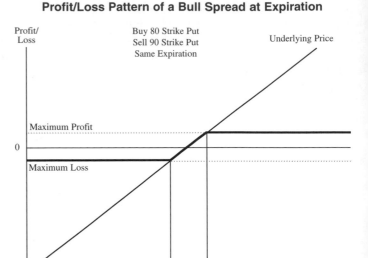

Profit/Loss Pattern of a Bull Spread at Expiration

Bulldog Bond: A sterling-denominated bond issued by a corporation that keeps its accounts in another currency.

Bullet Maturity Bond: A coupon-paying debt instrument with no repayment of principal until maturity.

Bullet Swap: A swap with a constant notional principal reflecting a constant risk-offset requirement, and/or the use of a debt security with full repayment of principal at maturity.

Bundesbank (Buba): The German central bank.

Bundle: A package of Eurodollar strips composed of two, three, five, seven, or ten years' accumulation of quarterly contracts. Bundles are used to create long-dated Treasury/Eurodollar (TED) spreads and in the hedging of some swap transactions. *See also Treasury/EuroDollar (TED) Spread, Stub (4), Pack.*

Bunds: German government bonds underlying the primary bond futures and options contracts denominated in deutschemarks.

Bunny Bond: A coupon bond that gives the investor the right to receive coupon payments in cash or in additional bonds with the same coupon as the underlying bond. The purpose is to offer the investor protection from reinvestment risk. *See Guaranteed Coupon Reinvestment Bonds, Reinvestment Risk.*

Burnout: Slowing of a mortgage's interest rate-linked prepayment rate when rates drop into a prepayment range for the second time in the life of a mortgage pool.

Business Day: In most countries/markets, any day on which banks and/or securities exchanges are open for business. Differences in national holidays have important implications for cross-border transactions and even for the nature and quality of data available from non-domestic markets for use in financial analysis.

Busted Convertible Security: A security trading so far below conversion value that its value as a straight debt or preferred stock obligation is much higher than its conversion value—causing it to trade much like a straight, or non-convertible, security.

Busted Planned Amortization Class (PAC) Bond: A planned amortization class tranche of a collateralized mortgage obligation (CMO) with a prepayment range above current market rates. The PAC prepayment schedule may no longer be feasible because of the rate movement, and the value of the PAC may be impaired. *See Planned Amortization Class (PAC) Bond.*

Butterfly Spread: Although a few traders use different definitions, the most common butterfly spread combines a vertical bull and a vertical bear spread with the same expiration date on all options and the same strike price on all short options. The often sought, but unobtainable, "perfect butterfly" requires no net premium payment, assuring the buyer of profit at any price between the upper and lower strike prices with no possibility of a loss. *This structure is sometimes called an Alligator Spread or a Sandwich Spread. See Condor, Call Spread.*

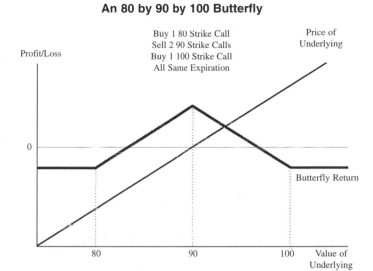

An 80 by 90 by 100 Butterfly

Buy Back: Purchase of a position to cover or offset a previously established short position.

Buy-In: (1) When a call is exercised against an option writing account that does not hold a sufficient position in the called security, the broker may buy in the necessary position for delivery to the optionholder. (2) In short selling, if no securities can be borrowed to continue a short position, the broker buys in securities for delivery, forcing the short seller to cover. This type of buy-in occurs in issues with large short interests and/or small floats.

Buy-Out of a Swap in Termination: The payment of a swap's market value to the net creditor to close out the transaction. Bookout is an earlier term for a similar transaction.

Buy-Write: A covered call position created by simultaneously buying the underlying and selling the call. *Also called Covered Call. See Covered Call (diagram).*

Buy-write Option UNitary DerivativeS (BOUNDS): An Americus Trust PRIME-like companion to the option exchanges' SCORE-like LEAPS proposed to fill the gap created by the expiration of the Americus Trust components. The functional equivalent of a covered call writer's position. *See also Americus Trust, Long-term Equity AnticiPation Securities (LEAPS).*

Buyer's Option: (1) A call option. (2) A contract for the delivery of securities on a date specified by the buyer at the time of the transaction.

Buyer's Right to Pay (BRP) Fixed Swaption: *See Payer's Swaption.*

Buying the Basis: Buying a deliverable instrument or index-equivalent position, and selling a futures position in an attempt to profit from a narrowing of the basis, i.e., from a low-risk, interest-like return. *Also called Cash-and-Carry Trade. See Cash Enhancement Strategy.*

Cabinet Trade: (1) A transaction in an inactive stock or bond. (2) An off-market transaction to close out a nearly worthless out-of-the-money option contract.

Cable: The exchange rate between the U.S. dollar and the British pound sterling. The rate was transmitted over the transatlantic cable from 1866, and the initial novelty of the communication method gave the exchange rate this name.

Cacall: An option to purchase a call. *See Compound Option (1) (diagram).*

Calamity Clause: A CMO provision that authorizes the issuer to pay some obligations out of principal if the reinvestment rate on principal during the interest period is below the bond coupon rate.

Calculation Agent: The party designated to calculate the amounts payable under a swap agreement or the value of a derivatives instrument.

Calendar: A list of new issues scheduled for offering in the near future.

Calendar Roll: A buy and sell combination trade where a futures or option position is closed in one contract month and opened on the same side of the market in a more distant calendar month. For example, a long position in a March futures contract is closed and a June contract is opened in a calendar roll.

Calendar Spread: Margin rules dictate that the option purchased in a calendar spread expires after the option is sold. The number of contracts purchased equals the number sold, and both options have the same strike price. For example, an investor who buys a December 80 call and sells a September 80 call is said to buy the Sept—Dec 80 call (calendar) spread. A calendar spread is most profitable when the price of the underlying is very close to the strike on the expiration date of the short option. *Also called Horizontal Spread, Time Spread. See also Bear Spread (diagram), Bull Spread (diagram), Call Spread.*

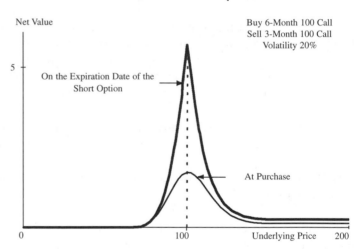

Value of a Calendar Spread

Net Value

Buy 6-Month 100 Call
Sell 3-Month 100 Call
Volatility 20%

On the Expiration Date of the Short Option

At Purchase

0   100   Underlying Price   200

Calibrated Model: A valuation model that produces prices consistent with available market information. The model values are forced to fit existing prices by constraining the time-varying parameter specifications, often at the expense of intertemporal insights.

Call-Adjusted Yield: The non-callable bond-equivalent yield on a callable bond. Equal to the basic yield to maturity less the expected opportunity loss (due to exercise of the issuer's call privilege). Similar adjustments are made in the calculation of call-adjusted duration and call-adjusted convexity. *See also Option-Adjusted Spread (OAS), Option-Adjusted Yield.*

Call Feature: *See Call Provision.*

Call Loan: A loan extended with the understanding that it can be called by the lender at will. Most loans collateralized by securities are made on a call basis. At one time, the broker's call loan rate was significant in money markets. Today, most call loans are based on LIBOR-type rates.

Call Loan Rate: The interest rate on short-term secured loans that can be cancelled (called) on twenty-four hours' notice.

Call Market: A variety of markets in which batches of buy and sell orders are collected for batch rather than continuous execution. *Also called a Walrasian Market.*

Call Option: An option to buy. Call options on securities are ordinarily issued for a period of less than one year, but the label is now commonly applied to longer contracts. *See Option, Terms of an Option Contract, Warrant, Basis. See also Forward Intrinsic Value, Volatility Value.*

Call Or Put (COP): *See As-You-Like Warrant.*

Call Premium: *See Premium (1), Call Price (1).*

Call Price: (1) The market price of an exchange-traded or over-the-counter call option. *Also called Call Premium.* (2) The price at which a callable security can be retired by the issuer. In traditional option terminology, a kind of strike price. In many cases, the call provision provides for a sequence of call prices that change over the life of the security.

Call Protection: Provisions in a bond indenture or preferred stock that designate a period of time during which the issuer cannot call an issue or during which the issuer must pay a premium over parity to retire the issue. *See Hard Call Protection, Soft Call Protection.*

Offsetting Payout Patterns of Long and Short Call Options

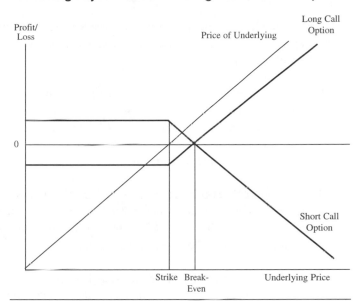

The Components of the Value of a Call

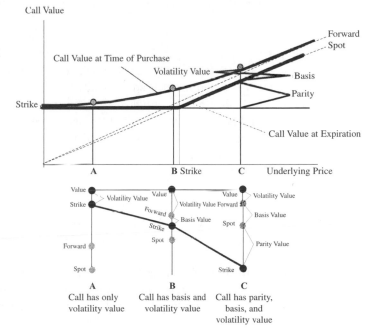

Call Provision: A term in a bond indenture that gives the issuer of a bond the right (option) to call the bond for redemption and/or refunding at certain prices and at certain times. This option can be evaluated approximately with techniques similar to those used in evaluating traded options, but the option to call a bond has some unique characteristics that complicate the analysis. *Also called Call Feature. See Embedded Option.*

Call Report: A quarterly financial report filed by a bank in compliance with regulatory requirements. The focus of the call report is the bank's credit risk exposure. *See also Data Filters.*

Call Risk: A lender's potential opportunity loss associated with premature prepayment of principal on a debt instrument. Call risk is a reinvestment risk, because it is usually impossible to reinvest the funds in a similar instrument with an equal yield.

Call Spread: A spread consisting of partially risk-offsetting long and short positions in at least two different calls on the same underlying stock. *See, for example, Bear Spread (diagram), Bull Spread (diagram), Butterfly Spread (diagram), Calendar Spread (diagram).*

Call Swaption: *See Receiver's Swaption.*

Callable Option or Warrant: In the hands of its holder, this is a long call or long put subject to a short call retained by the issuer of the long option. The issuer can limit the holder's profit by exercising its call and terminating the position during the life of the call feature. Ordinarily, the long call or put has a longer life than the option to terminate retained by the issuer.

Callable Securities: Bonds, preferred issues, and occasionally warrants that can be retired by the issuer. The right to call an issue is often subject to conditions such as a time delay and/or the payment of a premium over the face value of the security. If a security is called, the holder may lose some of the market value of the position. The terms under which the issue can be called are described in the issuance documentation. *See Prepayment Option.*

Callable Step-Up Note: A callable debt issue that features one or more increases in a fixed rate or a step-up in a spread over LIBOR during the life of the note. Most issuers of these notes have low credit ratings. Consequently, the purpose of the step-up is usually to encourage the issuer to refinance. If the issuer does not refinance, the higher rate is designed to compensate for the investor's acceptance of credit risk. Occasionally, a highly rated issuer will sell one of these bonds to implement a strongly held view that rates will decline and a replacement bond can be issued at a lower rate. *Also called Step-Up Coupon Note, Step-Up Bond, Increasing Rate Notes (IRNs). Compare with Convertible Reset Debenture. See also Multi-Step-Up Callable Bond or Note.*

Callable Swap: A swap contract that permits the fixed-rate payer to terminate the contract when interest rates decline to a specified level, or when a bond on which the fixed-rate payment is based is called. *See also Puttable Swap, Cancellable Swap, Retractable Swap.*

Called Away: Elimination of an underlying security position through the exercise of a call option (exercised against the position). Examples include a common stock position called away through the exercise of a short call option, and a bond position called by the issuer under call provisions embedded in the bond indenture.

Called Bond: A bond that the debtor declares due and payable on a certain date prior to maturity and in accordance with a call provision in the bond indenture. Investors need to be alert to bond calls because a called bond earns no interest after the payable date.

Cambistry or Cambism: Any technique used to determine the cheapest method of satisfying an obligation in a foreign currency. The art, science, or the operations side of foreign exchange transactions.

Cancellable Forward Exchange Contract: *See Break Forward (diagram).*

Cancellable Option: *See Break Forward (diagram). Also called Boston Option (1), Forward with Optional Exit (FOX).*

Cancellable Swap: One party to the swap (or sometimes both) has the right to cancel under certain circumstances. Ordinarily, the rates exchanged in the swap reflect the value of a cancellation option. *See also Callable Swap, Puttable Swap. Also called Collapsible Swap.*

Cancellation of a Swap: Early termination of a swap agreement with payment by one counterparty to the other of an amount equal to the net present value of the swap.

Candlestick Chart: Using a charting technique called *rosoku-ashi*, which originated in Japan, candlestick charts indicate the trading range for the day as well as the opening and closing price. If the close is higher than the open, the rectangle between the open and close is unshaded. If the open is higher, that area of the candlestick is shaded.

Cap: (1) A provision of a debt contract or a separate option agreement that, in effect, puts a ceiling or "cap" on an interest rate. A floating-rate borrower may buy an interest rate cap that limits interest cost to, say, 8%, even if rates go much higher. The form of the ceiling may vary. An embedded cap may actually impose a rate ceiling. A separate contract may pay the holder of the cap an amount equal to the amount by which market rates exceed the cap rate (times the notional principal). A cap usually consists of a strip or series of caplets—options putting a ceiling on rates for each rate reset period over the life of the cap. *Also called Interest Rate Cap, Ceiling. See also Caplet, Caption, Floor (1) (diagram).* (2) An option that puts a ceiling on rates or returns in foreign exchange or equity markets.

Candlestick Chart

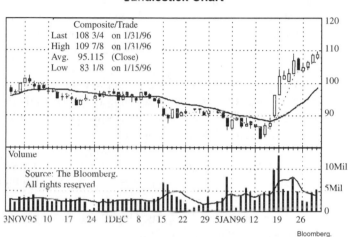

Bloomberg.

The Effective Interest Rate With and Without a Cap

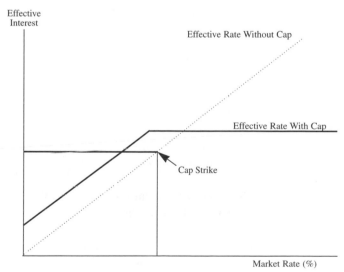

Cap and Floor: *See Equity Risk Reversal, Forward Rate Bracket, Interest Rate Collar, Range Forward Contract (diagram).*

Cap and Floor Certificate: A packaged cap and floor on rates. The cap and floor typically bracket a floating reference index rate over the life of the underlying instrument.

Cap Rate: The strike rate of a cap contract.

Capacity: (1) The business risk element of a credit transaction measured by the ability (capacity) of the debtor to service and ultimately repay the debt. (2) The legal right or authority to engage in a transaction. *See Ultra Vires Act.*

Capacity to Trade: The legal ability to enter into a binding contract of the specific type contemplated and to perform all fixed and contingent obligations under the contract. *See Ultra Vires Act.*

Capital: Funds at risk in an enterprise.

Capital Adequacy: A risk management concept requiring that the capital of a financial organization be sufficient to protect its counterparties and depositors from on- and off-balance sheet market risks, credit risk, etc. Capital requirements tend to be simple mechanical rules rather than applications of sophisticated risk management technology.

Capital Adequacy Directive: An agreement to require standard capital provisions for financial intermediaries doing business in the European Union (EU). This provision may be superseded, at least at first, by implementation of the Basle Convergence Agreement on bank capital by the nations of the EU. *See Basle Convergence Agreement, Risk Measurement.*

Capital Asset Pricing Model (CAPM): An asset valuation model describing the relationship between expected risk and expected return for marketable assets. The CAPM posits that the intercept of a regression equation between an asset's returns and the returns of systematic factors equals 0% in an efficient market, but it does not necessarily assume a single source of systematic risk. This classic model embodied in the security market line is not always empirically affirmed, but it is the most widely used approach to relative asset evaluation. *See Mean Variance (MV) Portfolio Model, Modern Portfolio Theory (MPT). See also E-V Maxim, Random Walk Hypothesis, Market Line.*

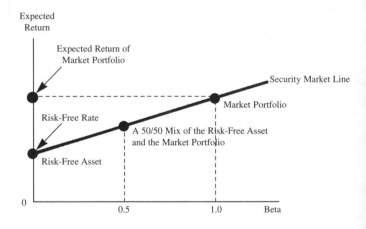

Securities Market Line of the Capital Asset Pricing Model (CAPM)

Capital, Assets, Management, Earnings, and Liquidity (CAMEL): A bank rating system or process that focuses on the five named characteristics.

Capital at Risk: Usually a measure of credit risk. Although maximum possible losses are sometimes brought up in discussions of capital at risk, the predominant approach is to measure capital at risk as a function of the probability distribution of economic loss. The probability distribution of economic loss is, in turn, a function of the distributions and correlations of potential replacement cost, default, and recovery. What may be described as the worst case scenario is usually a 95 or 90 percentile case, not the worst outcome imaginable. *See Value At Risk (VAR) (diagram), Worst Case.*

Capital Change: A stock split, stock dividend, merger, or spin-off that affects the number of shares of stock owned by an investor without necessarily affecting their aggregate value.

Capital Gains Distribution: A payment to a mutual fund or unit trust shareholder of gains realized on the sale of instruments held by the fund.

Capital Gearing: *Brit.* Short- and long-term debt as a percentage of net tangible assets.

Capital Guarantee Note: *See Equity-Linked Note (ELN) (diagrams).*

Capital Market Preferred Stock (CMPS): *See Convertible Adjustable Preferred Stock (CAPS).*

Capital Markets: The markets for corporate equity and intermediate- or long-term debt securities.

Capital Requirements: Equity or subordinated debt funding of a financial intermediary required by regulators to assure the stability and soundness of the institution. After a long period of relaxing capital requirements, recent trends have been in the direction of increasing capital and adjusting requirements to reflect the relative riskiness of an institution's assets and liabilities.

Capital Structure: Capitalization. The equity and longer-term debt obligations that fund an enterprise.

Capitalization Rate: The rate of interest used to discount a series of future cash flows to a present value. *Also called Discount Rate.*

Capitalized Option: *See Contingent Premium Option (diagram).*

Caplet: One of the interim period cap components in a multiperiod interest rate cap agreement. *See also Cap (1) (diagram), Caption.*

Capped Call: A long call position with a maximum payout—analogous in structure to a vertical bull spread position or an equity risk reversal. The terms under which the cap is exercised and the maximum call value may vary in different contracts, and markets and should be checked carefully. *Compare with Floored Put. See, for example, Bull Spread, Capped Index Options (CAPS) for payoff diagrams.*

Capped Floating-Rate Note: A floating-rate note whose maximum rate is fixed in terms of the reference index rate, holding the issuer's interest payment down in a high rate environment. The premium from the cap increases the effective yield at rates below the cap rate plus the premium. *See Participating Capped Floating-Rate Note.*

Capped Index Options (CAPS): An exchange-traded, single-contract, vertical option spread with European-style exercise plus an early exercise price trigger. CAPS incorporate in a single contract either two index calls or two index puts with the same expiration date and with strike prices 30 points apart. The two options are traded as a single, inseparable option spread contract. The early exercise

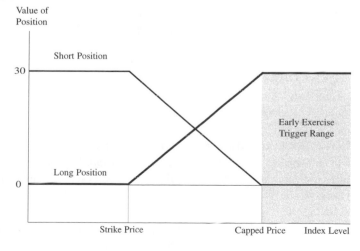

Call CAPS Payoff Pattern at Expiration

price trigger terminates the contract and provides for settlement at the maximum value of the CAPS if the underlying closes at or through the upper strike price on call CAPS or the lower strike price on put CAPS any time during the life of the contract. If the early exercise trigger does not terminate the CAPS sooner, automatic European-style exercise occurs at expiration. *See Automatic Cash-Out Call, Early Exercise Price Trigger, Capped Call, Exploding Option.*

Capped Lookback Calls: A call option with a lookback strike and a ceiling on the settlement price or rate or on the total value of the settlement.

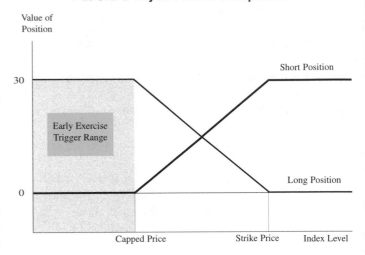

Put CAPS Payoff Pattern at Expiration

Capped Swap: An interest rate swap with an embedded cap on the floating-rate payment.

Capping: An illegal attempt to hold down the price of a financial instrument, often to discourage exercise or reduce the payout of a call option.

Caption: An option to buy a cap. At the expiration of a caption, the holder has the right to purchase a cap with a contractual strike rate for a prespecified premium. *Also called Interest Rate Caption, Option on a Cap. See also Cap (1) (diagram), Caplet, Compound Option (1) (diagram).*

Caput: An option to purchase a put. *See Compound Option (1) (diagram).*

Carrot-and-Stick Bond: A variant of the traditional convertible bond with a low conversion premium to encourage early conversion (the carrot), and a provision allowing the issuer to call the bond at a specified premium if the common stock is trading at a relatively modest percentage above the conversion price (the stick).

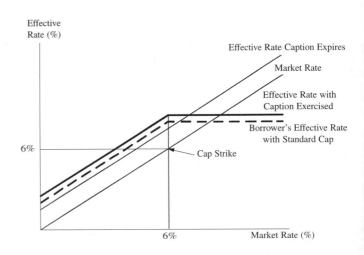

**Borrower's Effective Interest Rate
With and Without a Caption**

Carrying Charge Market: A forward or futures market where the forward price is higher than the spot price by approximately the net cost of purchasing the spot commodity or security and storing and/or financing it until the settlement date of the futures contract. The opposite of a Backwardation Market. *Also called Contango (1). See Basis (1), Forwardation. See also Backwardation (1).*

Cash-and-Carry Trade: An arbitrage-type position—typically consisting of a long position in an underlying and a short position in a futures contract—whose risk-offsetting features transform the net position into the equivalent of a short-term money market instrument maturing at the expiration of the futures contract. *Also called Buying the Basis. See Cash Enhancement Strategy, Index Arbitrage. See also Basis Trade (3).*

Cash Cow: A business that generates cash in excess of what is needed to maintain its facilities or earning power, and that is expected to continue to throw off cash without providing significant opportunities for growth through reinvestment of profits.

Cash Enhancement Strategy: A technique designed to create the risk equivalent of a short-term money market portfolio with a superior return. Arbitrage techniques are often used to obtain a higher rate of return at a very low level of risk. Techniques requiring the sale of an option or a yield curve shift (swap) may adversely affect returns in some circumstances. *See Buying the Basis, Cash-and-Carry Trade, Index Arbitrage.*

Cash Extraction Strategy: An underlying position is exchanged for an approximately risk-equivalent derivatives position that permits the investor to remove cash from the account. Adding back the cash return, the revised position should have a return pattern that replicates the original position very closely. Examples include replacing an equity or bond portfolio with futures contracts, and selling an in-the-money European put to replace a long position in a security or portfolio.

Cash Flow Matching: An asset/liability management technique that attempts to purchase a portfolio with periodic cash flows equal to expected liabilities for each period. *Also called Dedicating a Portfolio, Immunization of a Portfolio.*

Cash Flow Sensitivity Analysis: A combination and extension of Value at Risk (VAR) and Monte Carlo risk measurement techniques. Cash flow sensitivity analysis is designed for non-financial corporations where risk is more a function of cash flow disappointments than problems with the valuations of marketable financial instruments. *See also Value At Risk (VAR) (diagrams), Stress Testing.*

Cash Flow Swap: Usually a swap with irregular cash flows generated by specifically designated instruments or investment processes.

Cash-Futures Swap: *See Exchange of Futures for Physicals (EFP).*

Cash Index Participations (CIPs): *See Index Participations.*

Cash Management Account (CMA): A consumer account offered by a brokerage firm—initially in cooperation with a bank, but increasingly with a money market mutual fund providing deposit and checking privileges. These accounts have simplified consumers' management of their cash balances and have been a significant factor in disintermediation of retail bank deposits in recent years.

Cash Market: The market for securities, physical commodities, or other traditional investments.

Cash-on-Cash: A measurement of return on investment often used in the marketing of tax shelters and investments based on a specific project. Cash-on-cash measures the return on investment by dividing net cash earnings by the cash invested. Changes in likely cash flows over time and the expected life of the cash flows may not be analyzed adequately with this return measurement procedure.

Cash On Delivery (COD) Option: *See Contingent Premium Option (diagram).*

Cash-or-Nothing Option: Similar to an Asset-or-Nothing Option, except that the cash-or-nothing option pays out the exercise price to the holder of the option if the asset value is greater than the exercise price. The holder pays only the initial option premium, not an exercise price.

Cash Or Titles Option (COTO): Convertible instruments issued in Switzerland that let investors avoid the dividend withholding tax and let corporations raise capital. They typically had an expiration date up to twelve months in the future, and gave the holder the right to receive a cash dividend or exchange the COTO for new shares at a fixed price. COTOs ran into Swiss government opposition as a tax avoidance device.

Cash-Out Call Option with Rebate: *See Up-and-Out Call, Rebate. See also Exploding Option.*

Cash-Out Put Option with Rebate: *See Down-and-Out Put, Rebate. See also Exploding Option.*

Cash Secured Put: A short put position collateralized by a cash equivalent instrument that can pay the exercise price at the put's expiration. *Also called Covered Put Writing.*

Cash Settled Option: Although traditional option contracts call for delivery of the underlying in settlement following exercise of the option, many currency, fixed-income, stock index, and basket options, and some options on stocks with restricted transferability, are settled for cash equal to the difference between the strike price and the spot price of the underlying at the time of exercise. *See Cash Settlement (1).*

Cash Settlement: (1) In contrast to traditional stock and bond option contracts and most commodity futures, many currency, fixed-income, and stock index options and financial futures contracts are settled with a cash payment based on the difference between the settlement price and the strike (options) or the settlement price and the previous settlement price (futures). *See Cash Settled Option.* (2) An alternative to activating a swap at the expiration of a swaption is to survey the market and calculate the cash value of the swaption paid to the holder upon exercise. (3) Delivery of securities against cash for settlement on the trade date. *Also called Same Day Settlement.*

Catastrophe Futures and Options: Low-volume contracts listed on the Chicago Board of Trade that are designed to spread participation in insurance company losses and profits by attracting speculative capital to market-based underwriting participation.

Caveat Emptor: Literally, "let the buyer beware." The principle that a buyer is not entitled to rely on a seller's representations as truthful, but must verify the facts independently. A position increasingly rejected by courts. *See also Caveat Venditor.*

Caveat Venditor: Literally, "let the seller beware." The principle that the seller is responsible for any problem the buyer has with a product or service. Often the position embraced by law courts. *See also Caveat Emptor.*

Ceiling: *See Cap (1) (diagram).*

Ceiling Rate Agreement (CRA): A synthetic interest rate cap, often constructed with Eurodollar or other Eurocurrency futures options.

Central Bank: The government or quasi-governmental organization responsible for determination and implementation of a country's monetary policy and currency settlements. Examples include the Federal Reserve System in the U.S. and the Bank of England in the U.K.

Central Limit Theorem: The proposition that the distribution of a sum of independent, random variables, that are not themselves normally distributed, will approach a normal distribution if the number of observations in the sum is large enough. This theorem has been misused by advocates of certain option strategies by applying it to truncated return distributions. The sum of these truncated returns requires more time than any investor can count on to approach normality. Of even greater import, the truncation of extreme values has a lasting effect on very high or very negative return possibilities. *See also Binomial Model (diagram).*

Central Securities Depository (CSD): An operation that dematerializes or eliminates physical delivery and settlement of securities transactions. Once a security is delivered to the central depository, future transactions can be settled electronically or by paper confirmations exchanged by members of the depository.

Centrale de Lívraíson de Valuers Mobilières (CEDEL): One of two clearing houses for Euromarket securities. *See also Euroclear.*

Certainty Equivalent: The value of a certain prospect that yields the same level of utility as the expected utility of an uncertain prospect. For risk-averse investors this value is always lower than the expected value of a risky prospect. A risk-free investment that lies on the same indifference curve as some risky investments is the certainty equivalent of each of those risky investments.

Certificate of Accrual on Treasury Securities (CATS): Zero-coupon instruments created by stripping U.S. Treasury securities. *Also called Stripped Treasury Securities. See STRIPS.*

Certificate of Amortizing Revolving Debts (CARDs): Securitized credit card debt. *See Asset-Backed Security (ABS), Credit Card Receivable-Backed Security.*

Certificate of Automobile Receivables (CARs): Debt instrument collateralized by automobile loan paper. *See Asset-Backed Security (ABS).*

Certificate of Deposit (CD): A debt instrument issued by a bank. CDs are usually interest-bearing, although, like the medium-term notes issued by corporations, they can be used to embed a variety of financial instruments to achieve desired interest rate or equity return patterns.

Certificate of Government Receipts (COUGRs): A member of the feline family of stripped U.S. Treasury securities. *See Stripped Treasury Securities, STRIPS.*

Certificate of Participation (COP): A municipal obligation secured by relatively short-term leases on public facilities. In contrast to general obligation or revenue bonds, leases provide only limited investor protection if a facility is not essential to municipal operations. Default rates on COPs have been substantially higher than default rates on other municipals.

Certificateless Clearing: In contrast to the securities markets, where physical delivery of certificates showing ownership of stocks and bonds is now giving way to electronic book entry of positions, options and futures have always been traded with no more than a broker's confirmation slip as evidence of most transactions.

Ceteris Paribus: *Lat.* Under the assumption that other things are equal or that other variables are unchanged.

Cetes: Mexican Treasury bills.

Chameleon Option: An option that "changes its color" if certain conditions are satisfied. For example, a chameleon call option may change into an otherwise identical put option if the underlying asset's price falls below some prespecified level.

Chaos Theory: A branch of mathematics dealing with non-linear dynamic systems that produce results that appear random, but which in fact arise from a deterministic process. A chaotic system has a fractal dimension, and is highly dependent on initial conditions. Fractals are geometric structures that look similar when viewed at a wide range of magnifications; hence, an implication of small-scale patterns for large-scale phenomena—and vice versa.

Charm: An option derivative or sensitivity calculation that measures the change in delta in response to the passage of time with other variables unchanged: $\Delta\Delta/\Delta t$.

Cheapest To Deliver (CTD): For some physical commodity and fixed-income derivatives contracts, a variety of "grades" of the underlying can be delivered at any of several delivery points, or a number of eligible bonds or notes can be delivered in satisfaction of the short's obligation. The market price of the derivatives contracts reflects the assumption that the delivery requirement will be met by the short in the form of the cheapest commodity grade or instrument to deliver. *Also called Best Bond to Deliver. See Deliverable, Delivery Option.*

Cherry Picking: (1) In some bankruptcy proceedings, contracts favorable to the bankrupt have been enforced and related obligations to unsecured creditors have been abrogated. Swap offset and netting agreements and recent bankruptcy law changes are designed to prevent this cherry picking. (2) Selecting securities from the portfolio of a terminated manager for inclusion in the portfolio of the replacement manager.

Chi-Square Test: A statistical measure of goodness of fit, independence, or homogeneity. The chi-square test can be used to determine whether a sample of data is drawn from a normally distributed population by comparing the sample's frequency distribution with the normal distribution. It can also be used to determine whether two variables are independent by comparing their observed joint occurrence with their expected joint occurrence, assuming independence. Finally, it can be used to determine whether categories of a single variable are represented in the same proportions in two or more populations.

Chicago Mercantile Exchange Swaps Depository Trust Company (CME DTC): An organized swap collateral depository taking over the third-party collateral management function. *See also Collateralized Swap, Depository Trust Company (DTC), Hybrid Instruments Transaction Service (HITS), C-Trac+, Global Credit Support Service (GCSS).*

Chinese Wall: Usually a physical barrier as well as a set of policies and procedures designed to insure compliance with securities laws governing the separation of information available to an investment bank's corporate finance division or a commercial bank's lending division as distinct from information available to personnel dealing with customers on securities transactions and investments.

Choice LIBOR Swap: A swap giving the floating-rate receiver the right to receive the higher of LIBOR set at the beginning of the period or at the end of the period. *See also In-Arrears Swap (diagram).*

Choke: A tight collar, i.e. a collar with a narrow spread between its upper and lower strikes. *See Collar (2) (diagram), Range Forward Contract (diagram), Equity Risk Reversal (diagram).*

Chooser Option: *See As-You-Like Warrant.*

Chooser Swap: A swap with a range option payout embedded in a floating rate. The choice comes from the floating-rate receiver's ability to set the midpoint of the range on each reset date. *See also Wedding Band Swap.*

Christmas Tree: *See Ladder Trade (diagram). Also called Table Top.*

Chumming: *See Churning (3).*

Churning: (1) Excessive turnover of an investor's securities holdings, usually implemented or strongly encouraged by a securities salesperson who may face disciplinary action as a result of his activities. (2) Trading more for the sake of generating commissions or trading spreads than for the benefit of the account where the activity takes place. (3) Trading to create the appearance of activity, perhaps as part of an attempt at market manipulation. *Also called Chumming.*

Circuit Breakers: A complex series of rules adopted by securities and futures exchanges in the aftermath of the 1987 market break in an attempt to slow down market activity during major stock price movements. It is difficult to prove that these rules have done any harm—or any good. *See also Limit Move.*

Circus Option: *See Cross-Currency Swaption.*

Circus Swap: A combined currency and interest rate swap. For example, a currency coupon swap with $/LIBOR as the floating rate. Often used to link fixed-rate swaps in two currencies that do not have active swap markets. *See Currency Coupon Swap.*

City (of London): The approximately one-square mile area in London where financial activity is concentrated. *Also called Square Mile.* Compared figuratively to Wall Street in the U.S.

Class of Options: All listed option contracts of the same type covering the same underlying security, e.g., all listed IBM common stock call options.

Clean Hedge Instrument: A derivative security whose risk can be hedged with liquid exchange-traded securities and whose market risk exposure remains relatively constant. *See also Dirty Hedge Instrument.*

Clean Price: A bond price quoted exclusive of accrued interest. *See also Dirty Price.*

Clean Risk: (1) The risk that a swap counterparty will not make a required payment on a given reset day—as distinct from the risk of a cancellation and loss of mark-to-market value if the swap has a net present value. The risk of loss of a single swap payment. (2) *See Overnight Delivery Risk.*

Clean Up Provision: A feature of many amortizing instruments whereby the remaining principal is repaid and the instrument is cancelled if the remaining principal drops below a predesignated percentage of the initial face of the instrument.

Clearing: The process of settling a trade—including the deposit of any necessary collateral with the clearing corporation and exchange of any necessary cash and paperwork.

Clearing Broker or Member: An exchange member authorized to deal directly with the clearing corporation when settling a trade executed on the exchange floor or through an electronic order matching system. Parties to every trade exchange names or other information identifying their clearing member. The clearing member is responsible for any collateral or cash exchanges with the clearing corporation, carries the position, and is responsible for its ultimate settlement or disposition. Most investors find it convenient to deal with a limited number of clearing brokers. If they want the services of a larger number of executing brokers, they ask the executing brokers to "give up" the trade to a clearing broker, and the executing and clearing brokers share the commission. *See also Non-Clearing Member.*

Clearing Corporation: The affiliate or subsidiary of a futures or securities exchange that clears trades and holds performance bonds (margins) posted by dealers to assure performance on their own and customers' futures and options obligations. Called a clearing house in the U.K. *See Options Clearing Corporation (OCC).*

Clearing House: The British term for clearing corporation.

Clearing House Interbank Payment System (CHIPS): An interbank settlement and money/payment transfer system organized by the New York Clearing House Association, a group of the largest city banks. CHIPS has appropriate links to SWIFT and the FEDWIRE Communications System.

Cliquet Option: The French like the sound of "cliquet," and seem prepared to apply the term to any remotely appropriate option structure. (1) Originally a periodic reset option with multiple payouts or a ratchet option (from *vilbrequin à cliquet*—ratchet brace). *Also called Ratchet Option. See Multiperiod Strike Reset Option (MSRO), Stock Market Annual Reset Term (SMART) Note. See also Coupon-Indexed Note.* (2) *See Ladder Option or Note (diagram). Also called Lock-Step Option. See also Stock Upside Note Security (SUNS).* (3) Less commonly, a rolling spread with strike price resets, usually at regular intervals. (4) An exploding or knockout option such as CAPS (from *cliqueter*—to knock). *See Exploding Option.*

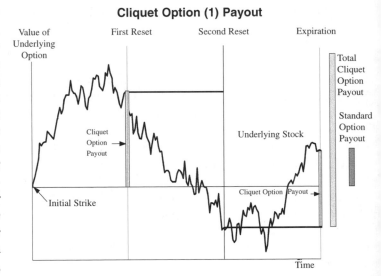

Cliquet Option (1) Payout

Close: (1) The price of the final trade, or alternately the closing trading range in a trading session. (2) The time period near the end of a trading session. (3) To eliminate a position through an offsetting purchase or sale.

Close-Out Netting: *See Netting Agreement.*

Closed-End Mutual Fund: An investment company with a fixed number of shares outstanding. Shares purchased in such a fund are purchased from another shareholder rather than issued in response to demand for new shares. In contrast to shares in an open end mutual fund, which can usually be redeemed at net asset value, a closed-end fund's shares can trade at a premium or discount.

Closed-Form Solution: A closed-form solution exists whenever the transitional density function is completely specified. A restrictive use of this term refers to solutions described in terms of a normal distribution function. Although all closed-form solutions come from analytic models, not all analytic models have closed-form solutions.

Closed Fund: A mutual fund that no longer offers shares for sale to the public, often because management cannot manage additional assets effectively. In some cases, present shareholders may buy more shares.

Closing Date: The date on which a transaction is completed, including the transfer of ownership and the payment and receipt of funds.

Closing Purchase Transaction: A transaction in which an investor terminates his short option or futures delivery obligation by purchasing a fungible contract having the same terms as a contract previously sold.

Closing Range: The high and low prices, or bids and offers, recorded during the period designated as the official close of some futures exchanges. *See also Opening Range.*

Closing Rotation: *See Rotation.*

Closing Sale Transaction: A transaction where an investor liquidates a long option or futures position by selling a fungible contract having the same terms as the contract previously purchased. *See also Opening Sale Transaction.*

CMO Swap: A swap based on a specific collateralized mortgage obligation with amortization of the notional principal linked to the repayment rate of a mortgage pool or the principal prepayment rate of a specific CMO tranche.

Co-opetition: A principle of game theory, holding that businesses succeed by combining cooperative strategies with competitive strategies. They cooperate to enlarge the pie and compete to divide it up. This approach is supported by the notion that your opponent does not have to fail for you to succeed.

Coberatura: *Mex.* A Mexican variation on a currency forward contract. An investor who wants to hedge a peso position pays forward points to lock in the spot rate. At settlement, the investor receives the difference between the initial spot rate and the spot rate at settlement. The Mexican government imposes a small withholding tax on any "capital gain" from the transaction.

Cockroach Theory: Like cockroaches, there is rarely just one adverse earnings surprise.

Cocktail Bond: *See Dual Option Bond.*

Cocktail Swap: A complex transaction involving several swaps of different types and usually more than two counterparties.

Coefficient of Determination: *See R^2 (Coefficient of Determination).*

Cointegration: An association between two time series that measures the extent to which fluctuations in one series offset fluctuations in another. Time leads or lags may be used, but a perfectly cointegrated and weighted pair of time series will sum to a straight line. Cointegration is used to model series and relationships characterized by persistence, and is often modeled with mean reversion techniques. *See R (Correlation Coefficient).*

Collapsible Swap: *See Cancellable Swap.*

Collar: (1) A feature of a debt contract or a separate agreement that puts both a cap (ceiling) and a floor (minimum) on the interest rate. *Also called Min Max.* (2) An option contract or set of contracts that limits downside risk in any underlying below a floor price and eliminates upside participation beyond a cap price. *Also called Fence or Fence Spread, Hedge Wrap. See Choke, Interest Rate Collar (diagram), Equity Risk Reversal (diagram), Floor (1) (diagram), Partial Collar (diagram), Participating Collar (diagram).*

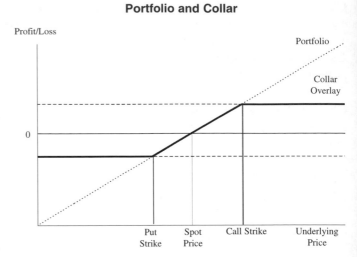

Portfolio and Collar

Collared Floating-Rate Note (FRN): A floating-rate note with an embedded collar. Usually the sale of the cap(s) brings in more premium than the investor pays for the floor(s), making this a common floating-rate note variation when short rates are low and the yield curve is steeply rising.

Collared Swap: An interest rate swap with an embedded collar constraining the floating-rate payment.

Collateral: An obligation or security linked to another obligation or security to secure its performance. For example, an option writer may deposit with his bank or broker common stock in the company on which an option is written as collateral to guarantee performance on the option. He may also deposit securities convertible into the underlying stock or completely unrelated securities with an appropriate market value. Collateral is also posted as a performance bond to guarantee performance on listed futures contracts and on various over-the-counter contracts.

Collateral Agreement: A provision in a risk management agreement that requires one party (a unilateral collateral agreement) or both parties (a bilateral collateral agreement) to provide collateral to guarantee performance under the agreement. Arrangements for marking positions to the market, measuring the collateral requirement, moving collateral around, and even providing a physical location for holding the collateral are not standardized across markets.

Collateral Trust Bond: A bond secured by securities owned by the issuing company. The securities are usually held by a trustee.

Collateralized Bond Obligation (CBO): A multitranche debt structure similar in some respects to a CMO structure. Low-rated bonds, rather than mortgages, usually serve as the collateral. The organization creating and promoting the structure usually holds the underlying equity and may also collect a fee. *See Collateralized Mortgage Obligation (CMO), Tranche.*

Collateralized Depositary Receipt (CDR): A generic financial instrument secured by the deposit of another financial instrument with the issuing depository institution.

Collateralized Increasable Yield Notes: A combination of medium-term notes and a commodity futures pool designed to produce a guaranteed minimum return (often zero) and upside participation linked to the performance of the futures pool.

Collateralized Lease Equipment Obligations (CEO or CLEO): Securitized equipment loans.

Collateralized Mortgage Obligation (CMO): A generic term for a security backed by real estate mortgages. CMO payment obligations are covered by interest and/or principal payments from a pool of mortgages. In addition, the term CMO usually suggests a non-governmental issuer. *Also called Fast-Pay/Slow-Pay Bonds or Serialized Mortgage-Backed Security* because they usually have a multitranche structure with interest and principal payments prioritized and segmented. *See also Collateralized Bond Obligation (CBO), Interest Only (IO) Obligation, Government National Mortgage Association (GNMA) Pass-Through Certificates, Mortgage-Backed Securities, Principal Only (PO) Obligation, Real Estate Mortgage Investment Conduit (REMIC), Z Bond, Stripped Mortgage-Backed Security (SMBS).*

Collateralized Security: A debt instrument secured by an asset or a pool of assets, often other securities.

Collateralized Swap: A swap contract under which one or both counterparties post collateral, usually with a third party, to insure performance on the agreement. The collateral may be deposited on the trade date of the swap, or it may be posted on demand only by the party who is the net creditor on the swap. Organized swap collateral depositories are being formed to take over the third-party collateral management function. *See Hybrid Instruments Transaction Service (HITS), Chicago Mercantile Exchange Swaps Depository Trust Company (CME DTC).*

Collect On Delivery (COD) Option: *See Contingent Premium Option (diagram).*

Color: An option derivative or sensitivity calculation that measures the change in gamma in response to the passage of time, other things equal: $\Delta\gamma/\Delta t$.

Combination Option: An option or group of options consisting of at least one put and one call. The component options may be exercised or resold separately, but they are originally traded as a unit. The term is increasingly applied loosely to any package of several different options. *See Option, Spraddle (diagram), Spread, Straddle (diagram), Strangle, Strap, Strip (2).*

Comfort Letter: A letter from an independent auditor to an underwriter describing the scope of the auditor's examination of an issuer's financial statements.

Commercial Paper: Short-term corporate debt obligations with maturities ranging up to 270 days. Like many money market instruments, they are usually priced at a discount to par.

Commercial Real Estate-Backed Bonds: Asset-backed securities with a single property or a commercial real estate portfolio as collateral. This structure is used to increase the liquidity of real estate loans.

Commission: A transaction fee charged by a broker for acting as agent in a transaction. *Also called Brokerage, Courtage. See also Broker.*

Committee for Improved Corporate Reporting (CICR): A unit of the New York Society of Security Analysts (NYSSA) that monitors trends in corporate reporting and changes in accounting standards. CICR educates the society's members and expresses the membership's views to accounting standards-setting bodies like the Financial Accounting Standards Board (FASB).

Committee on Investment of Employee Benefit Assets (CIEBA): An organization of employee benefit administrators whose members share insights into common problems and maintain dialogues with regulators.

Committee on Uniform Security Identification Procedures (CUSIP): A group established by the American Bankers Association to develop a uniform method of identifying securities in the U.S. Each security publicly traded in the U.S. is assigned a unique CUSIP number. Similar systems are in place in other countries and in the Euromarket.

Commoditization: A process of marketability enhancement in which illiquid financial contracts are modified for trading in more liquid and transparent markets. Securitization is a special case. Most observers consider this transformation desirable, but there are occasional references to commoditization as a cause of price fluctuations. In fact, prices do fluctuate in the less liquid market, but prices are harder to measure without liquidity.

Commodity: (1) A physical good typically produced in agriculture or mining, usually standardized or subject to grading or other classification, that can be the object of commercial transactions. The expansion of the legal definition of commodity in recent years has led many managers, analysts, and traders to refer to these as physical commodities. (2) Any economic good. (3) Any index, rate, security, or physical commodity that is or could be the underlying instrument or price determinant of a futures contract or other instrument regulated by the Commodity Futures Trading Commission (CFTC).

Commodity Exchange Act (CEA): The principal legislation governing the trading of commodities and futures in the U.S. This act, as amended, establishes the Commodities Futures Trading Commission (CFTC); sets out the circumstances under which the CFTC regulates, or can exempt from regulation, transactions in physical commodity and financial futures contracts; and incorporates the Shad-Johnson Agreement, which describes the division of authority and responsibility for regulation of financial contracts between the CFTC and the Securities and Exchange Commission (SEC.)

Commodity Futures Trading Commission (CFTC): The regulatory agency charged with regulation of futures and futures option markets in the United States.

Commodity Index Note: Some or all of any positive return on the note is tied to the performance of a specific physical commodity or commodity index, such as oil, gold, silver, the CRB index, etc. The participation in the commodity price may be in the form of an option or a forward component. Often issued by a producer of the underlying commodity. *Also called Commodity-Linked Note or Bond. Compare with Equity-Linked Note (ELN) (diagrams).*

Commodity-indexed preferred or debt Securities (CompS): A cash settled hybrid instrument that may or may not pay periodic interest or dividends, and settles at maturity at a price linked to the price of a single commodity.

Commodity Interest-Indexed Bond or Note: A debt instrument with a coupon rate linked to the price of a commodity, usually issued by a producer of the commodity. Unless otherwise indicated, the principal is not indexed. *Generically, a Coupon-Indexed Note.*

Commodity-Linked Note or Bond: *See Commodity Index Note.*

Commodity Option: An option to buy (call) or sell (put) a specific physical commodity or commodity futures contract at a given strike price within a specified time. Less frequently, an option on a financial futures contract. *See Option.*

Commodity Pool Operator (CPO): Section 1a(4) of the Commodity Exchange Act defines "Commodity

Pool Operator" as "any person engaged in a business that is of the nature of an investment trust, syndicate, or similar form of enterprise, and who, in connection therewith, solicits, accepts, or receives from others, funds, securities, or property, either directly or through capital contributions, the sale of stock or other forms of securities, or otherwise, for the purpose of trading in any commodity for future delivery on or subject to the rules of any contract market...." In short, the manager of a public or private futures fund.

Commodity Swap: A swap in which counterparties exchange cash flows based on a physical commodity price or return on at least one side. *See Swap (3).*

Commodity Trading Advisor (CTA): In the U.S., any person (in the legal sense) registered with the Commodity Futures Trading Commission "who, for compensation or profit, engages in the business of advising others, either directly or through publications, writings or electronic media, as to the value of or the advisability of trading in any contract of sale of a commodity for future delivery made or to be made on or subject to the rules of any contract market; [or] any commodity option authorized under section 4 (c) [of the Commodity Exchange Act]...or who, for compensation or profit, and as part of a regular business, issues or promulgates analyses or reports concerning [any of the foregoing]." The approximate futures market equivalent of a registered investment adviser in the securities market in the U.S.

Common-linked Higher Income Participation Security (CHIPS): A synthetic Preferred Equity Redemption Cumulative Stock (PERCS) issued by a financial intermediary or some other third party. *See Equity-LinKed Security (ELKS), Preference Equity Redemption Cumulative Stock (PERCS) (diagram). Also called Synthetic High-Income Equity-Linked Debenture (SHIELD), Synthetic PERCS.*

Common Market: A formal relationship among a group of European countries, also referred to as the European Economic Community (EEC), and more recently as the European Union (EU). The EU was established in 1958 in an attempt to integrate its members' economies through financial cooperation and free trade within the Community. The original members of the Common Market were: West Germany, France, Italy, Belgium, the Netherlands, and Luxembourg. As of the end of 1995, the EU had grown to include all of Germany, France, Italy, the U.K., Spain, the Netherlands, Belgium, Denmark, Greece, Portugal, and Ireland. Although the original motivation was political integration, most of the progress has been economic. *Most commonly called the European Union. See also European Monetary Union.*

Common Stock: The residual ownership securities class in a corporation. Common stockholders usually control the board of directors and management, and have rights to the benefits of the corporation's economic success once prior claims are satisfied.

Companion Collateralized Mortgage Obligation: A volatile CMO tranche that, for example, gets principal first or interest last to stabilize the cash flows to other tranches. *Also called Support Collateralized Mortgage Obligation. See Interest Only (IO) Obligation, Principal Only (PO) Obligation, Support (SUP) Bond.*

Comparative Statics: By comparing different equilibrium states associated with different parameters and exogenous variables, comparative statics addresses how a new equilibrium compares with a prior equilibrium. This analysis ignores the path of adjustment and focuses only on the initial and post-change states.

Competitive Currency Risk: Currency exchange rate risk that affects a firm's competitiveness in a product line also produced by a competitor whose costs are incurred in a foreign currency. If the competitor's currency weakens, his relative competitive position improves, because his costs decline relative to international competition. A producer facing competition of this sort can use currency contracts to match the competitor's cost structure for the duration of available contracts. *See also Economic Hedge, Economic Risk.*

Complement Rule: A reference to the parity relationship between European barrier options and standard options. The complement rule states that an "out" barrier option without rebate plus an otherwise identical "in" barrier option must have the same value as a standard option with otherwise identical terms.

Complete Market: A market where investors buy or sell combinations of securities that pay off in all desired states. More generally, a market where investors have a full range of risk/return choices. Investment opportunities are presented in the form of basic components, which the investor can assemble on a customized basis to conform to a personal utility function. One of the important contributions of derivatives instruments is to increase investor utility and issuer flexibility by increasing the range of choices and the completeness of markets.

Completion Portfolio or Fund: A selection of stocks or, less frequently, bonds that fills "gaps" in a portfolio and improves its tracking relative to a designated benchmark index. Completion funds are often used by pension plan sponsors or endowment investment funds to add types of assets not used by the portfolio's active managers. *Also called Fulfillment Fund.*

Complex Option: An option with an exercise price that can change and/or is subject to a change other than a price change in the underlying. *Examples include Quanto Note (diagram), Step-Up Option or Warrant, Step-Down Option or Warrant. See also Quantity Adjusting Option (QUANTO) (1).*

Compliance Procedures: Policies that ensure that a securities or futures firm's personnel follow rules imposed by regulators.

Component (COM) Bond: A collateralized mortgage obligation (CMO) composed of a combination of non-detachable components. The principal pay type and/or sequence of principal pay of each component may vary. An example with an unflattering name is the *Kitchen Sink Bond*, used to package CMO leftovers.

Composite Index: An index that combines figures relating to several variables or separate indexes, such as the exchange rates of several currencies. *See also Basket.*

Composite Option: *See Cross Option.*

Composite Swap: Most commonly, an equity-linked swap with the equity return denominated and paid in the natural currency of the equity market.

Compound Annual Growth Rate (CAGR): *See Geometric Mean Return.*

Compound Average Rate Option: An option to buy a currency average rate put or call. *See Average Price or Rate Option (APO, ARO) (diagrams), Compound Option (1) (diagram).*

Compound Exotic: A name devised by the financial press to add pizzazz to a structured note with one or more embedded equity or interest rate components combined with at least one currency component.

Compound Option: (1) An option on an option, such as a put on a call, a call on a put, a call on a call, or a put on a put. These options are used primarily in fixed-income and currency markets when the need for the risk protection afforded by an option is not certain, and the buyer of the compound option wants to pay a reduced initial premium. The contingency on the first option usually determines the need for the protection provided by the second option. Compound option techniques are often useful in evaluating early exercise options and in a variety of fixed-income option valuation applications. The compound option model of Robert Geske was the first stochastic volatility model. *Also called Option on an Option. See also Back Fee,*

Front Fee, Caption (diagram), Compound Average Rate Option, Floortion, Split-Fee Option, Strike Premium, Exotic Options. See also Cacall, Caput. (2) Occasionally refers to a call option on the shares of a leveraged company. Common shareholders, in effect, have a call option to "buy" the firm by paying off its debt. Alternately, shareholders cannot lose more than the cost of their shares if they abandon the firm to the debtholders. Robert Geske and others have used such examples to demonstrate that a call option on common stock can be usefully valued as an option on an option.

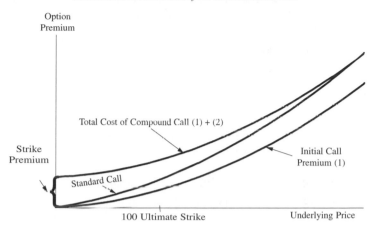

A Compound Call Option (1)
Strike Premium Fixed at Value of 100 Strike Six-Month Call

Option Premium

Total Cost of Compound Call (1) + (2)

Strike Premium

Initial Call Premium (1)

Standard Call

100 Ultimate Strike

Underlying Price

Compounding: The reinvestment of all periodic return in subsequent periods. For example, if an investment strategy generates a 10% total return in each of two consecutive periods, and the first return is reinvested in the strategy, then the cumulative compounded return over the two periods equals 21%, because the first 10% return generates an additional 1% return in the second period.

Compression Risk: The potential loss from a decline in yields that triggers call features on corporate debt or prepayment on mortgaged debt, and causes an issue to behave like a short-term note. A function of prepayment opportunities and incentives.

Comptant: Cash transaction on a Swiss or French stock exchange.

Comptroller of the Currency: *See Office of the Comptroller of the Currency (OCC).*

Concave Payoff Function: Relative to a linear payoff pattern, a return function that has lower returns at the extreme values of the underlying asset, and higher returns at values close to the average value of the underlying asset. Concavity is the result of reduced exposure to the performance of the underlying as the underlying increases, and increased exposure as the underlying decreases. *The opposite of Convexity.*

Concave Utility Function: A utility function with a positive first derivative and a negative second derivative with respect to wealth. Concavity implies that each increment to wealth conveys progressively smaller increments to utility. Investors with concave utility functions are risk averse and will reject a fair game. *See also Utility, Utility Theory.*

Concertina Swap: *See Rollercoaster Swap.*

Conditional Forward Purchase Contract: A forward agreement under which the long side of the contract has the right to cancel the purchase by paying a fee to the short on the contract maturity date. Alternatively, the cancellation fee can be eliminated if the trade price is sufficiently lower than the forward price. This contract and the conditional forward sale contract are variants of the break forward contract. *See also Break Forward (diagram).*

Conditional Forward Sale Contract: The mirror image of a conditional forward purchase contract. The short side of the contract has the right to abandon the agreement by paying a fee. If the trade price is sufficiently above the forward price, the fee is waived.

Conditional Mean: The forecast of the value of a time series at time t given information on the series up to time t − 1.

Conditional Prepayment Rate (CPR): A method of expressing the prepayment rate for a mortgage pool that assumes that a constant fraction of the remaining principal is prepaid each month or year. Specifically, the conditional prepayment rate is an annualized version of the single monthly mortality (SMM). *See also Single Monthly Mortality (SMM).*

Conditional Variance: The forecast of the variance of a time series at time t based on the time-varying evolution of the series' variance up to time t − 1.

Condor: A complex option spread that is similar to a butterfly except that the two short options have different strikes. This bird is extinct in portfolios that are transaction cost-sensitive. *See also Butterfly Spread (diagram).*

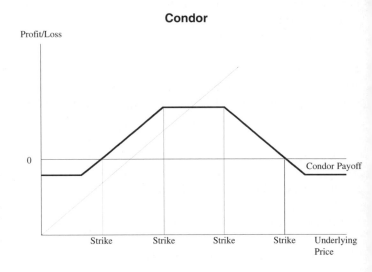

Conduit Financing: A form of financing in which a government or a government agency lends its name to a bond issue, although it is only acting as a conduit between a specific project and bondholders. The bondholders can only be repaid by the project's earnings, and not by the government or agency whose name appears on the bond.

Conduit Tax Treatment: The pass-through tax treatment accorded regulated investment companies, S corporations, many mortgage structures, partnerships, etc. *See also Pass-Through Securities.*

Confidence Intervals: An estimate of the probability (confidence) that an observation will fall within or outside a specified range. If the underlying data are normally distributed, a 68% confidence interval is estimated as the mean ± 1 standard deviation, and a 95% confidence interval is estimated as the mean ± 2 standard deviations. *See Normal Distribution.*

Conflict of Interest: A situation where the financial interests of an individual or institution are different from the interests of one or more of the institution's clients, or in which the interests of one client conflict with the interests of another.

Congeneric Company: A holding company or combined holding and operating company whose holdings and operations are complementary or similar in nature as opposed to conglomerate. Congenerics are most common in the financial and utility industries.

Conjectural Guarantee: A reference to a sovereign or regulator's unstated willingness to protect an investor or lender from loss due to failure of a creditor, because the creditor entity is essential to the operation of the financial markets or is "too big to fail." *See also Too Big To Fail Policy.*

Consols: Perpetual British government bonds. These bonds are available in both registered and bearer form and have no provisions requiring repayment of principal. *See also Renter.*

Constant Elasticity of Variance (CEV) Model: A probability-type option valuation model that incorporates a variance adjustment causing the absolute level of the variance to decline as the stock price rises, and to rise as the stock price declines. Empirically, most equity and interest rate volatilities do respond to price or rate changes in approximately this way.

Constant Maturity Swap (CMS): A variation of the fixed-rate-for-floating-rate interest rate swap. The rate on one side of the constant maturity swap is either fixed or reset periodically at or relative to LIBOR (or another floating reference index rate). The constant maturity side, which gives the swap its name, is reset each period relative to a regularly available fixed maturity market rate. This constant maturity rate is the yield on an instrument with a longer life than the length of the reset period, so the parties to a constant maturity swap have exposure to changes in a longer-term market rate. Although published swap rates are often used as constant maturity rates, the most popular constant maturity rates are yields on two- to five-year sovereign debt. In the U.S., swaps based on sovereign rates are often called constant maturity Treasury (CMT) swaps.

A standard fixed-for-floating interest rate swap is priced to reflect the arbitrage-enforced relationship between a fixed rate and the combined spot and forward rates implied by the yield curve. In contrast, the CMS is priced to reflect the relative values of either fixed or floating rates on one side and an intermediate-term fixed-rate instrument that covers a segment of the forward curve and moves out along the forward curve at each reset date. The CMS arbitrage relationship is more complex than the fixed-for-floating rate swap, but the principles that determine the pricing of other swaps apply to CMS.

In general, a flattening or an inversion of the curve after the swap is in place improves the constant maturity rate payer's position relative to a floating rate payer. The relative positions of a constant maturity rate payer and a fixed-rate payer are more complex, but the fixed-rate payer in any swap benefits primarily from an upward shift of the yield curve. *See Constant Maturity Treasury (CMT) Rate (diagram), Swap (1).*

Constant Maturity Treasury (CMT) Option: A put or rate cap structure created for payers of annuities, paying off if the synthetic Treasury rate rises above a strike rate. The covered CMT optionholder benefits from any rate decline after deduction of the CMT option premium. *See Constant Maturity Treasury (CMT) Rate (diagram).*

Constant Maturity Treasury (CMT) Rate: An interest rate benchmark index based on the yield of a synthetic security of appropriate maturity as interpolated from the Treasury yield curve. *See Constant Maturity Swap (CMS) for more detail. See Constant Maturity Treasury (CMT) Option.*

Constant Proportion Portfolio Insurance (CPPI): A portfolio insurance technique that exposes a constant multiple of a cushion over an investor's floor or "insured" value to the performance of the risky asset. For example, an investor with a $100 portfolio, a floor of $90,

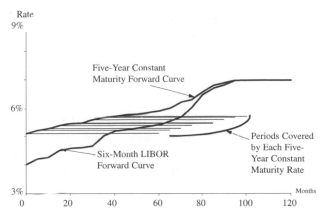

Constant Maturity Treasury (CMT) Rate

and a multiple of 5 allocates \$50 [5 × (\$100 − \$90)] to the risky asset, and the remaining \$50 to the riskless asset. The investor revises the exposures as the portfolio value changes. Unlike other portfolio insurance strategies, CPPI does not require the investor to specify a finite horizon. *See Portfolio Insurance, Floor (3).*

Constant Relative Risk Aversion: A description of risk aversion that holds that investors allocate the same percentage of wealth to risky assets as wealth changes.

Constant Spread Range Index Bond Security (CS-RIBS): A variation of the index range note, in which the range is reset at the end of each period to make the current level of the index rate (usually LIBOR) the midpoint of the target range during the next accumulation period. *See also Corridor Accrual Swap.*

Construction Loan Swap: *See Accreting Principal Swap (APS).*

Contango: (1) *See Carrying Charge Market, Forwardation. See also Backwardation (1).* (2) A charge made to a stock purchaser who wishes to delay delivery of and payment for his shares. The charge is based on interest on the amount of the transaction from the scheduled settlement date until the ultimate settlement.

Contingent Cap: An interest rate cap contract for which the buyer of the cap pays no upfront premium, but agrees to pay a predetermined premium if the cap has any value on its effective date. The premium for a contingent cap is much greater than the premium on an ordinary cap, but the premium is paid only if the cap is in the money at expiration. *See Contingent Premium Option (diagram).*

Contingent Claim: An option. A derivative asset whose value at any settlement date is determined by the value of one or more other assets. *See also Derivatives Instrument or Product (2).*

Contingent Currency Option: An option that protects a portfolio from currency losses only when the local return on the underlying portfolio falls below a prespecified value. This option is less expensive than an unconditional currency option, because of the diminished likelihood of concurrent losses on the currency component and asset component of the total portfolio. A special case of the *Contingent Payout Option. See Multi-Asset Option.*

Contingent Currency Risk: Currency exchange rate risk associated with a transaction that may or may not occur. A contract proposal, for example, may lead to currency exposure only if the contract is executed. This contingent currency exposure can be hedged with a traditional option, or, at a lower premium, with a specialized option designed for this problem. *See Contingent Hedge with an Agreement for Rebate at Maturity (CHARM). Also called Shared Currency Option Under Tender (SCOUT).*

Contingent Exchange Option: An option to exchange one asset (a managed portfolio, for example) for another asset (a benchmark portfolio, for example) when the managed portfolio underperforms the benchmark portfolio by a prespecified amount and simultaneously drops below a prespecified hurdle value. This option protects a portfolio manager from concurrently experiencing unfavorable absolute and relative performance. *See Exchange Option, Multi-Asset Option.*

Contingent Hedge with an Agreement for Rebate at Maturity (CHARM): A currency option designed for companies bidding on foreign contracts. If the company wins the contract, the option can be exercised like any other currency option. If the company loses, the option is void, but the issuer rebates a portion of the premium. Consequently, the value of the payoff depends on the buyer's ability to obtain business requiring currency protection as well as on currency movements. The rebate serves the dual function of relating the net premium to the value of the hedge and facilitating the hedging position taken by the currency option dealer. *See Contingent Currency Risk.*

Contingent Immunization: A fixed-income portfolio management technique with some characteristics in common with portfolio insurance in equity markets. The manager of a contingently immunized portfolio may have considerable flexibility in the yield and duration of the positions used in the portfolio as long as the positions perform well relative to the associated liability. If the portfolio performs poorly, the manager moves to a portfolio that matches (immunizes) the duration and return requirements of the liabilities. The shift to the immunized portfolio is total and irrevocable, as opposed to portfolio insurance strategies where the manager continually shifts funds between risky and riskless assets.

Contingent Liability: An off-balance sheet item that is a potential liability under certain circumstances. Examples include loan commitments, lines of credit, letters of credit, certain foreign exchange contracts, and judgments from pending litigation.

Contingent Order: An order to purchase or sell one security whose execution depends on the execution and/or the price of a trade in another instrument. Contingent orders are frequently used in the execution of futures rolls and option spread transactions and in the establishment and liquidation of option buy-writes. *See also One Cancels the Other Order (OCO).*

Contingent Payout Option: A variation on a standard option in which the holder's payout is contingent not only on the behavior of an equity rate or index price but on the behavior of a second financial or economic variable as well. One of the most common varieties of contingent payout options is an option on a specific stock index, with the investor's ability to collect a payout contingent upon an exchange rate relationship or an interest rate relationship. For example, an investor may feel that a decline in French interest rates will cause the CAC 40 index to perform extremely well over the next six months, but he may also believe that good stock performance will not be achieved unless French interest rates decline. To the extent that the correlation between stock prices and interest rates in France is less than perfect, the investor can reduce his premium outlay by purchasing an option on the CAC 40 with its payout contingent upon a specified movement in French interest rates. Depending on the correlations that the seller of the option anticipates, and how much of a movement in interest rates

Standard Option versus Contingent Payout Option on the CAC 40 Index

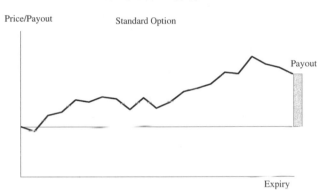

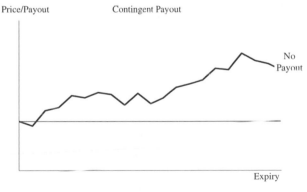

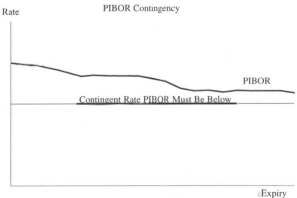

the option buyer is willing to specify, introducing this contingency might reduce the option premium substantially. *Also called Equity Rate Contingency Option, Contingent Currency Option, Dual Contingency Option, Stock Index Contingent Option. Compare with Contingent Premium Option. See also Interest Rate Contingent Option, Multi-Asset Option.*

Contingent Premium Option: A contract for which the buyer of the option pays no premium upfront, but agrees to pay a predetermined premium if the option has any value at expiration. The premium for a contingent premium option exceeds that for an ordinary option, but the premium is paid only if the option is in the money at expiration. *Also called Capitalized Option, Cash On Delivery (COD) Option, Collect On Delivery (COD) Option, Pay On Exercise Option. Compare with Contingent Payout Option, Deferred Premium Option. See also Boston Option (2), Contingent Cap, Contingent Premium Swaption, Exotic Options, Pay Later Option (PLO).*

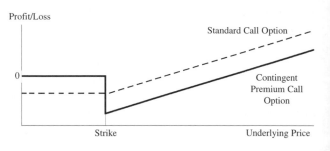

Contingent Premium versus Standard Call Option Value at Expiration

Contingent Premium Swaption: A contract conferring the right to buy or sell a swap on fixed terms. As with any contingent premium option, the holder pays a premium only if the option is in the money at the time of exercise or expiration, and the premium exceeds that for a standard swaption. *See also Contingent Premium Option (diagram).*

Contingent Swap: A swap agreement that takes effect only if some designated event occurs, such as an acquisition or an interest rate move. Usually one party, needing the risk adjustment of the swap in the event of this contingency, pays an option premium to the other party. A swaption is a special type of contingent swap, whose value and exercise are usually contingent on an interest rate. *See also Swaption.*

Contingent Takedown Option: An option to buy a fixed-income security, usually issued as a "kicker" (attached to another fixed-income security). This option gives the buyer of a bond or note an option to acquire a second bond with a similar coupon. *Also called Bond Warrant, Debt Warrant. See also Kicker.*

Contingent Value Rights (CVRs): A contingent instrument issued in an acquisition to give shareholders of the acquired company a consistently valued stake in the surviving company. CVRs may take the form of a put spread to guarantee that the total proceeds from the exchange of stock reach a certain value, or a call warrant with a payoff tied to the revenue or earnings of the acquired business.

Continuation Option: *See Installment Option (diagram).*

Continuous Compounding: The instantaneous reinvestment of income or total return. The continuously compounded return is equal to the natural logarithm of the quantity, 1 plus the periodic return. For example, a continuously compounded annual return of 9.53% corresponds to a 10% periodic return [9.53% = *ln* (1.10)], and e, the base of the natural logarithm, raised to the power of the continuously compounded return, gives the result of 1 plus the periodic return ($e^{0.0953} = 1.10$). *See e, Natural Logarithm.*

Continuous Market: Ideally, a market characterized by great depth and liquidity and by small price changes between successive transactions. Many financial models assume markets are continuous, but care must be taken that discontinuities do not lead to misapplication of a model. *See Dynamic Hedging.*

Continuous Probability Distribution: A probability distribution that assumes an infinite number of observations covering all possible values along a continuous scale. The normal distribution is a continuous probability distribution.

Continuous Return: The rate of return that, when compounded continuously, causes an investment to grow by a factor equal to 1 plus the periodic return. For example, $1 invested for one year at an annualized continuous return of 9.53% will grow to $1.10. The continuous return is equal to the natural logarithm of the quantity, 1 plus the periodic return:

$$0.0953 = ln\ (1.10)$$

Continuous Time: The notion that time progresses smoothly and without interruption. This assumption is important in the application of calculus to financial analysis. *See also Discontinuity Risk.*

Contract: (1) An over-the-counter risk management agreement. (2) The unit of trading on an option or futures exchange. The terms of the contract are set by the exchange with the concurrence of its regulator. Although mini-contracts with a lower value than standard contracts are sometimes introduced for the retail market, it is not possible to trade fractional contract units.

Contract for Differences: A diff or difference option or a forward contract with a value based on the difference between two rates or values. The term may have a specific legal or regulatory meaning in certain contexts. *See Diff or Difference Option (2).*

Contract Grade: A cash market instrument or physical commodity eligible for delivery in settlement of a futures contract. *See also Deliverable.*

Contract Month: The settlement or expiration month of an exchange-traded option or futures contract. *See also Delivery Month.*

Contract Period: A reference to the life of any risk management agreement, but especially to the effective term of a forward rate agreement (FRA).

Contractual Settlement Day Accounting (CSDA): A securities custody or safe-keeping arrangement between an investor and a custodian under which the investor is credited for all payments due and debited for all payments required on the nominal settlement day—even if the transaction does not actually settle because of a failure on the part of the custodian or the counterparty to a transaction. CSDA is usually available in relatively mature markets with good settlement procedures.

Contrarian Investment Theory: The proposition that an investment opinion contrary to the predominant opinion is, other things equal, a better predictor of market results than the more popular opinion.

Contribution: In operational cost analysis, total revenue less total variable cost.

Control Variate Technique: A variance reduction procedure used in conjunction with a numeric method, such as a Monte Carlo simulation, to improve the estimate of a derivative's price when only a limited number of sample paths is estimated. This procedure is useful in pricing two similar derivatives instruments with correlated pricing errors.

Convenience Yield: A premium earned by holders of a physical commodity—and sometimes by holders of a government bond in short supply in the REPO market. A convenience yield reflects the near-term scarcity of the underlying commodity or instrument. Analogous to a stock loan premium. *See also Backwardation (1).*

Conventional Option: An outdated term for an over-the-counter stock option.

Conventions of a Market: Most OTC financial and physical commodity products and markets have adopted standard terms or default provisions that are part of any agreement unless the parties agree to a different provision (examples include $ LIBOR as the default reference index rate in interest rate swaps and Telerate as the standard source of Treasury rates). The conventions of an exchange market cannot ordinarily be modified by a simple agreement of the parties to a contract.

Convergence: One of the tests of the quality of a derivatives market instrument is how closely the derivative's forward price converges to the cash market spot price at expiration. Some markets, such as the market in S&P 500 futures, are characterized by almost perfect convergence: An arbitrageur can be confident that a long stock index replicating portfolio sold at the opening on expiration day will match the value of the cash settlement on the related futures contract almost exactly. Where trading at the settlement price, and therefore convergence, is less certain, the pricing relationship between the underlying and the futures contract is more tenuous. Other things equal, markets with good convergence and close spot/futures trading relationships tend to be more liquid markets.

Conversion: (1) The process by which a put can be changed to a call and a call to a put. To convert a put to a call, the converter buys the put and the cash underlying and issues a call. To convert a call to a put, the converter buys the call, sells the cash underlying short, and issues a put. *See also Break Out, Reversal (2).* (2) The exchange of a convertible security for the underlying instrument. (3) Selling a call against a long outright forward currency position.

Conversion Premium (on a Convertible Bond): The additional amount or percentage that the purchaser of a convertible bond pays over parity with the underlying. Note the analogy to the concept of premium in the U.K. warrant market. *See also Premium (2) and (3).*

Conversion Price: The share price at which the face amount of a convertible bond or convertible preferred is converted into common stock.

**The Conversion (1) Equation:
Long Put**

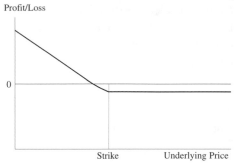

Plus Long Stock

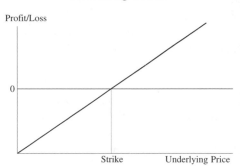

Equals Long Call

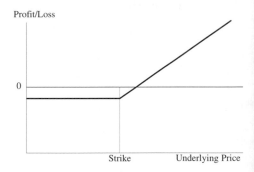

**Conversion Premium
(on a Convertible Bond)**

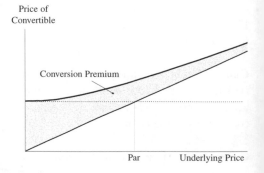

Conversion Ratio: The number of common shares an investor receives in exchange for a single convertible bond or convertible preferred share.

Conversion Spread: *See Equity Risk Reversal (diagram), Interest Rate Collar (diagram), Range Forward Contract (diagram). Also called Spread Conversion.*

Conversion Value: The value of a convertible security if converted immediately—after reflecting any change in the value of the underlying security resulting from the act of conversion. *Also called Parity Value.*

Convertible Adjustable Preferred Stock (CAPS): A floating-rate preferred issue, convertible by the holder on dividend payment dates into a variable number of the issuer's common shares. The shares received upon conversion are equal in market value to the par value of the preferred (usually subject to a cap on the number of shares). The convertible feature is designed to give the adjustable-rate preferred investor greater liquidity, and to protect the preferred investor's principal if the credit standing of the issuer declines. *Also called Capital Market Preferred Stock (CMPS).*

Convertible Adjustable-Rate Mortgages (Convertible ARMs): Adjustable-rate mortgages that are convertible into fixed-rate mortgages, usually upon payment of a service charge.

Convertible Bond With a Premium Put: A convertible bond issued at nominal or face value with an embedded put that entitles the bondholder to redeem it for more than its face value beginning at some future date. The put is exercised only if the underlying equity fails to appreciate by enough to make the bond worth more alive than dead. *See Liquid Yield Option Note (LYON).*

Convertible Capital Note or Security: A fixed-term debt instrument or preferred stock issued by a bank and convertible into perpetual preferred stock. In some issues, conversion to preferred may be encouraged or forced by the issuer, who may have the right to reduce the note coupons or simply to effect conversion. The perpetual preferred stock becomes Tier I bank capital under the Basle Capital Adequacy Directive. These notes are used primarily to assure a bank has access to additional capital in an emergency. *Also called Exchangeable Capital Security (X-Cap), Exchangeable Capital Unit, Preferred Purchase Unit. See also Equity Contract Notes, Perpetual Preferred Stock (Perp).*

Convertible Currency: If convertibility is unrestricted, any holder of a currency can exchange it for units of another currency at market rates. Some non-convertible currencies are used only for internal (domestic) transactions and other currencies are not convertible for all holders.

Convertible Exchangeable Preferred Stock: A convertible preferred issue that is exchangeable at the issuer's option for convertible debt with identical yield and identical conversion terms. Designed to permit an issuer to switch to a lower-cost (tax-deductible) obligation when its earnings become taxable.

Convertible Floating-Rate Note: An FRN with an embedded option permitting the issuer to convert the note into long-term fixed-rate bonds.

Convertible Gilts: U.K. government bonds that give the holder an option to convert them into longer-maturity bonds on specified terms.

Convertible Money Market Units (CMMUs): Unlike the more popular return of principal equity-linked notes, convertible money market units provide a high return if an equity-linked instrument appreciates, but provide full participation (except for the accumulated yield) in a downside move if the value of the equity instrument or index declines. While an equity-linked note provides a return pattern often reminiscent of a long call, the pattern of the convertible money market unit is similar to that experienced by a covered call writer. Someday a philosopher or psychiatrist will analyze why institutional investors generally sell covered calls rather than buy puts against their portfolios, but tend to buy equity-linked notes rather than convertible money market units. *Also called Synthetic High-Income Equity-Linked Debenture (SHIELD). See Equity-LinKed Security (ELKS), Structured Note.*

Return Pattern of Convertible Money Market Units

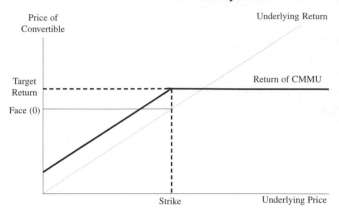

Convertible Option Contract: A currency option with a trigger price feature that converts the option into a forward foreign exchange contract when the exchange rate trades to or through the trigger price.

Convertible Reset Debenture: A convertible bond with a required upward interest rate adjustment, typically effective several years after issuance. The issuer may be required to reset the coupon high enough to give the debentures a market value at least equal to their face or par value. The purpose of the reset is to compensate the bondholder for any credit deterioration. The reset frequently encourages the issuer to refinance, or perhaps forces conversion. *Compare with Callable Step-Up Note.*

Convertible Security: A bond, preferred stock, or warrant that is convertible under prescribed circumstances into the common stock of a corporation or some other security with or without a supplementary payment of cash or "useable" securities.

Convertible Stock Note: A "debt" instrument that pays coupons and principal in the common stock of the issuer. A variety of mandatory convertible bond.

Convex Payoff Function: Relative to a linear payoff pattern, a return function that has higher returns at the extreme values of the underlying asset, and lower returns at values close to the average value of the underlying asset. Convexity is the result of increased exposure to the performance of the underlying as the underlying increases, and reduced exposure as the underlying decreases. *See Convexity (1) and (2) (diagrams).*

Convexity: (1) In a fixed-income instrument, convexity is a measure of the way duration and price change when interest rates change. A bond or note is said to have positive convexity if the instrument's value increases at least as much as duration predicts when rates drop, and decreases less than duration predicts when rates rise. Positive convexity is desirable to investors because it makes a position more valuable after

Convexity

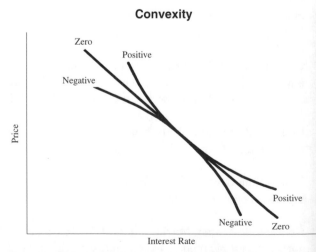

Source: *The Institutional Investor Focus on Investment Management*, ed., Frank J. Fabozzi. Cambridge, MA: Ballinger Publishing Co., 1989.

a price change than its duration value suggests. *See Convex Payoff Function.* (2) In an option position, convexity is a measure of the way the value of the position changes in response to a change in the volatility or price of the underlying instrument. A position with positive convexity (gamma) maintains or increases its value better than delta predicts when volatility increases or when prices change by a large percentage in either direction. A position with negative convexity loses value relative to delta's prediction when prices change in either direction. *Also called Curvature. The opposite of Concave Payoff Function. See also Gamma (1).*

Convexity Hedge: Another name for a reverse option hedge or a long straddle. The name comes from the tendency of these positions to increase in value with increasing volatility or a large one-time price movement.

Convexity Risk Premium: A measure of any difference between the actual option premium and the option's estimated fair value. The difference results from the unwillingness of option writers to sell options at their statistical fair value because of a recent period of extraordinary price movement in the underlying instrument.

Core Liquidity Provider: A large-scale market maker that is such a large factor in a market that bid-ask spreads would widen if it withdrew.

Corner: (1) The act of gaining control of enough of the items trading or available to trade in a market to dictate the prices and terms to other market participants. (2) The state of such control.

Correlation Coefficient: *See R (Correlation Coefficient).*

Correlation Risk: (1) The risk that the realized correlation between assets will be different than the assumed correlation, thereby rendering a portfolio riskier than anticipated. *See also Omega Risk.* (2) Basis risk. *See Basis Risk (3), Tracking Error.*

Corridor: (1) A combination of two caps, one purchased by a borrower at a set strike and the other sold by the borrower at a higher strike to, in effect, offset part of the premium of the first cap. The two-cap structure limits interest costs unless rates rise through the strike on the upper cap. At that rate, the borrower's interest costs begin rising again. *Also called Interest Rate Corridor. Compare with Floored Put (diagram).* (2) A collar on a swap created with two swaptions—the structure and participation interval is determined by the strikes and types of the swaptions. (3) A digital knock-out option with two barriers bracketing the current level of a long-term interest rate. The payout is some multiple (typically 2 or more) of the premium if the rate stays between the barriers. If either barrier is breached, there is no payoff.

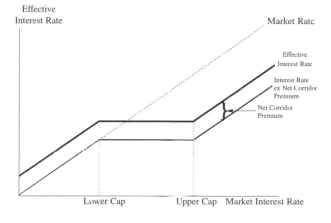

Effect of a Corridor (1) and its Premium on a Borrower's Interest Rate

Corridor Accrual Swap: An accrual swap (1) with interest accruing on one side only when the index price or rate falls within a fixed width range that can be reset at the start of each payment period, moving up or down with spot or forward prices or rates. *See also Constant Spread Range Index Bond Security (CS-RIBS), Corridor Swap.*

Corridor Bond or Note: *See Index Range Note.*

Corridor Swap: An interest rate swap where the payment obligation on one side accrues only on days when the reference rate is within a predetermined range or corridor—analogous to a range accumulation option or note. This swap is designed to implement a forecast on the volatility, range, or level of interest rates. *See also Corridor Accrual Swap.*

Cost-Benefit Analysis: A conceptually simple comparison of the costs and benefits of a capital expenditure, a government regulation, or any other decision or decision process.

Cost of Capital: The weighted average cost of each type of debt and equity capital issued by a corporation. Usually, the firm's cost of capital bears a relationship to the hurdle rate that investment projects must pass.

Cost of Carry: (1) The net out-of-pocket cost of holding a cash market position. (2) A model for the pricing of futures contracts, particularly financial futures, describing the fair value of the futures contract in terms of the net cost incurred to hold a long cash position and a short futures position through the settlement date of the futures contract. *See also Benefit of Carry.*

Cost Of Funds Index (COFI): An interest rate reference index based on the cost of funds to 11th District (U.S.) savings and loan associations. *See Cost Of Funds Index (COFI) Swap.*

Cost Of Funds Index (COFI) Swap: An interest rate swap with the floating payment stream linked to the 11th District Cost of Funds Index (COFI). This rate is often used in swaps with savings institutions as counterparties. *See Cost Of Funds Index (COFI).*

Cotation Assistée en Continu (C.A.C.): *Fr.* Literally, a continuous-time computer-assisted quotation system. The computerized market mechanism at the Paris Bourse from which the French CAC indexes take their name.

Counterparty: One of the participants in a swap agreement or any other financial contract.

Counterparty Risk: The expected cost of possible credit and "moral hazard" losses associated with the chance that a financial counterparty will default on contractual obligations. *See Moral Hazard. See also Credit or Counterparty Risk, pp. 5-6.*

Country Limit: A risk management policy that limits exposure to borrowers or counterparties in a particular country.

Country Risk: Legal, political, settlement, and other risks associated with a cross-border transaction into a specific country. *Also called Geographic Risk. Related to Sovereign Risk.*

Coupon: (1) The nominal annual rate of interest on a bond or note usually expressed as a percentage of the face value. (2) A piece of paper detached from a bearer bond and exchanged for a quarterly, semiannual, or annual interest payment.

Coupon-Indexed Note: A variable-rate note with the periodic coupon dependent on the performance of an embedded equity, currency, interest rate, or commodity index option. One variation is called a *Stock Market Annual Reset Term (SMART) Note. Also called Multiperiod Strike Reset Option (MSRO). See Commodity Interest-Indexed Note, Cliquet Option (1) (diagram).*

Coupon Stripping: *See Stripped Treasury Securities.*

Coupon Swap: A traditional fixed-for-floating interest rate swap.

Coupons Under Book Entry Safekeeping (CUBES): A program that allows holders of physical stripped coupons from Treasury securities to convert them to book entry form to reduce safekeeping and insurance costs.

Courtage: Brokerage or commission charges on a French or Swiss stock exchange. *See also Broker, Brokerage, Commission.*

Covariance: A measure of the correspondence between the movement of two random variables such as securities prices or returns. The correlation coefficient is a normalized covariance measure because it is independent of the units of measurement. Covariance is calculated as the product of the variables' standard deviations and their correlation coefficient. *See also R (Correlation Coefficient).*

Covariance Assets: Categories of investments added to a portfolio because their returns are not highly correlated with returns on the domestic stocks and bonds that are the fund's principal holdings. These low-covariance assets may not improve average returns, but they reduce return variation and, consequently, often increase compound returns. Examples of covariance assets might include real estate, foreign stocks and bonds, or gold mining shares. *See also Variance Drain.*

Covenant: A provision of a loan or risk management agreement that requires or prohibits certain actions by a borrower or a financial agreement counterparty. Covenants may limit dividends, require maintenance of working capital, set a ceiling on compensation, etc. If a covenant is violated, the instrument is considered in default. *See also Negative Pledge Clause.*

Cover: (1) To buy back instruments previously sold. Typically used to describe the closing of a short position. (2) A hedge position purchased from a third party to offset the market risk of a derivatives issuance or OTC risk management agreement. For example, many investment banks purchase cover for the option components of equity or index-linked instruments from one or more of the major financial intermediaries specializing in these products. (3) Collateral behind a security or obligation. (4) The contingencies for which an insurance company is liable under the terms of a policy.

Coverage: A ratio expressed as any of several measures of cash flow or income available to meet obligations divided by the size of the total or immediate obligations. *See also Fixed Charge Coverage, Interest Cover, Interest Coverage Ratio.*

Coverage Period: The interim period in a swap or other periodic reset agreement when a specific set of terms is effective. The aggregate of the interim coverage periods is the total coverage period of the agreement.

Covered Arbitrage: Creation of a synthetic foreign exchange forward contract with a pair of zero-coupon debt instruments denominated in each of the two currencies.

Covered Call: A short call option collateralized by a long position in the underlying. *See Buy-Write, Covered Writer. See also Naked Option.*

Covered Interest Arbitrage: A simple currency swap where the counterparties exchange currencies at the spot and forward rates simultaneously. The forward swap restores currency exposures to the original position without a currency gain or loss—making this a way to adjust exposure to a narrowing or widening of interest rate differentials rather than adjusting currency exposures. Covered interest arbitrage also insures interest rate parity, because the relationship prevents speculators from profiting by borrowing in a low interest rate country, simultaneously lending in a high interest rate country, and hedging the currency risk. *See Arbitrage, Interest Rate Parity. See also Forward Discount.*

Covered OPtion Securities (COPS): A short-term note with a high coupon and an embedded put that gives the issuer an option to repay principal and interest in U.S. dollars or an agreed foreign currency at an exchange rate set at issuance.

Covered Put Writing: *See Cash Secured Put.*

Covered Warrant: A stock, basket, or index warrant issued by a party other than the issuer of the underlying stock(s) and secured by the warrant issuer's holding in the underlying securities or the warrant issuer's general credit standing. Covered warrants are most common in Europe and parts of Asia. They are often issued by investment banks when transfer of the underlying security is temporarily or permanently restricted, when traditional warrants are not available, or when buyers want security and currency warrant combinations not otherwise available in the market. *Also called Synthetic Warrants, Third Party Warrants. See Foreign Stock Index Options, Warrants, and Futures,* Guaranteed Warrant, Equity Warrant, Guaranteed Exchange Rate Warrant, Warrant.

The Covered Call Writer's Profit/Loss Position at Expiration

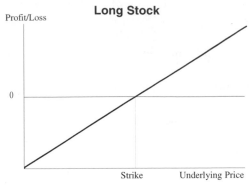

Long Stock

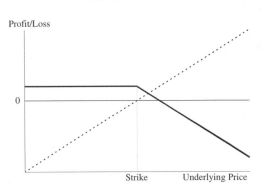

And Short Call

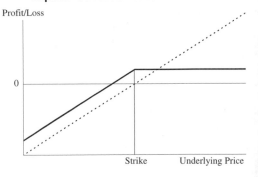

Equals Covered Writer's Position

Covered Writer: A call option writer who owns the underlying that is subject to option. An investor setting up an option hedge or writing multiple options may be covered with respect to part of the option position and uncovered with respect to the rest. *See Covered Call (diagram). See also Option Hedge (diagrams), Uncovered Writer.*

Cox-Ingersoll-Ross (CIR) Model: A single factor, analytic model used to value interest rate dependent claims. In a rigorous general equilibrium framework, the CIR model assumes that the short-term interest rate conforms to a square root diffusion model with mean reversion. Unlike the Vasicek mean reversion model, the CIR model does not permit negative interest rates.

Crack Spread: An oil refiner's operating margin embodied in the relative prices of crude oil and refined products' spot, futures, or forward contracts.

Crack Swap: A swap agreement based on the spread between crude oil and an appropriate basket of cracked and refined products.

Cram-Down Rules: Procedures in bankruptcy litigation that allow the bankruptcy court to implement a reorganization plan over the objections of a class of creditors. Specifically, these rules provide that secured claimants must retain their liens on the debtor's property, and their liens must be satisfied if the property is sold. The claims of unsecured claimants must receive full value, or no junior claimants will receive anything. Actual practice may deviate from these rules. *See Absolute Priority Rule (APR).*

Creation Unit: The minimum module for issue or redemption of shares in an EXchange-TRAded (EXTRA) Fund, usually between 25,000 and 300,000 fund shares, depending on the fund's policy. Existing EXTRA funds issue their shares in return for portfolio deposits of securities in multiples of the creation unit basket specified by the fund's distributor. With minor exceptions related primarily to accrued dividend payments, creations and redemptions are in kind, not in cash. EXTRA fund trading in the secondary market on the exchange is in individual fund shares issued in the creation.

Credit Card Receivable-Backed Security: Asset-backed instrument with consumer credit card obligations as the securitized collateral. *Also called Certificate of Amortizing Revolving Debts (CARDs).*

Credit Crunch: A reduction in the supply of credit that disrupts the credit extension process. Credit crunches are often associated with tightening monetary policy.

Credit Derivative: A highly generic term often used to describe one or more of the following instruments or arrangements: (1) a put or a call with a payoff dependent on the interest rate spread between a specific corporate debt instrument and sovereign debt denominated in the same currency. The most common example is the Treasury EuroDollar, or TED spread. Alternately, an option with a payoff dependent on the spread between indexes of similar maturity debt instruments such as the five-year swap rate and a five-year government bond rate; (2) a swap or embedded swap with the payments on one side mirroring the interest and principal payments of a basket of bonds rated below investment grade. The payer of the bond return is the nominal holder of the low-rated bonds, but the receiver actually takes the credit risk. The payment on the other side can be a fixed or floating rate as the parties agree; (3) an asset swap in the form of a stand-alone swap or structured note where one party holds a below-investment-grade issue and pays the interest called for under the bond indenture, in exchange for a traditional fixed or floating rate. The fixed or floating rate is greater than usual in compensation for the acceptance of any losses from default by the holder of the below-investment-grade issue. *See Credit Derivative Bond;* (4) a total return swap with the "fixed" rate based on the total return of a corporate bond because the bond's issuer is overrepresented in the fixed-rate payer's credit portfolio.

Credit Derivative Bond: A proposed pass-through product based on pools of low-rated bonds held by AAA- or AA-rated financial institutions. Prospective highly rated issuers sought AAA or AA ratings despite the fact that the issuer would have served only as a conduit: the cash flows of the lower-rated bonds would pass to the buyers of the credit derivative bonds without any credit enhancement. Credit rating agencies decided that the rating of the underlying bond pool was appropriate, and the product was stillborn. *See also Credit Derivative.*

Credit Enhanced Debt Securities: Bonds or notes with special investor protection that gives them a better credit standing than the ordinary debt of the issuer would have. To obtain enhanced credit, an issuer may pay a guarantor or endorser for a letter of credit or a surety bond that lends the guarantor's higher credit to the issuer. The purpose of credit enhancement is to achieve a lower net borrowing cost.

Credit Enhanced Vehicle (CEV): *See Derivatives Product Company (DPC).*

Credit Enhancements: Supplementary provisions of a financial contract designed to moderate losses from an adverse credit event or counterparty default. The most common enhancements are third-party guarantees and collateral deposits.

Credit Equivalent Amount: The result of translating the off-balance sheet liabilities of a financial intermediary into the approximate risk equivalent of loans.

Credit Equivalent Value (CEV): Monetary value of the credit risk exposure represented by an off-balance sheet transaction. CEV is the potential cost at current market prices of replacing the contract's expected net cash flows in the event of default by the counterparty. *See also Credit Line Usage, Maximum Potential Replacement Cost.*

Credit Event: Any event that triggers the payout of a credit derivative, such as a default event, a rating downgrade, or a price decline or rate advance in a reference instrument.

Credit Exposure in a Swap: Net credit exposure is the reduction in the present value of the net swap cash flows if the swap had to be replaced at current market terms for the remaining life of the original swap. This calculation usually assumes that an enforceable netting agreement is in place.

Credit Line Usage: The maximum potential replacement cost of an instrument requiring the extension of credit. *See also Credit Equivalent Value (CEV).*

Credit Option on BRAdy Bonds (COBRA): An option on the spread between the yield to maturity on a Brady bond and the yield to maturity on another bond, usually a comparable maturity Treasury.

Credit Quality Rating: *See Table of Bond Ratings (Appendix).*

Credit Risk: (1) Exposure to loss as a result of default on a swap, debt, or other counterparty instrument. (2) Exposure to loss as a result of a decline in market value stemming from a credit downgrade of an issuer or counterparty. Credit risk may be reduced by credit screening before a transaction is effected or by instrument provisions that attempt to offset the effect of a default

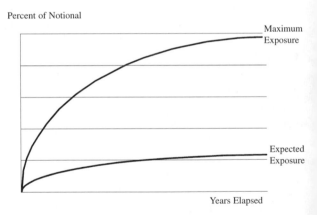

Credit Exposure in a Currency Swap

Percent of Notional

Maximum Exposure

Expected Exposure

Years Elapsed

Credit Exposure in an Interest Rate Swap

Percent of Notional Amount at Risk

Maximum Exposure

Expected Exposure

Years Elapsed

or require increased payments in the event of a credit downgrade. (3) A component of return variability resulting from the possibility of an event of default. (4) A change in the market's perception of the probability of an event of default, which affects the spread between two rates or reference indexes. *See, for example, Treasury EuroDollar (TED) Spread (diagram). See Credit or Counterparty Risk discussion, pp. 5-6.*

Credit Risk Option: A kind of put option that pays off to the holder if the creditworthiness of a bond issuer falls below a strike level. The strike and payout may be set in terms of credit ratings, rate spreads, or financial ratios. The option's value is a function of changes in the interest rate structure, credit spreads, and changes in total firm value.

Credit Risk Premium: The component of a debt instrument's yield (or price discount) that reflects the expected value (cost) of the risk of a possible default or downgrade. The credit risk premium is usually expressed in basis points (it can be hundreds of basis points).

Credit Sensitive Note: Fixed- or floating-rate note with an interest rate reset in the event of a change in the issuer's credit rating. *Also called Rating Sensitive Note. See Table of Bond Ratings (Appendix).*

Credit Spread: (1) *See Quality Spread.* (2) A listed option spread transaction that generates a net cash inflow into the investor's account when initiated. *Also called Back Spread (2).*

Credit Watch: An alert or warning issued by a credit rating agency in anticipation of a credit upgrade or downgrade. *See Table of Bond Ratings (Appendix).*

CREST: A certificateless settlement system in the U.K. that replaces the Institutional Net Settlement (INS) and Transfer Accounting Lodgment for Investor Stock MANagement for principals (TALISMAN) systems used to match and settle transactions on the London Stock Exchange. CREST is scheduled for implementation in July 1996. *See Institutional Net Settlement (INS) System, Transfer Accounting Lodgment for Investor Stock MANagement for principals (TALISMAN).*

Cross: An agency transaction where the same broker represents both parties.

Cross-Border Transaction: A trade in a foreign financial instrument.

Cross-Currency Basis Swap: An interest rate swap with both counterparties as floating-rate payers in their respective currencies. *Compare to Cross-Currency CRoss-Index Basis Swap (X-CRIBS).*

Cross-Currency Cap or Floor: An option setting a maximum (cap) or minimum (floor) on the spread between two reference index rates (usually LIBORs) denominated in different currencies. This option is cash settled, usually in one of the subject currencies, or embedded in a note. *See International Spread Option, Warrant, or Note, Spread Option (1).*

Cross-Currency Convertible Bond: A convertible bond denominated and with coupons paid in one currency that is convertible into shares of a common stock denominated and traded in a second currency. Conversion terms are stated as the number of shares exchanged for each bond. Depending on the relationship of the currencies at the bond's maturity, the bond may be converted even if the share price is unchanged or lower than the price at issuance. Alternately, the bond may be redeemed for cash in the denominated currency, if the share price rises while the shares' nominal currency declines.

Cross-Currency CRoss-Index Basis Swap (X-CRIBS): One party to this swap pays the LIBOR rate in his base currency and the other pays a floating rate based on the same LIBOR rate in a different currency. For example, one party pays U.S. dollar LIBOR on a notional amount denominated in dollars in exchange for the dollar LIBOR rate plus or minus a spread applied to a notional principal denominated in deutschemarks. For the party paying a LIBOR-based rate on a deutschemark notional principal, this swap might reflect a willingness to pay a floating rate set in another currency, combined with a preference to apply that rate to a notional amount in its own currency—as protection against a specific exchange rate risk. *Compare to Cross-Currency Basis Swap.*

Cross-Currency Option or Warrant Bonds: An embedded outperformance option struck at an exchange rate between two currencies. The premium is often in a third currency. These are popular exchange-traded derivatives in the U.S. *See Dual Option Bonds, Outperformance Option (diagram).*

Cross-Currency Settlement Risk: The risk that one party to a currency swap will default after the other side has met its obligation, usually due to a difference in time zones. *Also called Herstatt Risk* after a failed German bank that generated such a default on a large scale. *See also Settlement Risk.*

Cross-Currency Swap: *See Currency Coupon Swap.*

Cross-Currency Swaption: An option to pay or to receive the fixed rate in a cross-currency swap. *Also called Circus Option.*

Cross-Currency Warrants: Currency warrants in which neither of the two currencies determining the pay-out is the U.S. dollar, or, alternatively, the investor's base currency.

Cross Default: A provision of a loan or swap agreement stating that any default on another loan or swap will be considered a default on the issue with the cross-default provision. The purpose is to protect a creditor or counterparty from actions favoring another creditor.

Cross-Guarantee Contract: A proposed comprehensive insurance or guarantee mechanism under which financial institutions would pay and receive premiums to obtain and provide guarantees of each other's depository and counterparty obligations. These private guarantees would be market priced. Parties would exchange currently non-public information to assure an efficient market, and these contracts would replace existing deposit insurance. Existing credit ratings would be an initial input to the pricing process, but the market price for an institution's "insurance" would soon become the dominant measure of its soundness.

Cross Hedging: A technique used in a variety of markets to counter the risk of one instrument by taking a risk-offsetting position in another instrument whose risk characteristics do not perfectly offset the position to be hedged. Examples include hedging the risk of a 100-stock portfolio with futures contracts on the S&P 500, or doing a currency hedge on a portfolio of German stocks with Swiss franc forwards or options. Among the risks in a cross hedge are that different maturities of the offsetting positions will lead to a mismatch, that the market for one of the instruments will be highly illiquid, with correspondingly larger price fluctuations, and that differences in credit quality will affect the cross-hedge basis. *See Maturity Mismatch Risk.*

CRoss-Index Basis (CRIB) Swap: *See Rate Differential Swap, CUrrency Protected Swap (CUPS).*

Cross Option: An option on a foreign security, basket, or index struck at a value of the underlying instrument in the investor's base currency and priced and paid in the investor's base currency at exercise. *Also called Composite Option, Joint Option.*

Cross-Product Netting Agreement: A netting agreement between two counterparties providing that netting occurs not only within one line of financial instruments, such as interest rate products, but also across several product lines, such as interest rates, currencies, equities, physical commodities, etc.

Cross Rate: (1) The exchange rate between any two currencies. In practice, the term is most frequently applied to currency relationships that are non-standard in the country where the currency relationship is quoted. In U.S. markets, a yen/DM rate would be a cross-rate, but in Tokyo or Frankfurt, it would be one of the primary currency relationships traded. (2) The implied exchange rate between two currencies derived from their respective exchange rates relative to a third currency. For example, suppose the exchange rate between the dollar and the pound equals 1.5 dollars per pound, and the exchange rate between the dollar and the deutschemark equals 0.70 dollars per deutschemark. The implied cross rate between the pound and the mark equals 0.4667 pounds per deutschemark. This cross rate is found by dividing the dollars per deutschemark exchange rate by the dollars per pound exchange rate. The reciprocal of this value expresses the cross rate as deutschemarks per pound, which equals 2.1429. This value can also be found by dividing the dollars per pound exchange rate by the dollars per deutschemark exchange rate.

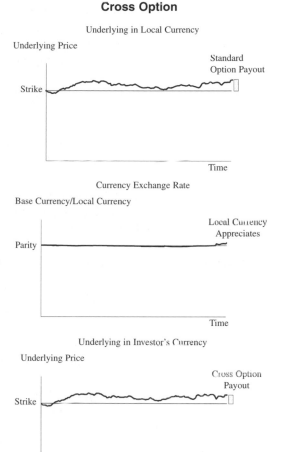

Cross Option

Underlying in Local Currency

Cross-Rate Options: Currency options on a currency pair that is not standard in the market where the options are traded. For example, in the U.S. market, standard options include sterling/dollar options, DM/dollar options, and options on any other currency relative to the U.S. dollar. A sterling/DM option would be a cross-rate option in the U.S., but standard in London or Frankfurt.

Cross-Rate Swap: *See CUrrency Protected Swap (CUPS), Rate Differential Swap.*

Cross-Sectional Regression Analysis: A regression analysis where the observations are measured at the same point in time or over the same time period but differ along another dimension. For example, an analyst may regress stock returns for different companies measured over the same period against differences in the companies' yields for the period.

Crossed Market: A market with the posted bid price higher than the offer. *Also called Backwardation (2). Compare with Locked Market.*

Crossing Network: An automatic or semiautomatic execution system that matches anonymous buy and sell orders in a call market at certain fixed times in the day and/or executes trades at a price established in the primary market on which the security is traded. *See also Fourth Market.*

Crowd: A group of exchange members organized around a specific floor location. Although members of the crowd may have a variety of functions, they trade a common list of securities, futures, or options.

Crown Jewels: The most desirable, and usually the most valuable, assets of a company that are often the primary target in a takeover.

Crush Spread: The soybean processor's operating margin—embodied in the relative prices of soybeans, soybean meal, and soybean oil and their futures contracts.

C-Trac+: A cash transfer and over-the-counter derivative collateralization service sponsored by Bankers Trust. *See also Global Credit Support Service (GCSS), Hybrid Instrument Transaction Service (HITS), Chicago Mercantile Exchange Depository Trust Corporation (CME DTC).*

Cum-Rights: With Rights. The time early in a rights offering when the purchaser of the stock also receives the rights.

Cumulative Auction Market Preferred Stock (CAMPS): *See Adjustable-Rate Preferred Stock (ARPS).*

Cumulative Preferred Stock: A preferred stock issue that requires payment of all passed dividends on that issue before payment of any common stock dividends.

Cumulative Probability Distribution: A probability distribution that measures, for example, the probability that a variable is less than or equal to a specified value. For a discrete distribution, the cumulative probability is calculated by summing the relative frequencies up to and including the value of interest.

Currency: Any form of money issued by a government or a central bank and used as legal tender and a basis for trade.

Currency Annuity Swap: A currency swap that does not call for an exchange of principal in different currencies at maturity.

Currency Average Rate Option: *See Average Price or Rate Option (APO, ARO) (diagrams).*

Currency Board: A currency exchange rate management technique that attempts to remove most functions of a central bank from the political process, and to eliminate discretionary changes in domestic money supply, interest rate policy, etc. Money is created only in response to an increase in foreign exchange reserves. Currency boards have the practical effort of pegging a smaller country's currency to a reserve currency.

Currency Coupon Swap: A variant on the standard currency or interest rate swap, where the interest rate in one currency is fixed, and the interest rate in the other is floating. The only difference from a traditional interest rate swap is the combination of the currency and interest rate features. *Also called Circus Swap, Cross-Currency Swap. A special case of CUrrency Protected Swap (CUPS).*

Currency Exchange Warrants (CEWs): A cash settled, American-style warrant often issued in conjunction with straight debt by a corporate issuer. The holder of the warrant is entitled to a cash payment at exercise if the spot rate in the target currency exceeds the rate designated as the strike.

Currency Forward: *See Outright Forward Currency Transaction.*

Currency-Hedged Foreign Bond: A bond with all coupons and principal payments in an investor's domestic currency, but with coupons sensitive to foreign interest rates. Foreign interest rate sensitivity can be achieved by making the coupon equal to a fixed rate plus a domestic floating rate (such as LIBOR) minus a foreign floating rate.

Currency Insurance: The currency market analog of portfolio insurance or contingent immunization, currency insurance is created either through dynamic hedging in cash or futures contracts or, more frequently, by using a sequence of short-term currency options to replicate the characteristics of a longer-term option.

Currency-Linked Notes: Debt structures with returns partly determined by changes in currency rates and, correspondingly, by interest rate differentials across currencies. Currency-linked instruments are available in isolation or combined with a variety of interest rate, equity, or index structures. *See also Deposit Notes.*

Currency-Linked Outperformance Units (CLOUs): A note with its return tied to an embedded outperformance option that increases in value at least partly in proportion to the relative change in two currencies.

Currency Option: Generically, the right, but not the obligation, to buy (call) or sell (put) a currency for another currency at a specified exchange rate (strike rate) during a specified period ending on the expiration date. *See Secondary Currency Option.*

Currency Overlay Management: The use of a separate currency manager to hedge currency exposures for an asset portfolio or corporate liability structure, rather than delegate currency decisions to the managers of the various equity or fixed-income portfolio segments or divisional financial managers. *See Overlay Risk Management.*

Currency Protected Instrument: A contract under which the return from a foreign market or instrument is translated back to the investor's home currency at an embedded exchange rate. *See also Rate Differential Swap (diagram).*

CUrrency Protected Swap (CUPS): An interest rate or other swap with one of the payment rates or returns denominated in a different currency than that used to state the notional principal amount. Both rates or returns are calculated against the base currency. *Also called CRoss-Index Basis (CRIB) Swap, Cross-Rate Swap, Currency Coupon Swap, Diff or Difference Swap, Differential Swap, Interest Rate Index Swap, LIBOR Differential Swap, Rate Differential Swap.*

Currency Quantity Adjusting Option (Currency QUANTO): *See Quantity Adjusting Option (QUANTO) (2).*

Currency Risk: (1) The probability of an adverse change in currency exchange rates. (2) The cost of an adverse change in currency exchange rates. (3) The product of (1) and (2), leading to an adverse variation in return or cost resulting from a change in currency exchange rates. (4) The component of return volatility in a cross-border asset class due to changes in foreign exchange rates. *Also called Foreign Exchange Risk.*

Currency Swap: In its simplest terms, the counterparties to a currency swap exchange equal initial principal amounts of two currencies at the spot exchange rate. Over the term of the swap, the counterparties exchange fixed- or floating-rate interest payments in their swapped currencies. At maturity, the principal amount is reswapped, usually at a predetermined exchange rate. In contrast to the parallel loan structure that swaps have largely replaced, netting agreements usually limit the parties' exposure to each other's credit to a single period net exchange and any increase in the "residual" value of each side of the swap.

Currency Swap Option: An option to buy or sell a currency swap at a specific exchange rate. The option is typically priced off the forward rate curve, with European-style exercise.

Current Coupon: An interest coupon on a bond giving a yield close to current rates on comparable instruments.

Current Exposure Method: A technique for estimating the credit risk of a swap transaction. Exposure is equal to the mark-to-market replacement cost of all contracts with a positive value. Some risk management systems add on an amount for potential credit exposure arising from future favorable price or rate changes. *Also called Current Presettlement Exposure.*

Current Presettlement Exposure: Exposure to loss from a counterparty default as of the date the exposure is measured. The replacement cost of a defaulted in-the-money contract. *Also called Current Exposure Method.*

Current Ratio: Current assets divided by current liabilities.

Current Yield: Annual dividend or interest divided by the current price of a stock or bond. *See also Yield.*

Curvature: *See Convexity, Gamma (1).*

Curve Risk: A measure of interest rate risk that emphasizes exposure to independent shifts in yield curve time buckets. Each time a bucket is shifted 50 basis points (0.5%), the simulated loss is measured. *See Absolute Risk, Spread Risk, Loss Limit.*

Cushion Bonds: High-coupon bonds selling at a premium to par that offer a higher yield to maturity and yield to first call than par bonds of the same issuer because of the greater likelihood of early call.

Custodial Account: An account in which securities or other assets are held, often by a bank or other depository institution, under a safekeeping agreement on behalf of one or more customers.

Custodian: A financial institution that holds securities in safekeeping for clients.

Custody Cost: Payment to a custodian for safekeeping and some recordkeeping services. *See Holding Cost.*

Customized Upside Basket Security (CUBS): An equity-linked note with a payout contingent on the average value of an underlying portfolio (basket) over the life of the note. *See Equity-Linked Note (ELN) (diagrams).*

Cybercash: *See Electronic Money.*

Cylinder: (1) *See Equity Risk Reversal.* (2) Purchase of a call or put and sale of another option of the same type with the same expiration date and a different strike. The buyer of a debit cylinder would pay a net option premium and the seller would receive a net option premium.

Daily Adjustable Tax-Exempt Securities (DATES): Variable-rate municipals that are remarketed daily at a market clearing rate.

Daily Earnings at Risk (DEaR): A measure of value at risk for a twenty-four-hour period, typically using a 95% confidence level. *See Value At Risk (VAR) (diagram).*

Daily Price or Trading Limit: The maximum amount that the price of a security, future, or option is permitted by an exchange to rise or fall in one day. The purpose of trading limits—much like the purpose of circuit breakers tied to market indexes—is to impose a cooling-off period on a turbulent market. *See Limit Up/Limit Down.*

Daily Settlement: The cash variation margin payment associated with most of the world's futures contracts. Futures market participants are charged for losses or credited with gains at the end of each trading day—and sometimes more frequently in turbulent markets.

Data Filters: Supplementary tests applied to bank call reports by the Office of the Comptroller of the Currency in an attempt to detect high levels of interest rate risk at reporting banks. *See also Call Report.*

Data Mining: Examining a large number of economic or financial variables, usually in a time series format, until the researcher finds one or more variables or relationships that seem to have predictive ability, but which, in fact, may result from the random arrangement of data. Often, the illusory predictive value disappears when the variable or relationships are applied to new data. *Also called Data Snooping. See Holdout Period. See also Model Mining.*

Data Snooping: *See Data Mining.*

Day Count Basis: *See Money Market Basis, Bond Basis.*

Day Trade: A day trade occurs when a security, option, or futures position is bought and sold during the same trading session.

Daylight OverDraft (DOD): (1) Intraday debit in a transaction settlement account at a clearing bank and/or at a clearing house or central bank. While these overdrafts are covered, one way or another, by the end of a business day, they expose the clearing bank, the clearing house and its members, or the central bank to some default risk. (2) Debit incurred by Federal Reserve member banks on an intraday basis. Until recently, no attempt was made to measure intraday exposure of an individual bank or of the system. Recognition of the risks involved in measuring the exposure only at each day's close of business has led to Fed charges based on average intraday overdrafts to encourage banks to monitor and manage this risk exposure.

Daylight Risk Exposure: A variant of settlement risk, daylight risk occurs when a party faces possible loss between the time a settlement payment is made and a corresponding payment is received (usually in another currency) on the same business day. *See also Overnight Delivery Risk, Settlement Risk.*

Deal: *Brit.* A transaction.

Dealer: A financial market intermediary who trades as a principal rather than as an agent. *See also Broker.*

Dealer Market: A market with communication mechanisms that permit market makers to buy and sell for their own and customer accounts by telephone or by communicating via a screen-trading system. Ordinarily, at least one side of each transaction in these markets is for a dealer's account.

Dealer-to-Dealer Broker: *See Inter-Dealer Broker (IDB).*

Dealing: *Brit.* Trading, usually as a principal.

Death Put: A provision of some small and otherwise illiquid bond issues that permits the estate of an original beneficial holder to put the bonds to the issuer at par upon the holder's death.

Debenture: (1) In the U.S., an unsecured bond or note. Neither principal nor interest payments are secured by a lien against specific property. (2) In the U.K., a secured or collateral-based debt instrument.

Debit Spread: An option spread that generates a net cash outflow in an investor's account when initiated. *See Front Spread.*

Debt/Equity Ratio: Long-term debt divided by equity capital, usually expressed as a percentage. *Also calculated as Equity/Debt Ratio.*

Debt-Equity Swap: A refinancing device that gives a debtholder an equity position in exchange for cancellation of the debt.

Debt Exchangeable for Common Stock (DECS): A debt issue with an embedded short put and long call combined with an interest coupon. The issuer is the issuer (or a block holder) of the underlying common stock; the DECS issue is ultimately convertible into the common. *Compare with Dividend Enhanced Convertible Stock (DECS), which is a preferred stock with a similar return pattern and the same acronym. Also called Automatically Convertible Enhanced Security (ACES), Preferred Redeemable Increased Dividend Equity Security (PRIDES), Protected Equity Participation (PEP), Fixed-Income Equity-Linked Debt (FIELD).*

Debt Instrument or Debt Security: Generically,

Stock and DECS Return Profiles

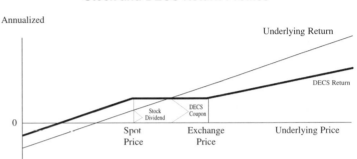

Composition of DECS

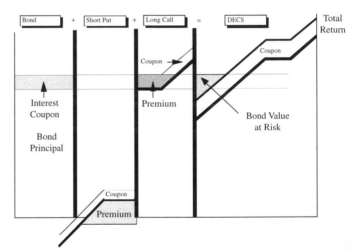

Exchange Rights/Obligations at Maturity of DECS

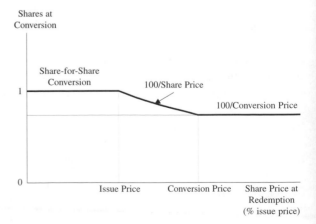

an obligation to repay a fixed amount, usually with periodic interest. A lump sum interest payment at maturity may be substituted for periodic payments in the case of a zero-coupon debt instrument. A more generalized term than Bond or Note.

Debt Service Costs: Annual cash requirements to meet interest and repayment obligations on debt. Coverage ratios with earnings before interest, taxes, depreciation, and amortization (EBITDA), or some other cash flow measure, as the numerator, and debt service costs as the denominator, are useful indicators of a debtor's ability to pay. *Compare to Fixed Charges. Also called Debt Service Coverage Ratios.*

Debt Service Coverage Ratios: *See Debt Service Costs.*

Debt Warrant: *See Contingent Takedown Option.*

Debt with a Mandatory Common Stock Purchase Contract: Notes with an embedded contract requiring the debtholders to buy sufficient common stock from the issuer to retire the debt issue in full at its scheduled maturity date. Before a change in the law, these notes were used as primary bank capital in the U.S. *See also Mandatory Convertible.*

Debt with Springing Warrants: A variation on usable bonds. Deep discount bonds (zero, low-coupon, or downgraded) can be used at par to exercise warrants when a triggering event like a hostile takeover attempt occurs. As this example suggests, these provisions occasionally serve as a takeover defense. *Also called Springing Warrants.*

Decay Factor: The rate at which a variable's value diminishes through time. For example, if a variable is set equal to Ae^{kt}, and A is greater than 0, k is negative, and t equals time, then the variable exhibits exponential decay. With exponential decay, a variable is reduced to half its value in the same amount of time, regardless of its starting value.

Decline Guarantee: A put option.

Decoupling: A reference to a departure from the typical relationship between two asset or asset class returns. In the U.S., for example, stock and bond returns tend to rise and fall together. These returns may diverge, i.e., decouple, in certain economic and financial environments.

Decoupling Trade: Any transaction designed to profit from a delinking or change in the spread relationship or correlation between or among two or more indexes, rates, or other financial relationships.

Dedicating a Portfolio: *See Cash Flow Matching, Immunization of a Portfolio.*

Deep Pockets: A reference to reliance by an investor, creditor, or litigant on the financial strength of an obligated parent or affiliate of the issuer, borrower, or lawsuit counterparty.

Default: Failure to meet an obligation, such as timely payment of interest or principal, maintenance of minimum working capital levels, etc. Upon an event of default, creditors are usually permitted to take steps to protect their interests. *Also called Event of Default.*

Default Exposure: The loss that would be incurred by a market participant if its counterparty defaulted. Default exposure is often measured using Monte Carlo techniques. Typically, the case associated with the 95% probability limit is defined, somewhat arbitrarily, as the "maximum default exposure." To complicate any loss calculation or estimate further, a default usually reduces the market value of an instrument, but rarely reduces it to zero within a short period. *See also Default Risk (2).*

Default Payment: The value of the payout of a credit derivative. The payout is usually equal to the mark-to-market decline in value of the underlying instrument; payment of par on the instrument in return for physical delivery; or, less frequently, a fixed percentage of the notional value of the instrument.

Default Risk: (1) The probability that a particular interest, principal, or swap payment or set of payments due from an issuer or a counterparty will not be forthcoming on schedule. (2) The cost of a payment default. Different financial transactions have different default probabilities, and because of the different magnitudes of associated net cash flows and principal exposures, different costs associated with the same probability of default. (3) The product of (1) and (2). *See also Default Exposure.*

Defeasance: A technique of liability immunization that permits a debtor to offset and eliminate a liability with the purchase of government securities or a special risk management contract. For tax, regulatory, contractual, or other reasons, the debt issuer may find it more appropriate to set aside certain assets—typically government bonds and/or cash equivalents—against a debt obligation, rather than repurchasing and cancelling the debt. Unless the dedication of the assets set aside for extinguishing the debt is irrevocable, both the assets and liabilities will continue to appear on the balance sheet.

Deferred Coupon Note or Bond: A debt instrument that pays no interest for a fixed period and then pays interest at a relatively high rate for the remainder of its life. *See also Deferred Interest Bond.*

Deferred Interest Bond: A bond that pays interest only at a future date or dates. A zero-coupon bond is the ultimate deferred interest bond, because it pays all interest and principal at maturity. *See also Deferred Coupon Note or Bond.*

Deferred Pay Securities: Instruments whose value accrues for some time before the issuer has to part with cash. Examples include zero-coupon bonds and payment in kind (PIK) securities.

Deferred Payment American Option: This structure, more common with puts than calls, permits an option-holder to freeze the underlying price at which an option will be exercised prior to the option's maturity. Under the deferred payment feature, the intrinsic value of the "exercised" option is not paid out until the scheduled maturity (expiration) of the option. The actual or implied carrying cost of the long underlying position that makes American puts more expensive than European puts remains with the put holder until expiration. This contract usually costs approximately the same as a European put, but provides some of the market timing possibilities of an American put. *Also called a Deferred Payout Option, and may be embedded in a Deferred Payment Note or Bond (2) or a Fixed Assurance Note. See also Shout Option (2), American Option, Bermuda Option, European Option, Japanese Option, Modified American Option, Quasi-American Option.*

Deferred Payment Note or Bond: (1) A bond issued to investors with payment to the issuer deferred for a fixed period, usually to facilitate the investor's use of the bond as collateral for a loan. *Also called Fixed Assurance Note (FAN).* (2) An equity-linked note or bond with an embedded deferred payment American option that permits early designation of the spot price to be used in calculating the payout, but defers the payout until maturity of the bond or note. *See also Deferred Payment American Option.*

Deferred Payout Option: *See Deferred Payment American Option.*

Deferred Premium Option: An option without an upfront premium. At expiration, the premium is paid or netted against any option payoff. The only differences from a standard option are the timing and size of the premium payment. The premium for a deferred premium option is higher by at least the interest cost of carrying the premium. *See Boston Option (2). Contrast with Contingent Premium Option (diagram). See also Installment Option (diagram), Pay Later Option (PLO).*

Deferred Start Option: Any of a variety of options that are traded before their effective lives commence, and perhaps even before their strikes and other terms are set. Typically, these options provide for selection of the strike and start date at the holder's option, constrained by a formula built into the option contract. Sometimes the terms are set entirely by formula, based on spot prices or rates on selected dates. *See, for example, Barrier Option, In Option, Deferred Strike or Strike Price Option.*

Deferred Start Swap: A swap with a forward start date. *See Deferred Swap, Forward Swap.*

Deferred Strike or Strike Price Option: An option that permits the buyer of the contract to set the strike price or rate at a fixed ratio to the spot price or rate at any time during an interval after the trade date. If the buyer does not set the strike earlier, it is determined by the spot at the end of the deferred start period. A deferred strike option is usually purchased when the buyer feels that current levels of volatility are relatively low, and there is an opportunity to obtain a commitment to issue an option at a lower implied volatility than the buyer expects to prevail when he wants to fix the strike on the option. The deferred strike option's premium as a percent of the ultimate strike and the other terms of the option contract are determined on the trade date. *See also Deferred Start Option, Exotic Options, Shout Option (1).*

Deferred Strike Option

Deferred Swap: Any swap where some or all payments are delayed for a specific period after their magnitude is determined—usually for tax or accounting purposes. *See Deferred Start Swap.*

Degenerate Swap: A swap based on only one forward rate. Essentially, this contract is a forward rate agreement (FRA) or a simple variation on this basic contract. Variations on a standard FRA might include unusual timing or calculation of the payment on one side of the contract. Calling this an FRA or a modified FRA avoids the connotations of the word "degenerate." *See Forward Rate Agreement (FRA).*

Delayed Convertible: A convertible security that cannot be converted immediately.

Delayed Reset Swap: *See In-Arrears Swap (diagram).*

Delayed Settlement: A provision of a risk management agreement that provides for a longer than usual time between the determination of settlement terms and the accounting and funds exchange of the settlement process.

Delayed Start Swap: A swap with a forward start date. *See Forward Swap.*

Deleveraged Constant Maturity-Linked Floating-Rate Note: A floating-rate note with the interest payment set relative to a constant maturity swap or sovereign rate. Deleveraging refers to the fact that the effective rate on one side of the swap is a fraction of the constant maturity rate, or a fraction of that rate plus a spread. Embedded floors are common in these notes.

Deleveraged Instrument: Any note, swap, or even option in which the participation rate in an interest rate or other index change is less than 100%. Examples include most participating equity-linked notes and floating-rate notes paying some fraction of a constant maturity rate. *See, for example, Step-Up Recovery Floater (SURF).*

Deliverable: A financial instrument or commodity that meets the settlement requirements of a futures or option contract. *See also Cheapest to Deliver (CTD), Contract Grade, Delivery Option.*

Delivery: The exchange of funds for a financial instrument, commodity, or for cancellation of a cash settlement obligation.

Delivery Day: The day on which the short in a futures contract makes delivery of the appropriate cash or underlying.

Delivery Factor: A coefficient multiplied by the settlement price of a financial futures contract to obtain the invoice price for a specific deliverable instrument. Commonly, delivery factors for interest rate contracts in the U.S. are based on an 8% yield.

Delivery Month: *See Contract Month.*

Delivery Option: In settlement of a futures contract, the seller often has a choice of tendering one of several instruments or grades of a commodity to satisfy his obligation. *See also Cheapest to Deliver (CTD), Deliverable.*

Delivery Price: *See Settlement Price (2).*

Delivery Risk: In a currency transaction, it has been impossible to settle both sides simultaneously, putting the full principal amount of the transaction at risk for a short period. New settlement procedures are reducing and will eventually eliminate this risk. *See Settlement Risk.*

Delivery Specifications: The provisions of a futures, forward, or option contract that detail the characteristics of the financial instrument(s) or commodity(ies) that are accepted as good delivery in settlement of the contract at expiration or exercise.

Delivery Versus Payment (DVP): A settlement procedure that coordinates the exchange of cash for securities or commodities to eliminate most settlement risk.

Delta Δ: (1) The change in option price for a given change in the underlying price or rate. The neutral hedge ratio. *See Black-Scholes Equation, Delta Hedge, Neutral Hedge Ratio, Delta/Gamma Hedge,*

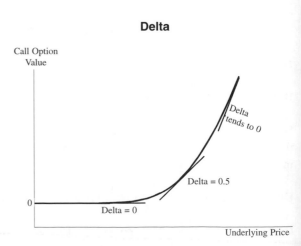

The Effect of Maturity on Call Deltas

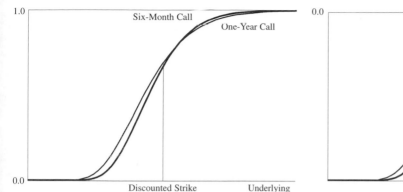

The Effect of Maturity on Put Deltas

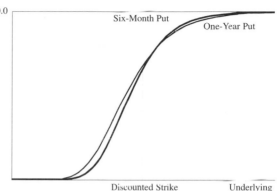

Delta-Gamma-Kappa-Rho Hedge, Hedge Ratio. (2) The smallest-capitalization issues on the London Stock Exchange. Delta stock quotes are not continually displayed on dealing screens. The other size classifications are alpha (α), beta (β), and gamma (γ). *See also alpha (α), beta (β), gamma (γ).*

Delta/Gamma Hedge: A risk-offsetting position—consisting in part of short-term option contracts—that neutralizes the market risk of an underlying position in an instrument with some embedded option features. The hedge offsets the current delta within a narrow range and attempts to match the change in delta (gamma) of the underlying position over a wider range of possible prices. In contrast to dynamic hedging or delta hedging, which relies on a series of transactions in the underlying, forwards, or futures to match changing deltas, a delta/gamma hedge has an option payoff pattern built in. *See also Delta (1), Delta Hedge, Dynamic Hedging, Neutral Hedge Ratio.*

Delta-Gamma-Kappa-Rho Hedge: A complex hedge involving at least two options with different expiration dates. This hedge is designed to eliminate exposure to the risks described by all four of these option price sensitivity measures. *See Delta (1), Gamma, Kappa, Rho.*

Delta Hedge: A risk-offsetting position that matches the market response of the base or underlying position over a narrow range of price or rate changes. Because one side of the net position has option characteristics, the position must be modified to maintain delta neutrality if the price or rate moves beyond a narrow range. *See also Delta (1), Delta/Gamma Hedge, Dynamic Hedging.*

Delta Neutral: A series of related instruments or a portfolio consisting of positions with offsetting positive and negative deltas that eliminate or neutralize the aggregate response to market movements over at least a limited range of prices or rates.

Dematerialization: Replacement of a physical or substantial item with electronic signals or bits in a memory register. Dematerialization in financial markets often occurs in stages. A stock certificate may be replaced by an accounting entry that can be printed out on demand, and ultimately by an all-electronic record. Any financial instrument, including money, can be dematerialized. *See Electronic Money.*

Department of Trade and Industry (DTI): The principal regulatory body in the U.K. responsible for the regulation of insurance companies, enforcement of corporate legislation, and prosecution of insider trading cases.

Depletion: The proportion of the cost of acquiring and developing a natural asset, such as oil or minerals, that is or has been amortized as an expense, much like depreciation. Depletion is a non-cash item charged against income and reflected as a reduction in the carrying value of the natural resource on the balance sheet.

Depo Rate: A deposit rate in the interbank market. As LIBOR is an offered rate, the corresponding depo rate is a bid rate, often called LIBID.

Déport: *Fr. See Backwardation (2).*

Deposit: Money or other liquid assets left at a depository institution to earn a return, as a liquidity reserve or in compensation for services provided by the institution.

Deposit Notes: A term deposit in a bank. Deposit notes, like medium-term notes, may serve as the basis for an equity or currency-linked risk management structure. *See Currency-Linked Notes, Equity-Linked Note (ELN) (diagrams).*

Depositary Receipt: Evidence of the deposit of a financial instrument with a custodian bank. *See also American Depositary Receipts (ADRs), Global Depositary Receipts (GDRs).*

Depository Institution: A financial institution that, usually among other businesses, accepts cash deposits for which it pays interest or provides services (e.g., checking) in return for the opportunity to invest or lend the proceeds from the deposits at a higher return than the cost of this source of funding. Examples include commercial banks, credit unions, and savings banks.

Depository Trust Company (DTC): A corporation owned collectively by broker-dealers and banks responsible for holding securities owned by its shareholders and their clients and for arranging the receipt, delivery, and monetary settlement of securities transactions. Once securities are on deposit, further transfers within the system can be accomplished electronically at low cost. *See Chicago Mercantile Exchange Depository Trust Company (CME DTC).*

Derivative Instrument or Product: (1) A contract or convertible security that changes in value in concert with and/or obtains much of its value from price movements in a related or underlying security, future, or other instrument or index. (2) A security or contract, such as an option, forward, future, swap, warrant, or debt instrument with one or more options, forwards, swaps, or warrants embedded in it or attached to it. The value of the instrument is determined in whole or in part by the price of one or more underlying instruments or markets. *Also called Contingent Claim.* (3) An instrument created by decomposing the return of a related underlying instrument or index. Examples include Americus Trust and Collateralized Mortgage Obligation (CMO) component instruments. (4) Occasionally limited to zero net supply contracts. This restrictive definition excludes warrants, convertibles, and CMO components. (5) In the financial press, any product that loses money.

Derivatives Operating Subsidiary: Distinct from special purpose vehicle (SPV) and derivatives product company (DPC), a derivatives operating subsidiary is designed to avoid some of the regulatory and, perhaps, capital restrictions that its bank or investment bank parent might face in certain derivatives markets.

Derivatives Product Company (DPC): A special purpose credit enhanced financial corporation designed to serve as a counterparty for swaps and other credit-sensitive derivatives instruments. Usually a subsidiary of a financial intermediary, a DPC carries a higher credit rating than its parent corporation, and is insulated in various ways from the parent's liabilities. *Also called Credit Enhanced Vehicle (CEV), Special Purpose Vehicle (SPV). See Bankruptcy Remote Entity, Enhanced Derivatives Product Company (EDPC).*

Derivatives Trading Manager (DTM): (1) The manager of a futures fund or a hedge fund specializing in derivatives instruments. (2) The manager of a derivatives trading desk.

Derman-Dupire-Rubinstein Models: *See Dupire-Derman-Rubinstein Models.*

Designated Investment Exchange (DIE): Any non-U.K. exchange recognized by U.K. regulators as suitable for use by U.K. investors.

Designated Order Turnaround (DOT) System: (1) An electronic order entry system developed and used by the New York Stock Exchange to expedite the execution of small market and limit orders by routing them directly to the specialist post on the floor. This system is actively used in program or portfolio trading in NYSE stocks. The proper name of the NYSE system is SuperDOT. (2) Generically, an electronic system that delivers orders to an exchange floor or other order matching system for automatic or semiautomatic execution.

Designated Primary Market Maker (DPM): A floor trader responsible for maintaining a two-sided market for a specific product on the Chicago Board Options Exchange. The DPM's responsibilities are much like those of a specialist on other exchanges. Creation of this category of floor member is a recognition of the advantages the specialist system enjoys when two exchanges are competing for order flow in the same product.

Designated Time Net Settlement (DTNS): A funds settlement system used in the Bank of Japan's BOJNET fund wire. As the name implies, net settlements are debited or credited to participating banks at designated times based on their net obligations to, or credits from, other banks. *See also Real Time Gross Settlement (RTGS).*

Destructured Asset Swap: A structured note combined with a swap structure that converts the note to a simple floating-rate note.

Detachable Warrants: Warrants originally issued with a bond or other security, that may be separated, traded, and/or exercised independently of the other security.

Diagonal Bear Spread: Whether puts or calls are used, this position involves the purchase of a relatively long-term option contract and the sale of a shorter-term contract with a lower strike price. Ordinarily, the number of contracts purchased equals the number of contracts sold. As the diagram indicates, the investor profits from a market decline, within limits.

Diagonal Bull Spread: Whether puts or calls are used, the option contract purchased expires later and has a lower strike price than the option sold. Ordinarily, the number of contracts purchased equals the number of contracts sold. As the diagram indicates, the investor profits from a market advance, within limits.

Value of a Diagonal Bear Spread

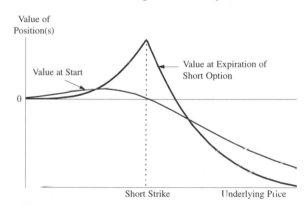

Value of a Diagonal Bull Spread

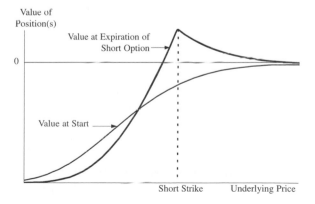

Dichotomous Variable: A variable that categorizes data into two groups, such as bankrupt versus solvent or energy versus non-energy company. *Also called Dummy Variable, Indicator Variable, Binary Variable.*

Diff or Difference Option: (1) An option on the forward interest rate differential (DIFF) between comparable instruments denominated in different currencies. (2) A spread or outperformance option with a payout linked to the price or rate difference between two underlyings. *See, for example, Yield Differential Warrant, Outperformance Option (diagram), Spread Option. See also Contract for Differences.*

Diff or Difference Swap: *See Rate Differential Swap (diagram), CUrrency Protected Swap (CUPS).*

Difference Check: The form of payment for a net settlement, such as the periodic net payment under a swap agreement where counterparty obligations are offset (netted).

Difference Equation: A discrete time version of a differential equation. While a differential equation treats time as a continuous process, a difference equation treats it as a sequence of discrete intervals.

Differential Equation: A continuous time equation that contains derivatives. For example, $dx/dy = 0$ is a first order differential equation. An nth order differential equation contains nth order derivatives.

Differential Swap: *See Rate Differential Swap (diagram), CUrrency Protected Swap (CUPS).*

Diffusion Process: A Markov process continuous in its time coordinate and its state space.

Digital Equity Note: An equity-linked note with an embedded digital or binary option payout.

Digital Option: *See Binary Option.*

Dilequant: A financial analyst who dabbles in quantitative analysis, but whose comprehension of the subject is superficial.

Dilution: The process that reduces the participation of equity owners in the earnings and market value increase of a company through the issuance or prospective issuance of new common stock or participating instruments. Warrants or other convertible securities issued by a corporation have a potential diluting effect on voting power and earnings per share, because they can lead to new share issuance. Exchange-traded options or third-party options or warrants do not dilute earnings because they are exercised into existing shares. In practice, unless a warrant or convertible issued by the company is quite large (relative to the common stock equivalent capitalization), the dilution effect is not a major consideration in the valuation of the underlying or derivatives on the underlying. Except for rare cases where a warrant or other convertible is sold or exchanged at less than a fair market price, dilution gets more analytical attention than it deserves. *See Warrant Dilution, Warrant.*

Diminishing Marginal Utility: The notion that investors derive less satisfaction with each incremental unit of wealth. It follows that investors suffer greater disutility from a decline in wealth than the utility that would come from an increase in wealth of equal magnitude.

Dint: *See Lookback Option.*

Direct Registration of Securities (DRS): An alternative to street name registration where securities are held in a registrar account for the beneficial owner. DRS is favored by regulators who want to facilitate same day securities settlement while giving shareholders the opportunity to participate in dividend reinvestment plans (DRIPS). Shareholders would not hold certificates that would have to be turned in to effect a transfer. *See Street Name.*

Dirty Hedge Instrument: A derivative security whose risk cannot be fully hedged with liquid exchange-traded securities and/or whose risk exposure changes over time or in response to changes in a secondary underlying variable. *See also Clean Hedge Instrument.*

Dirty Price: The price of a bond including accrued interest. Outside domestic U.S. bond markets and the Eurodollar markets, most bonds trade "dirty." *See also Clean Price.*

Disagio: *Swiss.* The discount on a bond relative to par, expressed as a percent. *See also Agio.*

Disclaimer: *See Hedge Clause.*

Disclosure Document: Although the term can be used more generally, it usually refers to a booklet published by the Options Clearing Corporation. This disclosure document outlines the risks associated with various kinds of options trading and various options positions. It must be given to option clients at or before the time their account is approved for option trading.

Disclosure Risk: The risk that mandatory or voluntary disclosure of company information will put an enterprise at a disadvantage when it needs to make future transactions to roll its positions over, control its risks, or otherwise modify its financial position.

Discontinuity Risk: Exposure to loss from failure of market prices or rates to follow a "smooth" or continuous path. A classic example is the risk investors faced in the October 1987 stock market break. *Also called Market Gapping. See Market Price Discontinuities discussion, p. 5.*

Discount Bond: A debt instrument, such as a Treasury bill or a coupon or principal payment stripped from sovereign or other debt, that pays no periodic interest but trades at a discount from its ultimate settlement value at maturity.

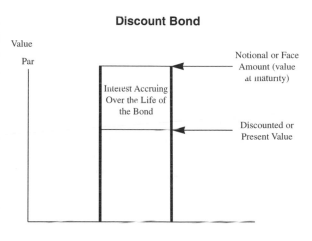

Discount Bond

Discount Currency: A currency whose debt market is characterized by interest rates higher than the rate prevailing in the investor's or liability manager's reference (domestic) currency. For many years, sterling was a discount currency with respect to most of the world's major currencies. High interest rates in sterling denominated instruments and low forward exchange rates implicitly predicted that a holder of pounds would be able to buy fewer dollars or DMs at a future date than could be bought in the spot market. *See also Interest Rate Parity, Premium Currency.*

Discount Factor: In interest rate term structure analysis, the reciprocal of the quantity, 1 plus the spot rate of interest, raised to the maturity of the instrument. Thus, if the spot rate of interest equals 8%, and the term to maturity equals 5, the discount factor equals $(1/1.08)^5 = 0.6806$. The discount factor must fall between 0 and 1. It approaches 0 as term to maturity approaches infinity, and it approaches 1 as term to maturity approaches 0. Although the discount factor decreases at a decreasing rate with term to maturity, it adjusts price as a percentage of value proportionately with time.

Discount Instrument: (1) A debt instrument, such as a Treasury bill or a coupon or principal payment stripped from sovereign or other debt, that pays no periodic interest but trades at a discount from its ultimate settlement value at maturity. *See Zero-Coupon Bond (diagram).* (2) Any fixed-rate bond with a below market coupon, so named because this low-yielding instrument trades at a discount to its par or notional value. (3) A reference to a security selling at less than its theoretically fair or expected value.

Discount Swap: A swap based on the coupon of a discount instrument(s) as the fixed-rate payment. Rather than add a spread to the fixed-rate payment, the parties may agree to a balloon payment by the fixed-rate payer at maturity, based on the size of the discount at the start date. *Also called Non-Par Swap, Off-Market Coupon Swap. Compare with Low-Coupon Swap.*

Discount Yield: Some money market instruments, principally Treasury bills and commercial paper, are priced on the basis of a discount from par value. The discount yield is expressed as a percentage equal to the annualized discount divided by par value. *See also Add-On Yield.*

Discrete Average: An average calculation based on a number of fixed points rather than on a continuous series.

Discrete Payoff Bull Note: A high fixed-rate note with repayment of principal at one of two levels: par or substantially less than par. The principal repayment depends on the level of a specified interest rate denominated in a currency other than the base currency of the note. The lower prepayment level may apply if the foreign rate rises (or falls) beyond an agreed level.

Discrete Time: The notion that time progresses in distinct and separable intervals.

Discretionary Order: An order entered by an agent with authority to exercise judgment on timing, price, or even on the instrument to be bought or sold. Some discretionary authority can be granted orally; but discretion beyond time and price is usually conferred in written form.

Discretize: To transform time from a continuous process to a discrete process.

Discriminant Analysis: A type of regression analysis that classifies the dependent variable into discrete groups based on two or more continuous independent variables. For example, a cross section of bonds might be classified as "likely to default" or not based on the values of independent variables such as the companies' debt/equity ratios and earnings growth.

Disintermediation: A broad change in financial relationships characterized by a decline in the traditional deposit and lending relationship between banks and their customers and an increase in direct relationships between the ultimate suppliers and users of financing. The securitization of collateral, the rise of money market funds for investment of cash reserves, the growth of communications networks, and the implementation of rigid bank capital requirements have all contributed to this trend. Disintermediation has drastically changed the roles played by various financial intermediaries and non-financial firms in the risk management process. *See also Intermediation, Loan Participation, Securitization.*

Distressed Security: A financial instrument (usually debt) that is in default, or in substantial risk of default, and has lost, or stands to lose, much of its value.

Distribution: (1) *See Normal Distribution, Lognormal Distribution (diagram)*. (2) The sale of securities by dealers to investors. (3) To technical analysts: a liquidation or bearish change in securities holdings.

Distribution-Free Statistics: *See Non-Parametric Statistics.*

Distribution-Free Test: A statistical test that does not rely on any assumption about the distribution of the population from which a sample is drawn. *Also called Non-Parametric Test.*

Diversification: An approach to investment management analyzed and popularized by Harry Markowitz and encouraged by widespread acceptance of the usefulness of the capital asset pricing model (CAPM). With diversification, risk can be reduced relative to the average return of a portfolio by distributing assets among a variety of asset classes, such as stocks, bonds, money market instruments, and physical commodities, as well as by diversifying within these categories and across international boundaries. Diversification usually reduces portfolio risk (measured by return variability) because the returns (both positive and negative) on various asset classes are not perfectly correlated. *See Modern Portfolio Theory, Non-Systematic Risk, Systematic Risk, Variance Drain.*

Impact of Number of Securities Held on Risk Level of Portfolio

Source: Hagin, Robert L. *The Dow Jones-Irwin Guide to Modern Portfolio Theory.* Homewood, IL: Dow Jones-Irwin, 1979.

Dividend Arbitrage: Techniques used to obtain part or all of an investor's return in the form of dividend payments. These techniques are often referred to as dividend capture when practiced in the U.S. Dividend capture may be practiced if dividends are treated more favorably than other forms of investment return for tax, regulatory, or accounting purposes. Certain American, German, and Japanese investors, among others, have found dividends particularly attractive at times. *See also Dividend Capture Program.*

Dividend Capture Program: Any techniques designed to take advantage of the relatively favorable tax treatment accorded intercorporate dividends in the U.S. Stock may be traded frequently to "capture" as many quarterly dividends as possible subject to holding period requirements in the tax code. Dividend capture strategies have been less common in the U.S. since 1986 tax law changes. *See also Dividend Arbitrage, Dividend Stripping.*

Dividend Cross-Over Method: A technique used to approximate the relative attractiveness of a convertible bond and its underlying equity. The dividend cross-over method estimates the date on which the rising common stock dividend will equal the convertible coupon. This approach is meaningful only when the convertible is deep in the money and a reliable dividend growth forecast is available.

Dividend Enhanced Convertible Stock (DECS): A preferred stock issue with an embedded short put and long call and a higher-than-market dividend rate. The issuer is the issuer (or a block holder) of an underlying common stock, and the DECS issue is ultimately convertible into the underlying common. *Compare with Debt Exchangeable for Common Stock (DECS)*, a variation of convertible debt with a similar return pattern and the same acronym. *Also called Yield Enhanced Stock (YES), Preferred Redeemable Increased Dividend*

Equity Security (PRIDES). See Equity-LinKed Security (ELKS), Automatically Convertible Enhanced Security (ACES).

Dividend ReInvestment Program (DRIP): A service that permits shareholders in a corporation to receive dividends in the form of additional shares of stock. The dividends are treated as cash dividends for tax purposes, but the stock is usually purchased without a commission charge and often at a discount to market value. The corporation may encourage shareholder loyalty and obtain a steady, if modest, source of new equity capital.

Dividend Stripping: A misnamed reference to the process by which German investors have taken maximum advantage of the favorable tax treatment of German corporate dividends received by domestic investors. Roughly comparable to dividend capture in the U.S., except that, in Germany, investors enjoy favorable dividend tax treatment, not just corporations, as in the U.S. *Also called Dividend Washing. See Dividend Capture Program.*

Dividend Swap: A transaction in which an investor exchanges an underlying stock or index's current dividend for increased upside (only) equity participation. The dividend is essentially used to buy a call option.

Dividend Washing: *See Dividend Stripping.*

DK'd Trade: An uncompared transaction. The initials stand for "don't know," and the transaction appears on the records of only one of the two putative parties to the trade. *Also called Out-Trade.*

Do-Nothing Option: An option whose payout is linked to the realized range of the underlying asset's price path. The option's payout increases as the price range of the underlying asset decreases. The do-nothing option structure is a way for an investor to obtain a payout that increases in a low-volatility environment without selling an option.

Dollar Bond Index-Linked Securities (Dollar BILS): Floating-rate, zero-coupon notes with an effective interest rate (determined retrospectively by the change in the value of a specific index) that measures the total return on a long-term bond. Used primarily for asset liability matching or portfolio immunization.

Dollar Cost Averaging: A long-term investment strategy that calls for an investor to commit a fixed dollar amount at fixed intervals to the purchase of common stocks or a common stock fund without regard to increases or decreases in the price of the underlying security(ies).

Dollar Risk Premium: The expected return on a foreign asset translated at spot exchange rates into U.S. dollars minus the U.S. risk-free rate. Expressed another way, the risk premium on a foreign asset for a U.S. investor with no currency hedging. Comparable risk premium calculations are made for investors keeping their accounts in other currencies. *See also National (Asset) Risk Premium.*

Dollar Roll: A special repurchase agreement transaction where the security transferred to the investor as collateral is a mortgage-backed instrument. Because mortgage securities are more diverse than Treasury securities, borrowers may receive different securities than they delivered when they repay the loan. Dollar rolls are an inventory management tool for mortgage securities dealers as well as a short-term financing/lending instrument. *See also Repurchase Agreement (Repo), (RP).*

Dollar Value of a Basis Point (DV 01): *See Value of a Basis Point (PV 01 or PVBP).*

Dollar-Weighted Return: The rate of return that discounts a portfolio's terminal value and interim cash flows back to its initial value. Equivalent to a portfolio's internal rate of return. The dollar-weighted return can be misleading for purposes of performance measurement, because it is influenced by the timing and magnitude of contributions and disbursements beyond the control of the portfolio manager. An alternative measure of performance is the time-weighted rate of return, which controls for cash flows. *Also called Internal Rate of Return, Yield to Maturity. See also Time-Weighted Rate of Return.*

Dollarization: A reference to the use of U.S. dollars as a measurement of value and a medium of exchange in an economy with a weak or unstable currency. Other reserve currencies may fill similar functions.

Dollarized Bull Note: A fixed-rate medium-term note denominated in dollars, but with principal payments indexed to the performance of a non-dollar interest rate.

Dollarized Derivatives Security: An instrument with all cash flows denominated and paid in U.S. dollars. Not necessarily similar to a quanto, because the exchange rate translation may be at the spot exchange rate at the time a payment is due.

Dollarized Yield Curve Note (DYCN): A medium-term note with an embedded rate differential swap agreement. The note's yield is a function of a specified non-dollar interest rate, but all interest and principal payments are made in dollars at an exchange rate that may be set in advance (a quanto note) or set at the spot rate in effect on the payment date. If the payouts are not quanto-style, the dollar payouts are strictly for convenience in position and portfolio accounting.

Dollars at Risk (DAR): Value at risk denominated in dollars.

Domino Theory: The notion that a default or financial stress at one institution will precipitate defaults or financial stress within other institutions, causing a ripple effect throughout the financial system because of interconnected assets and liabilities.

Don't Know (DK): A refusal to settle a trade by one counterparty because its operations department has no record of or instructions to complete the trade. In a volatile market, DKs can be an important source of settlement risk.

Double Barrier Option: An option with two instrikes, outstrikes, or trigger prices. *See, for example, Rebate Strangle Option. See also Barrier Option.*

Double-Declining Balance (DDB): Accelerated depreciation method using twice the rate of annual depreciation. As the table indicates, DDB provides a faster write-off in early years and the total depreciation is the same with both methods.

Four Year Depreciation Charges
(in percent of original asset value)

Year	Straight Line	DDB
1	25	50
2	25	25
3	25	12.5
4	25	12.5

Double Option: (1) An option to buy (call) or sell (put) but not both. Exercise of the call causes the put to expire and exercise of the put causes the call to expire. Double options have been used primarily in unlisted commodity option trading, but they are also found in OTC financial structures. (2) In the operation of a bond sinking fund, the issuer is often permitted to purchase "double" the mandatory number of bonds for the sinking fund at par. *Also called Option to Double.*

Double Rated: *Brit.* Callable securities.

Double Taxation Agreement: One of numerous bilateral treaties that reduces the tax bill in a stockholder's home country by eliminating or reducing the domestic tax on foreign dividends or by giving a tax credit for dividend withholding taxes paid abroad.

Down-and-In Call: A contract that becomes a standard call option if the underlying drops to the instrike price. The strike price of the resulting standard option may be identical to the instrike price or it may be at any other level the parties to the contract agree on. *See Barrier Option, Instrike.*

Down-and-In Put: A contract that becomes a standard put option if the underlying falls to the instrike price. The strike price of the resulting standard option may be identical to the instrike price or it may be at any other level the parties to the contract agree on. *See Barrier Option.*

Down-and-In Call

A. Option Activated | B. Instrike Not Breached

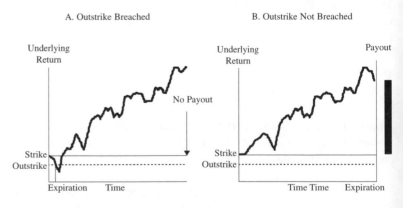

Down-and-Out Call: A call option that expires if the market price of the underlying drops below a predetermined expiration (outstrike) price. *Also called Special Expiration Price Option. See Barrier Option, Out Option.*

Down-and-Out Put: A put option that expires if the market price of the underlying drops below a predetermined expiration (outstrike) price. *Also called Special Expiration Price Option, Cash-Out Put Option with Rebate. See Out Option, Barrier Option.*

Down-and-Out Call

A. Outstrike Breached | B. Outstrike Not Breached

Downgrade Risk: The risk that an issuer's debt securities' ratings will be lowered because of a deterioration in its financial condition.

Downside Probability: The probability that an investor will not achieve a target (minimum) return. *See*

Target Return, Average Downside Magnitude.

Downside Put: An out-of-the-money put option.

Dragon Bonds: Debt instruments priced in U.S. dollars but sold largely in and through Hong Kong; functionally equivalent to Eurobonds.

Drawdown: Percentage loss measured from the high value of an account or fund. Many types of futures accounts and some general accounts are terminated if losses exceed a previously agreed upon drawdown from the initial investment or a recent high. In evaluating a commodity trading advisor's (CTA) performance, the maximum cumulative loss over a period of months is often cited as a measure of the risk the manager has taken.

Drawdown Swap: *See Accreting Principal Swap (APS).*

Dressed: A covered or hedged position. The opposite of naked.

Dressed Option: A short futures option collateralized by a risk-offsetting position in the underlying futures contract. A dressed call option—comparable to a covered call—is a short call collateralized by a long position in the underlying futures contract. The name originated as a contrast to naked or uncovered options.

Drift: (1) The mean value of a random variable that follows a Markov process. (2) A measurement of the value of the difference in convexity between two instruments. Specifically, the standard deviation of forward rate changes times the standard deviation of zero-coupon bond returns times the correlation of forward rate changes with zero-coupon bond returns.

Droit de Timbre: *Fr.* Stamp tax.

Drop-Lock Floating-Rate Note: A floating-rate instrument that converts into a fixed-rate note when the reference index rate drops below a preset trigger rate.

Drop-Lock Swap: An interest rate swap agreement with a provision that resets the fixed-rate payment if market rates change by an agreed amount.

Dropout Price: *See Outstrike.*

Dual Contingency Option: *See Contingent Payout Option (diagram).*

Dual Coupon Swap: A fixed-for-floating interest rate swap agreement with an embedded call option giving one party the right to require that periodic settlements be made in an alternate currency if exchange rates move against the base currency used in the swap.

Dual Currency Bond: Generically, a fixed-income instrument that pays a coupon in a base currency (usually the currency of the investor) and the principal in a non-base currency (typically the currency of the issuer). This generic structure is subject to many variations. *Also called Adjustable Long-term Puttable Securities (ALPS). See also Alternative Currency Option, Foreign Currency Bond, Foreign Interest Payment Security (FIPS), Indexed Currency Option Notes (ICONs), Principal Exchange Rate-Linked Securities (PERLS), Reverse Dual Currency Bond, Variable Redemption Bonds.*

Dual Currency Option: An option that settles in either of two currencies at the choice of the optionholder.

See Alternative Currency Option, Exotic Options.

Dual Currency Option Bond: *See Dual Option Bond.*

Dual Currency Swap: A swap used to hedge the issuance of a dual currency bond, incorporating an option and other components to transfer the unwanted features of the dual currency bond from the issuer to a financial intermediary who, in turn, will probably disaggregate and reassemble the components.

Dual Index Floater or Note: A debt instrument with coupon rates linked to the difference between two market indexes, typically a constant maturity Treasury (CMT) rate and LIBOR. Often a deleveraged instrument.

Dual Listing: Listing of a security or futures contract for trading on more than one exchange. In spite of the ordinary meaning of dual, the listings can extend to three or more exchanges. The latter situation is also called *Multiple Listing.*

Dual Option: *See Outperformance Option (diagram).*

Dual Option Bond: A bond with an embedded option giving the investor a choice of currencies for interest and principal payments. *Also called Cross-Currency Option or Warrant Bonds.*

Dual Trading: A controversial practice where a floor trader trades for her firm's account as well as for the accounts of customers during a single trading session.

Duet Bond: A bond with interest and principal payments linked to the exchange rate between two currencies on the date of payment. An exchange rate movement may have a leveraged rather than a simple percentage impact on the size of the payments.

Dumbbell Strategy: A duration-matching method that takes advantage of the shape of the yield curve to improve performance while meeting an average duration target with a combination of instruments with shorter and longer durations than the target duration.

Dummy Variable: *See Dichotomous Variable.*

Dupire-Derman-Rubinstein Models: Non-standard option and option portfolio hedging models pioneered by Bruno Dupire, Emanuel Derman, Mark Rubinstein, and others. These models share a focus on the volatility smile and term structure and an ability to incorporate these features into a valuation. An important application of these models is the hedging of dealer books. They promise to reduce hedging costs, and, consequently, to reduce the transaction costs of non-standard options. *Also called Derman-Dupire-Rubinstein Models, Rubinstein-Dupire-Derman Models. See Smile (diagram), Term Structure of Volatility.*

Duration: *See Macaulay Duration, Modified Duration, Option-Adjusted Duration, Effective Duration, Adjusted Duration, Partial Duration.*

Duration Bogey: The level of asset or liability duration sought in the management of a portfolio.

Duration Gap: The difference between the duration of an asset portfolio and the duration of its associated liabilities.

Duration Matching: *See Immunization of a Portfolio.*

Duration Risk Management: The use of modified duration measurements for a group of assets and/or liabilities to quantify and control exposure to interest rate risk.

Duration-Weighted Swap: A swap with one of the payments dependent on the effective rate at more than one point on the yield or swap curve. For example, a two-year swap might have payments dependent, in part, on three-, four-, and five-year forward or swap rates, rather than just on a single rate.

Durbin-Watson Statistic: A test for first-order autocorrelation (correlation between successive values) in the residuals of a regression analysis. The Durbin-Watson statistic is approximately equal to $2(1-R)$, where R equals the correlation coefficient measuring the association between successive residuals. As the Durbin-Watson statistic approaches 2, it is more likely that the residuals are independent of each other, at least successively. With economic and financial data, it is often possible to reduce autocorrelation in the residuals by transforming the data into percentage changes.

Dutch Auction: An auction system where the price of the item being auctioned is gradually reduced until it elicits a responsive bid. Dutch auctions are used to sell U.S. Treasury bills and to set rates on some remarketed floating-rate debt instruments and preferred stocks.

Dutch Auction Interest and Dividend Reset: Provisions of some floating-rate notes and adjustable-rate preferreds that determine rates by reoffering the securities in the marketplace on each reset date. The organization conducting the Dutch auction accepts bids and allocates notes or preferred shares to successful bidders at the highest market clearing price (lowest successful bidder's yield). *Among the instruments with similar features are Market Auction Preferred Stock (MAPS), Auction Rate Note, Money Market Preferred Stock (MMPS). See also Lender's Option—Borrower's Option (LOBO), STated Rate Auction Preferred Stock (STRAPS).*

Dutch Auction Rate Transferable Securities (DARTS) Preferred Stock: *See Adjustable-Rate Preferred Stock (ARPS).*

Dynamic Asset Allocation: Typically used as a synonym for dynamic hedging or portfolio insurance. *See also Asset Allocation.*

Dynamic Hedging: A technique of portfolio insurance or position risk management in which an option-like return pattern is created by increasing or reducing the position in the underlying (or forwards, futures, or short-term options on the underlying) to simulate the delta change in value of an option position. For example, a short stock index futures position may be increased or decreased to create a synthetic put on a portfolio, producing a portfolio insurance-type return pattern. Dynamic hedging relies on liquid and reasonably continuous markets with low to moderate transaction costs. *See Continuous Market, Delta Hedge, Delta/Gamma Hedge, Portfolio Insurance.*

Dynamic Overwriting: A call option writing strategy that mandates an increase in the short call position as the price of the underlying rises. The dynamic overwriter may begin by selling calls covered by 10% of the underlying position. If the price of the underlying rises, he repurchases these calls at a loss and sells calls with a higher strike and a greater aggregate premium against 20% of the underlying position, and so on. In effect, the dynamic overwriter counts on mean reversion in the price of the underlying as he increases a short position most aggressively when the position is proving most unprofitable. Results of this strategy—measured by the performance of the option position alone—are characterized by long periods of modest profitability interrupted by enormous losses when the market rises sharply. *See also Overwriting.*

e: The base of natural logarithms. The value e is equal to 2.71828. e is also equal to the limit of the function $[1 + (1/n)]^n$, as n approaches infinity. e is used to convert continuous returns into periodic returns. For example, if e is raised to the power 0.0953, it equals 1.10, which is the terminal value of 1 compounded continuously at this rate. Thus the periodic return equals:

$$e^{\text{continuous return}} - 1$$

See Logarithm, Natural Logarithm.

E-V Maxim: The proposition, first put forth by Harry Markowitz, that an investor should choose the portfolio that offers the highest expected return for a given level of variance. *See Efficient Frontier.*

Early Exercise: Exercise of an American-style put or call option before its expiration date.

Early Exercise Price Trigger: The provision of CAPS contracts under which the CAPS option terminates early with settlement at its maximum value if the underlying index is priced at or through the cap or outstrike price at the close of any trading session. *Also called Trigger Option. See also Capped Index Options (CAPS) (diagrams).*

Early Redemption (Put) Option: An embedded feature of some bonds with both fixed and floating rates that permits the holder to sell the bonds back to the issuer or to a third party at par or close to par if interest rates rise and/or if the quality of the issuer's credit declines. *Bonds with these options are usually called Put Bonds, Puttable Notes, or Puttable Bonds.*

Early Termination Date: The date on which the final obligations of the parties to a risk management agreement are calculated in the event of a default.

Earnings Before Interest and Taxes (EBIT): A measure of enterprise cash flow, largely replaced in recent finance literature by *Earnings Before Interest, Taxes, Depreciation, and Amortization (EBITDA).*

Earnings Before Interest, Taxes, Depreciation, and Amortization (EBITDA): A measure of enterprise cash flow that is replacing *Earnings Before Interest and Taxes (EBIT).*

Earnings Yield: The reciprocal of the price/earnings ratio, expressed as a percent.

Écart: *Swiss.* The difference between the price of a company's bearer shares and its registered shares. The latter can often be owned only by Swiss nationals and generally trade at a discount to the bearer shares.

Econometric Model: A series of mathematical relationships, typically estimated by regression techniques, used to forecast the values of economic and financial variables.

Economic Hedge: (1) Most commonly a currency hedge to offset the factor of production cost advantage of a competitor with a depreciating currency. *See Competitive Currency Risk.* (2) A hedge based on statistically measured sensitivity to a risk factor rather than the number of units of exposure. For example, a globally diversified portfolio may allocate 20% to German securities, but its economic exposure to the deutschemark may be different depending on the sensitivity of the other assets to changes in the value of the German currency.

Economic Rent: Excess over a competitive rate of return attributable to owning an asset or resource whose supply is limited, at least in the short run.

Economic Risk: Exposure to changes in exchange rates, local regulations, product preferences, etc., that favor the products or services provided by a competitor. *See Competitive Currency Risk.*

Economic Statistics Effect: A tendency for some option implied volatilities to rise in anticipation of the release of economic data or company results, and to drop as soon as the data is released because the uncertainty surrounding the release is gone.

Economic Value Added (EVA): A corporate performance measurement and analysis technique that stresses the importance of cash flow increments above the market-determined weighted average cost of capital. Often stated as:

$$EVA = NOPAT - (Capital \times WACC)$$

where **NOPAT** = net operating profit after tax, and **WACC** = weighted average cost of capital. Comparison of the EVA and franchise factor literature is often useful. *See also Net Operating Profit After Tax (NOPAT), Weighted Average Cost of Capital (WACC).*

Economically Targeted Investment (ETI): A project not expected to meet an investor's minimum rate of return hurdle, but which is undertaken to further non-investment objectives or to satisfy legal or regulatory mandates.

Edge: A dealer's expected profit on a transaction.

Edge Act Corporation: A corporation organized under Section 25(a) of the Federal Reserve Act (The Edge Act) to engage principally in foreign banking activities. *Also called Agreement Corporation.*

Effective Date: *See Start Date.*

Effective Duration: The ratio of the proportional change in bond value to the infinitesimal parallel shift of the spot yield curve. Equal to modified duration if the yield curve is flat. *See Modified Duration, Partial Duration, Macaulay Duration, Option-Adjusted Duration.*

Effective Rate or Yield: The net interest rate an investor receives (or a borrower pays) after the premium of a cap or floor is added to or subtracted from the contractual rate of interest.

Efficient Frontier: A continuum of portfolios that have the highest expected returns for their given levels of standard deviation plotted in dimensions of expected return and standard deviation. *See also Efficient Plane.*

Efficient Holder of an Instrument: Tax and regulatory considerations often make certain financial instruments unattractive to some potential users. Dividend withholding taxes often make foreign investors inefficient holders of a country's common stocks. Mark-to-market taxation makes tax-free

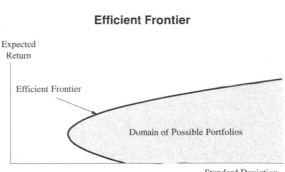

Efficient Frontier

accounts the most efficient holders of equity-linked notes in the U.S. Some countries forbid certain investors to own some financial instruments. Many derivatives transactions are designed to place an underlying instrument in the hands of an efficient holder and the beneficial interest in other hands.

Efficient Market: A trading market where the current price reflects all available information from past prices and volumes. In this market, past price and volume patterns cannot provide meaningful predictions of future price movement. These minimum features describe a weak form efficient market. More stringent requirements describe semistrong and strong forms. Efficiency is categorized by the strength of the efficiency that can be proven.

> **Weak Form:** There are no dependencies in past price changes that a technician can use to predict future changes. Prices are a random walk.
>
> **Semistrong Form:** The current price reflects all publicly available information that could affect the price.
>
> **Strong Form:** The current price reflects all relevant information, whether publicly available or not.

Also called Market Efficiency. See also Random Walk Hypothesis, Modern Portfolio Theory.

Efficient Plane: A surface of portfolios that have the highest expected returns for their given levels of standard deviations and their tracking error plotted in dimensions of expected return, standard deviation, and tracking error. A portfolio that lies on the efficient plane is not necessarily efficient in two dimensions, such as expected return and standard deviation or expected return and tracking error. *See Efficient Frontier (diagram).*

Efficient Portfolio: A portfolio whose risk/return characteristics fall on the efficient frontier, i.e., at a given level of risk no portfolio has a higher expected return, and for a given expected return no portfolio has a lower level of risk.

Efficient Portfolio Management: A set of standards in the U.K. for prudent management of investment accounts, including those for unit trusts and life assurance (insurance) companies. The standards call for economically appropriate transactions, i.e., transactions that reduce risk, reduce cost, or generate additional capital or income.

Eigenvalue: In factor analysis, a statistic used to measure the fraction of the variation in a security's return that is accounted for by a particular factor.

Eigenvectors: In factor analysis, linear combinations of securities comprising both long and short positions, that explain virtually all the covariation in the returns of a sample of securities. Eigenvectors are proxies for factors. *See Multifactor Model.*

Either-Or Option: *See Alternative Option (diagram).*

Elasticity: (1) A measure of the response of one value to a relative change in another. For example, if volume is not affected materially by a given percentage change in price, it is said to be inelastic to price. If volume increases greatly when prices are cut slightly and drops sharply with a small price increase, volume is highly elastic to price. (2) Used colloquially as an equivalent of delta or neutral hedge ratio. Note that delta is an absolute change measured in currency units, so this use is not strictly consistent with the origins of the term in economics. (3) Delta times the underlying price divided by the option or warrant price. *Equivalent to Gearing, Leverage Factor.*

Election Warrant: A warrant whose ultimate payoff or redemption value is likely to depend on the results of an election.

Electric Fence: A long position in an underlying instrument that sells forward at a premium is combined with a long lookback put on the full value of the underlying and a short lookback call covering enough of the notional value of the underlying to generate a premium equal to the put premium. An electric fence has a complex payoff depending on the put payout and the ultimate value of the underlying. It is safe to assume that this will never be a widely used instrument.

Electricity Forward Agreement (EFA): A contract calling for the delivery of and payment for electric power in a future period. EFAs are used much like oil derivatives contracts to fix or hedge energy costs.

Electronic Data Gathering Analysis and Retrieval System (EDGAR): A system implemented by the Securities and Exchange Commission to permit electronic filing and public retrieval of SEC-mandated financial reports. EDGAR took a great deal longer to implement than anticipated, and the Commission has received considerable criticism for its attempts to eliminate other means of access to corporate filings.

Electronic Money: The ultimate (so far) dematerialization of money, electronic money exists only as debit and credit transfers over a network. Electronic accounts may be printed on paper to give them physical substance, but an exclusively electronic manifestation is increasingly common. *Sometimes called Cybercash. See also Dematerialization.*

Electronic Trade Confirmation (ETC): As the name implies, a paperless trade.

Eligible Swap Participant: Eligible swap participants are the only parties permitted to enter into swap agreements that are exempt from regulation by the Commodity Futures Trading Commission (CFTC). There is a long list of eligible swap participants, including banks and trust companies, savings associations, insurance companies, commodity pools, corporations, partnerships, proprietorships, and other organizations such as trusts, employee benefit plans, governmental entities, broker/dealers, futures commission merchants, and any natural person with total assets exceeding $10 million. There are asset and net worth requirements for some of the other eligible swap participants as well as the requirement for individuals. *Also called Appropriate Person. See also Swap Rules.*

Embedded Loss: *See Unrealized Loss.*

Embedded Option: An option that is an inseparable part of another instrument. Most embedded options are conversion features granted to the buyer or early termination options reserved by the issuer of a security. A common example is the call provision in most corporate bonds that permits the issuer to repay the borrower earlier than the nominal maturity of the bond. The homeowner's option to repay mortgage principal early—resulting in early liquidation of a mortgage-backed security—is another common embedded option. *Also called Embeddo, Imbedded Option. See Call Provision, Latent Call Option, Latent Warrant, Prepayment Option (2).*

Embedded Securities Lending Credit: *See Securities Lending Credit.*

Embeddo: *See Embedded Option.*

Emerging Issues Task Force (EITF): A committee of the Financial Accounting Standards Board (FASB) responsible for providing timely guidance on emerging accounting issues. The task force includes accountants and financial industry representatives as well as the chief accountant of the SEC. EITF is a mechanism whereby FASB can provide accounting guidance on issues of small and intermediate significance without release of a formal financial accounting standard.

Emerging Market: (1) Any market that has introduced public trading of securities since roughly 1970. (2) Any market that is not one of the ten largest securities markets in the world. There is no uniform standard for inclusion or exclusion from the emerging market category, and small markets are called "emerging" even when trading activity has been declining and economic prospects are grim.

Emerging Market Warrants: Covered or guaranteed options or warrants on common stocks, stock baskets, indexes, or bonds traded in an immature market often characterized by some combination of restrictions on foreign ownership, discontinuous trading, inadequate investor protection, and/or limitations on currency convertibility. The creator or writer of these warrants insulates the buyer from some of these undesirable market characteristics in return for a warrant premium that is bigger than volatility alone can justify.

Empirical: Based on the analysis of actual data or experience. A conclusion based on observation rather than speculation or deduction. Empirical studies are undertaken to test or to suggest a hypothesis.

Employee Retirement Income Security Act (ERISA): The legislation that established regulation of the administration, investment, and risk management policies of pension (defined benefit) and profit-sharing (defined contribution) employee benefit plans in the U.S. *See also Prudent Expert Rule of ERISA.*

Employee Stock Ownership Plan (ESOP): A trust organized under the provisions of the original ERISA legislation to permit a sponsoring company to transfer shares of its stock in tax-deductible contributions for the ultimate benefit of the company's employees upon their retirement. ESOPs are defined contribution pension plans with the maximum annual contribution limited to 25% of the company's payroll. For some companies the shares held by an ESOP have become a significant part of the corporate capitalization.

End User: Usually a reference to the entity for which a financial instrument is created or to whom it is sold by a broker or dealer.

End Users of Derivatives Association (EUDA): A derivatives end users' information-sharing and coordination organization formed in the aftermath of a number of end user derivatives losses.

Endorsed Bond: *See Guaranteed Bond (2).*

Endorsement: In OTC transactions, a creditworthy guarantor sometimes endorses a derivatives contract to guarantee performance. Clearing corporations perform an analogous function for listed options and futures.

Endowment Warrant: Although the buyer makes an upfront payment called a "premium," an endowment warrant is a long-term margined stock purchase instrument with almost none of the contingency features usually associated with warrants. The premium payment is based on a calculation of the estimated dividends the underlying stock will pay over ten years. The premium payment per share is equal to the current stock price less the value of a ten-year amortizing margin loan that the forecast dividends would liquidate. If the actual dividend is equal to or above the forecast, the loan is repaid in ten years or less, and the investor owns the stock outright as soon as the loan is repaid. If the dividend payments are below expectations, the investor can pay off the remaining loan and receive the shares. Alternately, the investor can sell the net position at the end of ten years. Endowment options were introduced in Australia, primarily as a way to introduce limited leverage into retirement accounts.

Enhanced Derivatives Product Companies (EDPCs): AAA-rated subsidiaries of lower-rated financial intermediaries that serve as counterparties or issuers of risk management products. *See Derivatives Product Company (DPC).*

Enhancement of a Position: The use of arbitrage-type substitution techniques to improve the return from a position without materially changing its risk characteristics.

Enterprise Value: The market value of a corporation's total capitalization: equity plus debt, less the value of assets peripheral to the firm's core businesses.

Equilibrium Condition: An equation that describes a prerequisite for the attainment of equilibrium. For example, quantity demanded = quantity supplied is an equilibrium condition for the market model.

Equitize Cash: To purchase an equity futures, forward, or options synthetic position and collateralize it with a previously held cash equivalent position.

Equity Basket Option: An option on a portfolio consisting of more than one stock or stock market index. Portfolios or baskets can be composed of stocks from one or a few industries, or they can be designed to replicate broad market indexes. In the latter case, a basket may be used rather than the full index, because some index components do not trade actively or are subject to substantial market impact. One basket application combines several indexes to make a basket of indexes.

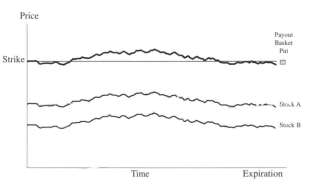

Performance of a Stock Basket, Component Stocks, and Payout of an Equity Basket Put

Apart from baskets designed to replicate or combine indexes, the primary motivation for trading a basket is that an investor expects the index or other grouping of stocks incorporated in the portfolio to move significantly over the life of the option. The investor wants to take advantage of the fact that premiums are usually lower on basket options than on separate options on each of the basket's components. *See Basket.*

Equity Buyback Obligation Rights (EBORs): Puts sold by the issuer of the underlying stock and guaranteed by a creditworthy third party giving the holder the right to sell the company's stock at a fixed (strike) price for a designated period. EBORs are sold to signal confidence in the corporation's outlook, not as part of a stock repurchase program.

Equity Contract Notes: Debt issued by a bank with mandatory convertibility into common stock. Counted as primary bank capital under earlier capital rules. *Also called Convertible Capital Note or Security, Exchangeable Capital Security (X-Cap), Exchangeable Capital Unit. See also Mandatory Convertible.*

Equity/Debt Ratio: *See Debt/Equity Ratio.*

Equity Enhanced Dedication: A form of portfolio insurance using a dedicated bond portfolio as the reserve asset and common stocks or stock index futures as the risky asset. This technique is designed to maintain a minimum pension surplus (or a ceiling on underfunding), while providing equity exposure and a chance to increase the ratio of assets to liabilities.

Equity Forward: A forward contract for the purchase and sale of an equity instrument or index at a future date.

Equity Gearing: Usually equivalent to the *Debt/Equity Ratio.*

Equity Index LIBOR-Linked Installment Premium Option: An equity index installment option with the level of each installment premium determined by the level of LIBOR on the date the installment is due. The LIBOR link can be set to cause small or relatively large changes in the installment premium level as interest rates change. The reason for this pattern might be to reflect the investor or dealer's view of the link between interest rates and the level of the equity index.

Equity Index-Linked Note: *See Equity-Linked Note (ELN) (diagrams), Index-Linked Bonds or Notes.*

Equity Index Participation Note: *See Equity-Linked Note (ELN) (diagrams).*

Equity Index Warrants: *See Index Warrants.*

Equity-Indexed Annuity (EIA): Any of several forms of equity-linked notes (ELN) wrapped in an annuity to achieve tax deferral.

Equity-Linked Certificate of Deposit (ELCD or ECD): A variation on the equity-linked note with a bank as the issuer. In the U.S., these instruments usually carry FDIC deposit insurance and the issuer may impose a penalty for early withdrawal. Ordinarily, an ELCD does not trade in a secondary market. *See Equity-Linked Note (ELN) (diagrams). See also Market-Linked CD, Market Index Deposits (MIDs).*

Equity-Linked Debt Placement: *See Equity-Linked Note (ELN) (diagrams).*

Equity-Linked Foreign Exchange (Elf-X) Option An elf-X put option enables an investor to sell a foreign stock position or portfolio at a future date (the expiration date of the option contract) without risk of foreign exchange loss. Specifically, an elf-X put gives the holder the right to sell the currency received on the stock sale at an exchange rate fixed in advance, usually the spot rate in effect when the option is created. An elf-X call provides the right to buy enough currency at the strike exchange rate to purchase a specified foreign equity position without fear that foreign currency appreciation will increase the cost of the position in the investor's home currency. While elf-X puts and calls provide currency protection, the price of the stocks can move against an investor while the elf-X option is in place.

The principal, or face amount of the option, is a function of the future value of a spe-

Equity-Linked Foreign Exchange (Elf-X) Option

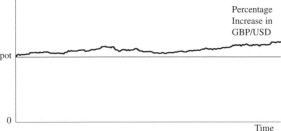

Step One: Calculate the Currency Change (GBP) versus (USD)

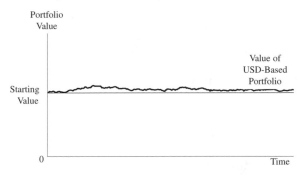

Step Two: Calculate the Change in USD Portfolio Value

Step Three: Elf-X Payout = (Percentage Increase in GBP/USD × (USD Value of Portfolio at Expiration) = Dollars That Can Be Sold for Pounds at the Strike Rate

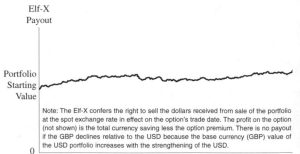

Note: The Elf-X confers the right to sell the dollars received from sale of the portfolio at the spot exchange rate in effect on the option's trade date. The profit on the option (not shown) is the total currency saving less the option premium. There is no payout if the GBP declines relative to the USD because the base currency (GBP) value of the USD portfolio increases with the strengthening of the USD.

cific underlying equity portfolio, not a fixed amount set at the time the option is purchased. One difference between the quanto and the elf-X option is that the exchange rate is fixed at the spot rate with a quanto, and the option payout in the investor's base currency is dependent on the equity or index percentage return in the equity's natural currency. If the equity or index percentage return is not in the money in the position's natural currency at maturity, there is no quanto option payout, regardless of the currency change.

In contrast, the elf-X option has no payout if the exchange rate does not change in the direction required under the terms of the put or call option. For example, an elf-X put on dollars relative to sterling has no payout if sterling depreciates relative to the dollar. The option pays out if sterling appreciates, but the size of the payout is also a function of the performance of an underlying equity portfolio or index. If the portfolio appreciates, the payout increases in proportion to the portfolio value. *Also called Portfolio Currency Protection Option (PCPO). Compare with Quantity Adjusting Option (QUANTO) (1).*

Equity-Linked Note (ELN): A security that combines the characteristics of a zero- or low-coupon bond or note with a return component based on the performance of a single equity security, a basket of equity securities, or an equity index. In the latter case, the security is typically called an equity index-linked note. Equity-linked notes come in a variety of styles. The minimum return may be zero with all of what would normally be an interest payment going to pay for upside equity participation. Alternatively, a low interest rate may be combined with a lower rate of equity participation. The participation rate in the underlying equity instrument may be more or less than dollar for dollar over any specific range of prices. The participation may be open ended (the holder of the note participates proportionately in the upside of the underlying security or index, no matter how high it goes), or the equity return component may be capped. Other things equal, a capped return is associated with a higher rate of participation up to the cap price. *Various versions of this instrument are known as Capital Guarantee Note, Equity-Linked Debt Placement, Equity-Linked Certificate of Deposit (ELCD or ECD), Equity Participation Notes (EPNs), Indexed Notes, Index-Linked Bonds*

Composition of an Equity-Linked Note (ELN)

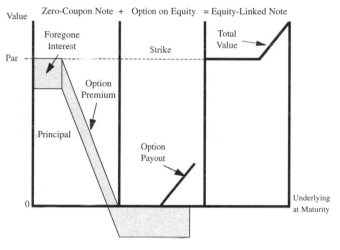

Capped Return Note

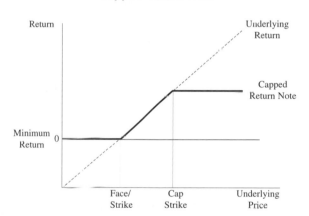

Participating Return Note

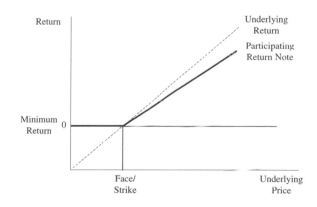

or Notes, Equity Index Participation Note, Equity Index-Linked Note, Equity Participation-Indexed Certificates (EPICs), Index Principal Return Note, All-Ordinaries Share Price Riskless Index Notes (ASPRINs), Geared Equity Capital Units (GECUs), Performance Index Paper (PIP), Customized Upside Basket Security (CUBS), Structured Upside Participating Equity Receipt (SUPER), Portfolio Income Note (PIN), Market Index Deposits (MIDs), Market-Indexed NotE (MINE), Market Index Target-Term Security (MITTS), Stock Index Growth Notes (SIGNs), Stock Index Insured Account, Stock Index Return Security (SIRS), Stock Performance Exchange-Linked Bonds (SPELBonds), Guaranteed Return Index Participation (GRIP), Guaranteed Return on Investment (GROI) Certificate, Index Growth-Linked Units (IGLUs), Index Participation Certificate, Protected Equity Note (PEN), Protected Equity Participation (PEP), Protected Index Participation (PIP), Safe Return Certificate, or as a variety of "money back" certificates. While the names may provide a clue to the structures, each issuer seems to have at least one proprietary name for some version of these instruments. Investors must look at the structure and pricing of the units offered and compare them with more familiar names and structures. *Compare with Commodity Index Note. See Securitized Options, Standard & Poor's Index Notes (SPINs), Structured Note. See also Guaranteed Index Unit, Deposit Notes, Market-Linked CD, Synthetic Convertible Debt (2), Money Back Certificates.*

Equity-LinKed Security (ELKS): An enhanced dividend, capped return instrument modeled on Preference Equity Redemption Cumulative Stock (PERCS). Unlike PERCS, which are issued by the corporation that issued the underlying, ELKs are issued by a third party, frequently a financial intermediary. *Also called Common-linked Higher Income Participation Security (CHIPS), Yield Enhanced Equity-Linked Debt Security (YEELDS), Performance Equity-Linked Redemption Quarterly Paid Security (PERQS), Convertible Money Market Units (CMMUs) (diagram), Market Index Deposits (MIDs), Synthetic PERCS. See Dividend Enhanced Convertible Stock (DECS).*

Equity Option: A put or call, often exchange listed, with a single common stock issue as the underlying. *Also called Stock Option.*

Equity Participation-Indexed Certificates (EPICs): *See Equity-Linked Note (ELN) (diagrams).*

Equity Participation Notes (EPNs): *See Equity-Linked Note (ELN) (diagrams).*

Equity Premium Puzzle: A reference to the difficulty of explaining the size of the observed equity risk premium (return premium) using standard asset return models. Brown, Goetzmann, and Ross suggest that survivorship bias in equity markets overstates the equity premium experienced by investors. *See Equity Risk Premium, Survivorship Bias.*

Equity Range Note: A stock or stock index range note with the payout dependent on the behavior of a stock or stock index relative to a designated price range. *See Index Range Note.*

Equity Rate Contingency Option: *See Contingent Payout Option (diagram).*

Equity Redeemable Bond: *See Preference Equity Redemption Cumulative Stock (PERCS) (diagram).*

Equity Risk Premium: (1) The earnings yield on an equity benchmark index minus the risk-free rate.

Composition of an Equity Range Note

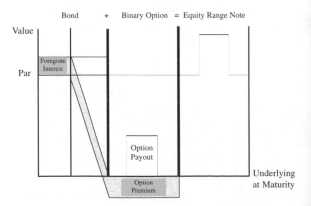

(2) Less frequently, the earnings yield on the equity benchmark minus an intermediate or long-term bond yield. *See also Equity Premium Puzzle.*

Equity Risk Reversal: A contract or pair of contracts that in combination provide a payoff pattern in an equity instrument similar to the interest rate collar or range forward contract in fixed-income and currency markets, respectively. The term "risk reversal" is also used to describe the comparable interest rate and currency market positions. In the most common structure, the investor buys a put that provides downside protection and pays for the put with the sale of a call, which caps upside return. Although there is no necessary connection between the premium paid for the put and the premium received for the call, most users elect a zero premium risk reversal rather than pay or receive a net premium. Some users fail to appreciate that

Payoff Pattern of an Equity Risk Reversal

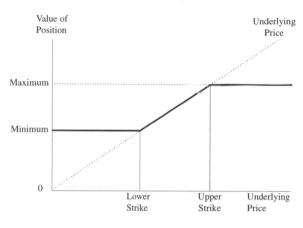

they may have to make payments on the short option. These payments may be covered by failure to participate in the price movement of the underlying in some structures. *Also called Min Max, Zero Cost Hedge, Collar (2) (diagram), Fence or Fence Spread, Cylinder (1), Risk Reversal, Spread Conversion, Conversion Spread, Forward Rate Bracket, Range Forward Contract (diagram), Tunnel Option, Hedge Wrap, Cap and Floor. See also Choke, Interest Rate Collar (diagram), Free Collar, Knock-In Risk Reversal (diagrams), Zero Cost Collar, Zero Cost Option.*

Equity Structured Call And Put Exposure (ESCAPE): The functional equivalent of an equity-linked note created with options to avoid adverse tax consequences.

Equity Swap: A swap with payments on one or both sides linked to the performance of equities or an equity index. Equity swaps are normally used to (1) initiate and maintain cross-border equity exposures either in an index or a specific stock portfolio; (2) temporarily eliminate exposure to an equity portfolio without disturbing the underlying equity position; or

Equity Swap

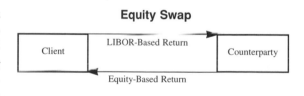

(3) increase, reduce, or eliminate market exposure to a single issue or a narrow stock portfolio, or obtain greater diversification for a limited period of time without disturbing an underlying position.

Equity Warrant: A put or call with a single common stock issue as the underlying. The issuer may be the issuer of the underlying or a third party. Third-party warrants are called covered warrants. *See Covered Warrant, Warrant.*

Equity Yield Enhancement Security (EYES): An equity-linked instrument with a single stock as the underlying, a coupon that exceeds the dividend on the underlying stock, and a capped return. The higher coupon is purchased with the proceeds from the cap. A synthetic (dealer issued) preference equity redemption cumulative stock (PERCS). *See Preference Equity Redemption Cumulative Stock (PERCS) (diagram). Also called Yield Enhanced Stock (YES), Performance Equity-linked Redemption Quarterly paid Security (PERQS).*

Equivalent Martingale Probability (EMP): Martingale probability values are equivalent to risk neutral probability values. EMPs are not actual probabilities; rather, they are probabilities used to determine expected prices under conditions of no arbitrage. The term "equivalent martingale" reflects the fact that the current value of a derivative security divided by the current value of a money market account is equal to the future expected value of the derivative security divided by the value of the money market account at the future date.

Escalating Swap or Escalating Principal Swap: *See Accreting Principal Swap (APS).*

Escrow Receipt: A document providing evidence of the existence of collateral. An escrow receipt may be used to protect a securities firm carrying a customer's short option position. The escrow receipt certifies that collateral adequate to protect the broker and the clearing corporation has been deposited with the bank or trust company issuing the escrow receipt.

Escrowed To Maturity (ETM) Bonds: De facto defeasance of a municipal with Treasury securities in escrow to meet all coupon and principal payments.

Euler's Theorem: Euler's theorem states that if a function is linearly homogeneous, that is, homogeneous of degree 1, the function can be rewritten in terms of weighted partial derivatives. For example, if the Black-Scholes option pricing function is linearly homogeneous with respect to the underlying asset price (S) and the strike price (X), then the option price (C) can be expressed as:

$$C = S\ \delta C/\delta S + X\ \delta C/\delta X$$

Euro: A proposed Eurocurrency for use in a limited number of countries—a partial replacement for the ECU, which seems fated to survive only as a unit of account for a few supranational agencies. *See European Currency Unit (ECU) Bond.*

Euroclear: One of two clearing houses for securities traded in the Euromarkets. *See also Centrale de Lívraison de Valuers Mobilières (CEDEL).*

Eurocurrency: (1) Technically, a Eurocurrency is a deposit claim on the domestic banks of the country whose currency is used to denominate the claim, deposited in a bank located outside the country—including foreign branches of the currency-issuing country's domestic banks. (2) Dollars, DM, yen, pounds, or any other currency deposit or instrument outside the formal control of the issuing country's monetary authorities. The "Euro" prefix describes only the geographical origins of the first markets in securities denominated in these unregulated currencies. Today many Euromarkets are located in Asia and elsewhere around the world. *Also called Eurodollars, Eurosterling, etc.*

Eurodollars: *See Eurocurrency (2).*

Euromarkets: Markets in securities and futures denominated in Eurocurrencies and sold to investors based outside the country that is home to the currency used as the unit of payment and valuation for the instrument. *See Interest Equalization Tax (IET).*

European Currency Unit (ECU): A weighted basket of currencies of members of the European Economic Community (EC). Over time, the composition and weighting of the ECU would have become increasingly stable if original agreements remained in force. While the ECU remains in use as a unit of account for certain organizations like the European Bank for Reconstruction and Development (EBRD), the name for the proposed common currency is the Euro.

European Currency Unit (ECU) Bond: A Eurobond denominated in the ECU. The provisions of these bonds vary, but ordinarily interest and principal can be paid in ECUs or in any of the ECU constituent currencies at the option of the holder. In most cases, the exchange rate would be the spot rate in effect at the time of the payment. *See also Euro.*

European Exchange Rate Quotation Convention: In currency markets, the practice of quoting exchange relationships in terms of the number of units of the foreign currency per dollar. Quotations in French francs per dollar or DM per dollar would be expressing the exchange rate relationship in the European convention. *See also American Exchange Rate Quotation Convention.*

European Monetary System (EMS): A set of rules establishing the European Currency Unit (ECU) and the Exchange Rate Mechanism (ERM) by which most members of the European Economic Community have committed to maintain exchange rate relationships within narrow bands.

European Monetary Union: A plan that would replace the currencies of member countries with the Euro. The outlook for incorporating more than a few currencies in a single currency plan is clouded. *See also Common Market, European Snake.*

European Option: A put or call that can be exercised only on its expiration date. The term has nothing to do with where the option is traded or what underlies it. Stock options listed on European option exchanges are usually American-style options in the sense that they can be exercised prior to the expiration date. *See also American Option, Bermuda Option, Deferred Payment American Option, Japanese Option, Modified American Option, Quasi-American Option.*

European Snake: An exchange rate agreement reached in 1976 whereby the countries in the European Monetary Union (EMU) agreed to establish mutual exchange rate parities with narrow margins and to let their currencies float within a wider band with respect to the U.S. dollar. *See also European Monetary Union.*

European Union: *See Common Market.*

Eurosterling: *See Eurocurrency (2).*

Eurowarrants: Warrant contracts traded in the Euromarkets, originally in London and Zurich, but increasingly in Asian markets.

Event Arbitrage: A subset of risk, merger, convertible, or distressed securities arbitrage that counts on a specific event, such as a contract signing, regulatory approval, judicial decision, etc., to change the price or rate relationship of two or more financial instruments and permit the arbitrageur to earn a profit.

Event of Default: *See Default.*

Event Risk: Exposure to loss from a change in the credit quality of an issue or issuer resulting from a merger or acquisition, leveraged buyout, product failure, or some other development with a major impact on the issuer's business or capitalization.

Event Risk Covenant: A bond provision that requires redemption of the bond at par in the event of a corporate takeover, merger, or anti-takeover restructuring that would dissipate significant corporate assets. *Also called Poison Put (1).*

Event Study: A study of the relationship between a particular event or class of events and the response of a variable of interest. For example, a researcher may be interested in the relationship between company stock repurchases and stock returns. The researcher measures the returns in the period prior to and after the day a stock repurchase is announced for a sample of securities. Although the dates of the stock repurchase announcements differ across time, the pre-event and post-event periods are uniform in relation to the event. The researcher tests to see if the average returns in the pre-event and post-event periods are significantly different from each other.

Ex-Dividend: Without the dividend. Stocks sell ex-dividend on the first business day when a normal transaction would not lead to settlement in time to give the buyer the right to receive the dividend. A stock normally trades ex-dividend well before the payment date of a dividend.

Ex-Dividend Date: The date on which the buyer of a stock is no longer able to purchase the stock the regular way and still receive a specific dividend payment. A holder of the stock who sells on the ex-dividend date is entitled to retain the dividend when it is paid.

Ex-Pit Transaction: *See Exchange of Futures for Physicals (EFP).*

Ex-Rights: The period, late in a rights offering, when the purchaser of the stock no longer receives the rights. When the stock is trading ex-rights, the rights may still trade separately.

Ex-Warrants: An instrument sold without the warrants that were attached to the instrument at the time of its issuance.

Exchange: A formal marketplace or procedure for trading tangible or intangible property. The trading process is usually accompanied by standard procedures for settling trades.

Exchange Clearing HOuse (ECHO): A U.K.-based competitor of Multinet and IBOS in currency transaction clearing and collateralization. S*ee also Multinet, Inter-Bank On-Line System (IBOS).*

Exchange de Taux d'Intérêt: *Fr.* Interest rate swap agreement.

Exchange Delivery Settlement Price (EDSP): *See Settlement Price (2).*

Exchange for Swap: A technique, analogous to an Exchange of Futures for Physicals (EFP) transaction used by banks to avoid taking physical delivery of commodities. A dealer takes the bank's futures positions into its own account and swaps the commodity return for a funding rate.

Exchange of Futures for Physicals (EFP): A technique (originated in physical commodity markets) whereby a position in the underlying is traded for a futures position. In financial futures markets, the EFP bypasses any cash settlement mechanism built into the contract and substitutes physical settlement. EFPs are used primarily to adjust underlying cash market positions at a low trading cost. An EFP by itself will not change either party's net risk position materially, but EFPs are often used to set up a subsequent trade that will modify the investor's market risk exposure at low cost. *Occasionally called Against Actuals (AA), Cash-Futures Swap, Ex-Pit Transaction. See Basis Trade (1), Portfolio Trade.*

Exchange Option: An option to surrender one asset in exchange for another. Not to be confused with Exchange-Traded Option. *Also called Margrabe Option, Outperformance Option (diagram). See Contingent Exchange Option, Exchange-Traded Contracts.*

Exchange Rate Agreement (ERA): A synthetic agreement for forward exchange (SAFE), much like a forward rate agreement in the interest rate market, that increases or decreases in value as the spread between two forward currency exchange rates, say, three months and six months forward, moves up or down. Note that in contrast to a forward exchange agreement (FXA), the ERA is settled with reference to two forward rates rather than a forward and the spot rate on settlement. Usually related to some other risk position rather than a stand-alone position. *See also Forward Rate Agreement (FRA), Forward Exchange Agreement (FXA), Synthetic Agreement for Foreign Exchange (SAFE).*

Exchange Rate Mechanism (ERM): A commitment on the part of members of the European Monetary System (EMS)—most members of the European Economic Community (EC)—to maintain relatively fixed currency exchange rates. For most member currencies, fluctuations around a bilateral central rate with regard to every other currency in the ECU are to be maintained at ±2 1/4% from an agreed upon relationship. Tables of current minimum and maximum exchange rate parity relationships have been used to predict exchange rate intervention and central bank monetary policies.

Exchange-Traded Contracts: Standardized options and futures listed and traded on an organized exchange. These contracts meet many end user risk management needs and are used by major financial intermediaries to manage their diverse positions. *See also Exchange Option, Over The Counter (OTC).*

EXchange-TRAded (EXTRA) Funds: Modified unit trusts or mutual fund-type investment funds characterized by a dual trading process. Fund shares are created or redeemed in large blocks through the deposit of securities to, or delivery of securities from, the fund's portfolio. Secondary trading, in lots as small as a single fund share, takes place on a stock exchange. The dual trading process permits the fund shares to trade close to net asset value at all times. EXTRA funds are usually more tax efficient than comparable conventional funds. *See Frozen Index Funds.*

Exchangeable Auction Rate Preferred Stock: An auction rate preferred stock exchangeable at the issuer's option for auction rate notes on any dividend payment date. The purpose of this form is to permit the issuer to replace the preferred dividend that is paid from after-tax earnings with tax-deductible interest when the issuer's income becomes taxable.

Exchangeable Capital Security (X-Cap): *See Convertible Capital Note or Security, Equity Contract Notes.*

Exchangeable Capital Unit: *See Convertible Capital Note or Security, Equity Contract Notes.*

Exchangeable Debt: A bond or note issue that is "convertible" into the shares of a company other than the issuer of the debt instrument. This structure has been used primarily by corporations to sell a large position in the shares of another company.

Exchangeable Payment-In-Kind (PIK) Preferred Stock: The issuer has the option to convert the PIK stock into debt. *See also Pay-In-Kind (PIK) Securities.*

Exchangeable Preferred Income Cumulative Shares (EPICS): *See Monthly Income Preferred Share (MIPS).*

Exchangeable Zero-Coupon Swap: A specialized swap in which the end user who is originally scheduled to receive a fixed sum at maturity (the zero-coupon payment) sells the dealer an embedded option to convert the single payment to a series of fixed payments. The end user benefits from this structure if volatility declines and rates are relatively stable to declining.

Execution Cost: Usually the directly and easily measurable cost of trading—less comprehensive and far less meaningful than transaction cost. *See also Implementation Shortfall, Transaction Cost.*

Execution Risk: The chance that a desirable transaction cannot be executed within the context of recent market prices or within limits proposed by an investor. Unless a financial intermediary is willing to act as a dealer (principal) and guarantee a specific execution—within the rules of a marketplace—investors face execution risk in virtually all financial instruments. *See also Unwinding Risk, Roll-Over Risk.*

Executive Equity Swap: An equity swap in which one of the counterparties is a corporate insider. The executive usually tries to reduce exposure to her employer's stock price with the swap.

Exercise Limit: A limit on the number of exchange-traded option contracts that can be exercised by one holder within a specified time period. Related to position limits.

Exercise Notice: A notification—ultimately reaching an option seller—that the buyer of an option wishes to exercise and obtain the appropriate cash settlement or physical delivery of the underlying.

Exercise of an Option: Purchase or sale of the underlying at the strike price by the holder of a call or put. In cash settled option markets, exchange of the option position for cash.

Exercise Price: In some markets, the term "exercise price" designates the total amount or aggregate exercise price paid in exercise of the option. The exercise price for an underlying unit is more commonly called strike or strike price.

Exercise Procedure: The process detailed in an option contract, or in the rules of an exchange or clearing corporation, for the exercise of an option.

Exhaust Price: The price of a security at which the equity of a margin account would be exhausted.

Exit Bond: A modified or rescheduled bond, usually issued by a low-rated sovereign borrower to a long-term creditor. The name comes from provisions that exempt the holder of the bond from further rescheduling or a future lending obligation based on its position in this instrument.

Exotic Derivatives: A pejorative term used to describe many derivatives instruments that contain more than one elementary financial instrument. Instruments tarred with this brush include such basics as inverse floaters, equity-linked notes (ELNs), virtually any instrument with a currency adjustment or translation, and practically all interest rate-based structured notes. In some cases, the term refers to instruments with complex or leveraged payout patterns.

Exotic Options: Options with unusual underlyings, strike price calculations, strike price determinations, payoff mechanisms, or expiration conditions. *Also called Non-Standard Options. Often called Specialty Option. See, for example, Average Price or Rate Option (APO, ARO) (diagrams), Barrier Option, Compound Option (1) (diagram), Contingent Premium Option (diagram), Deferred Strike or Strike Price Option, Dual Currency Option, Lookback Option, etc., Strike.*

Expectations Hypothesis: An hypothesis about the relationship between interest rates and term to maturity holding that the current term structure of interest rates is determined by the consensus forecast of future interest rates. Suppose that the spot interest rate for a one-year instrument is 6% and the spot interest rate for a two-year instrument is 7%. According to the expectations hypothesis, this term structure arises because investors believe a one-year instrument one year in the future will yield 8.01%, because investors can achieve the same return by investing in a one-year instrument today and a one-year instrument one year from now, as they can by investing in a two-year instrument today. Based on the expectations hypothesis, an upward sloping yield curve implies that investors expect interest rates to rise. A flat yield curve implies that investors expect interest rates to remain unchanged. A downward sloping yield curve indicates that investors expect rates to fall. *See Yield Curve (diagrams).*

Expectations Model: A theory of forward or futures price determination that emphasizes the importance of price or return expectations. While expectations may play a role through the interest rate structures that determine cost of carry, few observers today assign an independent role to expectations in financial forward or futures price determination.

Expected Credit Loss: The long-term average cost of defaults anticipated in a swap or debt instrument investment program. Theoretically, this cost should be recovered from swap spreads and interest rate premiums.

Expected Return: The probability-weighted mean of the set of possible returns from an investment.

Expected to Accrue Return on Nominal (EARN) Warrant: *See Range Accumulation Option or Warrant.*

Expected Value: For any investment instrument, the probability-weighted sum of all possible outcomes. *Also called Mathematical Expectation.*

Expected Volatility: The value for the underlying's volatility that an option analyst anticipates over the life of the option. *Also called Forecast Volatility. See also Implied Volatility (IV).*

Expert System: An "artificial intelligence" decision-making process modeled on the knowledge and decision-making process of human experts.

Expiration Cycle: One of three cycles that U.S. stock option exchanges used from the mid-1970s to the mid-1980s. Beginning in 1985, the exchanges began to modify the traditional cycles to allow four rather than three expiration months to trade at once, and to allow at least two near-term expiration months at all times. Other markets usually have relatively simple rules for listing new expiration months.

Expiration Date: (1) The date after which an option is void. An option buyer must decide whether to exercise on or before this date. *See also Extension (2), Option.* (2) The final settlement date of a futures or forward contract.

Expiration Price: An outstrike price in a barrier or out option.

Expiry: The British term for (1) the option or futures expiration process, and (2) the expiration date.

Exploding Delta: A reference to the extremely wide variation in an at-the-money option's hedge ratio just prior to expiration. *Also called Pin Risk.*

Exploding Option: (1) A collar or equity risk

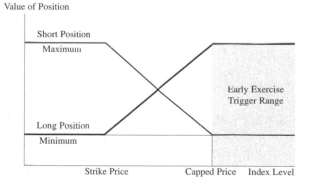

Payoff Pattern of Exploding Call Spread

reversal structure in which the short option "explodes" (expires), and the long option pays off at maximum value when the underlying trades through the outstrike price, either instantaneously or as of the close of a trading session. *See Barrier Option, Capped Index Options (CAPS) (diagrams), Path-Dependent Option, Cliquet Option (4) (diagram).* (2) An out option. *See Up-and-Out Call, Out Option, Kick-Out Option, Knockout Option, Cash-Out Call Option with Rebate, Cash-Out Put Option with Rebate, Touch Option, Up-and-Away Option, Vanishing Option.*

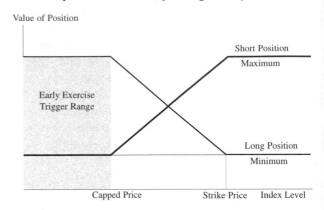

Payoff Pattern of Exploding Put Spread

Value of Position

Short Position

Maximum

Early Exercise
Trigger Range

Long Position

Minimum

Capped Price   Strike Price   Index Level

Exponential Moving Average: An averaging method that weights recent data more heavily (at a geometric rate) than data from the distant past.

Exposure Draft (ED): A proposed statement of financial accounting standards issued by the FASB for public comment. The exposure draft represents the FASB's considered judgment on a specific accounting issue. Subject to comments received and possible additional deliberation, an exposure draft may become a Statement of Position (SOP), mandating a Financial Accounting Standard (FAS). *See Financial Accounting Standard (FAS), Financial Accounting Standards Board (FASB), Statement of Position (SOP).*

Exposure Management: *See Risk Management.*

Extended Bond: A replacement bond with identical security but a more distant maturity offered to an issuer's bondholders in lieu of repayment of principal on the original bond schedule.

Extendible Note: (1) An open-ended debt obligation that resets every few years to a new interest rate based on negotiations between the issuer and the investor. At each renegotiation date, the investor has the option to put the notes back to the issuer, if the new rate the issuer proposes is unacceptable. (2) A combination of a traditional bond or note and an embedded option that gives the issuer or the holder the right to terminate or to extend the maturity of the note at a prespecified interest rate on one or more exercise dates. *Compare to Retractable Note.*

Extendible Swap: One or both parties to a swap have an option to extend the swap for an additional period beyond the original maturity date.

Extension: (1) The tendency of some mortgage pools to prepay principal more slowly than average or than predicted by standard formulas. (2) An agreement between the buyer and the writer of an over-the-counter derivative instrument to lengthen the life of the contract beyond the original expiration date. Extensions are not common because both parties have to agree to the extension and to the price to be paid for it. There is no mechanism for extension of a specific listed option or futures contract. *See also Expiration Date (1).*

Extension Risk: (1) The risk or cost associated with slower than anticipated repayment of mortgages, either because the underlying mortgage pool has unusual characteristics or because interest rates have remained too high to stimulate repayment or refinancing. (2) Corporate debt has extension risk if rates rise prior to an expected refinancing date prior to the debt's ultimate maturity. *Compare to Reinvestment Risk.*

Extension Swap: A swap with a forward start date that coincides with the termination date of an existing swap with otherwise similar terms. The forward start date swap effectively extends the life of the initial swap.

Extinguishable or Extinguishing Option: *See Out Option.*

Face Value: (1) Value of a bond or other debt instrument at maturity. *Also called Par.* (2) Notional principal amount of a forward, future, option, or swap.

Facility: A stand-by borrowing arrangement that can be used with little or no advance notice. *See Note Issuance Facility (NIF).*

Factor: (1) In the mortgage market, the ratio of the principal outstanding to the original balance of the mortgage pool, expressed as a decimal. (2) *See Multifactor Model.* (3) A traditional financial intermediary who finances low-rated enterprises by purchasing their receivables. *See also Forfeiting.*

Factor Analysis: A statistical technique for uncovering common sources of variability in data. For example, factor analysis uncovers the underlying factors in security returns. It is limited, however, in that the factors are statistical constructs and not easily associated with economic or financial variables. *See Multifactor Model.*

Factor Model: *See Multifactor Model.*

Fail: A trade that does not clear on the settlement date. *See also Settlement Risk.*

Fair Game: A game between two participants in which the expected outcome is equal for both participants but all the stakes go to the winning player. A risk-averse person will reject a fair game.

Fair Value Basis: The value or range of values of the difference between the forward or futures price and the spot price that offers no opportunity for profitable arbitrage at current carrying costs. For example, if the maximum risk-free lending rate is 6.0%, and the minimum borrowing rate is 6.2%, the fair value basis of a zero-coupon bond future one year out would be a range between 6.0% and 6.2% over spot. The range will be greater after transaction costs. In actual markets, participants' opportunity sets are different, and the fair value basis may range between a single point and a relatively wide interval. In some markets, such as DAX futures in Germany, there are structural arbitrage profits available and these may disappear only slowly over time. *Also called Fair Value Premium. See Basis (1).*

Fair Value of an Option: The option value computed by a probability-type option valuation model. The fair value of an option is the price or premium at which both the buyer and the writer of the option should expect to break even, neglecting the effect of commissions and other trading costs and after an adjustment for risk. Fair value is an estimate of where an option should sell in an efficient market, not where it will sell. The fair value of an option is also defined as parity plus basis plus insurance value. *Also called Fair Value Premium. See also Black-Scholes Equation, Parity (2), Insurance (2), Normal Price of an Option.*

Fair Value Premium: *See Fair Value Basis, Fair Value of an Option, Forward Intrinsic Value.*

Fairness Opinion: A valuation of a physical asset, a security, or a company prepared by an investment bank or some other presumably independent individual or organization. The opinion addresses the fairness or adequacy of a takeover proposal, recapitalization, or other corporate transaction.

Fairway Bond: A range accumulation note or index range note. The name comes from golf: when the rate is in the range, just as when a drive stays in the fairway, all is well. When the rate is outside the range, the feeling is like that of a shot that hooks or slices into the rough. *See Index Range Note.*

Falcon: A covered warrant with the issuer's obligation collateralized by enough shares to fully meet the underlying equity delivery obligation upon exercise of the warrant. *See Covered Warrant.*

Fallen Angel: A corporate bond whose investment rating has been reduced, usually from investment grade to a speculative rating, as a result of deterioration in the credit quality of the issuing corporation. *See Junk Bond, Rising Star.*

Falling Interest RatE Adjustable-Rate Mortgage (FIREARM): In contrast to the traditional adjustable-rate mortgage where the interest rate increases (usually subject to a ceiling) or decreases, the interest payment on a FIREARM adjusts downward when interest rates decline, but remains stable when interest rates advance. The rate on a FIREARM is capped at the lowest payment rate set after the issuance of the mortgage.

Fast-Pay/Slow-Pay Bonds: A reference to the expected cash flow patterns of CMO tranches with early and late access to interest and principal payment streams. *See Collateralized Mortgage Obligation (CMO).*

Fat-Tailed Distribution: A reference to the tendency of many financial instrument price and return distributions to have more observations in the tails and to be thinner in the midrange than a normal distribution. Assets prone to price jumps tend to exhibit fat-tailed distributions. *See Leptokurtosis, Lognormal Distribution (diagram), Normal Distribution.*

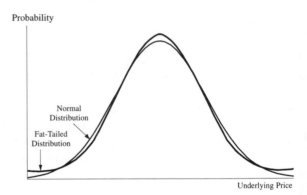

The Shape of a Fat-Tailed Distribution

Federal Agency Non-Guaranteed (FANG): Debt instruments issued by federal agencies that do not carry a Treasury guarantee.

Federal Deposit Insurance Corporation (FDIC): The regulatory organization responsible for collecting deposit insurance fees and administering the bank depository insurance fund in the U.S.

Federal Deposit Insurance Corporation Improvement Act of 1991 (FDICIA): Deposit insurance reform legislation enacted in response to greater than expected claims on deposit insurance funds during the late 1980s. Among the important provisions of FDICIA is endorsement of the enforceability of netting agreements in swaps and other notional contracts.

Federal Financial Institutions Examination Council (FFIEC): An interagency coordinating body consisting of the Controller of the Currency, the Chairman of the FDIC, members of the Board of Governors of the Federal Reserve System, the Office of Thrift Supervision, and the chairman of the National Credit Union Administration. Together, these five regulatory agencies have primary regulatory jurisdiction over domestic banks and other thrift institutions as well as the U.S. branches of foreign banks.

Federal Funds: Excess funds held by the Federal Reserve Banking system on behalf of depository institutions. The institutions lend these funds to one another, usually on an overnight basis.

Federal Open Market Committee (FOMC): A twelve-member body consisting of the seven members of the Federal Reserve Board and five of the twelve Federal Reserve Bank Presidents. The President of the Federal Reserve Bank of New York is a permanent member, and the other Federal Reserve Presidents serve on a rotating basis. The Committee is the primary policy-making body in the determination of objectives for the growth of money and credit. Its decisions are implemented through purchases and sales of U.S. government securities in the open market. The FOMC is also the principal policy-making body with respect to Federal Reserve operations in foreign exchange markets.

Federal Reserve Board (FRB): Seven Governors of the U.S. Central Bank appointed by the President of the U.S., with the advice and consent of the Senate, responsible for management of the Federal Reserve System.

Federal Reserve System: Central Bank of the U.S. created by Congress in 1914 and responsible for most aspects of U.S. monetary policy. The Federal Reserve System is largely independent of the executive branch.

Federation International des Bourses de Valeurs (FIBV): An international organization of securities exchanges that attempts to develop common policies and practices.

FEDWIRE System: The Federal Reserve Bank's communication system used to transfer payments in U.S. dollars.

Fence or Fence Spread: (1) *See Collar (2) (diagram), Equity Risk Reversal (diagram), Interest Rate Collar (diagram), Range Forward Contract (diagram), Forward Rate Bracket.* (2) *See Electric Fence.*

Feynman-Kac (FK) Theorem: The FK theorem provides a method for solving any differential equation subject to boundary conditions by using probability theory. For example, the Black-Scholes formula is a solution to a parabolic differential equation, and the Cox-Ross risk neutral valuation based on the FK theorem provides an alternate solution.

Fiduciary: A person or institution standing in a relationship of trust to one or more entities. In the financial risk management context, a fiduciary often manages or acts as custodian of money or property for another and must exercise a high standard of care imposed by law or contract.

Fiduciary Call: A call is purchased and the present value of its aggregate exercise price is invested in money market instruments placed in escrow to cover the cost of possible exercise. The implication is that the cash deposit reduces overall portfolio risk by preventing call purchases that increase leverage.

Fiduciary Put: A put is written and its aggregate exercise price is invested in money market instruments placed in escrow to assure that adequate cash will be available in the event of exercise. As with the fiduciary call, the cash deposit prevents the use of options to increase leverage.

Filtration: The inference of correct information from noisy or incomplete information.

Financial Accounting Standard (FAS): The letters FAS followed by a number (i.e., FAS 109) refer to a Statement of Position from the Financial Accounting Standards Board (FASB). These statements provide definitive accounting guidance on many topics for U.S.-based entities. *Also called Statement of Financial Accounting Standards (SFAS). See also Exposure Draft (ED), Statement of Position (SOP).*

Financial Accounting Standards Board (FASB): The professional quasi-regulatory organization with primary responsibility for determination of financial reporting standards in the U.S. The SEC has the power to override FASB standards. *See Exposure Draft (ED), Statement of Position (SOP).*

Financial Engineering: The development and creative application of financial technology to solve financial problems and exploit financial opportunities. (International Association of Financial Engineers.) The art (with contributions from science) of creating desirable cash flow and/or market value patterns from existing instruments or new instruments to meet an investment or risk management need. The creations of financial engineers are typically based on traditional instruments such as bonds and notes with forward and futures contracts, options, and swap components added.

Financial Futures Contract: A regulated, exchange-traded futures contract with a financial instrument as the underlying. Examples include futures contracts on debt instruments, currencies, and stock indexes. *See Futures Contract.*

Financial Institutions Recovery, Reform, and Enforcement Act (FIRREA): An act that made thrift institutions subject to Federal Reserve Board capital requirements and, together with revisions in the federal bankruptcy code, assured the enforceability of netting for swap agreements subject to U.S. law.

Financial Instrument: Cash, evidence of an ownership interest in an equity, or a contract that is *both*:
- a (recognized or unrecognized) contractual right of one entity to (1) receive cash or another financial instrument from another entity, or (2) exchange other financial instruments on potentially favorable terms with another entity.
- a (recognized or unrecognized) contractual obligation of another entity to (1) deliver cash or another financial instrument to another entity, or (2) exchange financial instruments on potentially unfavorable terms with another entity. (From a FASB exposure draft.)

Financial Instruments Project: An undertaking by the FASB to clarify accounting for a wide variety of financial instruments, particularly more complex financial instruments developed in recent years. The financial instruments project has led to a number of Statements of Principle from the FASB and the development of Exposure Drafts that are becoming accounting standards.

Financial Intermediary: A bank, securities firm, or other financial institution that collects deposits and makes loans, facilitates fund transfers and risk management transactions, and/or facilitates the flow of capital between operating units and the economy. *Also called Intermediary.*

Financial Leverage: Usually defined as total assets divided by shareholders' equity.

Financial Reporting Exposure Draft (FRED): The U.K. Accounting Standards Board's (ASB) equivalent of the FASB's exposure draft in the U.S. *See Accounting Standards Board (ASB), Exposure Draft (ED).*

Fine Print: Contract provisions, often in a small type font, that may create problems if both contracting parties are not fully alert to their contents. *See also Boilerplate.*

Finite Difference Method: A numeric method used to estimate a derivative's price by converting a differential equation into a set of difference equations. The implicit finite difference method establishes a relationship between each of three derivatives prices at time t and one derivatives price at time t + 1. The explicit finite difference method establishes a relationship between one derivative's price at time t and each of three derivative's prices at time t + 1. The implicit method is more accurate than the explicit, but it is also more computationally demanding.

Firewall: Barrier designed to prevent losses or risks taken in one part of a financial institution from weakening other parts of the institution.

Firm Price: A price at which a trader is willing to trade for a limited period of time. *Compare to Indicative Price (2). See also On the Wire.*

First Loss Guarantee: A form of credit enhancement where an investor has additional recourse to a third party for a stated percentage of any obligation or a percentage of any losses. A common feature of securitized loan packages.

First Passage Option: An option that has a random payoff at a random time, such as a stock option that pays its intrinsic value when the price of another asset reaches a prespecified value.

First Passage Time: The time until a prespecified state is first entered. The distribution of first passage time is often of interest in solving problems stated in terms of the time until an event (such as bankruptcy) occurs.

Fisher Effect: The notion, advanced by Irving Fisher, that the nominal interest rate should change in a one-to-one relationship with the expected rate of inflation.

Fisher Report: A discussion paper published by the Bank for International Settlements in September 1994. The working group that prepared the paper was chaired by Peter R. Fisher of the Federal Reserve Bank of New York. The formal title of the report is "A Discussion Paper on Public Disclosure of Market and Credit Risks by Financial Intermediaries."

Fixed/Adjustable-Rate Preferred Stock (FRAP): A variation on the adjustable-rate preferred that increases the dividend rate if the intercorporate dividend exclusion percentage is lowered in the future.

Fixed Assurance Note (FAN): *See Deferred Payment Note or Bond (1), Deferred Payment American Option.*

Fixed Charge Coverage: The ratio of earnings before interest, taxes, depreciation, and amortization to fixed charges. *See also Coverage, Interest Coverage Ratio.*

Fixed Charges: Usually interest on debt, but may include some mandatory debt principal repayments. *Compare to Debt Service Costs.*

Fixed Exchange Rate Equity Note: *See Quanto Note (diagram).*

Fixed Exchange Rate Foreign Equity Option: *See Quantity Adjusting Option (QUANTO).*

Fixed Exchange Rate System: The currency exchange rate structure under the Bretton Woods agreement that calls for central bank intervention to maintain exchange rates within a very narrow band.

Fixed-Fixed Currency Swap: Both parties to the swap are fixed-rate payers in their respective currencies.

Fixed-Floating Swap: A basic interest rate swap agreement of a fixed rate for a floating rate in the same currency. *See also Asset Swap, Interest Rate Swap (diagram).*

Fixed-Income Equity-Linked Debt (FIELD): *See Debt Exchangeable for Common Stock (DECS).*

Fixed Interest Rate Substitute Transaction (FIRST): A two-tranche floating-rate note structure where one tranche is a traditional floater and the other is a reverse floater. The net effect of the offsetting tranches is to make the issuer a fixed-rate payer. *See also Residual Interest Bonds (RIBs).*

Fixed-Rate Mortgage: The traditional residential mortgage loan in the U.S. with a fixed interest rate set at closing and equal monthly payments that amortize all principal and interest at maturity.

Fixed-Rate Payer: (1) A party to an interest rate swap agreement whose payment is based on a swap rate, the coupon of a long-term fixed-income instrument, or is otherwise set at the same level during each payment interval. Often called the buyer of the swap or said to be long the swap. *Also called Swap Buyer.* (2) The issuer of a fixed coupon note or bond.

Fixing: (1) Setting a price or rate for a future period based on the relationship of market prices or rates and contractual terms. (2) *Brit.* Short selling.

Flat: (1) A bond price quotation excluding accrued interest. (2) A reference to the terms of trading of certain bonds that are in default or that pay interest only to the extent that interest is earned. When a bond is traded flat, it means that the price includes consideration for any or all of the unpaid interest accruals. (3) A zero price or yield spread between two (usually related) financial instruments.

Flexible Auction Rate Preferred Stock (FLEX): *See Auction Rate Preferred Stock (ARPS).*

FLexible EXchange (FLEX) Option: A semi-customized, exchange-traded put or call option issued by a clearing house. Customization is limited to expiration date, strike, and exercise style (European or American).

Flight to Quality: A reference to attempts by investors to shift from high-risk to low-risk investments in response to a development that stimulates perceptions of increased risk.

Flip Bond: A bond with an embedded Bermuda swaption (exerciseable at each reset date). The bond pays a below market floating rate but allows the holder to "flip" the bond and receive fixed on some or all future coupon payment dates.

Flip-Flop Bond or Note: (1) A flexible, variable-rate instrument that lets the issuer shorten or lengthen the term of the note to reflect rate opportunities available on the rate reset date. (2) An instrument with an embedded option that allows an investor to switch between two types of securities. For example, between a long-term and a short-term fixed-rate note, or between a note and equity.

Floatation: *Brit.* Initial public offering (IPO).

FLOating Auction Tax Exempts (FLOATs): A synthetic tax-exempt (municipal) floating-rate note. *See Select Auction Variable-Rate Securities (SAVRs).*

Floating Exchange Rates: The currency exchange rate structure since the collapse of the Bretton Woods agreement. Exchange rate relationships have been constrained by bilateral and multinational agreements, but the rigid rate parity of the former fixed-rate structure is not in force.

Floating-Floating Swap: *See Basis Rate Swap.*

Floating-Rate ENhanced Debt Security (FRENDS): Securitized note backed by a leveraged buyout loan participation.

Floating-Rate Mortgage: *See Adjustable-Rate Mortgage (ARM).*

Floating-Rate Note (FRN): A fixed principal instrument, often used as the basis for a swap, with a long or even indefinite life and a yield reset periodically relative to a reference index rate to reflect changes in short- or intermediate-term interest rates. *Also called Adjustable-Rate Instrument, Adjustable-Rate Note. See also Reverse Floating-Rate Note (diagram), Participating Capped Floating-Rate Note, Leveraged Reverse Floating-Rate Note.*

Floating-Rate Payer: (1) A party to an interest rate swap agreement who is required to make variable interest rate payments determined by the reference index rate named in the swap contract. Often called the seller of the swap or said to be short the swap. *Also called Swap Seller.* (2) The issuer of a floating-rate note (FRN) or adjustable-rate preferred stock (ARPS).

Floating-Rate Rating Sensitive Note: A type of floating-rate note in which the quarterly reset is based on a variable spread over the reference index rate. The spread increases if the issuer's debt rating declines. *See Table of Debt Ratings (Appendix).*

Floating Strike Asian Option: *See Average Strike Rate Option (ASRO).*

Floating Strike Option: *See Average Strike Rate Option (ASRO).*

Floor: (1) A feature of a debt contract or a separate agreement that puts a minimum or floor on the interest rate of a floating-rate instrument. *Also called Interest Rate Floor. See also Cap (1) (diagram), Collar (2) (diagram), Floortion.* (2) A long put that limits the downside risk in a long equity position or portfolio. (3) In Constant Proportion Portfolio Insurance (CPPI), the minimum value the portfolio is permitted to reach. *See Constant Proportion Portfolio Insurance (CPPI).*

Floor Broker: A member firm employee, or, less frequently, an exchange employee who executes orders on an exchange floor.

Floor/Ceiling Swap: A swap with a built-in interest rate collar that constrains the floating-rate payment between floor and ceiling rates as in a separate interest rate collar structure.

Floor Rate: The strike rate of a floor contract.

Floored Put: A put position with a maximum payout limited by the terms of the contract—analogous to a bearish vertical put spread and similar in form to a reverse equity risk reversal.

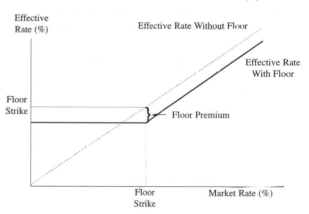

Effective Interest Rate With a Floor (1)

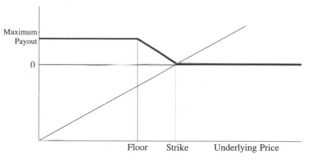

Payout of a Floored Put

The terms on which the floor provision comes into effect vary considerably by market and should be checked carefully. A put CAPS with its "exploding" early exercise price trigger is a variety of floored put. *Compare with Capped Call, Corridor (1) (diagram). Also called Limited Put.*

Floorlet: One of the interim period floors in a multiple period floor agreement.

Floortion: An option on a floor (1). The holder of a floortion has the right to buy a floor at a contractual strike price for a prespecified premium at the expiration of the floortion. *Also called Option on a Floor. See also Floor (1) (diagram), Compound Option (1) (diagram).*

Flush-Out Provision: A feature of a warrant to purchase common stock that permits the issuing company to reduce the specified exercise price of the warrant at various times and for varying periods during the life of the warrant to encourage early exercise of the warrants.

Focused Range Accumulation Note: A variant of the range accumulation note for investors who have more faith in their ability to predict short-term rates during the period immediately ahead than in their longer-term forecasting ability. The accrual index ratio calculated during a short initial measurement period is multiplied by the reference index rate plus a spread on each reset date. The rate still floats with market rates, but a good initial forecast can lock in a premium rate over the entire life of the note.

Fonds d'État: *Fr.* Government bonds.

Fonds Garantis: *Fr.* Guaranteed bonds.

Force Majeure Clause: A contract provision that excuses one or both parties from part or all of their obligations in the event of war, natural disaster, or some other event outside the parties' control.

Forced Conversion: Involuntary conversion of a warrant or convertible instrument undertaken to preserve the value of the holder's position. Forced conversion occurs when the issuer exercises a bond call provision in a convertible bond or is acquired by another firm for cash.

Forecast Distribution: A probability distribution of prices or rates that a market participant expects on the basis of analysis or insight. A forecast distribution is notable primarily when its shape or mean is inconsistent with standard distributions or basis calculations. *See also Implied Distribution.*

Forecast Volatility: *See Expected Volatility. See also Implied Volatility (IV).*

Foreign Currency Bond: A debt instrument with a coupon paid in a different currency than the proceeds of issuance. The principal payment at maturity is in the same currency as the coupon or converted to the currency of issuance at the spot rate of exchange at maturity. *See also Dual Currency Bond.*

Foreign Exchange: Cash market or forward claims payable abroad and denominated in a foreign currency. Foreign money.

Foreign Exchange Markets (FX, Forex): Cash, forward, futures, and options markets in currencies.

Foreign Exchange Risk: *See Currency Risk (2).*

Foreign Interest Payment Security (FIPS): A perpetual reverse dual currency bond with a periodic put back to the issuer at par. Coupons are in the currency of the issuer, and the put is at par in the currency of the investor. *See also Dual Currency Bond, Reverse Dual Currency Bond.*

Foreign Property Rule: A Canadian law that limits the percentage of a pension fund that can be invested in foreign assets. Historically, the percentage was 10%, but it has risen to 20%.

Foreign Stock Index Options, Warrants, and Futures: These exchange-traded contracts, most common in the U.S., provide exposure to CFTC/SEC-approved foreign stock indexes (typically the Nikkei, or Japan index; the FTSE-100; the DAX; or the CAC-40). The index level is translated into dollars for pricing and settlement purposes, and, in most warrants and options, the exchange rate is fixed at issuance for the life of the contract. *See also Covered Warrant, Guaranteed Exchange Rate Warrant, Guaranteed Warrants.*

Forfeiting: Non-recourse financing of longer-term receivables, similar to factoring. *See also Factor (3).*

Forward: A contractual obligation between two parties to exchange a particular good or instrument at a set price on a future date. The buyer of the forward agrees to pay the price and take delivery of the good or instrument and is said to be long the forward, while the seller of the forward, or short, agrees to deliver the good or instrument at the agreed price on the agreed date. Banks are often involved as credit intermediaries and collateral may be deposited, but cash is not exchanged until the delivery date. *See also Futures Contract.*

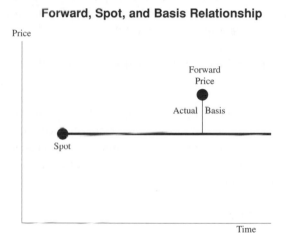

Forward, Spot, and Basis Relationship

Forward Band: A zero (premium) cost interest rate collar.

Forward-Based Derivatives Contract: An instrument that can be analyzed as a portfolio of forwards. Examples include futures contracts and swaps.

Forward Break: *See Boston Option (1), Break Forward.*

Forward Cap: An interest rate cap with a deferred start date.

Forward Currency Swap: A currency swap with a forward start on terms agreed upon in advance. Used to hedge or lock in some combination of interest rates and currency rates relative to an expected change in financing or operations.

Forward Discount: A price relationship in which the forward price, usually a currency exchange rate, is below the spot price. A forward contract sells at a discount to the spot rate when foreign interest rates are above domestic interest rates. Specifically, the forward exchange rate for a period equals the spot exchange rate multiplied by the ratio of 1 plus the domestic rate to 1 plus the foreign rate. *See Covered Interest Arbitrage.*

Forward Exchange Agreement (FXA): A contract whose value at maturity is based on differences between a forward currency exchange rate on the start date and the spot rate at settlement. *See also Zero-Coupon Currency Swap, Exchange Rate Agreement (ERA).*

Forward Intrinsic Value: Parity plus basis. The intrinsic value of an option (parity) plus the fair value basis on the forward underlying the option contract. A European option should not sell for less than its forward intrinsic value in an efficient market. The forward intrinsic value of a call is always above the traditional intrinsic value measurement, except in some cases when there is a dividend to be paid prior to expiration. The forward intrinsic value of a European put is always less than the put's traditionally measured intrinsic value, except when there is an impending dividend. *Also called Fair Value Premium. See Basis (1) (diagram), Call Option (diagrams), In-The-Money Forward, Intrinsic Value of an Option.*

Forward Outright Rate: The actual forward exchange rate as distinguished from the swap rate premium or discount. The rate used in an outright forward contract. *See Outright Forward Currency Transaction.*

Forward Plus: *See Participating Range Forward.*

Forward Point Agreement: A swap agreement under which one party pays fixed forward points set at the time of agreement and the other party pays floating forward points based on relative interest rates in the two currencies at a series of future dates.

Forward Points: A number added to or subtracted from the spot currency exchange rate to calculate a forward price.

Forward Premium: A price relationship in which a forward price, often a currency exchange rate, is at a premium to the spot price. This relationship, common in financial markets, often reflects the possible carrying cost of the underlying instrument. In exchange rate markets, it reflects the relative level of interest rates in the two countries whose currencies are involved, and indicates that interest rates are lower in the base currency country.

Forward Rate: *See Forward Yield Curve.*

Forward Rate Agreement (FRA): A contract determining an interest rate to be paid or received on a specific obligation beginning at a start date in the future. A notional principal contract like an FRA need not be with the party on the other side of the obligation that the FRA contract is linked to. Any gain or loss on the FRA is like a gain or loss on an option or futures contract. It is a function of the return of an underlying position. *Also called Future Rate Agreement (FRA). See Degenerate Swap, Exchange Rate Agreement (ERA).*

Forward Rate Bias: The empirical tendency of forward exchange rates to overestimate changes in spot exchange rates. According to the theory of uncovered interest arbitrage, forward exchange rates are unbiased predictors of future spot exchange rates, implying that a forward contract's expected return equals 0%. It is an empirical fact, however, that during the modern floating-rate era, the forward exchange rates of the major currencies have predicted larger subsequent changes in the spot rates than have occurred. Forward contracts that have sold at discounts have produced positive returns on average, while forward contracts that have sold at premiums have produced negative returns on average. *See also Uncovered Interest Arbitrage, Prediction Bias.*

Forward Rate Bracket: A contingent forward contract often used in currency markets. The investor can take advantage of favorable price moves to the upper end of the contract range while remaining protected against moves below the lower end of the contract range. Within the range, the contract settles at the spot rate and the customer pays no option premium. The payoff pattern is similar to an interest rate collar or equity risk reversal in fixed-income and equity markets, respectively. *Also called Fence or Fence Spread, Spread Conversion, Cap and Floor, Knock-In Risk Reversal (diagram), Range Forward Contract (diagram) in cur-*

rency markets. See also Equity Risk Reversal (diagram), Interest Rate Collar (diagram).

Forward Rate Curve: *See Forward Yield Curve.*

Forward Reserve Option: *See Break Forward (diagram).*

Forward Spread: The difference between any two forward rates or prices. A forward spread may be used in calculating the payoff—and the value—of a financial contract.

Forward Spread Agreement: (1) A specialized forward rate agreement that settles at the index rate (usually LIBOR) at the time of settlement plus or minus an agreed spread. (2) A forward that settles at the basis between two agreed-upon rates on settlement day.

Forward Start Agreement: A risk management agreement whose effective life does not start until a future date set by agreement or contingent on a specific event. Ordinarily, all terms of the contract are set at the trade date. *Contrast with Spot Start.*

Forward Start Swap: *See Forward Swap.*

Forward Surprise: The component of a currency's return that exceeds the rate of return implied by the forward rate. For example, if, at the beginning of the period the forward rate equals 1.50, and the spot rate equals 1.55, the forward implied return is:

$$(1.50/1.55) - 1 = -3.23\%.$$

If the spot rate at the end of the period equals 1.53, the forward surprise equals:

$$[(1.53/1.55) - 1] - [(1.50/1.55) - 1] = 1.94\%$$

Forward Swap: A swap agreement where the period covered by the exchange begins at a future date. Often priced as two partially offsetting swaps—both starting immediately, but one ending on the deferred start date of the forward swap. For example, a one-year swap and a five-year swap could partially offset to create a four-year swap, starting one year forward. *Also called Forward Start Swap, Deferred Start Swap, Delayed Start Swap.*

Forward Volatility Agreement: A contract analogous to a forward rate agreement or a forward exchange agreement that settles at a value determined by the difference between the contractual volatility level determined on the trade date and an implied or actual volatility determined on or near the settlement date.

Forward with Optional Exit (FOX): *See Break Forward, Boston Option (1), Cancellable Option.*

Forward Yield Curve: An interest rate curve derived point by point from the traditional yield curve, the forward curve is used to price many interest rate derivative instruments. The forward curve shows the implied forward interest rate for each period covered by the yield curve. The diagrams under the listing for yield curve illustrate forward rate curves for both normal and inverted yield curve environments. *Also called Forward Rate, Forward Rate Curve. See also Implied Forward Interest Rate, Term Structure of Interest Rates, Yield Curve (diagrams), Zero-Coupon Yield Curve.*

Forwardation: *Brit.* Opposite of *Backwardation (1). See Carrying Charge Market, Contango (1).*

Fourchette Option: *Fr.* Any of a variety of spread- or range-contingent option payout structures.

Fourier Transform: A technique for solving differential equations.

Fourth Market: Direct trading between institutional investors, either without the services of a broker or dealer or using a broker's back office only to clear the trades. *See also Crossing Network, Primary Market, Secondary Market, Third Market.*

Fractal: *See Chaos Theory.*

Fractional Exposure: An estimate of an institution's maximum potential mark-to-market exposure to a specific counterparty between the calculation date and the maturity of all open contracts. Usually expressed as a decimal fraction or percent of the creditor institution's capital.

Framing: The context in which a problem or question is posed. Behaviorists have conducted tests to demonstrate that people give opposite answers to identical questions conditioned on how the question is framed. Framing can distort the results of political polls, market surveys, and financial analyses.

Franchise Factor: A measure of the impact of above market return investments on a company's price/earnings multiple. It is equal to the return premium (relative to the expected market return) from new business investments, divided by the product of the return on equity for existing businesses, and the expected market return. A franchise factor of 2 indicates that the company's price/earnings multiple will increase two units for each unit gain in book value (in present value terms). An approach to the valuation of investments proposed by Martin Leibowitz and Stanley Kogelman. *Comparison of the Economic Value Added (EVA) and Franchise Factor literature is often useful. See also Franchise Value, Growth Equivalent of Franchise Investments.*

Franchise Value: The present value of an enterprise's prospective new investments, reflecting the application of a franchise factor that captures the enterprise's ability to earn an above market rate of return on a specific level of investment. *See also Franchise Factor, Growth Equivalent of Franchise Investments.*

Fraption: An option on a forward rate agreement. *Also called Interest Rate Guarantee (IRG).*

Fraud: Deliberate deceit or intentional misrepresentation or concealment of a material fact to cheat or prejudice the legal rights or conduct of another to secure unfair or unlawful gain.

Free Boundary Problem: When solving a differential equation subject to a boundary condition, a free boundary problem arises if any of the boundary conditions change with the passage of time. The pricing of an American put option is a well-known free boundary problem.

Free Cash Flow (FCF): The remaining net operating profit after taxes (NOPAT) after necessary investments have been deducted. *See also Net Operating Profit After Tax (NOPAT).*

Free Collar: A zero net premium cost collar or equity risk reversal. The premium on the cap and the floor offset one another. *See Interest Rate Collar (diagram), Equity Risk Reversal (diagram).*

Free Of Tax to Residents Abroad (FOTRA): Certain U.K. securities that are exempt from withholding taxes to holders filing proof of non-U.K. residency.

Free-Standing Derivative: A distinction made in some FASB statements to distinguish elemental derivatives contracts (such as futures, forwards, swaps, and options) from more complex instruments that incorporate embedded options (such as equity-linked notes (ELNs), bonds with an issuer's call provision, and currency-linked debt or equity instruments). *See Trading Derivative.*

Frequency: The periodic schedule of rate or price readings used to calculate the payoff of an average rate or price option.

Frequency Distribution: A summarization of data that shows the percentage of the observations falling within specified ranges. The ranges collectively account for all the data.

Frogs: Floating-rate notes with coupons reset quarterly or semiannually to the coupon on the current thirty-year Treasury bond. Used in yield curve swaps.

Front Contract or Front Month Contract: The near month futures contract.

Front Fee: The premium on the first leg of a compound option. *See also Compound Option, Back Fee.*

Front Spread: An option spread with a net premium outflow, usually because the long option is further in the money, closer to the money, or has a longer life than the short option. *Also called Debit Spread.*

Front Stub Period: The first interim period in the life of a swap or other periodic reset agreement. The value date to the first payment date if that period is different (usually shorter) than subsequent periods. *See Stub (2). See also Back Stub Period.*

Frontrunning: The practice (illegal in the U.S.) of effecting a transaction on the basis of material non-public information about an impending order or trade. Regulators have introduced the fuzzy concept of inter-market frontrunning to emphasize the relationships among options, futures, and cash markets.

Frozen Index Fund: The taxable investor's hypothetical ideal of diversification and tax efficiency, a frozen index fund consists of a fixed portfolio of stocks that does not change in composition as a result of a portfolio manager's decision or as a result of component companies being merged or liquidated in taxable transactions. The tax advantage of a frozen index fund is that it distributes only ordinary cash dividends, never taxable capital gains. A U.S.-based taxable investor defers any capital gains indefinitely, often permitting heirs to take advantage of the tax-free step up in basis at the original buyer's death. EXchange TRAded (EXTRA) Funds come closest to the ideal. *See EXchange-TRAded (EXTRA) Funds, Standard & Poor's 500 Depositary Receipts (SPDRs).*

Fugit: Expected time to exercise of an American option. *Also called Target.*

Fulcrum Point: Broadly, an inflection point on a graph where the value or payout pattern of an instrument changes direction. Narrowly, the price or rate at which an instrument's value at maturity reaches a maximum.

Fulfillment Fund: *See Completion Portfolio or Fund.*

Full Investment Note (FIN): An equity-linked note that mirrors the performance of the stocks in a mutual fund portfolio and extends that performance to the fund's cash reserves. A FIN permits the fund to perform as if it were fully invested at all times despite the fact that the fund keeps an adequate reserve for possible shareholder redemptions. The FIN also helps reduce problems caused by the short-short rule. *See also Short-Short Rule.*

Full Two-Way Payment (FTP) Clause: A preferred settlement clause in the ISDA swap agreement that requires settlement of a swap at its full value even if that requires a net payment to a defaulting counterparty. *See also Limited Two-Way Payment (LTP) Clause.*

Functional Regulation: Regulation of products, markets, and market participants based on the function the product or market serves. *Compare to Institutional Regulation.*

Fund of Funds: A financial intermediary organized as a corporation, business trust, or partnership that accepts equity investments and buys shares of other funds that, in turn, hold securities or commodities.

Fundamental Analysis: Appraisal of macroeconomic data (levels and trends) and the interaction of economic data with information from company financial statements and operations with the objective of predicting the company's cash flow and earnings and, ultimately, the investment value of its securities.

Fundamental Financial Instruments: As identified by the FASB, these include unconditional receivables (payables), conditional receivables (payables), forward contracts, options, guarantees or other conditional exchanges, and equity instruments. Most practitioners would list equity, debt, forwards, swaps, and options.

Funding: Issuing a security to obtain means of payment.

Funding Cost: The security issuer's cost of obtaining means of payment necessary to finance its operations. Expressed as the cost of a single instrument, a class of instruments (debt or equity), or as an average cost of capital to obtain all the enterprise's funding.

Funding Ratio (FR): In asset/liability management, the market value of assets divided by the present value of future liabilities. If the ratio exceeds unity (or 100%), the obligations are said to be overfunded. If the ratio is less than 100%, the obligations are underfunded. *See also Funding Ratio Return (FRR).*

Funding Ratio Return (FRR): The percentage change in the funding ratio during a measurement period, usually one year. The funding ratio return is a joint function of the asset/liability structure, the allocation and return on assets, and the discount structure of liabilities. *See also Funding Ratio (FR).*

Funding Risk: The potential for unanticipated costs or losses due to a mismatch between asset yields and liability funding costs. The risk may be due to different maturities of assets and liabilities, changes in credit quality, or a variety of other causes. In addition to these basis-type risks, funding risk can take the form of inability to meet cash or collateral requirements, forcing premature liquidation of a position.

Funds: Cash or equivalents such as federal funds or clearing house funds used to settle a transaction.

Fungibility: The standardization and interchangeability of listed option and futures contracts and certain other financial instruments with identical terms. Fungibility permits either party to an opening transaction to close out a position through a closing transaction in an identical contract. All financial contracts with identical terms are not necessarily fungible, a fact that can increase risk in some markets. *See also Offsetting Transaction.*

Future Rate Agreement (FRA): *See Forward Rate Agreement (FRA).*

Future Value: The value of an instrument or cash at a designated future date. The future value may be calculated by applying a compound return factor to the present value.

Futures and Options Funds (FOFs): Unit trusts offered in the U.K. that are able to make limited use of derivatives instruments. *Also called Authorized Futures and Options Funds (AFOFs). See also Geared Futures and Options Funds (GFOFs).*

Futures Commission Merchant (FCM): A broker executing commodity and financial futures and futures options transactions.

Futures Contract: An agreement, originally between two parties, a buyer and a seller, to exchange a particular good for a particular price at a date in the future. All terms are specified in a contract common to all participants in a market on an organized futures exchange. The contract must be for a specific amount of a good for delivery at a specific time as required by the exchange with the price determined in a public marketplace by "open outcry" or on an electronic limit order book system. Futures contracts can be traded freely with various counterparties without material counterparty credit risk. After a trade is cleared, the exchange clearing corporation is the ultimate counterparty for all contracts, so the only credit risk is the creditworthiness of the exchange's clearing corporation. No credit intermediary is necessary, but margin deposits must be posted as performance bonds with the clearing broker, and, in turn, with the exchange clearing corporation. Typically, variation margin payments mark futures positions to market at least once a day. *Also called Listed Futures Contract. See Financial Futures Contract. See also Forward (diagram).*

Futures Contract on Individual Stock: A simple, single stock futures contract priced, valued, and margined much like a stock index futures contract. These instruments have been introduced on Swedish and Australian issues, and are proposed for stocks in Britain and Hong Kong. The attraction of single stock futures contracts is based on their generally low margin requirements and the ability to avoid transfer and dividend withholding taxes. Not permitted in the U.S.

Futures-Style Options: A proposed contract to replace many traditional options on futures contracts. Unlike traditional options, the buyer of a futures-style option does not prepay the premium. Buyers and sellers post margin, as in a futures contract, and the option premium is marked to the market daily. Valuation differs from traditional futures options primarily in the analysis of the timing of cash flows associated with the buyer's non-payment of an upfront premium.

FXNET: *See Multinet.*

G-Hedge: An interest rate collar with an upfront premium and a symmetrical range on either side of the forward rate.

Game Theory: An approach to managerial decision-making and economic analysis in an environment that does not conform to the assumptions of perfect competition. Game theory is probably most applicable in oligopolistic markets, where the actions of competitors are interdependent. A key element of game theory is that the actions of each agent are not known in advance by the other agents.

Gamma γ: (1) The change in delta divided by the dollar change in the underlying instrument's price. The second derivative of the option price with respect to the price of the underlying. A measurement of the rate

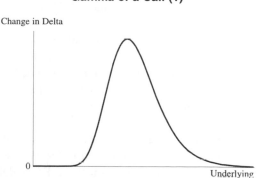

Gamma of a Call (1)

of change of the rate of change in the option price with respect to the underlying price. If the gamma of a position is positive, an instantaneous move either up or down in the underlying will give the position a higher value than the static delta would predict. A positive gamma indicates a position with positive convexity. *Also called Curvature. See also Convexity (2).* Delta-gamma-kappa-rho hedge. (2) The smallest electronically quoted stocks on the London Stock Exchange. *See also Alpha (α), Beta (β), and Delta (δ).*

Gamma Distribution: One of a family of standardized distributions suggested by Bookstaber as a possible form for certain securities' price behavior. Gamma distributions can have fat tails and are usually skewed.

Gap Analysis: *See Maturity Gap.*

Gap Management: *See Maturity Gap.*

Gap Option: An option in which the strike price determines the size of the payoff, but a different constant determines whether or not the payoff is made. For example, a gap call option pays $8 if the underlying price is $8 above the strike and the gap is $5. If the underlying price less the strike is less than the gap, there is no payoff.

Garman-Kohlhagen Model: A currency option evaluation model similar in structure to the Black-Scholes option model with separate terms for foreign and domestic interest rates. Biger and Hull published essentially the same model at about the same time. *Also called Biger and Hull Model.*

Garn-St. Germain Act (1982): Legislation that liberalized investment policies for savings and loan associations in the U.S., leading to substantial losses covered by deposit insurance in the late 1980s.

Gaussian Distribution: *See Normal Distribution.*

Geared Equity Capital Unit (GECU): An open-ended, usually leveraged, equity-linked note. Leverage is obtained by setting the minimum value of the note below the amount the buyer pays for it. *See also Guaranteed Index Unit, Equity-Linked Note (ELN) (diagrams).*

Geared Futures and Options Fund (GFOFs): Unit trusts offered in the U.K. that use futures and options to obtain leveraged market exposure. *See also Futures and Options Funds (FOFs).*

Geared Zero-Coupon Convertibles: A complex variant of standard zero-coupon convertibles (LYONS) with a minimum redemption value below par, leveraged exposure to the performance of the underlying common stock up to a capped price, no conversion premium or interim put provision, no call provision, and exercise only at maturity.

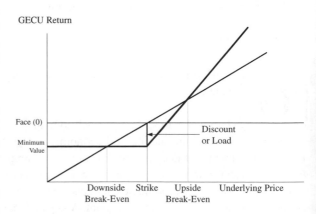

Geared Equity Capital Unit (GECU) Payout

GECU Return

Face (0)

Minimum Value

Discount or Load

Downside Break-Even   Strike   Upside Break-Even   Underlying Price

Gearing: The price of the underlying divided by the price of the call or warrant. The term, also called nominal gearing, is widely used in the U.K. warrant market, and in other markets (such as the Japanese warrant market) developed on the U.K. model. The gearing ratio is of limited value in any analysis of

Warrant Price, Premium, and Gearing for a Four-Year Warrant

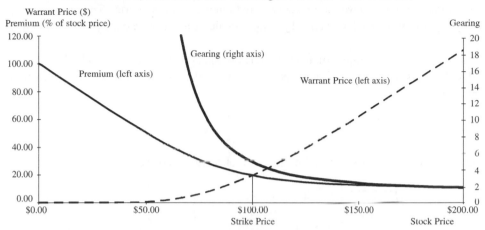

option or warrant price relationships. Effective gearing, which is a related concept, is only slightly more useful. The latter is the traditional gearing measure multiplied by the call option or warrant delta. Effective gearing is also called elasticity. *See also Premium (2) (diagrams), Premium/Gearing Ratio (diagram), Leverage Factor, Elasticity.*

Geisha Bond: *See Shogun Bond.*

Geld und Brief: *Ger.* Bid and asked. Note that the letter "g" designates a bid and the letter "b" an asked price in a German language price table.

General Obligation (GO) Bond: A bond backed by the ability of a sovereign or municipal issuer to levy taxes on real property and on business activities in its jurisdiction. General obligation bonds are backed by the full faith, credit, and taxing power of the issuer.

General Repo Rate: *See Special Repo Rate.*

Generalized AutoRegressive Conditional Heteroskedasticity (GARCH) Model: An extension of the ARCH class of models that allows lagged conditional variances to enter the equation. GARCH models have both a longer memory and a more flexible lag structure than ARCH models. *See AutoRegressive Conditional Heteroskedasticity (ARCH) Model. See also Heteroskedastic, Mean Reversion.*

Generalized Least Squares: A regression technique used when the error terms from an ordinary least squares regression display non-random patterns, such as autocorrelation or heteroskedasticity. *See also Ordinary Least Squares, Least Squares Regression Line (diagram).*

Generally Accepted Accounting Principles (GAAP): Established accounting rules in the U.S. administered by the FASB and largely delineated by Statements of Financial Accounting Standards (SFAS) issued by the FASB.

Generally Accepted Risk Principles (GARP): A catchy title for a checklist of risk management musts and must nots proposed by Coopers & Lybrand. The list lives up to the title.

Genetic Algorithm: A set of instructions that is applied to a problem and then tested to determine how well the instructions meet established performance criteria. Instruction sets that perform poorly are discarded, while instructions that perform well are preserved and mutated for a new trial. The process is repeated until a satisfactory algorithm is found. Genetic algorithms are designed to mimic the process of natural selection.

Gensaki Rate: The repurchase agreement (repo) rate on Japanese government bonds. The gensaki rate rivals the yen LIBOR rate as an indicator of short-term rates in yen-denominated instruments. *See also Repurchase Agreement (Repo), (RP).*

Geographic Risk: *See Country Risk.*

Geometric Average: The nth root of the product of n observations or values.

$$\text{If } n = 3, x = \sqrt[3]{a * b * c}$$

Indexes based on geometric averages have been uncommon since the index underlying the Value Line Index contracts was changed to an arithmetic average. A geometric average is smaller than a corresponding arithmetic average unless all observations are equal. *See also Mean.*

Geometric Brownian Motion (GBM): A stochastic process in which price changes follow a stationary random walk in continuous time. This specification of price movement implies that, conditioned on the current price, the distribution of continuously compounded returns at the end of any finite time interval will be normal. *See also Brownian Motion, Arithmetic Brownian Motion.*

Geometric Return: The geometric return is calculated by adding 1 to each single period return, multiplying these values (called wealth relatives) together, taking the nth root of the product, and subtracting 1. It is also called the constant rate of return because an investment compounding at the geometric return grows to the same value that the actual returns produce. The geometric return is approximately equal to the arithmetic return less one-half the variance of the returns. *Also called Time-Weighted Return. See also Variance Drain.*

Gilt-Edged Market Maker (GEMM): A primary dealer in British government securities.

Gilts: Bonds issued by the government of the U.K. and named after the gilded edge on the bond certificate.

Gini Coefficient: A measure of dispersion within a group of values, calculated as the average difference between every pair of values, divided by two times the average of the sample. The larger the coefficient, the higher the degree of dispersion.

Giro Bank: A European financial intermediary specializing in a book-entry transaction settlement process that does not require actual use of money.

Girsanov's Theorem: A change of probability measure to accommodate different drift assumptions of Brownian processes. Suppose there are n independent and identically distributed random variables, X_1, X_2, ..., X_n. Each variable is normally distributed with mean μ_i and variance σ^2 under a specified probability measure. Then, under an appropriate change of probability measure determined from Girsanov's formula, the random variables are distributed with a different mean but the same variance. Girsanov's theorem applies to Brownian motion (independent and normally distributed increments), and, in general, to solutions of multi-dimensional differential equations. *Also called Measure of Change Theorem. See also Brownian Motion, Radon-Nikodym Derivative.*

Give Up: (1) A procedure in securities or commodities trading where the executing broker passes information on and verification of a transaction to another broker for clearance and settlement. The two brokers split any commission generated on the transaction in accordance with a previously agreed upon formula. (2) In the U.S., a portion of a fixed securities commission (prior to 1975) passed from the executing broker to another broker on the instructions of the client. This give up is compensation for services rendered by the broker receiving it.

Glass-Steagall Act: The legislation that facilitates federal deposit insurance for banks by prohibiting banks from certain "risky" activities, such as owning brokerage firms or engaging in many investment banking activities. The constraints of Glass-Steagall have been eroding steadily, and many observers consider its ultimate repeal almost a non-event.

Global Asset Allocation: Active management of commitments to asset classes and markets in a number of countries, frequently combined with passive or index management within markets. To keep trading costs manageable, global asset allocation adjustments are typically made in futures and options markets.

Global Credit Support Service (GCSS): An OTC derivatives collateralization service sponsored by Luxembourg-based Cedel. *See also Hybrid Instrument Transaction Service (HITS), Chicago Mercantile Exchange Depository Trust Corporation (CME DTC), C-Trac+.*

Global Depositary Receipts (GDRs): The Euromarket analog of American Depositary Receipts (ADRs). GDRs are issued and cleared by the Euromarket depositories, rather than by banks. *See also American Depositary Receipts (ADRs), Depositary Receipt.*

Global Hedge: A hedge covering the unwanted risks of a portfolio or an entire organization on an aggregate basis, taking advantage of any natural risk offsets and using broad spectrum hedging instruments. Global hedging is a low-cost approach to risk management available to large financial intermediaries, nonfinancial enterprises, and investors. A global hedge does not usually qualify for hedge accounting treatment. *Also called Macro Hedge. Compare with Micro Hedge. See also Portfolio Approach to Risk Management.*

Globalization: The trend toward looking at economic and financial issues, instruments, and portfolios from a worldwide rather than a single-country viewpoint.

Globex: An electronic "exchange" or trading mechanism designed to trade a variety of securities and derivatives. Initially, Globex has traded instruments when their primary markets are closed.

Going Concern Value: Earning power of an enterprise's assets plus its goodwill.

Gold Loan: A loan denominated in ounces of gold and payable in either gold or currency at the spot rate (of gold) at the time of repayment. Interest payments may also be linked to the price of gold.

Gold Standard: An informal international exchange rate and payment system lasting roughly from 1870 to the beginning of World War II, under which each country committed to exchange its currency for a specific quantity of gold. This agreement caused exchange rates to remain fixed for extended periods. Commitment to the gold standard required countries to maintain gold reserves. To discourage investors from converting currencies into gold, countries had to deflate their currencies during periods of trade deficits and inflate their currencies during periods of trade surpluses.

Golden Parachute: A takeover prevention or takeover impact reduction strategy that gives the top management of the target company large termination packages if their positions are eliminated as a result of a hostile takeover.

Good Delivery: Delivery at settlement of funds or instruments that meet the requirements of a market.

Good 'Til Cancelled (GTC) Order: An order to buy or sell a security or future placed with a broker and subject to specific terms of the order until the order is executed or cancelled. *Also called Open Order.*

Good Will: The value of an established business as a going concern in excess of its tangible book value. *See also Negative Good Will.*

Governing Law: The legal system of the sovereign jurisdiction that interprets an agreement.

Government National Mortgage Association (GNMA) Pass-Through Certificates: Debt securities collateralized by residential mortgage debt and guaranteed as to payment of interest and principal by the GNMA, an agency of the U.S. government. *See Collateralized Mortgage Obligation (CMO), Mortgage-Backed Securities.*

Graduated Payment Mortgage (GPM): A mortgage finance contract in which payments start at a relatively low level and rise for a period of time—usually to a stable level that holds until maturity.

Grant Date: (1) The start date of an employee stock option. (2) The effective start date of a deferred start date option.

Grave Dancer: *See Bottom Fisher.*

Gray Market: As the name suggests, a market whose existence might be outside the traditional regulatory framework, though probably not strictly illegal. Gray markets spring up when local regulations prohibit the transfer of certain ownership interests, particularly from domestic to foreign investors, or in advance of a public offering when shares may trade on a when-issued basis in advance of the availability of actual shares for sale.

Greeks: Option derivatives or sensitivities usually (but not always) designated by a Greek letter. Examples include sigma σ, Delta Δ, gamma γ, kappa κ, Tau T, "vega," rho ρ, theta θ, and Omega Ω, each of which is defined herein alphabetized by the English language spelling of the Greek letter. *See Appendix.*

Green Shoe Option: A right granted by a securities issuer to its underwriter giving the underwriter an over-call on 10%-15% of the stated size of the issue to meet heavy investor demand. This provision of many underwriting agreements is named after the Green Shoe Company, which first granted such an option to an underwriter.

Greenmail: A takeover target's more or less voluntary repurchase of shares held by a hostile would-be acquirer, usually at a price significantly above market. Some transactions of this nature are now illegal.

Gross Replacement Value (GRV): The cost of replacing all contracts of a given type or with a given counterparty that have a net present value, before any adjustment for possible netting agreements. *See also Net Replacement Value (NRV), Net-to-Gross Ratio (NGR).*

Gross Settlement: A method of making payments between parties in which each party makes a separate payment on each transaction between them. Gross settlement arrangements are giving way to various net settlement arrangements to reduce credit/settlement risk and expense.

Group of 7 (G-7): A group of countries and a loose organization of national economic and monetary authorities committed to working out economic and currency exchange rate issues. Members are the appropriate officials and organizations in the U.S., Japan, Germany, the U.K., France, Italy, and Canada.

Group of 10 (G-10): An organization of central banks, inevitably linked to the Bank for International Settlement (BIS) by concern for payments systems. Like the Group of 20 (G-20), the number does not reflect the actual membership, which is eleven central banks: U.S., Germany, Japan, U.K., France, Italy, the Netherlands, Belgium, Sweden, Switzerland, and Canada.

Group of 30 (G-30): A private organization sponsored by central banks and major commercial and investment banks. The G-30 assembled an international task force that developed plans for faster, standardized clearance and settlement of domestic and international securities transactions, which has led to shorter settlement times in many markets. A later task force examined risk management procedures, particularly as they pertain to derivatives instruments, and made recommendations for improvements in risk management procedures by financial and non-financial corporations. Follow-up surveys indicate a remarkably high rate of adoption of these risk management standards.

Group of 20 (G-20): An organization with members from less than twenty major commercial banks. The G-20 addresses international clearance and settlement issues, as well as other topics important to its members.

Group Rotation: An active investment strategy that emphasizes shifts from one investment sector to another to find groups with favorable prospects.

Growth Equivalent of Franchise Investments: A measure of the present value of all (corporate) franchise investments that adjusts for irregular cash flows. *See Franchise Factor, Franchise Value.*

Growth Management: An equity management style that emphasizes the recent past and expected future ability of a company to increase its earnings per share at an above average rate. Growth managers look for strong earnings growth records, evidence of market dominance, and indications that growth will continue, or even accelerate. *See also Style Management.*

Guarantee: A contractual or statutory commitment to accept responsibility for repayment of another entity's loan or similar obligation. *See also Keepwell Agreement.*

Guarantee Fund: Assets available to cover a failing company's obligations to selected creditors. Guarantee fund arrangements to benefit policyholders are most common in the insurance industry. Similar funds, often supplemented by government guarantees, are found in the securities industry and in banking.

Guaranteed Bond: (1) A bond on which the payment of principal, interest, or both has been guaranteed by a party other than the issuer. (2) Outside the U.S., a structured note or bond—usually an equity-linked note—that promises a return of all or most of the original investment at maturity, plus participation in favorable movements in an underlying index or instrument. *Also called Endorsed Bond. See Principal Protected Note.*

Guaranteed Coupon Reinvestment Bonds: A bond or note structure that gives the holder a series of options to receive each interest coupon in cash or to reinvest it in the same bond at par on the interest payment date. A holder electing to reinvest all coupons in this way would create the equivalent of a zero-coupon bond. The appeal of the guaranteed coupon reinvestment bond is that it gives a holder flexibility to avoid the reinvestment risk associated with having to reinvest coupons at lower rates than the original yield on the bond. *Also called Bunny Bond.*

Guaranteed Exchange Rate Option: *See Guaranteed Exchange Rate Warrant, Quantity Adjusting Option (QUANTO) (1).*

Guaranteed Exchange Rate Warrant: Covered warrants on non-U.S. stock indexes issued in the U.S. by a sovereign or financial intermediary with the currency exchange rate at maturity fixed at the spot rate in effect at issuance. *Also called Secondary Currency Option, Guaranteed Warrant*—but all guaranteed warrants do not fix the exchange rate at issuance. *See Guaranteed Exchange Rate Option. See also Covered Warrant, Quantity Adjusting Option (QUANTO) (1), Foreign Stock Index Options, Warrants, and Futures.*

Guaranteed Index Unit: Zero-coupon or low-yield note combined with capped or uncapped participations that provide upside exposure to changes in the value of an equity index. *See Equity-Linked Note (ELN) (diagrams), Geared Equity Capital Unit (GECU) (diagram).*

Guaranteed Investment Contract (GIC): An obligation issued by an insurance company in return for a payment by an investor. The terms of GICs vary greatly, but they typically offer a relatively high initial return guarantee and impose some restrictions on the investor's ability to withdraw funds. A similar contract offered by a bank is called a Bank Investment Contract (BIC), or Bank Deposit Agreement (BDA). The failure of several insurance companies that were active issuers of GICs has led investors and marketers to look for synthetic GICs that offer a similar return pattern with lower risk. *See Synthetic Guaranteed Investment Contract (Synthetic GIC), Participating Account.*

Guaranteed Minimum Reinvestment Rate: A provision of some CMO tranches that assures investors they will be able to reinvest their periodic cash flows at a fixed rate, usually close to the nominal yield of the tranche carrying the guarantee.

GUAranteed Rate on Delivery (GUARD): *See Break Forward (diagram).*

Guaranteed Return Index Participation (GRIP): Equity index-linked note, typically with less than 100% participation in the index. *See Equity-Linked Note (ELN) (diagrams).*

Guaranteed Return on Investment (GROI) Certificate: A combination of a note and collar or equity risk reversal position guaranteeing investors a minimum return with a cap on the maximum return. *See Equity-Linked Note (ELN) (diagrams).*

Guaranteed Return Structure (GRS): Any structured product that guarantees a minimum value at maturity (e.g., most equity-linked notes) or guarantees a minimum return based on levels reached by the underlying during the life of the instrument (e.g., ladder options).

Guaranteed Warrant: A stock index warrant issued by a sovereign or a corporation in the U.S. market. *See also Covered Warrant, Guaranteed Exchange Rate Warrant, Foreign Stock Index Options, Warrants, and Futures.*

Guts: *See Mambo Combo.*

H

Haircut: (1) The margin or, more frequently, the capital tied up when a financial intermediary takes a position. (2) A commission or fee for execution of a transaction (uncommon). (3) The collateral held by the lender in a REPO transaction.

Hammersmith and Fulham, London Borough of: A local government in the U.K. that was extremely active in sterling swaps between 1986 and 1989. Swap volume was very large relative to underlying debt, suggesting large-scale speculation by the borough council. The speculation was unsuccessful, and a local auditor ruled that the transactions were *ultra vires*—beyond the powers of the council. The House of Lords sitting as the High Court ultimately upheld the auditor's ruling. The "legal" risk of some risk management contracts was established at considerable cost to the London financial community. *See also Legal Risk.*

Handle: The first few digits of a financial instrument or an interest rate or currency exchange rate. These digits change relatively infrequently as prices fluctuate, so a quote will often omit this handle, or "big figure," particularly in a busy trading environment. *Also called Big Figure.*

Hard Call Protection: A period when a bond is not callable for early redemption by the issuer under any circumstances. Hard call protection is often more important with convertible bonds than with straight bonds. *See also Call Protection, Soft Call Protection.*

Harmful Warrant: A warrant detached from its carrier bond. It usually conveys the right to buy an instrument other than an indentured bond.

Harmless Warrant: A warrant permanently attached to a callable bond. It usually conveys the right to purchase more of the same bond.

Harmonic Average: The inverse of the arithmetic average of inverse terms. With **n** as the number of observations and r_i as the underlying rate or price, the harmonic average is:

$$\frac{n}{1/r_1 + 1/r_2 + \ldots + 1/r_n}$$

The harmonic average is used in the pricing of certain non-standard options and when averaging ratios—such as fixed charge coverage and price earnings ratios.

Hazard: A risk or source of risk. Used primarily in insurance.

Heath-Jarrow-Morton (HJM) Model: An analytic model used to value interest rate dependent claims that incorporates the entire term structure of interest rates. The underlying instruments in the HJM model are the forward rates, each of which is permitted to have a different volatility. The HJM model is a calibrated model. It is calibrated by using the observed volatility term structure, rather than by constraining time-varying parameters. It is sometimes criticized for computational expense, especially when the process leads to a non-recombining tree.

Heaven and Hell Bond: A variety of dual currency bond with principal redemption linked directly to the change in the spot exchange rate from issuance to maturity. *See Variable Redemption Bonds.*

Hebel: *Ger.* Leverage.

Hedge: (1) Among professional traders and position managers, a position or combination of positions taken to profit from an expected change in a spread or relative value; basis arbitrage. *See also Basis (1)*. (2) In popular use, a position or combination of positions that reduces some type of risk, usually at the expense of expected reward. Risk hedging is typically accomplished by making approximately offsetting transactions that largely eliminate one or more type of risk. (3) In the narrower sense, the term often indicates partially offsetting a long position in one security with a short or short equivalent position in a related security. *See also Long Hedge, Option Hedge, Reverse Option Hedge, Spread (5)*.

Hedge Account: (1) An account in which a risk reduction position is carried. (2) Designation of a trader's futures position as a hedge account can be important in obtaining favorable margin requirements and an exemption from speculative position limits on futures contracts.

Hedge Accounting: While the rules for hedge accounting vary across borders, nearly universal requirements are that (1) the transactions that are part of the hedge must be designated by the enterprise as constituting risk-offsetting transactions, (2) there must be risk reduction as a result of the combined transactions, and (3) there must be correlation between the underlying transaction and the risk management transaction taken as a hedge. The purpose of hedge accounting is to provide a match of related gains and losses and to avoid distorting financial reports. The SEC and members of the FASB are engaged in complex discussions over some aspects of the use of hedge accounting in financial reporting. This discussion may lead to differences between the economic effect of a risk management transaction and its reflection in financial reports. The growth in mark-to-market accounting worldwide is leading to a reduction in hedge accounting applications.

Hedge Clause: A statement—usually in a small type font—that appears on a securities research report or market letter that may disclaim responsibility for losses the reader or user of the report may incur as a result of errors or omissions in the report. Hedge clauses may also reveal potential conflicts of interest that might be deemed to affect any recommendations contained in the report. *Also called Disclaimer.*

Hedge Fund: A private pool of assets managed intensely and often aggressively. A wide variety of financial instruments may be used and the managers of the fund are typically paid a percentage of any profits. In spite of the name, many such funds do little or no hedging, and risk exposures vary greatly. Funds offered in the U.S. have a limited number of holders (usually limited partners), and partners must meet certain requirements in terms of net worth, minimum investment, etc.

Hedge Ratio: *See Neutral Hedge Ratio, Delta (1)*.

Hedge-To-Arrive Contract: A grain forward contract, often cash settled.

Hedge Wrap: *See Equity Risk Reversal (diagram), Collar (2) (diagram)*.

Hedged Inverse Floating-Rate Note: In effect, a combination of an inverse floating-rate note based on a foreign rate and a principal currency swap to hedge direct currency exposure.

Hedged Swap: An unmatched swap, usually in a dealer's inventory, where the dealer has undertaken transactions, perhaps in the futures market or in related instruments, to offset interest rate or other risks of the position. Contrasts with market swaps, where the dealer's market, riding on two mirror positions, is offset with another swap.

Hedgilator: (1) Someone who is a hedger in terms of a market move in one direction and an option-holder/speculator in terms of a move in the opposite direction. (2) Someone who delays hedging in the hope that a hedge will not be necessary.

Hedging Instrument: A contract, security, or other instrument that can partially or fully offset some type or element of risk.

Held for Risk Management (HRM) Derivative: A distinction made in some FASB statements. A free-standing derivative position that is part of a reporting enterprise's hedging or risk management activities. The value of this position is marked to market to a below-the-line equity account during each accounting period. A related position is in place, and both positions pass through earnings only when the risk management purpose has been achieved and/or disposal of the related position has been reported. *See also Trading Derivative.*

Hell or High Water Clause: A guarantee, usually by a parent corporation or an unaffiliated guarantor, to meet bond or lease obligations if the primary obligor does not perform. The guarantee is not contingent on the performance of any other obligation by any party.

Herfindahl Index: A measure of industry concentration. The value of the index, H, is the sum of the squares of the market shares of all firms in an industry:

$$H = \sum_1^n (\text{share}_i)^2$$

Industry concentration can be an indication of the effectiveness with which competitors engage in anti-competitive activity, or, less conspiratorially, the extent to which competitors might be insulated from the aggressive pricing that is characteristic of many commodity industries.

Herstatt Risk: *See Cross-Currency Settlement Risk, Presettlement Credit Risk, Settlement Risk.*

Heteroskedastic: A distribution characterized by a changing (non-constant) variance or standard deviation. *See also Generalized AutoRegressive Conditional Heteroskedasticity (GARCH) Model.*

Hidden Orders: Certain computerized (screen trading) market systems permit market participants to place a bid or offer for a larger amount than they are willing to expose to view. This hidden order becomes effective if and only if a firm order on the other side of the market is entered under conditions meeting the requirements of the hidden bid or offer. Globex and the Paris Bourse are two markets that permit hidden orders.

High Contact Condition: The limiting value of a function when one of the independent variables is specified at its highest possible value. For example, in the valuation of a put option, if the underlying is set equal to infinity, the limiting value of the put is zero.

High-Coupon Swap: A swap where a fixed-rate payment is above the market rate (any underlying bond or note is selling at a premium). The receiver of the high coupon may pay an upfront fee as compensation for the higher cash flow. *Also called Premium Swap, Non-Par Swap. See Off-Market Coupon Swap.*

High-Low Floater: A floating-rate note with a premium rate up to a cap level on the reference index rate. If the market rate is above the cap rate, the note becomes a reverse floater; its yield declines as the reference rate appreciates further. A high-low floater is a yield enhancement device for investors who expect no more than a modest rise in floating rates over the life of the agreement.

High-Low Option: A cash settled call option contract with a payout equal to the difference between the high and the low price or rate touched during a period, times the contract multiplier. A similar payout can be created as a combination lookback call and lookback put. *See Range Straddle.*

High Water Mark: (1) The all-time high value of a fund or an investment account. (2) The previous relative high value of an account subject to an incentive fee arrangement. Frequently, a manager cannot collect an incentive or performance fee until the fund's value exceeds this high water mark.

Higher of Proceeds or Market: The short-seller's or issuer's equivalent of *Lower of Cost or Market (LCM)*.

Highly Leveraged Transaction (HLT): As defined by several U.S. federal agencies, (1) a transaction that at least doubles a borrower's liabilities and results in a leverage ratio higher than 50%, or (2) a transaction that results in a leverage ratio higher than 75%, or which is designated as a highly leveraged transaction in a bank syndication loan. *See also Leveraged Derivatives Transaction (LDT)*.

Hindsight Currency Option: An option giving the buyer the retroactive right to buy a currency at its low point (call) or to sell a currency at its high point (put) within the option period. Generically, a lookback option. *See also Lookback Option*.

Historical Volatility: The variance or standard deviation of the change in the underlying's price, rate, or return during a designated period in the past. Historical volatility may or may not be a useful indicator of future volatility, but it is often used as such. *See also Implied Volatility (IV)*.

Ho-Lee Model: An analytic model used to value interest rate dependent claims. The Ho-Lee model incorporates the entire term structure of interest rates. This model was the first no-arbitrage interest rate model. It implicitly assumes constant and identical volatility for all spot and forward rates. A limitation is that the model does not incorporate mean reversion, a widely documented empirical tendency.

Hockey Stick Payoff Pattern: The traditional kinked return pattern of an option strategy valued at expiration. Also the return pattern of an immunized portfolio.

Holding Company: A parent corporation that holds all or the majority of the stock of its operating subsidiaries. The parent may also have non-financial or other operating divisions of its own.

Holding Cost: Annualized expenses associated with maintaining an ongoing position in a security or market. Includes custody costs and any property or income tax, including withholding tax. *See Custody Cost*.

Holdout Period: The measurement period for data used to test a model whose parameters are estimated from data for a different period. *See Out-of-Sample Data. See also Data Mining*.

Home Equity Loan (HEL): A consumer loan secured by a second mortgage on the borrower's residence. The mortgage provides collateral for an asset-backed security issued by the lender, and, sometimes, tax-deductible interest payments for the borrower.

Homogeneous Function: A function is said to be homogeneous of degree y if multiplication of each independent variable by the value x changes the value of the function by the amount x^y. For example, the Black-Scholes option pricing function is homogeneous of degree 1 (also called linearly homogeneous) with respect to the underlying asset price and the strike price (y = 1). Therefore, if each independent variable is multiplied by 2 (i.e., x = 2), the value of the option will increase by a factor equal to 2^1.

Homoskedastic: A condition of constant variance or standard deviation in dependent variables for given values of the independent variable in different populations being sampled and compared in a regression analysis.

Hope for A Market STabilization in a givEn Range (HAMSTER): The currency market equivalent of a Range Accumulation Option (RAO). *See Range Accumulation Option or Warrant.*

Horizontal Spread: *See Calendar Spread (diagram).*

Host Bond: A debt instrument originally issued with detachable warrants. Often useable at par to exercise the warrants. *See Useable Security.*

Hull-White Model: An analytic model used to value interest rate dependent claims that incorporates the entire term structure of interest rates. The model extends the Ho-Lee model to allow for mean reversion. The Hull-White model incorporates the volatility term structure (similar to the Heath-Jarrow-Morton model) and time-varying parameters (similar to the Ho-Lee model).

Hung Convertible: A convertible bond or preferred stock issue whose conversion cannot be forced by the issuer, usually because it is selling below parity or because the issue is protected from calls until a certain date or price level is reached.

Hurdle Rate: (1) The minimum or required rate of return that a proposal must exceed to justify a capital investment. (2) The minimum return an investment manager must achieve before she starts to earn an incentive or performance fee. *See also Incentive Fee.*

Hybrid Debt: Any combination of a debt instrument and an equity, currency, or commodity forward, option, or swap. A variant of hybrid security. *See Structured Note.*

Hybrid Instrument Rules: Regulations adopted by the Commodity Futures Trading Commission (CFTC) exempting certain instruments that have some characteristics of a security and some characteristics of a future from regulation by the Commission under the Commodities Exchange Act. The most important common thread in these rules is that the commodity- or futures-linked value must be less than 50% of the value of the hybrid instrument. *See Synthetic Convertible Debt (2).*

Hybrid Instruments Transaction Service (HITS): A clearing, settlement, and collateral management service, offered by the Chicago Board of Trade Clearing Corporation, for non-standardized instruments— essentially interest rate products. *See Collateralized Swap. See also Chicago Mercantile Exchange Depository Trust Company (CME DTC), C-Trac+, Global Credit Support Service (GCSS).*

Hybrid Security: Generically, a complex security consisting of virtually any combination of two or more financial instrument building blocks—bond or note, swap, forward or future, or option. *See also Structured Financial Transaction (2).*

Hypothecation: Deposit and pledge of collateral to secure a loan or other obligation.

Hypothesis Testing: A test to distinguish between a null hypothesis and an alternative hypothesis. For example, one may wish to test whether or not a coin is fair. The null hypothesis is that the coin is fair, and the alternative hypothesis is that it is biased. If a series of coin tosses produces a result that is only 3% likely given a fair coin, one would reject the null hypothesis, assuming 95% confidence is required. If, by contrast, the experiment produces a result that is 20% likely given a fair coin, one would fail to reject the null hypothesis that the coin is fair. It is not permissible to accept the alternative hypothesis. Only acceptance or failure to reject the null hypothesis is allowed in hypothesis testing. If a test fails to reject the null hypothesis, it is said to lack sufficient power to accept the alternative hypothesis. *See also Type I Error, Type II Error*

Ichibu: *Jap.* The first section (large companies) of the Tokyo Stock Exchange.

Idiosyncratic Return: That part of an asset's return that cannot be explained by exposure to pervasive factors. It is attributable to a factor or factors unique to a particular company. In a linear model of return, it is equal to the error term. It is also called the non-systematic component of return.

Idiosyncratic Risk: *See Non-Systematic Risk.*

Illiquid: Not readily convertible into cash. Illiquid assets can only be sold with difficulty or at a lower value than their nominally quoted price. *See also Liquidity.*

Imbedded Option: *See Embedded Option.*

Immediacy Cost: In trading, the cost associated with the decision to trade quickly, rather than take a chance on a better (or worse) price by entering a limit order away from the market or adopting some other more patient trading tactic. *See also Immediacy Demand.*

Immediacy Demand: In trading, the strongly felt need to buy or sell quickly. *See also Immediacy Cost.*

Immediate or Cancel: A type of order that is cancelled automatically if it cannot be filled as soon as it is revealed in the market.

Immediate Repackaging of a Perpetual (IRP): Combining a newly issued perpetual floating-rate instrument with a fixed-rate or zero-coupon bond to create cash flow/swap patterns of greater interest to investors.

Immunization of a Portfolio: A risk management technique designed to ensure that a portfolio of debt instruments will cover a liability coming due at a future date or over a period in the future. The typical approach to immunization is to invest in a portfolio with a Macaulay duration equal to the duration of the liabilities and a present value equal to the present value of the liabilities. This technique implicitly assumes that any shifts in the yield curve will be parallel shifts. *Also called Dedicating a Portfolio, Duration Matching, Cash Flow Matching.*

Impact Forward: A collared forward contract. *See Range Forward Contract (diagram).*

Implementation Shortfall: The difference between the calculated performance of a "paper" portfolio and the actual performance of an identical real portfolio based on actual market transactions. *See also Transaction Cost, Execution Cost, Market Impact.*

Implied Binomial Tree: A progression of prices for the underlying asset of options with different strike prices that begins with the asset's current price and evolves period by period through a bifurcation process. The locations of the nodes of the tree conform to the relationship between the options' implied volatilities and strike prices. The implied binomial tree is interpreted as the expected or implied probability distribution of the underlying asset. *See also Implied Distribution, Smile, Binomial Model (diagram).*

Implied Correlation: A factor in the pricing of multimarket financial instruments, implied correlation reflects a dealer's expectation of the relationship between two or more primary valuation parameters. For example, evaluating a swaption in terms of caps or floors requires analysis of the correlations among volatilities of a number of forward rates. Implied correlations among currency exchange rate pair volatilities are reflected in the pricing of their cross-rate options.

Implied Distribution: A probability distribution developed from prices of various at- and out-of-the-money options with a common expiration date. The implied distribution is notable primarily when its shape differs materially from the normal or lognormal distribution. The implied distribution, like many historical distributions, often has relatively fat tails and negative skewness. *See also Forecast Distribution, Implied Binomial Tree, Smile, Skew.*

Implied Duration: When a futures contract is added to a portfolio—either as a long or short position—the duration of the deliverable or underlying bond may be used as an estimate of the effect of the futures contract on the duration of the portfolio.

Implied Forward Interest Rate: The interest rate for a specific forward period calculated from the incremental period return in adjacent instruments on the spot zero-coupon yield curve. *See Forward Yield Curve, Yield Curve (diagrams), Zero-Coupon Yield Curve.*

Implied Repo Rate: The maximum cost of financing a position that is consistent with or discounted by the return available from a cash/futures arbitrage position. For example, an investor evaluating a cash-and-carry trade, such as buying a stock portfolio and selling a stock index futures contract, will calculate the expected return (dividends plus futures basis) as a money market rate. The implied repo rate is the break even financing rate for this arbitrage position. *Also called Return to Hedged Portfolio (RHP).*

Implied Standard Deviation (ISD): *See Implied Volatility (IV).*

Implied Volatility (IV): The value of the price or rate volatility variable that would equate current option price and fair value. Alternatively, the value of the volatility variable that buyers and sellers appear to accept when the market price of an option is determined. Implied volatility is calculated by using the market price of an option as the fair value in an option model and calculating (by iteration) the volatility level consistent with that option price. Volatility is nearly always stated as annualized standard deviation in percent of face amount or rate. *Also called Implied Standard Deviation (ISD). See also Expected Volatility, Historical Volatility.*

Implied Zero-Coupon Swap Curve: A yield curve for zero-coupon notes derived from the traditional yield curve and used to value fixed-rate swap payments. *See Zero-Coupon Yield Curve.*

Imputation System of Corporate Taxation: Most major industrial countries outside North America give shareholders a tax credit approximately equal to the corporate tax paid on dividend distributions paid from domestic earnings. This system effectively eliminates much double taxation of dividends.

Imputed Value: Information about the value of a non-traded asset inferred from information about the values of traded assets.

In Arrears: (1) Late in making payments. (2) A characteristic of a financial instrument that sets certain payment terms at the end of the period covered by the payment rather than at the beginning. *See, for example, In-Arrears Swap.*

In-Arrears Swap: A structure much like a traditional interest rate swap agreement except that the floating

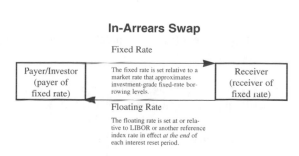

In-Arrears Swap

Fixed Rate

| Payer/Investor (payer of fixed rate) | The fixed rate is set relative to a market rate that approximates investment-grade fixed-rate borrowing levels. | Receiver (receiver of fixed rate) |

Floating Rate

The floating rate is set at or relative to LIBOR or another reference index rate in effect *at the end* of each interest reset period.

rate is set in-arrears—based on the reference index rate at the end of the reset period—and applied retroactively to the entire period. *Also called Arrears Swap, Back End Set Swap, Delayed Reset Swap, Swap-In-Arrears (SIA), LIBOR In-Arrears Swap, Reset Swap. See also Choice LIBOR Swap, Modified Following, In Arrears (2).*

In Option: An option that begins to exist as a standard option only if a particular barrier price is reached prior to the expiration date of the option. Examples include a down-and-in call, a down-and-in put, and up-and-in puts and calls. *See Touch Option, Path-Dependent Option, Kick-In Option, Knock-In Option. See also Barrier Option, Deferred Start Option.*

In the Money: A term referring to an option that has intrinsic value because the current market price of the underlying exceeds the strike price of a call or is below the strike price of a put. For example, a call exerciseable at $100 is said to be 3 points in the money when the underlying bond is selling at $103. *See also At the Money, In-the-Money Forward, Out of the Money.*

In-the-Money Forward: A reference to an option that is "in the money" when the spot price or rate of the underlying is compared to the forward price or rate used in valuing the option at expiration. *See Forward Intrinsic Value, In the Money.*

In-the-Money Lookback Option: A lookback option variation that pays off based on the better of an initial in the money strike or a more profitable strike reached during the life of the option.

Incentive Fee: An investment management fee that varies depending on the manager's performance. Incentive fees are common for funds invested in futures markets, but if the manager is a registered investment advisor (RIA), there are restrictions. Specifically, Rule 205-3 under the Investment Advisors Act of 1940, as amended, requires "among other things, that: (a) the client being charged the incentive fee have at least $500,000 under the management of the RIA or a net worth in excess of $1,000,000; and (b) that any incentive compensation paid to the RIA be based on the net gains in the client's accounts for a period of not less than one year." Except for mutual funds, the manager is not usually required to pay the client when the managed portfolio underperforms the benchmark; hence the incentive component of the fee can be thought of as an option granted to the manager to exchange the performance of the benchmark portfolio for the managed portfolio. In exchange for this option, the base component of the fee is usually set below the flat fee that the manager would otherwise charge.

Incentive Stock Options: Long-term (typically five-year) call options offered by a firm to key employees to increase their compensation and encourage behavior consistent with the interests of shareholders. The tax and accounting treatment of these options is constantly under fire, but they are an established component of executive compensation in the U.S.

Incentive Trade: A pretrade agreement between an institutional customer and a broker may provide for the broker to share in any gain from a better than average order execution and to be penalized for an inferior execution.

Inchoate Instrument: An incomplete financial instrument that can be perfected by the addition of a payee's name, an amount, etc.

Income Bond: A contingent interest bond with coupon payments dependent on earnings. Ordinarily, the principal repayment is not contingent. *Compare to Participation Bond.*

Income Warrants: Warrants that pay interest as well as carrying an exercise right.

Increasing Rate Notes (IRNs): Debt obligations on which the coupon rate increases by predetermined amounts or to predetermined levels at specified time intervals. An increasing rate structure can be used to defer a portion of interest expense to later years, or, when used in connection with a bridge loan, to compensate investors for increasing risk associated with the issuer's delay in redeeming the notes through refinancing or from the proceeds of asset sales. *See Callable Step-Up Note.*

Independent Risk Oversight (IRO): The practice of establishing an independent individual or organizational unit responsible for monitoring and enforcing adherence to prudent risk limits and risk policies for an enterprise.

Index: A number calculated by weighting a number of prices or rates according to a set of predetermined rules. A financial market index is a statistical construct that measures price changes and/or returns in stock, fixed-income, currencies, or futures markets. The purpose of the index calculation is to provide a single number whose behavior is representative of the movements of a variety of prices or rates and indicative of behavior in a market. Indexes serve as underlyings for a number of products, particularly in equity and fixed-income markets.

Index Allocated Principal (XAC) Bond: A CMO whose principal paydown is allocated according to the value of some index. *See also Indexed Principal Swap (IPS).*

Index Amortizing Note: A debt obligation with many characteristics similar to the fixed-rate side of an index amortizing swap. In the case of the note, the principal is repaid according to an amortization schedule linked to a specific index (usually LIBOR). Index amortizing notes are usually designed to behave similarly to a CMO with an embedded prepayment option. As market interest rates increase, and presumably mortgage prepayment rates decline, the maturity of an index amortizing note will extend. As rates decline and mortgage prepayment rates increase, the average life of an index amortizing note will contract. In common with many mortgage-backed instruments, the prepayment characteristic linked to interest rates gives the holder of the note negative convexity. *See Amortization.*

Index Amortizing Swap: An interest rate swap agreement with a notional principal amount that declines as a function of a short-term money rate such as LIBOR. The use of an index protects the fixed-rate receiver from unanticipated or erratic prepayment risk. A flaw in the structure is that actual prepayment risk to the fixed-rate payer—who often holds mortgage securities—is usually greatest and least stable when the reference index rate is lowest. *Compare with Indexed Principal Swap (IPS). Also called Amortizing Interest Rate Swap. See Amortizing Swap.*

Index Arbitrage: An investment strategy that attempts to earn higher than money market returns while taking risks comparable to those of a money market instrument, or to earn higher than stock index returns while taking risks comparable to those incurred by an investor in a stock index fund. The higher returns are made possible by a trading strategy that shifts cash between long and short stock positions and money market positions, and buys and sells stock index futures contracts in response to deviations in the stock index futures basis from its fair value. *See also Arbitrage, Cash Enhancement Strategy, Cash-and-Carry Trade, Portfolio Trade, Program Trading, Market Neutral Investment Strategy.*

Index Fund: A fund designed to track the performance of a market index. Most common among stock funds but used in other markets as well.

Index Growth-Linked Units (IGLUs): A combination of a note and a collar or equity risk reversal position. As the name implies, the underlying is usually an index, but it may also be a small basket of stocks.

See Equity-Linked Note (ELN) (diagrams).

Index-Linked Bonds or Notes: Debt instruments with principal and/or interest payments linked to the performance of an inflation or stock market index. *Also called Equity Index-Linked Note, Real Yield Security (REALS). See Equity-Linked Note (ELN) (diagrams).*

Index Participation Certificate: An equity index-linked note—usually one that provides more or less than 100% participation in the movement of the index and more or less than a full return of principal at maturity. *See Equity-Linked Note (ELN) (diagrams).*

Index Participations: Instruments introduced by the Philadelphia Stock Exchange and the American Stock Exchange in 1989 to provide small investors with a low-cost way to obtain an index equivalent portfolio. A federal court held that index participations were futures contracts, and hence could not be traded on securities exchanges. The index participations, which had attracted fair investor interest, were delisted because of this regulatory obstacle. The AMEX introduced a replacement product, Standard & Poor's Index Depositary Receipts (SPDRs, pronounced spiders). SPDRs became the first entry in a new class of instruments called EXchange-TRAded (EXTRA) Funds. *Also called Cash Index Participations (CIPs).*

Index Portfolio: A securities portfolio designed to track the performance of a specific benchmark index.

Index Principal Return Note: *See Equity-Linked Note (ELN) (diagrams).*

Index Range Note: A note with a coupon determined largely or entirely by an embedded range accumulation option. Equity indexes, currency exchange rates, and interest rates are among the underlying indexes, prices, or rates that can determine the payoff. Index range notes are used primarily to enhance interest rate yields when an investor has confidence in a forecast. LIBOR Range Notes are the most common variety. *Also called Accretion Bond Index Range Note, Corridor Bond or Note, Range Floater, Range Accrual Note, Accrual Note, LIBOR Range Note, Range Accumulation Note, Fairway Bond. See also Binary Swap, Range Accumulation Option or Warrant, Equity Range Note (diagram).*

Index Tracking: A reference to the correlation between a portfolio's return and the return on a benchmark index, or, alternately, to the portfolio's tracking error relative to the index. Many equity indexes and enhanced index portfolios are managed with close attention to index tracking. *See also Tracking Error.*

Index Warrants: Put and call options on an index or index futures contract with an original life of more than one year. Index warrants are issued by corporate or sovereign entities or cleared and guaranteed by option clearing houses. Pricing of these instruments in the marketplace often depends on investors' ability or inability to sell the warrants short or on the ability of new issuers to license an index to supply new warrants. *Also called Equity Index Warrants.*

Indexation: (1) A passive or nearly passive investment strategy that attempts to replicate the return of a benchmark index in a fund. (2) The practice of linking the coupon on a debt security to an index of inflation.

Indexed Coupon Note: A debt instrument with a fixed principal due at maturity, but with coupons that vary with the behavior of an interest rate, equity, currency, commodity, inflation, or other index.

Indexed Currency Option Notes (ICONs): A variant of the dual currency bond, with all payments in one currency but with the principal payment indexed to a currency exchange rate at maturity. If the exchange rate is less than an agreed rate, the bondholder receives the face value of the note minus an amount that (typically) increases as the exchange rate declines. Within this generic structure, a number of variations are possible, including a reversed version that provides that the principal payment increases with a decline in the exchange rate. This structure has attracted more publicity than users. *See Reverse Dual Currency Bond. See also Dual Currency Bond, Principal Exchange Rate-Linked Securities (PERLS).*

Indexed Inverse Floater: *See Reverse Floating-Rate Note.*

Indexed INverse FLOating-rate Security (Indexed INFLOS): *See Reverse Floating-Rate Note.*

Indexed Notes: The generic combination of a zero-coupon bond and an embedded index option feature "purchased" with the present value of what would normally be the periodic yield on the bond. The option provides the noteholder with participation in the performance of the index. The participation can be either open-ended or capped, and more or less than 100% of the movement of the index. The underlying can be any of a wide variety of indexes. *See also Equity-Linked Note (ELN) (diagrams), Participation, Real Yield Security (REALS).*

Indexed Principal Swap (IPS): An amortizing fixed-for-floating-rate swap with a fixed rate above the market rate for a constant notional principal swap, and an amortization rate that decreases as rates rise and

Comparison of an Indexed Principal Swap and a Plain Vanilla Fixed-for-Floating Swap

LIPS example: four-year maximum life, one-year lockout, coupon 4.51%, one-year swap rate 3.55%, 5% cleanup call
Plain vanilla example: four year fixed-for-floating, coupon 5.12%

A. Notional Principal Outstanding

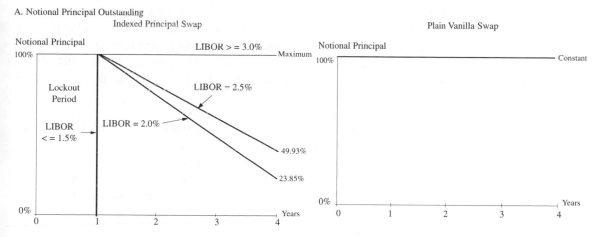

B. Percentage of Notional Principal Subject to Reinvestment Risk Due to Amortization or Lock-In to Low Rates

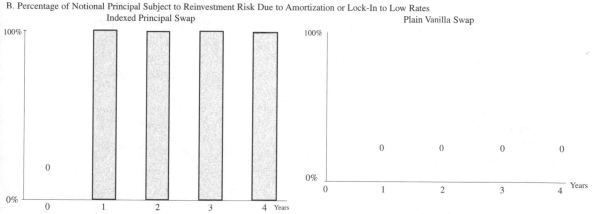

increases as rates fall. The most common variety is a mortgage replication swap. *Also called LIBOR-Indexed Principal Swap (LIPS). Compare with Index Amortizing Swap. See Amortizing Swap, Index Allocated Principal (XAC) Bond, Mortgage Replication Swap.*

Indexed Strike Cap: A special purpose cap giving customized interest rate protection at reduced cost, usually with knock-in or knockout features. Indexed strike caps are used to reduce interim costs when cost is an important issue, but they allow higher interest costs under other circumstances. The diagram illustrates an application called an N-cap because of the shape of its payoff pattern. In the example, the cap buyer holds a 5.0% knockout cap and a 6.5% knock-in cap. Both caps have an 8.0% trigger rate. The cost of funds is capped at 5.0%, plus the cost of the indexed strike cap structure unless rates rise to 8.0%. At 8.0% the knockout and knock-in features are activated and the net cost of funds jumps. The logic is that a borrower

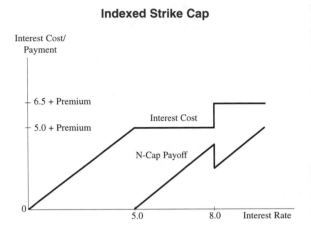

Indexed Strike Cap

will be able to pay higher rates in an 8.0% rate environment because business will be stronger and competitors will also be paying high rates. Many other cost patterns are possible.

Indicative Optimized Portfolio Value (IOPV): A calculation of the approximate intraday net asset value of an optimized index EXchange-TRAded (EXTRA) fund. The calculation is based on the intraday value of the fund's creation basket rather than the value of the previous day's closing fund portfolio. An implicit assumption behind this calculation is that any difference between the actual portfolio and the target portfolio represented by the creation basket will be adjusted quickly and with little price impact. *See also EXchange-TRAded (EXTRA) Fund, Creation Unit.*

Indicative Price: (1) Bid and offer price provided by a market maker for the purpose of evaluation or information, not as the firm bid or offer price at which she is willing to trade. *Also called Nominal Quotation.* (2) A preliminary estimate of the price at which a financial instrument might be created. Indicative prices are quoted to customers for planning or valuation purposes, but they do not form the basis for an actual transaction without further discussion. *Compare to Firm Price. See also Subject Bid or Offer, Workout Market.*

Indicator Variable: *See Dichotomous Variable.*

Indifference Curve: Plotted in dimensions of expected return and standard deviation, a curve connecting all combinations of expected return and standard deviation to which an investor is indifferent, because all these combinations convey the same amount of expected utility. This curve is typically positively sloped and convex (with expected return on the vertical axis), and its point of tangency with the efficient frontier marks the investor's optimal portfolio. *See Optimal Portfolio.*

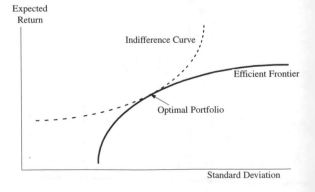

Indifference Curve Tangent to the Efficient Frontier

Individual Equity Future (IEF): A futures contract introduced by the Sydney Futures Exchange based on individual stocks. Similar products trade on the OMLX in London.

Infinite Ladder Option: A ladder option without a cap or a limit on the number of rungs on the ladder. Minimum payouts are locked in at any multiple of the percentage return threshold no matter how high the underlying rises. In contrast to most ladder options with a preset number of rungs, this instrument has an open-ended lock-in feature. *See Ladder Option or Note (diagram).*

Inflation Derivative: An instrument with a producer or consumer price index used as the basis for a swap or other index rate payment. Inflation-linked derivatives are often more difficult to hedge than traditional interest rate instruments, but several countries, including the U.K., Sweden, and Canada, have inflation-linked government bonds. In other countries there are few, if any, natural sellers of the inflation rate. The demand for inflation protection often exceeds readily available supply—even in countries where inflation-linked instruments are available. *Also called Inflation-Linked Debt, Real Yield Security (REALS). See Retail Price Index (RPI).*

Inflation-Linked Debt: *See Inflation Derivative, Real Yield Security (REALS).*

Inflation Rate Interest-Indexed Bonds: *See Real Yield Security (REALS).*

Inflation Risk: The opportunity cost incurred if the return from investing—typically in a note or bond—does not offset the loss in purchasing power due to inflation.

Information Coefficient (IC): Correlation between the actual values of a forecasted variable and its predicted values. An IC equal to 1 indicates perfect forecasting skill; an IC equal to 0 indicates no forecasting skill.

Informationless Trades: Trades initiated for reasons other than short-term profit expectations or risk control, such as sales to raise cash or purchases to reinvest income or cash flows into a portfolio. *See Liquidity.*

Initial Margin: The collateral deposit or performance bond deposited with a broker at the time a derivatives position or an underlying security position is taken. Initial margin may be set by government regulators (the Federal Reserve Board on securities in the U.S.), or by the exchange where the instrument is traded (futures contracts). If the broker carrying the position and handling the trade feels the minimum margin does not give her firm and its customers adequate protection, she may set a higher minimum margin. *See also Margin.*

Initial Public Offering (IPO): An issuer's first public sale of common stock, or less frequently, other securities.

Initial Value Problem: A problem in the valuation of contingent claims in which a partial differential equation is solved subject to conditions about the terminal value of the underlying asset but not about the path of the underlying asset price. This might have been more appropriately named a terminal value problem.

Insider Trading: Open market trading in the securities of a company by someone who has special information not publicly available. This information may be obtained because of the trader's position within the company or his relationship with a person with access to such information because of a relationship with the company. Partly as a result of a series of insider trading scandals in the 1980s, insider trading is now illegal in nearly all major international markets.

Insolvency: (1) Inability to meet financial obligations on an ongoing basis. (2) Inability to meet a specific solvency test imposed by a regulatory organization.

Installment Option: An installment option has two characteristics that differentiate it from a standard option: (1) the option premium is paid periodically—usually monthly or quarterly—over the life of the option, and (2) the holder has the right to stop making payments, thereby terminating the option on the due date of the first missed payment. The significance of the latter is that if the option is not worth the present value of the remaining payments, the holder does not have to continue to make payments. In return for the right to terminate payments, the premium charged for an installment option—if all payments are made—is greater than the premium for a standard option.

Installment options appeal to investors willing to pay a little extra for the opportunity to terminate payments and stop losses if the investment position is not working out. Installment options may have particular appeal in markets where most or all option contracts are traded OTC rather than on exchanges. An OTC option premium can be difficult to recover—even in part—if the option is out-of-the-money when an investor's viewpoint on the market price of the underlying changes. While most OTC option market makers quote two-sided markets in their products, their bid-ask spreads may expand at times. In this context, an installment option can be a partial remedy to concerns over OTC option marketability. If an installment option is selling below the value of making an installment to keep it alive, the investor need not be concerned about losing the value of a fully paid for standard option. She can simply walk away from the installment option on any installment payment date. Unless the option is an American-style contract, however, it usually makes sense to continue payments on installment options that have a net present value on a payment date. *Also called Continuation Option, Pay as You Go Option. See also Deferred Premium Option.*

Comparison of the Profit/Loss of Installment and Standard Put Options Under Two Price Scenarios

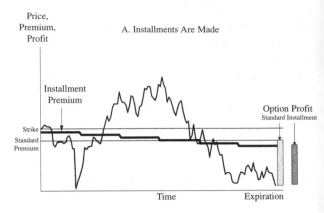

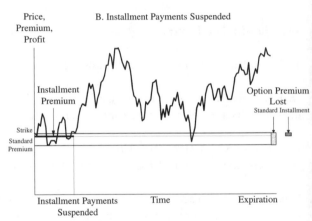

Instinet: An electronic securities order matching (trading) and information system used primarily by professional traders and investors.

Institutional Net Settlement (INS) System: An obsolete London Stock Exchange settlement system being replaced by CREST. *See CREST.*

Institutional Regulation: Regulation of all functions as they are associated with a particular financial institution, such as a bank or an insurance company. *Compare to Functional Regulation.*

Instrike: The trigger or barrier price at which an in option—such as an up-and-in put or a down-and-in call—becomes a standard option. *See Down-and-In Call (diagram).*

Insurable Interest: A necessary relationship between the holder of an insurance policy and the risk covered by the policy. The insured must suffer a demonstrable loss if the contingency insured against occurs.

Insurance: (1) A risk/return pattern characteristic of options that limits (or insures against) price or rate movements through a predetermined (strike) price or rate in exchange for the explicit or implicit payment of an option (insurance) premium. (2) The component of an option or of a more complex instrument that provides this risk limitation feature. In contrast to a straight hedging transaction that eliminates risk symmetrically over all price ranges, an insurance position creates an asymmetric risk/return pattern. *See also Fair Value of an Option, Volatility Value.* (3) An arrangement under which one party to a contract (the insurer) in return for a consideration (the premium) indemnifies another party (the insured) against a specific loss, damage, or liability arising from specified uncertain events.

Insurance Risk: For a property casualty insurance company, insurance risk is the ratio of annual premium income to total capital and surplus.

Integrity Risk: (1) In portfolio or basket trading, delivery of a portfolio that contains one or more highly illiquid positions that increase execution cost and risk. Portfolio traders usually guard against integrity risk by requiring general information on the size, trading activity, and volatility of each position in the basket. (2) *See Moral Hazard.*

Intellectual Risk: The risk that the employees capable of controlling a firm's business will leave the firm.

InterBank On-Line System (IBOS): A London-based currency payment management system. *See also Multinet, Exchange Clearing HOuse (ECHO).*

Interchangeable Bond: A bond that may be converted from coupon to registered form, or from registered form to coupon. (The option to convert from registered to coupon is rare.)

InterDealer Broker (IDB): A brokerage firm operating in the sovereign bond or OTC derivatives market that acts as an intermediary between major dealers to facilitate interdealer trades that can help dealers balance their books. Interdealer brokers take no principal risk, and operate on very small spreads, but they may handle extremely large transactions. *Also called Dealer-to-Dealer Broker.*

Interdealer Trades: Trades between dealers. These trades are of concern to regulators and investors because they create a mutual dependency on each dealer's financial strength. *See also Domino Theory.*

Interest: Money paid for the use of borrowed funds.

Interest Cover: *Brit. See Coverage.*

Interest Coverage Ratio: *See Coverage, Fixed Charge Coverage.*

Interest Equalization Tax (IET): A U.S. federal tax that became effective in 1963, the IET of 15% on interest received from foreign borrowers was designed to restrict foreign debt issues sold into the U.S. market. Its actual effect was to stimulate development of the Euromarkets and drive dollar-based financing activity to London. The tax was removed in 1974. *See Euromarkets.*

Interest Only (IO) Obligation: A tranche of a CMO or similar instrument whose owner receives only the interest or some part of the interest paid on mortgages in the underlying pool. IO tranches are not uniform. The value of a protected income only stream usually increases if rates decline slowly and moderately, but the holder of a companion or support IO tranche may receive interest payments only until repayments reach a certain fraction of the face value of the pool. Rapid repayment of mortgage principal in a sharply lower-rate environment reduces the total value of a pool's interest payments. If a specific IO tranche is designed to be affected first by prepayments, the interest payments available for that tranche can disappear quickly. The mortgage prepayment option and payments dependent on its exercise or non-exercise have proven to be difficult to predict, and consequently to evaluate. *See also Collateralized Mortgage Obligation (CMO), Companion Collateralized Mortgage Obligation, Mortgage-Backed Securities, Stripped Mortgage-Backed Security (SMBS), Planned Amortization Class (PAC) Bond, Prepayment Option, Principal Only (PO) Obligation, Tranche.*

Interest Rate Cap: *See Cap (1).*

Interest Rate Caption: *See Caption.*

Interest Rate Collar: A combination of an interest rate cap and an interest rate floor. The buyer of the collar purchases the cap option to limit the maximum interest rate he will pay, and sells the floor option to obtain a premium to pay for the cap. The effect of the combination is to confine interest rate payments to a range bounded by the strike prices of the cap and floor options. On the other side of the trade, an asset manager might sell a cap and give up the potential for unlimited upside yield in return for the assurance of a minimum return obtained by using the proceeds from the cap to purchase a floor. *Also called Cap and Floor, Fence or Fence Spread, Range Forward Contract (diagram), Forward Rate Bracket, Equity Risk Reversal (diagram), Conversion Spread, Spread Conversion. See also Collar (2) (diagram), Free Collar, Mini-Max Strategy.*

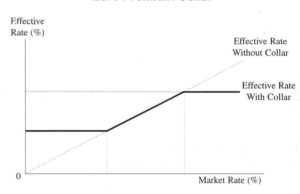

Interest Rate With and Without Zero Premium Collar

Interest Rate-Contingent Option: An option on an equity, physical commodity, or foreign exchange rate that is contingent upon a particular interest reference rate being above or below a certain level, or within a certain range. For example, an investor might buy a call on a stock index with the right to exercise the call contingent on a LIBOR rate being above a designated level at expiration of the option. *Generically a Contingent Payout Option (diagram).*

Interest Rate Corridor: *See Corridor (1) (diagram).*

Interest Rate Differential (DIFF): The yield spread between two otherwise comparable debt instruments denominated in different currencies.

Interest Rate Floor: *See Floor (1) (diagram).*

Interest Rate Guarantee (IRG): An option on a forward rate agreement (FRA) or an interest rate futures settlement rate. A lender's IRG is a call on the forward or futures rate, and a borrower's IRG is a put on the forward or futures rate. *Also called Fraption.*

Interest Rate Index Swap: *See Rate Differential Swap, CUrrency Protected Swap (CUPS).*

Interest Rate Option: (1) A right but not an obligation to pay or receive a specific (strike) interest rate on a predetermined principal for a set interval. (2) A cap or a floor.

Interest Rate Parity: The principle by which forward currency exchange rates reflect relative interest rates on default risk-free instruments denominated in alternative currencies. Currency forward rates and interest rate structures reflect these parity relationships. Currencies of countries with high interest rates are expected by the market to depreciate over time, and currencies of countries with low interest rates are expected to appreciate over time, reflecting (among other things) implied differences in inflation. These tendencies are reflected in forward exchange rates as well as in interest rate structures. Any opportunity to earn a certain profit from interest rate discrepancies will be arbitraged away by hedging the currency risk. If interest rate parity holds, an investor cannot profit by borrowing in a low interest rate country and lending in a high interest rate country. For most major currencies, interest rate parity has not held during the modern floating-rate regime. *See also Covered Interest Arbitrage, Discount Currency, Forward Rate Bias, Premium Currency, Purchasing Power Parity (PPP).*

Interest Rate Reset Notes: Interest on these notes is reset several years after issuance to the greater of the initial rate or a rate sufficient to give the notes a market value greater than the face amount. The reset provision is designed to offer the buyer of a long-term debt instrument some protection from loss of principal due to rising interest rates or a decline in the issuer's debt rating.

Interest Rate Risk: (1) An adverse variation in cost or return caused by a change in the absolute level of interest rates, in the spread between two rates, in the shape of the yield curve, or in any other interest rate relationship. (2) Exposure to accounting or opportunity loss as a result of a relative or absolute change in interest rates. Varieties of interest rate risk include prepayment risk, reinvestment risk, volatility risk, call risk, and long-term rate risk. A variety of instruments are available to reduce or eliminate most kinds of interest rate risk.

Interest Rate Swap: Generically, a fixed-rate for floating-rate swap in a single currency, but including any swap with payments on both sides determined by interest rate levels. *Also called Swap de Taux D'Intérêt. See Amortizing Swap, Swap, Asset Swap, Fixed-Floating Swap, Rate Differential Swap (diagram). See also LIBOR In-Arrears Swap.*

Interest Rate Swap

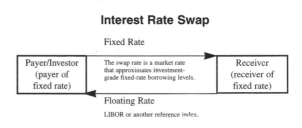

Interest Rate Swaption: *See Swaption.*

Intermarket Surveillance Group (ISG): ISG's membership of twenty-three self-regulatory organizations from five countries is committed to confidential market information-sharing for regulatory purposes and to regulatory coordination.

Intermarket Trading System (ITS): An electronic communications network that links the New York Stock Exchange, Nasdaq, and other stock exchanges in the U.S. The purpose of the ITS is to assure that a customer's order is filled at a price no worse than the best bid or offer available on any of the interconnected exchanges.

Intermediary: *See Financial Intermediary.*

Intermediation: Flow of funds from securities into the banking system. *See also Disintermediation, Loan Participation.*

Internal Model Approach to Capital Management: Bank for International Settlements (BIS) market risk capital requirements permit banks to use internal models to estimate market risk exposures as long as the internal models indicate requirements as high as or higher than industry standard models. The use of internal models has been linked to the precommitment capital standard, particularly in the U.S. *See also Precommitment Capital Standard.*

Internal Rate of Return (IRR): (1) The discount rate that equates the present value of future cash flows with the market value of a financial instrument, or the present valued cost of an investment. More than one internal rate of return may be consistent with a given set of cash flows. (2) A compound interest rate at which the net present value of cash inflows from a project is equal to the net present value of cash outlays. Net present value analysis and real option analysis are increasingly replacing IRR calculations as the basis for capital expenditures.

International Association of Financial Engineers (IAFE): An organization of financial economists, financial engineering practitioners, and what are loosely called "rocket scientists" who meet to share their knowledge and improve their professional skills. The organization also accredits educational programs in its specialty.

International Monetary Fund (IMF): An international organization established in 1944 as part of the Bretton Woods Agreement, the IMF has the authority to lend foreign exchange to member countries conditioned on their pursuit of sound economic policies. These loans are to be used to stabilize exchange rates. Member countries are required to make a payment of gold and currency to fund the IMF's lending activities, and their voting privileges in setting IMF policies are proportional to their financial contributions.

International Organization of Securities Commissions (IOSCO): An organization of securities commissioners and administrators from more than sixty countries. IOSCO's primary mandate is to facilitate and coordinate international securities regulation and to promote consistency in regulation across borders.

International Spread Option, Warrant, or Note: An instrument with a return pattern linked to cross-border interest rate spreads. The payoff at maturity can be set to increase as spreads increase or as spreads decline. *Also called Spread Warrant. See, for example, BOATs, Cross-Currency Cap or Floor.*

International Swaps and Derivatives Organization (formerly International Swap Dealers Association) (ISDA): The principal derivatives industry trade organization. ISDA develops and publishes master agreements for swaps and other OTC derivatives contracts. ISDA agreements serve as industry standard documentation for a variety of financial instruments.

Interpolation: A method for inferring a value from known higher values and lower values. For example, if y is a function of x, and we know the values for y_0 and x_0 and y_1 and x_1, we can interpolate the value for y given a value for x as approximately equal to:

$$y_0 + [(x - x_0)/(x_1 - x_0)] * (y_1 - y_0)$$

Also called Linear Interpolation.

Interquartile Range: The difference between the value of the observation that falls at the bottom of the first quartile in a population, and the value of the observation at the top of the fourth quartile. Often used as a measure of dispersion when a population does not match a standard normal or lognormal distribution. *See also Box Plot.*

Intrinsic Value of an Option: The amount, if any, by which an option is in the money. *See Basis (1), Forward Intrinsic Value, Parity.*

Invariance Propositions: An application of the law of one price to corporate finance. These propositions, put forth by Merton Miller and Franco Modigliani, argue that the value of a firm is invariant to its capital structure and dividend policy. If a leveraged firm is undervalued, investors can purchase its debt and its shares. The interest paid by the firm is offset by the interest received by the investors, so the investors end up holding a pure equity stream. Alternatively, if an unleveraged firm is undervalued, investors can borrow funds to purchase its shares. The substitutability of individual debt for corporate debt guarantees that firms in the same risk class will be valued the same, regardless of their respective capital structures. Dividend policy is irrelevant because repurchasing shares has the same effect as paying dividends; thus issuing shares and paying dividends is a wash. Although the cash component of an investor's return may differ as a function of dividend policy, the investor's total return, including price change, should not change with dividend policy. *Also called Modigliani-Miller Hypothesis.*

Inventory Turnover Ratio: The ratio of sales to average inventory with both numerator and denominator being valued at either selling price or original cost. Inventory turnover is a measure of a management's ability to use resources efficiently.

Inverse Floater: *See Reverse Floating-Rate Note.*

INverse FLOating Security (INFLOS): A synthetic tax-exempt (municipal) reverse floating-rate note. The complement of *Select Auction Variable-Rate Securities (SAVRs). See Municipal Derivative, Reverse Floating-Rate Note.*

Inverted Curve Enhancement Swap (ICE Swap): A swap agreement that places a floor under the floating rate (in an inverted yield curve environment) in exchange for a higher fixed rate.

Inverted Market: *See Backwardation (2).*

Inverted Yield Curve: *See Yield Curve (diagrams).*

Investment Grade: A bond or note rated Baa or higher by Moody's, BBB or higher by Standard & Poor's, or comparably by other rating agencies. *See Table of Bond Ratings (Appendix).*

Investment Grade Consensus: A bond rated Baa, BBB, or higher by two or more rating agencies.

Investment Letter: A feature of an agreement to purchase securities with restricted transfer provisions. The buyer acknowledges in a letter to the seller that the securities are purchased for investment rather than for prompt resale. Securities purchased under an investment letter can typically be resold only 1) to certain qualified buyers, 2) after registration by the issuer, or 3) after the passage of an agreed time period. *See also Letter Stock (1).*

Investment Management Regulatory Organization (IMRO): A self-regulatory organization in the U.K. whose members manage investment portfolios, including pension funds.

Investment Value: *See Bond Value.*

Iota (I): *See Skew Measure.*

Irredeemable Debt Instrument: (1) A bond with a fixed maturity that is not subject to prior redemption by the issuer; (2) a perpetual financial instrument or an instrument with no fixed maturity, sometimes called debenture stock when issued by a corporate enterprise. This instrument is illustrative of the fine line between debt and equity securities.

Issuance Facility: *See Note Issuance Facility (NIF).*

Issuer: The legal entity that issues and usually assumes any obligations of a security or other financial instrument.

Issuer's Option Bond: A debt instrument that, in return for a higher yield than the issuer would otherwise have to pay, gives the issuer an unusual option. The option may range from a put requiring the investor to accept the issuer's common stock for the bond's principal at maturity, to the right to retire the issue at maturity, partly with cash and partly with a new issue of bonds. In the latter case, the issuer's option may be an option to extend maturity. *See also Mandatory Convertible.*

Itayose: *Jap.* A call market at the exchange opening that treats all orders as if they arrived at the same time.

Iterative Solution: A solution arrived at by trial and error. An analyst calculates the implied volatility of an option with iterative techniques. Various values for volatility are substituted into the Black-Scholes equation until the theoretical option value agrees with the option's market price. The bisection method and the Newton-Raphson method are particularly efficient iterative procedures.

Ito Process: A generalized Wiener process in which the parameters are time and/or state dependent. *See Ito's Lemma.*

Ito's Lemma: A relationship that makes it possible to deduce the stochastic process followed by a function of a variable. The function is deduced from the stochastic process followed by the variable itself. Ito's lemma is important in the derivation of a number of option models. *See also Brownian Motion.*

J

Japanese Option: At the time trading was initiated in TOPIX stock index options on the Tokyo Stock Exchange and in Nikkei-225 options on the Osaka Stock Exchange, these options were exerciseable each Thursday during the life of the option contract. In early 1992, the exercise was changed to European style on options expiring after June 1992. When used today, Japanese option may be a reference to an option with fixed periodic exercise rights or a slightly confused reference to an Asian or average rate option. *See also Modified American Option, Semi-American Option, American Option, Bermuda Option, Deferred Payment American Option, Quasi-American Option, European Option, Limited Exercise Option.*

Jellyroll: A transaction in offsetting long and short synthetic stock or stock index positions created from options with identical strike prices but different expiration dates. Closing transactions in the near expiration options and opening transactions in the distant expiration options are used to roll a synthetic stock position to a more distant expiration. *See also Box Spread (2), Synthetic Stock, Time Box.*

Jensen Measure: A measure of investment performance estimated from the intercept of a regression of a portfolio's excess returns over the risk-free return on a benchmark's excess returns. The benchmark is usually the market portfolio. The Jensen measure is suitable for evaluating a portfolio's performance relative to other portfolios, because it is based on systematic risk rather than total risk. *Also called Alpha (2).*

Johnson-Shad Agreement: *See Shad-Johnson Agreement.*

Joint Option: *See Cross Option (diagram).*

Jump: The maximum change in the rate of a floating-rate note with a step-up cap. *See Lookback Step-Up Cap, Step-Up Cap.*

Jump Process: A description of a stochastic price or rate change mechanism or process that includes occasional moves larger than traditional random processes would generate. Analytically, jump processes may be viewed as combinations of a traditional random process and a second process generating the larger moves. *See also Kurtosis, Mixed Jump Diffusion Process, Price Jump, Poisson Jump.*

Jump Z Bond: An accrual tranche of a collateralized mortgage obligation (CMO) that jumps ahead of other tranches in priority of principal repayment when a trigger condition occurs.

Junior/Senior Structure: A collateralization or subordination structure that improves the security behind a senior obligation by subordinating collateral or cash flow to a junior obligation only after the senior obligation is satisfied. *Also called A/B Structure.*

Junk Bond: A bond carrying a rating below Baa (Moody's) or BBB (S&P). Some speculative bonds are originally issued with below investment-grade ratings, and others, known as "fallen angels," decline from their initial investment-grade ratings. *See Fallen Angel, Rising Star.*

Kappa κ: Change in option price in response to a percentage point change in volatility. Kappa measures the sensitivity of option value to a change in implied volatility. Tau, vega, and zeta are also used to designate this relationship. *See also Delta-Gamma-Kappa-Rho Hedge.*

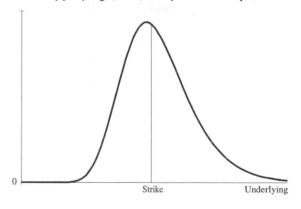

Kappa (Vega, Tau, Zeta) of a Call Option

Kassenverein: *Ger.* Securities clearing house.

Keepwell Agreement: A special form of guarantee in the form of a promise by a corporate parent to keep a subsidiary solvent. *See also Guarantee.*

Kerb Trading: Trading after an official exchange closing—often contrary to exchange rules.

Key Rate Duration: *See Partial Duration.*

Kick-In Option: A knock-in option with the instrike in the money. In-the-money barrier options have been blamed for certain incidents of instability in currency markets. *See In Option, Kick-Out Option.*

Kick-Out Option: A knockout option with the outstrike in the money. In-the-money barrier options have been blamed for some incidents of instability in currency markets. A dealer can avoid exposure to the instability by selling kick-in and kick-out options of the same type (call or put) with a common barrier. Hedging costs and risks may be greatly reduced if one option kicks in when the other kicks out. *See Out Option, Kick-In Option.*

Kicker: A right, warrant, or other low-value security added to a debt or stock offering to improve the market reception of the entire issue. *Also called a Sweetener. See also Contingent Takedown Option.*

Killer Bees: The staff experts in a takeover or takeover defense effort, including investment bankers, accountants, attorneys, tax specialists, etc.

Kitchen Sink Bond: An obligation of a secured investor trust that may be formed to provide an outlet for less popular collateralized mortgage obligation (CMO) tranches. Trust portfolios, and hence these bonds, are hard to value. The name reflects the miscellaneous composition of the underlying portfolio. The high credit rating of the bonds may not reflect the market risks—including prepayment risk—built into the issue. *See Secured Investor Trust.*

Knock-In Cap Option: A path-dependent option that pays off only if the underlying rate changes (usually falling) by a designated amount before rising through the cap strike.

Knock-In Option: Down-and-in or up-and-in barrier options activated at specific price or rate levels. *See In Option.*

Knock-In Premium Cap: A cap on a floating rate with the cap strike substantially above current rates and a trigger rate that must be breached before any premium payments are required. The trigger rate usually lies somewhere between the current rate and the cap strike. The holder of the cap pays a premium on reset dates only when the reference index rate is above the trigger rate. The premium (for each period) rises as the trigger rate is closer to the cap strike. This structure is used to reduce cap premiums when a floating-rate payer believes rates will not rise significantly and the chance of needing cap protection is small. It is important to emphasize that it is the cap premium, not the cap protection, that is subject to being knocked in. The fact that a premium is not always paid means that the premium will be larger than a standard cap premium when it is paid. *See also Knock-Out Premium Cap.*

Knock-In Risk Reversal: An equity risk reversal or comparable structure in currency markets with one or more knock-in option components. *See Equity Risk Reversal (diagram), Forward Rate Bracket.*

Knockout Forward: *See Break Forward (diagram).*

Knockout Option: A term descriptive of down-and-out or up-and-out puts and calls embedded in a structured risk management instrument or traded separately. *See Out Option.*

Knockout Premium Cap: A cap on a floating rate

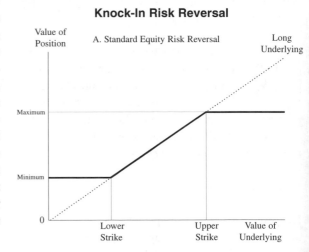

Knock-In Risk Reversal

A. Standard Equity Risk Reversal

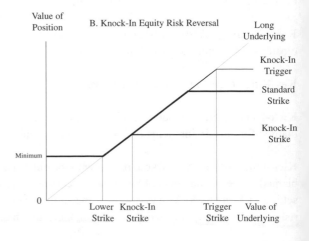

B. Knock-In Equity Risk Reversal

with a premium trigger knockout rate below current rates. If the reference index rate drops below the trigger rate, the cap holder stops making cap premium payments—but retains full cap protection. A knockout premium cap may have a lockout period during which cap premiums are paid before the knockout feature becomes effective. *See also Knock-In Premium Cap.*

Knockout Seagull: A seagull-shaped multi-option structure with knockout options on the down-swept portion of the seagull's wings. If the knockout triggers are breached, the wings straighten as in the diagram. *See also Rebate Strangle Option.*

Payoff Pattern of a Knockout Seagull

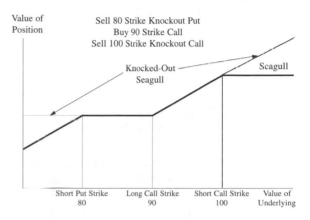

Knockout Swap: A swap that terminates if a designated instrument or index—usually an interest rate—moves above or below an agreed upon level.

Knockout Warrant: Provisions should be checked carefully because there can be many kinds of knockout warrants. One type combines a long call or a long call spread with a knockout put that assures the holder of a minimum return, unless the price of the underlying exceeds the knockout trigger price some time during the life of the option. If the knockout price is reached, the put expires and the put's minimum return protection expires with it.

Know Your Customer (KYC) Rule: A requirement in many regulatory regimes that a broker or dealer be familiar with the investment or funding objectives and policies of a customer, and actively discourage or even reject transactions that may be inappropriate or hazardous for the client—or for the broker/dealer.

Kolmogorov-Chapman Equation: The Kolmogorov-Chapman equation determines the exact functional form of the transitional probability function necessary to price derivative securities in a continuous time framework. Just as the Black-Scholes formula is the solution to a partial differential equation, the transitional density function underlying the Black-Scholes formula (the lognormal density function) is the solution to the Kolmogorov-Chapman equation. If stock prices follow geometric Brownian motion, the Kolmogorov-Chapman equation shows that ending stock prices are lognormally distributed.

Kolmogorov-Smirnov Test: A non-parametric test used to determine if two samples are likely to be from the same population.

Kurtosis: A measure of the extent to which observed data fall near the center of a distribution or in the tails. A kurtosis value less than that of a standard, normal distribution indicates a distribution with a fat midrange on either side of the mean and a low peak—a platykurtotic distribution. A kurtosis value greater than that of a normal distribution indicates a high peak, a thin midrange, and fat tails. The latter, a leptokurtotic distribution, is common in observed price, rate, and return time series data. *See also Jump Process, Leptokurtosis, Risk.*

L

Ladder Cap: A variation on the step-up cap structure in which the "jump" or periodic coupon increase is based on the highest rate level yet achieved, rather than the rate at the previous reset date. *See also Step-Up Cap.*

Ladder Option or Note: An index or currency warrant or option or equity index-linked note that provides an upward reset of its minimum payout when the underlying touches or trades through certain steps or threshold levels or attains a certain level on designated reset dates. For example, if the underlying trades through a price 35% above the strike, the holder of the warrant may be guaranteed a minimum payout equal to the value of the warrant at that price even if the index subsequently declines. A series of steps can ratchet the minimum payout up the ladder, providing protection from a later decline in the index. *Also called Lock-Step Option, Step-Lock Option or Note, Cliquet Option (2) (diagram), Ratchet Option. See Infinite Ladder Option. See also Shout Option (3).*

Ladder Trade: The contemporary purchase of one option and the sale of two other options at successively higher strike prices (in the case of calls) or lower strike prices (in the case of puts). The objective is to participate in the price movement of the underlying within a specific range for a low or zero option premium outlay. *Also called Christmas Tree, Table Top.*

Lambda λ: The percentage change in an option price, divided by the percentage change in an underlying price. A measurement of the option's leverage—equivalent to the leverage factor. *See Leverage Factor.*

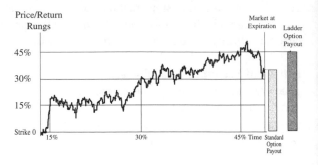

Payout of a Ladder Option or Note at Expiration

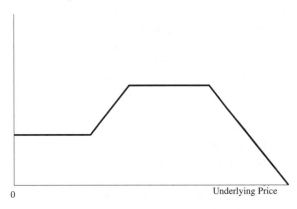

Payout Pattern of a Ladder Trade

Large-Cap Investment Manager: An equity portfolio manager who specializes in large companies. In the U.S., for example, her benchmark might be the S&P 500 Stock Index.

Latent Call Option: An option retained by the issuer of a convertible bond or convertible preferred stock that permits the issuer to force the holder to redeem it for a predesignated call value or to convert it to common stock. *See Embedded Option, Mandatory Convertible.*

Latent Warrant: A warrant embedded in a convertible bond or convertible preferred stock that gives these instruments their convertibility. The latent warrant's strike is the convertible's exercise price. *See Embedded Option.*

Lattice: The network of lines and nodes created in the expansion of a binomial or trinomial option pricing model. *See Binomial Model (diagram), Trinomial Model (diagram).*

Law of Large Numbers: The principle that a simple mean, range, standard deviation, or relative frequency (probability) calculation is usually more accurate with a large sample than with a small sample.

Law of One Price: The economic principle that the same item or closely equivalent items must sell for the same price or related prices in the marketplace. It follows that identical cash flows should command the same price, thereby denying investors the opportunity to profit from riskless arbitrage.

Least Squares Regression Line: A straight line fitted to a set of data by minimizing the sum of squared deviations of the observed data from the line. *See also Generalized Least Squares, Ordinary Least Squares.*

Fitting a Least Squares Regression Line

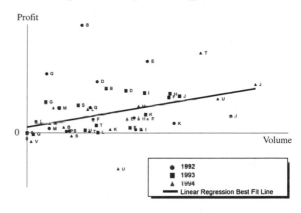

Leg: (1) One of several components of a combination option. (2) A phrase used by traders to describe a procedure where one of two offsetting positions is taken in the hope that a subsequent change in the price of the other position will permit execution of the entire trade on favorable terms. When this procedure does not work, the trader "gets legged." If a trader "lifts a leg," he closes one of the offsetting positions in the hope of an unhedged profit on the other. *See also Lifting a Leg.*

Legal List: A list of investments created by a regulatory regime that specifies a limited number of assets or classes of assets that may be purchased and held by a financial intermediary or a specific purpose fund. Legal lists have been largely supplanted by variations of the prudent man rule or market risk criteria in recent years.

Legal Right of Setoff: A contractual right to net obligations with a bankrupt counterparty. In the U.S., recent changes in the bankruptcy law have largely established netting rights in swaps and related risk management agreements if netting is covered in the master agreement between the parties. Other jurisdictions are moving in this direction in a competitive response. *See also Netting Agreement.*

Legal Risk: The most important legal risks in financial risk management are legal capacity, or *ultra vires* risk (the risk that a counterparty is not legally capable of making a binding agreement), and regulatory risk (the risk that a statute or a policy of a regulatory body conflicts with the intended transaction). *See also Hammersmith and Fulham, London Borough of, Ultra Vires Act. See Legal and Regulatory Risk discussion, pp. 6-7.*

Lender Option: A floor on a floating-rate agreement.

Lender's Option–Borrower's Option (LOBO): A floating-rate instrument that permits the lender to nominate a revised rate at periodic reset dates, and lets the borrower decide whether to pay the rate or redeem the bond. *Compare with other floating-rate reset mechanisms, such as Dutch Auction Interest and Dividend Reset. See also Puttable Extendible Notes.*

Leptokurtosis: A property of a probability distribution that gives a higher peak, a thinner midrange, and fatter tails than a normal distribution. Asset returns are likely to have a leptokurtic distribution if they are subject to frequent price jumps. *See also Kurtosis, Fat-Tailed Distribution (diagram).*

Less Developed Countries (LDCs): Countries with lower per capita incomes, greater dependency on commodity prices, less fully developed capital markets, and, often, less favorable credit ratings than major industrial countries.

Letter of Credit (LC): A document issued by a bank on behalf of a customer authorizing the customer or a third party to draw drafts on the bank up to a stipulated amount and under specified terms and conditions. The letter of credit may be a conditional commitment or it may be irrevocable if a fee has been paid by the customer. One type of LC guarantees that the bank will meet a customer's obligation if the customer is unable or unwilling to meet it.

Letter Stock: (1) Common or preferred stock sold subject to an investment letter from the purchaser who agrees not to sell it in the open market until a future date, when the company promises to register it for public sale or when the restriction on sale expires through the passage of time. These shares may be bought and sold by sophisticated investors before they are registered, but they usually trade at a discount to fully registered shares. *See also Investment Letter.* (2) *See Target Stock.*

Lettre de Faire: *Fr.* A medieval forward contract.

Level Payment Swap: Converts the cash flows from an amortizing debt instrument into a fixed swap payment at the periodic payment level of the amortizing debt. The notional value that the other swap payment is based on usually has no relationship to the unamortized principal of the amortizing debt.

Leverage: An investment or operating position subject to a multiplied effect on profit or position value from a small change in sales quantity or price. Leverage can come from high fixed costs relative to revenues in an operating situation, or from debt or an option structure in a financial context. *See also Premium (2) (diagrams).*

Leverage Factor: The expected or actual percentage price change in value of an option or other derivatives position in response to a 1% change in the cash value of the underlying. Equal to gearing if the option delta equals 1. For all values of delta, leverage equals delta, times underlying price, divided by warrant or option price per underlying unit. Sometimes expressed as a ratio rather than as a percent. *See also Lambda (λ), Gearing, Elasticity.*

Leveraged BuyOut (LBO): Any of a variety of techniques used to replace much of the equity in a corporate capitalization with debt. LBOs in the 1980s led to opportunities (and need) for risk management and refinancing in the 1990s.

Leveraged Capped Floater: A floating-rate note with an embedded short cap on a face amount greater than the face amount of the note. The note's coupon declines as interest rates rise above the cap rate, because the loss on the cap grows faster than the gain on the underlying note rate.

Leveraged Derivatives Transaction (LDT): As defined in an agreement between the Federal Reserve Bank of New York and Bankers Trust Company (December 4, 1994), a derivatives transaction "(i) where a market move of two standard deviations in the first month would lead to a reduction in value to the counterparty of the lower of 15 percent of the notional amount or $10 million, and (ii) for notes or transactions with a final exchange of principal, where counterparty principal (rather than coupon) is at risk at maturity, and (iii) for coupon swaps, where the coupon can drop to zero (or below) or exceed twice the market rate for that market and maturity, and (iv) for spread trades that include an explicit leverage factor, where a spread is defined as the difference in the yield between two asset classes." A leveraged derivative transaction may require special disclosure and documentation. *See also Highly Leveraged Transaction (HLT), Leveraged Floating-Rate Note, Leveraged Reverse Floating-Rate Note, Leveraged Structured Note, Leveraged Swap.*

Leveraged Floating-Rate Note: A variable-rate note with the floating rate set at a multiple of the reference index rate less a fixed rate or spread. *See also Leveraged Derivatives Transaction (LDT).*

Leveraged Recapitalization: An increase in the debt and a corresponding reduction in the equity of a corporation through a formal recapitalization plan in the form of a leveraged buyout, an extraordinary dividend, or a large stock repurchase.

Leveraged Reverse Floating-Rate Note: A structure similar to a reverse floating-rate note, except that the multiplier of the fixed rate in effect at the time the position is established is greater than 2, and the floating reference index rate is multiplied by that multiplier less 1, to give a payoff to the reverse floating-rate note that responds more than proportionately in reverse to changes in floating rates. *See Floating-Rate Note (FRN), Leveraged Derivatives Transaction (LDT), Reverse Floating-Rate Note.*

Leveraged Structured Note: Any of a variety of structured notes in which a rate or spread relationship is multiplied to arrive at the ultimate coupon or principal repayment. While these notes are leveraged within a range, there is usually a floor and a ceiling to the possible coupon or payment at maturity. *See also Leveraged Derivatives Transaction (LDT).*

Leveraged Swap: A swap agreement usually embedded in a structured note or similar instrument, in which the swap payments are expressed relative to a multiple of a notional amount, usually the face or principal amount of the underlying structured note or a multiple of a rate spread. Leveraged swaps are used primarily to minimize the cost of "hiring" the issuer of the structured note that serves as the carrier vehicle for the swap structure. The issuer receives a cost of funding reduction, and embedding the swap in leveraged form concentrates this funding cost reduction on a smaller base, reducing the total cost of creating the instrument. *See also Leveraged Derivatives Transaction (LDT).*

Liability: An obligation to make a payment to another.

Liability-Based Swap: A swap driven by a floating-rate borrower's decision to transform a floating-rate liability into a fixed-rate obligation, or a fixed-rate borrower's decision to swap for a floating rate. In either case, the motivation to swap comes from a desire to modify liabilities.

Liability Manager: A pension plan administrator, corporate financial officer, or other individual responsible for the management of financial liabilities, such as pension obligations, a corporation's liability structure, etc. *See also Asset Manager.*

Liability Risk Management: The application of risk control techniques to management of the payment obligations of a corporation, pension plan, insurance company, or any entity contractually obligated to make payments to debtors or beneficiaries over time.

LIBID: *See London Interbank BID Rate (LIBID).*

LIBOR: *See London InterBank Offered Rate (LIBOR).*

LIBOR Differential Swap: *See Rate Differential Swap (diagram), CUrrency Protected Swap (CUPS).*

LIBOR EuroDollar (LED) Spread: A yield curve spread at the very short end of the yield curve. This spread is ordinarily very narrow and relatively stable.

LIBOR In-Arrears Swap: *See In-Arrears Swap (diagram), Interest Rate Swap (diagram), Reset Swap, Swap.*

LIBOR Index Principal Swap (LIPS): *See Indexed Principal Swap (IPS), Swap, Treasury Rate Index Principal Swap (TRIPS).*

LIBOR Range Note: *See Index Range Note, Range Accumulation Option or Warrant.*

LIBOR^2 Swap: A fixed-for floating-rate swap with the floating rate calculated by squaring LIBOR expressed as a percentage (e.g., $(3.0\%)^2 = 9.0\%$). The LIBOR squared payer expects low rates and is willing to sell convexity in return for a high fixed rate. Receiving LIBOR squared can help to hedge a dealer's short options positions. These swaps are particularly useful in hedging exposure to changes in volatilities that are not linked to a specific price or rate level. They can be used in place of index amortizing swaps to hedge exposure to demand deposit withdrawal and credit card loan valuations at a bank. LIBOR squared caps and floors and LIBOR cubed instruments trade infrequently. *See also Power Bond (1), Turbo Swap.*

Life Assurance and Unit Trust Regulatory Organization (LAUTRO): A self-regulatory organization in the U.K. that regulates life insurance and unit trust (mutual fund) products and associated marketing organizations.

Lifetime: The term or tenor of a financial instrument or agreement.

Lifting a Leg: Closing out one of two or more risk-offsetting or modifying positions to increase profit by capturing a favorable trend in a market. *See also Leg (2).*

LIMEAN: The arithmetic average of LIBOR and LIBID in the same currency. *See also London InterBank Offered Rate (LIBOR), London Interbank BID Rate (LIBID).*

Limit Move: The maximum price change permitted by an exchange in a single trading session. Many futures exchanges impose limits on price changes in physical commodities except in the spot month. Except for the Japanese exchanges, daily price limits in financial instruments were uncommon, and were being phased out until the 1987 market break led to renewed interest in circuit breakers and price limits. *See also Circuit Breakers, Limit Up/Limit Down.*

Limit Option: *See Barrier Option.*

Limit Order: A purchase or sale order with restrictions on the maximum price to be paid or the minimum price to be received.

Limit Up/Limit Down: A condition that restricts trading on a futures exchange when prices rise (limit up) or fall (limit down) by the daily price limit imposed by the exchange. While some markets may close for the session when prices are at the limit, a more common practice is to permit sellers to hit limit bids or buyers to lift limit offers after the limit is reached. Occasionally, a market that is locked limit up or down early in a session will move away from the limit in response to the arrival of news and orders. *Also called Daily Price or Trading Limit. See Limit Move, Trading Limit (2). See also Lock-Limit, Price Limits.*

Limited Exercise Option: *See Bermuda Option, Japanese Option.*

Limited Liability Company (LLC): A corporate structure that may have the limited liability characteristics of a corporation and the tax pass-through characteristics of a partnership.

Limited Put: *See Floored Put (diagram).*

Limited Two-Way Payment (LTP) Clause: An optional clause in the ISDA swap agreement that permits the non-defaulting party to avoid any net liabilities to the defaulting party, while claiming any net balance due from the defaulting party. This clause has been criticized as inequitable by market participants and bankruptcy litigants. It is now used less frequently, partly because some jurisdictions will not enforce netting agreements if an LTP clause is part of a master agreement. *Also called Walkaway Clause. See also Full Two-Way Payment (FTP) Clause.*

Linear Interpolation: *See Interpolation.*

Linear Programming: A mathematical procedure for optimizing an objective function subject to inequality constraints and non-negativity restrictions. In portfolio optimization, an inequality constraint might take the form of a minimum or maximum allocation to certain assets. A non-negativity restriction implies that negative allocations are unacceptable. In a linear program, the objective function as well as the inequality constraints are all linear functions; hence the name.

Linked Asset: An asset held for, or committed to, the payment of specific liabilities or obligations.

Liquid Asset-Backed Securities (LABS): *See Securitization.*

Liquid Yield Option Note (LYON): A zero-coupon convertible, callable (by the issuer), puttable (by the investor) bond issued by a corporation. The combination of LYON features usually assures a positive return—at least until the expiration of the last opportunity to put the security back to the issuer at a premium over the issue price. The total return, if the company prospers and the common stock performs well, will be less than the return earned by common shareholders. The payout pattern of a LYON is roughly similar to some types of equity-linked notes. *See also Zero-Coupon Convertible Debt, Convertible Bond With a Premium Put, Synthetic Zero-Coupon Convertible Bond.*

Liquidate: Close a position.

Liquidity: A market condition where enough units of a security or other instrument are traded to allow large informationless transactions to be absorbed by the marketplace without significant impact on price stability. *See Illiquid, Informationless Trades.*

Liquidity Preference Theory: An hypothesis about the term structure of interest rates (the relationship between interest rates and term to maturity), holding that investors demand a premium for bearing interest rate risk. The extent of the premium increases with term to maturity but at a decreasing rate. The two reasons behind the decreasing rate of increase are that duration, a measure of a bond's price sensitivity to interest rate changes, increases at a decreasing rate with term to maturity, and that long-term interest rates are typically less volatile than short-term interest rates.

Liquidity Premium: An extra component of yield required to compensate an investor for the possibility that an adequate resale market may not develop for a security.

Liquidity Risk: (1) An adverse cost or return variation stemming from the lack of marketability of a financial instrument at prices in line with recent sales. Liquidity risk may arise because a given position is very large relative to typical trading volumes, or because market conditions are unsettled. Liquidity risk is usually reflected in a wide bid-ask spread and large price movements in response to any attempt to buy or sell. (2) In a depository institution, the cost or penalty associated with unanticipated withdrawals or the failure to attract expected deposits. Liquidity risk is usually managed by limiting holdings of illiquid positions, by matching asset and liability maturities, and by limiting any maturity gap. *Also called Marketability Risk. See Liquidity Risks discussion, pp. 4-5.*

Listed Futures Contract: *See Futures Contract.*

Listed Option: An option contract traded on a securities or futures exchange.

Listed Security: Any security admitted for trading on a generally recognized or regulated securities exchange.

Load: (1) The difference between the selling price of shares in some open-end investment companies (mutual fund or unit trust), and the net asset value of the underlying securities. (2) A sales charge for investing in a fund or other financial instrument. (3) A discount on a contingent forward sale or similar agreement that finances the implied premium "paid" for a break forward. *See also Break Forward.*

Loan-Based Certificates: Asset-backed instruments with consumer loan paper as collateral.

Loan Equivalent: The practice of translating so-called off-balance sheet commitments, such as swaps and other financial instruments, into the credit equivalent exposure represented by a loan. This approach is useful in overcoming the tendency to overstate the size of swap, option, and forward transactions by listing notional or face amounts. *See also Maximum Potential Replacement Cost, Notional Principal Amount.*

Loan Participation: A synthetic debt instrument created when a bank sells a share in a loan with a life under one year to a non-bank investor. Sale of the loan participation reduces the assets the bank carries, and provides attractively priced financing to a borrower too small to have its own commercial paper program. The loan participation also provides a slightly higher yield, administrative simplicity, and diversification to a buyer of short-term debt instruments. Asset-backed commercial paper often accomplishes some of the same objectives. *Also called Participation Agreement. See also Disintermediation, Intermediation, Asset-Backed Commercial Paper (ABCP).*

Local: A floor trader/market maker on an exchange (used most frequently in futures markets). *Also called Pit Broker.*

Local Return: The rate of return denominated in the currency of an asset's home country. The asset's rate of return to a foreign investor equals:

$$(1 + \text{local return}) * (1 + \text{currency return}) - 1$$

Lock-In Clause: A provision in a subordinated loan agreement preventing payment of interest or repayment of principal (even at maturity) if the payment brings the issuer's capital below a designated level imposed by law or regulation.

Lock-In Effect: The tendency of taxes on transactions or profits to inhibit trading out of a position.

Lock-In Option: A binary option used primarily in currency markets that pays off as long as the underlying stays inside the designated range throughout the life of the option. Some variants pay off as long as the underlying is inside the range at expiration. *See also Binary Option (diagram), Lockout Option.*

Lock-Limit: An imbalance in supply and demand at a daily price limit, usually in a futures market. Trading is not possible because the futures contract has reached the daily price limit, and few orders are arriving on the unpopular side of the trade. *See also Limit Up/Limit Down. Compare with Locked Market.*

Lock-Step Option: *See Ladder Option or Note (diagram), Cliquet Option (2) (diagram).*

Lock-Up Option: A stock option granted to a prospective merger partner or an exchange of stock options between two prospective merger partners designed to cover the losing party's expenses if the prospective partner is acquired by another firm. Lock-up options typically have such great value that they prevent a third party from breaking up the proposed merger or acquisition.

Locked Market: A confused market where bids and offers are temporarily identical. Identical bids and offers can occur routinely in some fixed-income markets because the trader who hits a bid or lifts an offer may pay the commission for both parties. *Compare with Crossed Market, Lock-Limit, Backwardation (2).*

Lockout Option: A binary option used primarily in currency markets that pays off only if the underlying breeches the upside or downside barrier at least once during the life of the option. Some variations must breech both upside and downside barriers or be outside the range at expiration. *See also Binary Option (diagram), Lock-In Option.*

Lockout Period: A time interval, usually early in the life of a security, when a call, conversion feature, or some other provision is not operative.

Logarithm: The power to which a base must be raised to yield a particular number. For example, the exponent 2 is the logarithm of 16 to the base 4, because 4 squared equals 16. Most financial applications use logarithms to the base 2.71828, denoted by the letter e. These are called natural logarithms and have a special property. The natural logarithm of the quantity 1 plus a periodic rate of return, equals the continuous rate of return. For example, the natural logarithm of 1.10 equals 9.53%. If one invests \$1 at a continuously compounded annual rate of 9.53% for one year, it would grow to \$1.10 by the end of the year. *See e.*

Logarithmic Transformation: The conversion of values to their logarithms, usually so that equal percentage changes have equal status. For example, in regressions that attempt to explain differences in security returns by differences in capitalization, capitalization is usually converted to its logarithm.

Logit Regression Analysis: A type of regression analysis used when the dependent variable is a dummy variable; that is, it can only have the values 1 or 0. Logit analysis is used to predict whether an event such as bankruptcy will happen. The independent variables may or may not be dummy variables.

Lognormal Distribution: Prices are said to have a lognormal distribution if the logarithm of the price has a normal distribution. To illustrate, if a stock is priced at \$100 per share, and prices have a normal distribution, the distribution of prices is the familiar bell-shaped curve centered at \$100. If the prices have a lognormal distribution, then the logarithm of the price has a bell-shaped distribution about $\log_n 100 = 4.6051702$. The logarithm of the prices is equally likely to be 5.2983174 or 3.912023, i.e.,

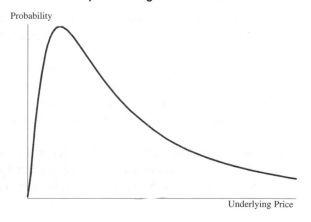

The Shape of a Lognormal Distribution

Probability

Underlying Price

4.6051702 ± 0.6931472 corresponding to prices of $200 and $50, respectively. If the lognormal probability density curve is plotted as a function of price rather than as a function of the logarithm of price, the curve appears positively skewed with tails more nearly depicting the observed behavior of stock prices. Lognormality arises from the process of return compounding. *See Normal Distribution, Brownian Motion, Fat-Tailed Distribution (diagram), Distribution.*

Logwealth Utility Function: A function relating utility to wealth first proposed by Daniel Bernoulli, who assumed that utility is equal to the natural logarithm of wealth. The logwealth utility function implies that a gain in wealth conveys a smaller increase to utility than the reduction in utility imparted by a loss in wealth of equal magnitude. Risk aversion follows from this asymmetry.

Lombard Rate: The DM interest rate applicable to collateralized loans. Named for the medieval bankers of Northern Italy.

London Clearing House Ltd. (LCH): The central clearing counterparty for most exchange-traded futures and option contracts in the U.K. The relationships among the customer, the broker, and the clearing house are slightly different in the U.K. and the U.S., though the function of each is similar.

London InterBank BID Rate (LIBID): The interest rate at which banks in London accept short-term deposits. The other side of the market from LIBOR. *See London InterBank Offered Rate (LIBOR), LIMEAN.*

London InterBank Offered Rate (LIBOR): The primary fixed-income index reference rates used in the Euromarkets. Most international floating rates are quoted as LIBOR plus or minus a spread. In addition to the traditional Eurodollar and sterling LIBOR rates, yen LIBOR, DM LIBOR, Swiss franc LIBOR, etc., are also available and widely used. *See also London InterBank BID Rate (LIBID), LIMEAN.*

Long: (1) Ownership of an investment position, security, or instrument. (2) A position that benefits from a rising market. (3) An investor whose position is such that she benefits from a rising market.

Long Bond Yield Decrease Warrants (Turbos): Originally, two-year warrants struck at the interest rate on thirty-year U.S. Treasury bonds. The warrants act like put warrants on rates or call warrants on the bond price.

Long Dated Forward: A forward contract with a settlement date more than one year in the future.

Long Dated Option: Traditionally, any option with an initial life of more than a year. Today, the term usually refers to instruments with an initial life in excess of two or three years.

Long Hedge: A risk-offsetting position that protects an investor or liability manager from an opportunity loss in the event of price appreciation in an underlying before a desired position can be established. An example might be a long call or a long futures or forward position taken in anticipation of a cash inflow that will finance a cash market investment. *See Anticipatory Hedge (1), Hedge.*

Long Position: (1) The holdings of the buyer of a security or other instrument. (2) A holding that appreciates in value when market prices increase, such as long stocks, bonds, futures, or call options, or short put options. Note that the holder of a put is long the contract or instrument, but profits when the market price declines.

Long-Short Portfolio: *See Pairs Trading.*

Long-term Equity AnticiPation Securities (LEAPS): Exchange-traded options with an original life of two years or more. Both puts and calls are available, and LEAPs become fungible with ordinary exchange-traded options as their remaining life falls into the maturity range of traditional exchange-listed options. *See also Buy-write Option UNitary DerivativeS (BOUNDS).*

Long-Term Rate Risk: Exposure to adverse fluctuations in long-term interest rates. The exact nature of the risk depends on whether risk is viewed from the perspective of an asset manager or a liability manager, and how the current asset or liability structure compares with the desired structure. Many instruments and techniques are available to manage long-term interest rate risks.

Long the Basis: A hedged position consisting of a long position in the cash instrument or actual and a short position in a future or forward. The opposite position would be short the basis. *See also Basis (1).*

Longitudinal Study: A study through time of a variable or group of variables. For example, a researcher may perform a cross-sectional regression analysis each month to measure the relationship between variation in book value and return for a sample of stocks. An examination of month-by-month changes in this relationship would constitute a longitudinal study.

Lookback Currency Option: A put or call option that gives its holder the right to buy, in the case of a call, or sell, in the case of a put, a foreign currency at the most favorable exchange rate available during the life of the option. Lookback options—with the lookback period covering the entire option period—are the most common type of reset options used in the currency markets. Improvement in the strike of a lookback currency option is based on daily exchange rate observations made over the life of the option.

    The value of the lookback call at expiration is at least as great as the value of the standard option, with a strike equal to the

Lookback Currency Option

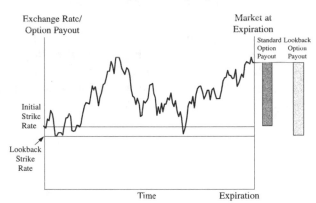

underlying exchange rate at the time of the option purchase. The price of a lookback currency option is usually several times the price of an at-the-money standard option at the outset of the contract. If the options were traded in the secondary market during their life, the relationship between the value of the lookback currency option and an otherwise comparable standard option would depend increasingly on two relationships: (1) the distance between the lowest exchange rate (in the case of a call) and the current exchange rate, and (2) the time remaining in which the exchange rate could continue to move in a favorable direction or, alternatively, establish an even lower strike rate and then appreciate. In general, the narrower the trading range has been, the lower the value of the lookback currency option as expiration approaches. *See also Best Buy Option, Partial Lookback Warrant or Option.*

Lookback Option: A call (put) option giving the holder the retroactive right to buy (sell) the underlying at its minimum (maximum) within the lookback period. *Also called Dint, Best Strike Option, Lookback Strike Option. See also Barrier Option, Best Buy Option, Best-Price Option, Hindsight Currency Option, Path-*

Dependent Option, Exotic Options, No-Regrets Options, Strike Bonus Option. Compare to Lookback Price Option (diagram).

Lookback Price Option: An option giving the holder the retractive right to cash in the contract at its maximum value within the lookback period. *Compare to Lookback Option.*

Lookback Step-Up Cap: A step-up cap structure that uses the lowest level of the reference index rate in the prior period as the base for calculating the maximum increase in the capped rate level. A variation of the step-up cap structure, where the periodic increase (called the "jump") is based on the lowest level the reference index rate reaches during a specific reset period. Because this feature reduces the strike on the cap, the jump is typically larger, and/or the cap premium greater than with a standard step-up cap. *See Step-Up Cap, Jump.*

Lookback Strike Option: *See Lookback Option, Partial Lookback Warrant or Option.*

Lookforward Option: An option giving the buyer the prospective right to the difference between the spot (strike) price at the beginning of a period and its high (call) or low (put) over that period. Functionally equivalent to a *Lookback Price Option.*

Lorenz Curve: A graph format used to illustrate income distribution or market concentration.

Loss Aversion: The notion that individuals assign more importance to losses than they assign to gains. Loss aversion implies that investors are less inclined to sell assets at a loss than they are to sell assets that have gained in value—even if expected returns are the same.

Loss Limit: The maximum loss considered acceptable in the simulation of a specific type of risk, usually in a worst case or stress test analysis. *See Absolute Risk, Curve Risk, Spread Risk, Worst Case.*

Lot: A standard contract, usually the minimum unit of trading.

Lottery Option: *See Binary Option (diagram).*

Comparison of Standard and Lookback Price Call Options

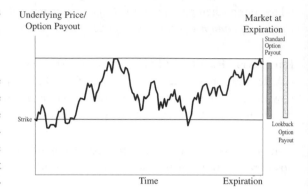

Comparison of Standard and Lookback Strike Call Options

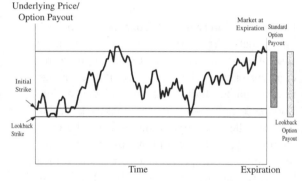

A Lorenz Curve of U.S. Family Income Distribution

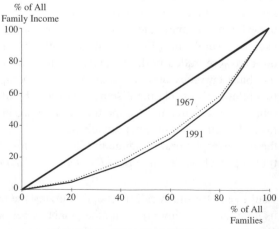

Source: Schwartz, Elaine, *Econ 101 1/2*, New York: Avon, 1995, p. 356.

Louvre Accord: An agreement by ministers of the major industrialized countries, reached at a 1987 meeting held in the Louvre, to maintain then current exchange rate levels. In the wake of a 1985 agreement to lower the value of the dollar, the ministers feared that the dollar might overshoot its natural level on the downside.

Low-Coupon Swap: An interest rate swap agreement with fixed-rate payments below current market rates. The floating-rate counterparty usually receives a front-end or back-end fee to compensate for the swap's positive net present value to the fixed-rate payer. Low-coupon swaps may be tax motivated. *Also called Non-Par Swap. Compare with Discount Swap. See Off-Market Coupon Swap.*

Low Exercise Price Options (LEPOs): An option introduced in Switzerland and Finland and under consideration in other countries to avoid the stamp duties sometimes imposed on stock trading, to facilitate the equivalent of short sales, and to create a risk transfer and financing instrument for shares that are not freely transferable. LEPOs have strike prices very close to zero, and hence provide all the features of stock ownership except voting rights and dividends. LEPOs may be cash settled if there are restrictions on transfer of the underlying to foreign investors. *See also Single Issue Options, Zero Strike Price Options.*

Low Outlay Geared Option (LOGO): A low premium call option that offers gradually declining upside participation. The payout formula of a LOGO at maturity is any positive value of the expression:

(Underlying Price at Maturity – Strike)/
Underlying Price at Maturity

As a LOGO goes in the money, its payout relative to a traditional option is gradually reduced, as if by multiplying the standard option payout by the ratio of the strike to the underlying price at maturity.

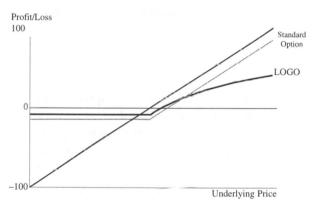

LOGO vs. Standard Option

Lower of Cost or Market (LCM): An accounting policy that values assets at historic cost or market value, whichever is lower. Recent changes in accounting rules are moving valuation policies away from historical cost and toward mark-to-market or fair value accounting. *See also Higher of Proceeds or Market.*

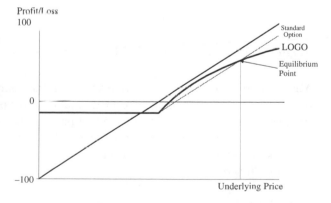

**LOGO vs. Standard Option:
Equivalent Premium Outlay**

Lower Partial Moment: A measure of downside risk computed as the average of the squared deviations below a target return. This measure is more general than semivariance, which is computed as the average of the squared deviations below the mean return. *See also Semivariance.*

Maastricht Treaty: A treaty among western European countries to promote economic cooperation and to establish a single European currency. In 1991, these countries met at Maastricht, the Netherlands, and agreed on a timetable and rules to implement a single European currency. They conditioned membership in this currency union on the maintenance of narrow bands around parity exchange rates, and on control of inflation and government deficits. In 1992, the reunification of Germany motivated the Bundesbank to pursue a tight monetary policy that forced other European countries to raise interest rates when their economies were mired in recession. Speculators sold the weaker European currencies, forcing a general realignment of exchange rates in August 1993. This experience dampened enthusiasm for a unified currency.

Macaulay Duration: The present value-weighted time to maturity of the cash flows of a fixed payment instrument or of the implicit cash flows of a derivative based on such an instrument. Originally developed as a market risk measurement for bonds (the greater the duration or "average" maturity, the greater the risk), duration has proven useful in analyzing equity securities and fixed-income options and futures. The diagram shows Macaulay duration as a balancing of present values of cash flows. *See also Modified Duration, Effective Duration, Option-Adjusted Duration, Partial Duration.*

Macro Hedge: *See Global Hedge.*

Macroeconomic (Macro) Swap or Option: A risk management agreement designed to offset some elements of quantity or business cycle risk by linking one or both payments of a standard swap or a swap or spread option to macroeconomic indexes. Obstacles to use of these instruments include (1) weak or inconsistent correlations between economic indexes and the related business risk; and (2) the reluctance of accountants and regulators to treat them as hedging instruments for reporting purposes. *See Global Hedge.*

Macaulay Duration of a 10% Coupon 4-Year Bond in an 8% Yield Environment

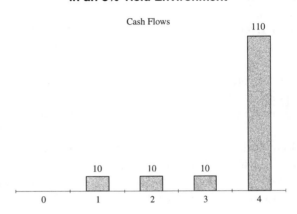

Cash Flows

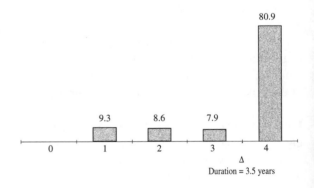

Present Value of Cash Flows and Duration

Duration = 3.5 years

Maginot Spread: *See BOAT Spread.*

Maintenance Margin: In addition to the initial margin, or performance bond, posted in futures, options, and securities markets, each market requires participants to post additional margin if the initial margin is not adequate to ensure that participants will meet their obligations. There is usually no maintenance margin requirement on long option positions, because they must be fully paid for in most markets. Maintenance margin is usually called variation margin in futures markets. *See also Variation Margin, Margin.*

Making a Market: Posting continuous two-sided (bid and asked) prices and being prepared to trade at those prices during normal market hours.

Mambo Combo: A combination of an in-the-money call and an in-the-money put, both long or both short. For example, a short 80 strike call plus a short 90 strike put is a short mambo combo, with the underlying between 80 and 90. This dance can facilitate a floor trader's cash management, but it holds few attractions for most investors. *Also called Guts.*

Mambo Combo

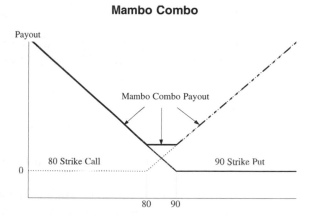

Managed Derivatives Fund (MDF): A futures fund or a hedge fund specializing in derivatives instruments.

Managed Futures Accounts: An approach to fund management that uses positions in government securities, futures contracts, and options on futures contracts in a portfolio. Some managers specialize in physical commodity futures, but most find they must trade a variety of financial and non-financial contracts if they have much money under management. Physical commodity markets alone will not accommodate a large fund.

Management's Discussion and Analysis (MD&A): An unaudited textual section of a corporate annual report that, among other information, usually includes a discussion of the risks the corporation faces and the steps taken to control those risks. The MD&A also describes the firm's recent performance, management policies, and an analysis of important year-to-year changes.

Managers of Managers (MOM): An investment advisor or commodity trading advisor (CTA) who selects and monitors the performance of multiple fund managers, each of whom manages part of the funds controlled by the MOM.

Mandarin Collar: A traditional collar structure with the possibility of an enhanced payout. The enhanced payout occurs in a low-volatility environment from a binary option that pays off if the underlying stays inside the collared range for the life of the instrument. The enhanced payout can alternately be evaluated in terms of up-and-out or down-and-out options that eliminate the extra payout for staying in the range. The collared range is usually narrow.

Mandate: (1) A contract or agreement to provide a service in exchange for a fee. (2) A law, rule, or regulation.

Mandatory Conversion Premium Dividend Preferred Stock (MCPDPS): *See Preference Equity Redemption Cumulative Stock (PERCS).*

Mandatory Convertible: An equity-like instrument that provides a higher yield or whose principal is denominated in a stronger currency than the underlying common stock at the time of issuance. On or before a contractual conversion date, the holder must convert this instrument into the underlying common stock. Mandatory convertibles are used when a traditional equity issuance would not be possible without placing severe market pressure on the underlying stock, or because the common stock yield or the stock's native currency is unattractive to potential purchasers. *Also called Preferred Purchase Unit, Debt with a Mandatory Common Stock Purchase Contract, Equity Contract Notes, Issuer's Option Bond. See also Latent Call Option.*

Manipulation of a Market: (1) A market corner followed by a short squeeze. (2) Buying or selling to establish a trend and then reversing the position to trade against the trend. The latter form of manipulation cannot be expected to be successful without fraud or major market inefficiencies.

Marché: *Fr.* Market.

Margin: The required equity or other performance bond that an investor must deposit to collateralize an investment position. *See also Initial Margin, Maintenance Margin, Margin Call, Variation Margin, Performance Bond (1).*

Margin Call: A demand from the broker or dealer carrying a customer's position for additional cash or collateral to guarantee performance on a position that has moved against the customer. *See also Margin.*

Margin of Solvency: Usually measured as assets minus liabilities.

Marginal Utility: Within the context of portfolio optimization, the increase in a portfolio's expected utility associated with a small increase in exposure to one of its assets.

Margrabe Option: The right to exchange one asset for another. Named after William Margrabe, the author of an article on how to value it. *Also called Exchange Option. See Outperformance Option (diagram).*

Mark to Market: To value a position or portfolio at current market prices. Marking to market is the only way to monitor risk and profit and loss effectively, and most enterprises are moving to daily marks to market of financial instruments. Marking positions to market is required with increasing frequency by accounting standards-setting bodies and regulators around the world.

Mark-to-Market Swap: Any swap settled by payment of the instrument's net value to the creditor counterparty on a periodic schedule (daily, monthly) or whenever the net value exceeds an agreed threshold amount. Bilateral marks to market are most common; but payments only when the counterparty with the lower credit rating is the debtor also occur. Too frequent marks to market may risk classification of a swap as an illegal off-exchange futures contract in the U.S.

Mark to Model: To price a position or portfolio at prices determined by using a financial model to interpolate between or among the market prices readily available. A mark to model is less reliable than a mark to market, because it depends on the realism of the assumptions in the model and may attribute a degree of liquidity to the instruments being priced that may not be present. With many complex financial instruments, where no ready market is available, a mark to model is the only practical valuation technique.

Market: (1) Prices at which a market maker is willing to buy and sell a particular instrument. If a market maker is willing to buy XYZ at 10 1/2, and sell XYZ at 11, his market is "10 1/2 at 11" for XYZ. A market maker's quote usually indicates size as well as price. (2) Location (physical or electronic) where transactions take place.

Market-Adjusted Debt (MAD): The mark-to-market value of an enterprise's debt.

Market Auction Preferred Stock (MAPS): *See Auction Rate Preferred Stock (ARPS), Dutch Auction Interest and Dividend Reset.*

Market Efficiency: *See Efficient Market.*

Market Gapping: *See Discontinuity Risk.*

Market-If-Touched Order: (1) In a dealer market, a contingent order that becomes a market order if the underlying instrument trades or is bid or offered at or beyond the limit price. (2) In an exchange market, an order to buy or sell at the best price available in the marketplace after a transaction has occurred at a specified price level.

Market Impact: The effect of the positions bought or sold on the price paid or received for a security. For example, if the market for a single lot is 1/2 to 5/8, and a sale of 10,000 shares occurs at 1/4, the market impact is said to be the nominal bid at 1/2 minus the sale price at 1/4, or 1/4. Market impact is often the largest component of trading cost for a large transaction and for a large investor. *See also Transaction Cost.*

Market Index Deposits (MIDs): Bank certificates of deposit or deposit notes with a return linked to the performance of an index, usually a stock market index. *See Equity-Linked Note (ELN) (diagrams), Equity-Linked Certificate of Deposit (ELCD or ECD).*

Market Index Target-Term Security (MITTS): An equity-linked note, usually without periodic coupon payments and with a single payoff at maturity. *See Equity-Linked Note (ELN) (diagrams).*

Market-Indexed NotE (MINE): *See Equity-Linked Note (ELN) (diagrams).*

Market Line: *Also called Securities Market Line. See Capital Asset Pricing Model (CAPM).*

Market-Linked CD: An equity-linked certificate of deposit. *See Equity-Linked Note (ELN) (diagrams), Equity-Linked Certificate of Deposit (ELCD or ECD).*

Market Maker: (1) Any dealer who regularly quotes both bids and offers and is ready to make a two-sided market. (2) A trader on the floor of an exchange who enjoys certain trading privileges in exchange for accepting an obligation to help maintain a fair and orderly market. *See Market Maker discussion, pp. 2-3.*

Market Neutral Investment Strategy: An approach to portfolio management that relies on the investment manager's ability to make money through relative valuation analysis, rather than through market direction forecasting. Although approaches vary, market neutral investment techniques usually generate gains in all or nearly all market scenarios. Market neutrality can be implemented with offsetting futures positions or with offsetting short and long positions. The offset is not necessarily measured in units of dollar exposure, but rather in relative variability units. Market neutrality does not insure non-volatile returns or positive returns. *See, for example, Index Arbitrage, Pairs Trading.*

Market Risk—The Viewpoints of Three Participants

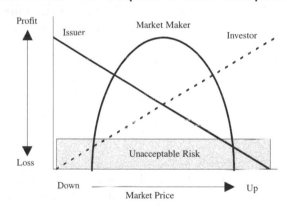

Market on Close Order (MOC): A type of order frequently used in portfolio trading and in related futures and options transactions that instructs the broker to execute the order at the closing price for the day. In futures markets, a market on close order is executed within the closing range. Under current New York Stock Exchange rules, a market on close order is assured of execution at the closing price if it is entered by a certain time. Investors using market on close orders should be aware of the probable effect a large order will have on the closing price.

Market Order: An order to buy or sell at the best price available when the instructions reach the marketplace.

Market Portfolio: The theoretically available portfolio consisting of all assets that an investor might purchase and hold in an investment portfolio. A cornerstone of the *Capital Asset Pricing Model (CAPM)*.

Market Risk: Exposure to an adverse variation in costs or returns resulting from a change in a market price or rate. *Also called Absolute Market Risk. See Market Risk discussion, pp. 2-3.*

Market Timing: Shifting in and out of asset groups and specific instruments on the basis of expectations that some are undervalued or overvalued relative to others, and that these discrepancies will soon be corrected.

Marketability Risk: *See Liquidity Risk (2).*

Markov Process: A stochastic process with the property that its present value alone provides just as much information about its future value as does its entire history up to and including the present value. A Markov process implies that only the present value is needed to forecast future values. *See also Brownian Motion, Square Root Law.*

Markovian: The absence of memory in a time series. Also called time independence.

Married Put: A stock put option and shares of the underlying stock bought on the same day and identified on a taxpayer's records as "married." *A special case of the Protective Put.*

Martingale Process: (1) A stochastic process with a finite first moment and the property that, conditioned on the entire history up to and including the present, the expected value of all future increments is zero. This is equivalent to the assumption that the expected value at any future moment equals the value of the process at the present moment. Stock prices are considered to follow a martingale process, because if currently available information implies that the expected value of a future increment is positive, then investor demand will drive up the current price, thereby eliminating the expected gain. *Also called Diffusion Process. See also Brownian Motion, Stochastic Process.* (2) Interestingly, this term has its earliest applications in probability and random processes as the name of a betting system in which the gambler doubles his wager at each loss until a win gains him a net amount equal to his original bet—or he goes bankrupt. This usage was common in the nineteenth and early twentieth centuries.

Maruyu: A traditional Japanese savings deposit system centered on accounts in the Japanese Post Office Savings Bank. These and other savings deposits enjoy important tax benefits. Efforts to increase income on these deposits have occasionally affected markets many time zones away from Japan.

Master Swap Agreement: Comprehensive documentation of standard terms and conditions covering all swap transactions between two counterparties. Usually based on standard documents prepared by the International Swap and Derivatives Association (ISDA).

Matched Book: A portfolio of offsetting assets and liabilities with equal maturities and equal value so that market risks cancel each other out.

Matched Hedge: A hedge that uses a financial instrument based on the same asset as the asset to be hedged in the underlying portfolio. This type of hedge contrasts to a cross hedge, which uses a different but correlated financial instrument to hedge an underlying asset, or a basket hedge, which uses a group of financial instruments collectively correlated with the asset to be hedged.

Matched Swap: (1) A swap covered on one side by an underlying bond or note with terms similar to, but offsetting, that side of the swap. (2) A swap paired with a mirror swap to offset market risk.

Materiality: The principle under which insignificant, inconsequential, and unimportant data and information are excluded from financial reports. In general, judgment as to what is material has been left to the preparers of specific financial statements. There are, however, specific standards for materiality in some instances.

Mathematical Expectation: *See Expected Value.*

Matrix Price: An estimated price or value for a fixed-income security. Matrix prices are based on quoted prices for securities with similar coupons, ratings, and maturities, rather than on specific bids and offers for the designated security. The name "matrix price" comes from the practice of interpolating among values for similar instruments arranged in a matrix format. These model prices must be used with care and with understanding that a specific position may be highly illiquid.

Maturity: The date on which the life of a financial instrument ends through cash or physical settlement or expiration with no value.

Maturity Gap: An early approach to the measurement of interest rate risk. For each period out to the longest maturity, the market values of rate sensitive assets and rate sensitive liabilities are measured. The size of the gap in each period is multiplied by the change in interest rates to be evaluated. The results are summed to give the effect on the cumulative net interest income or expense. This approach has been largely abandoned for newer techniques based on asset and liability duration and on value at risk. *Also called Gap Analysis.*

Maturity Mismatch Risk: The risk that, due to differences in maturities of the long and short positions in a cross hedge, the value of the risk offsetting positions will fail to move in concert. *See Cross Hedging.*

Maverick Risk: The risk of straying too far from the herd in implementing an investment or risk management policy. *Sometimes used interchangeably with Tracking Error.*

Maximum Likelihood Estimation: A method for estimating the parameters of the population from which sample data is drawn. For all possible parameters, compute the probability of observing the sample statistic. The maximum likelihood estimate is the parameter associated with the highest probability. For example, suppose someone observes a cab numbered 23, and wishes to estimate the number of cabs in the entire fleet. It is also known that the taxi company numbers its cabs from 1 to the total number of cabs in the fleet. The maximum likelihood estimate is 23, because there is a 0% probability that the number of cabs is less than 23, and a less than 1/23 chance that the number of cabs is any number greater than 23.

Maximum Maturity Bonds: Collateralized mortgage obligation (CMO) tranches that will be retired by minimal required principal payments in a known time period.

Maximum Potential Replacement Cost: The credit line usage required to carry a financial instrument in position. *See also Credit Equivalent Value (CEV), Loan Equivalent.*

Maximum Rate Note: *Another, perhaps misleading, name for Reverse Floating-Rate Note (diagram).*

May Day: A reference to the elimination of fixed securities commissions in the U.S., in May 1975.

Mean: Most commonly, the arithmetic average of a population or a sample of observations. *Also called Arithmetic Average. See also Geometric Average, Median.*

Mean Reversion: The name given diverse processes by which variables such as prices, rates, and volatilities tend to return to a mean or average value after reaching extremes. *Also called Ornstein-Uhlenbeck Process, Red Noise. See also AutoRegressive Moving Average (ARMA) Models, Volatility AutoRegressive Integrated Moving Average (VARIMA) Model, Generalized AutoRegressive Conditional Heteroskedasticity (GARCH) Model.*

Mean Tracking Error Utility Function: A function that defines the relationship between the degree of satisfaction an investor receives and combinations of expected return and tracking error against a benchmark. This utility function assumes that investors are indifferent to a portfolio's total volatility.

Mean-Variance (MV) Analysis: The process of identifying and evaluating portfolios that offer the highest expected return for given levels of variance. *See Efficient Frontier (diagram), Modern Portfolio Theory.*

Mean-Variance Tracking Error Utility Function: A function that defines the relationship between the degree of satisfaction an investor receives, and combinations of expected return, variance, and tracking error against a benchmark. This utility function assumes that investors are simultaneously concerned with both absolute risk and relative risk.

Mean-Variance Utility Function: A function that defines the relationship between the degree of satisfaction an investor receives and combinations of expected return and variance. This utility function assumes that investors are indifferent to a portfolio's tracking error against a benchmark.

Measure of Change Theorem: *See Girsanov's Theorem.*

Median: The middle observation in an ordered distribution. After the mean, the most common measure of central tendency. It is often used instead of the mean because it is less sensitive to extreme values. *See also Mean.*

Medium-Term Notes (MTN): Plain vanilla debt instruments with a fixed rate and fixed maturity (typically less than seven years, but occasionally much longer). Medium-term notes are the basic component of the debt issuance programs of many investment-grade borrowers. A medium-term note yield can serve as the base rate for a swap payment and an MTN component can be part of a hybrid security.

Member Firm: A corporation, partnership, or sole proprietorship that holds a seat or membership on a securities or futures exchange.

Mental Accounting: The tendency to categorize funds or items of value even though there is no logical basis for the categorization. For example, individuals often segregate their savings into separate accounts to meet different goals, even though funds from any of the accounts can be applied to any of the goals.

Mezzanine Financing: A class of subordinated debt used in leveraged buyouts (LBOs).

Micro Hedge: To offset portfolio or enterprise risk on a position-by-position basis. *Compare with Global Hedge.*

Mid-Cap Investment Manager: An equity portfolio manager who specializes in mid-sized companies. In the U.S., for example, his benchmark might be the S&P Mid-Cap 400 index.

Middle Market (or Mid-Market) Price or Quotation: (1) The mean between the best bid and the best offer quoted by market makers. (2) The mean of two or more recent prices.

Middle Office: In contrast to the front office (sales production, corporate finance, etc.) and the back office (settlements, clearances, record maintenance, custody, etc.), the middle office refers to a group that draws on the resources of both the front and the back offices to manage the risk exposures and often the technology of a financial organization.

Migration Analysis: A technique to estimate maximum likely credit losses based on the historic migration from an initial credit rating service grade to lower grades over a specified time period. The technique is based on the general principle that credit losses occur only over time, and that an AAA credit rarely defaults without moving through lower credit grades first.

Mil or Mill: A tenth of a cent: $0.001.

Milking: Illegally stripping a corporation of its assets before an ownership change or bankruptcy.

Min Max: *See Collar (1) (diagram), Equity Risk Reversal (diagram).*

Min Max Option: *A Best-Of or Worst-Of Option. See Alternative Option (diagram).*

Mini-Max Floater: A floating-rate note with an embedded collar.

Mini-Max Strategy: Generically, any interest rate risk management structure that provides participation and protection while attempting to minimize any option premium payment. This is often accomplished by selling a cap or floor to offset the cost of a corresponding floor or cap. *See Interest Rate Collar (diagram).*

Mini-Premium Option: A variant of the contingent premium option, in which no initial premium is paid but for which the option purchaser agrees to pay set amounts if the underlying price moves in the money to specific levels over the life of the option. This creates, in effect, a kind of stepped participating forward agreement. The risk to the holder is that the underlying will change direction after premiums have been paid, and finish out of the money.

Minimum Acceptable Return (MAR): A risk/return constraint imposed on the management of a portfolio of assets. The MAR is linked to the nature and level of the liabilities that the portfolio is designed to fund.

Minimum Price Fluctuation: *See Tick.*

Minimum Variance Hedge Ratio: The ratio of futures contracts to a specific spot position that minimizes the variance of the profit from the overall hedged position and is invariant to the cost of the hedge.

Ministry of Finance (MOF): The principal regulator of financial markets in Japan.

Mirror Swap: (1) An offsetting or contra-swap designed to eliminate the market exposure of an earlier swap position. (2) A swap between a derivatives products company (DPC) and its parent or an affiliated company designed to take most market exposure out of the credit enhanced vehicle (CEV).

Mismatched Payment Swap: A swap agreement under which the parties make payments at different times and/or at different intervals, exposing one or both parties to settlement risk.

Mixed Jump Diffusion Process: A stochastic process that combines a jump process with a diffusion process. *See Jump Process, Kurtosis, Price Jump, Poisson Jump.*

Mode: (1) The most common observation in a sample. (2) An infrequently used measure of the value that appears most frequently.

Model Mining: The process of first observing an event and then developing a theoretical model with a particular set of assumptions so that the model's implications conform to the previously observed event. *See also Data Mining.*

Modeling Risk: An adverse variation in cost or return stemming, usually indirectly, from errors in the assumptions built into a model or from a failure to model the behavior of an instrument, index, price, or rate correctly.

Modern Portfolio Theory (MPT): A variety of portfolio construction, asset valuation, and risk measurement concepts and models that rely on the application of statistical and quantitative techniques. Among the concepts and models associated with MPT are: portfolio theory, the capital asset pricing model (CAPM), arbitrage pricing theory, and the Black-Scholes option pricing model. *See Black-Scholes Equation, Arbitrage Pricing Theory (APT), Capital Asset Pricing Model (CAPM) (diagram), Diversification (diagram), Efficient Market, Mean Variance (MV) Analysis.*

Modified American Option: *See Deferred Payment American Option. Also called Quasi-American Option. See also American Option, Bermuda Option, European Option, Japanese Option.*

Modified And Combinable Remic (MACR): A kind of super-Remic (real estate mortgage investment conduit) that lists all possible cash flow combinations in the registration documents, and lets investors mix and match to create desired instruments without originating a new security.

Modified Duration: A measurement of the change in the value of an instrument in response to a change in interest rates. The primary basis for comparing the effect of interest rate changes on prices of fixed-income instruments. The formula shows the small difference between modified and Macaulay duration. Many applications are not sensitive to the difference, and modified and Macaulay duration numbers are often used interchangeably. *Also called Adjusted Duration. See also Macaulay Duration, Duration, Effective Duration, Partial Duration, Option-Adjusted Duration.*

$$D_{mod} = [1/(1 + [y/f])] \, D_{mac}$$

where D_{mod} = modified duration; y = yield to maturity; f = frequency of coupon payment, and D_{mac} = Macaulay duration.

If Macaulay duration is 6, yield is 7% (0.07), and the bond pays interest twice a year:

$$D_{mod} = [1/(1 + [0.07/2])] \, 6 = 5.8$$

Modified Following: In a swap or other interim reset agreement, variable terms are usually "modified following" a designated date, usually a combined payment and reset date. *Compare with In-Arrears Swap.*

Modigliani-Miller Hypothesis: The proposition (largely responsible for winning Nobel prizes for its proposers) that, in an efficient capital market with no tax distortions, the relative proportion of debt and equity in a corporate capitalization does not affect the total market value of the firm. Corporate financial officers and financial engineers continue to search for market inefficiencies and tax-related opportunities that can lower a corporation's cost of capital in the real world. *See Invariance Propositions.*

Momentum Investor: A market participant who increases or reduces his level of market participation to "go with the flow"—increasing market exposure when the market is rising, and decreasing market exposure when the market is falling. Trend-following technical traders and portfolio insurance practitioners are two examples of those who use this approach. *For contrast, see Asset Allocation.*

Monetary Model: A model of exchange rate determination that is an extension of the quantity theory of money to an open economy. There are two variations of the monetary model: the flexible price monetary model and the sticky price monetary model. The flexible price model assumes that purchasing power parity holds and that changes in relative price levels automatically translate into changes in exchange rates. The sticky price model assumes that prices are sticky in the short run. Thus, a change in the nominal money supply causes a change in the real money supply, resulting in interest rate changes and capital flows. These capital flows cause the exchange rate to overshoot the changes that would have occurred had prices adjusted instantaneously.

Money Back Certificates: Hybrid instruments that promise the investor the return of her original investment at a minimum. Cash that might ordinarily be paid as yield goes to pay for exposure to any of a variety of equity, interest rate, commodity, and/or currency exposures. These hybrids are usually best analyzed by dividing the original investment into a zero-coupon bond that will appreciate to the value of the original investment over the life of the instrument to provide the money back component and the balance used to buy an option, invest in a commodity pool, etc. *See, for example, Equity-Linked Note (ELN) (diagrams), Money Back Options or Warrants.*

Money Back Options or Warrants: Similar to money back certificates, but the warrant structure may permit only a partial refund of the warrant investment in the event of an adverse move in the underlying. *See Money Back Certificates, Redeemable Warrant.*

Money Market Basis: A day count fraction equal to actual days divided by 360, except in the U.K. and several commonwealth countries, where the denominator is 365 or actual days. *See also Bank Basis, Basis (3), Bond Basis.*

Money Market Preferred Stock (MMPS): Preferred stock featuring dividends reset at a Dutch auction. These go by a variety of names, including cumulative auction market preferred stock (CAMPS), market auction preferred stock (MAPS), fixed-rate auction preferred stock (FRAPS), Dutch auction rate transferable securities (DARTS), short-term auction rate cumulative preferred stock (STARS), and stated rate auction preferred stock (STRAPS). *See Auction Rate Preferred Stock (ARPS), Dutch Auction Interest and Dividend Reset.*

Money Spread: *See Vertical Bull Spread (diagram), Vertical Bear Spread (diagram).*

Moneyness: (1) The characteristic of being sufficiently like cash to be used as a medium of exchange in the settlement of transactions. (2) The degree to which an option is in the money and behaving more like a forward contract than an option.

Monte Carlo Method: (1) In option evaluation, a numerical probability approach to the valuation of path-dependent options that cannot be easily decomposed into a series of standard options with analytic solutions.

The Monte Carlo technique is also used when there is reason to believe that the underlying return-generating process does not match a standardized distribution. In applying the Monte Carlo method, an analyst generates a series of prices for the underlying(s) using a model that approximates the market's price-generating process. An average (expected) option value at expiration for each underlying or set of underlyings is determined and discounted to a present value. The quality of the result depends on the realism of the price- or return-generating process. (2) A sampling technique used to fix and evaluate cases in risk management stress testing. (3) A procedure for simulating the probable distribution of a strategy's return by repeatedly sampling from a population with a presumed distribution.

Monthly Income Preferred Shares (MIPS): A complex instrument based on an intracompany loan between a limited liability issuer and its parent company. The instrument is designed to give the parent equity treatment for regulatory, rating, and capital purposes, and tax deductibility for the coupon on the instrument. Some versions of this instrument may achieve the desired tax objective, but all tax issues have not been resolved. *Also called Exchangeable Preferred Income Cumulative Shares (EPICS), QUarterly Income Capital Securities (QUICS), QUarterly Income Preferred Securities (QUIPS), Trust Originated PReferred Securities (TOPRS).*

Monthly OverNight Average (MONA) Swap: A swap with a floating rate determined by the average overnight lending rate over a period (a month in this specific version), rather than by a fixed-term LIBOR rate on a reset date. *See also Taux Annuel Monétaire (TAM).*

Moral Hazard: The risk that a party to a transaction has not entered into a contract in good faith, has provided misleading information about its assets, liabilities, or credit capacity, or has an incentive to take unusual risks in a desperate attempt to earn a profit before the contract settles. *See also Integrity Risk (2), Agency Costs, Moral Risk, Counterparty Risk.*

Moral Obligation Bond: A municipal security backed by the issuer's or a related entity's stated intention to repay, but not by its full faith and credit.

Moral Risk: Exposure to loss resulting from a willful, improper, or illegal act by an agent or counterparty. *See also Moral Hazard.*

Mortgage: A lien or claim against real property that can serve as security for a loan.

Mortgage Bond: A corporate or other entity's debt security secured by a mortgage lien against certain real property of the issuer.

Mortgage Over Treasury Option (MOTO): A cash settled call on the spread between a specific mortgage-backed security or index yield and a selected Treasury security yield. The value of the option is affected by the mortgage repayment rate, and, hence, by the level and volatility of interest rates.

Mortgage Participation Certificate: An early attempt to package mortgages that ultimately led to the securitized mortgage obligation.

Mortgage Prepayment Cap: An OTC option contract that protects the holder of the cap from a return loss if the prepayment rate in a specific mortgage pool exceeds a strike expressed relative to a PSA prepayment rate. Although they are uncommon, prepayment floors are also available. *See also Prepayment Option, Public Securities Association (PSA) Prepayment Model.*

Mortgage Replication Swap: A variety of indexed principal swap where the fixed-rate side is based on a mortgage-style rate and amortization schedule. The rate is often a real mortgage rate or a premium over a benchmark Treasury issue. The amortization rate is a real or preset amortization schedule. *See also Indexed Principal Swap (IPS).*

Mortgage-Backed Securities: Debt instruments collateralized by residential, commercial, or industrial real estate mortgages. *See also Collateralized Mortgage Obligation (CMO), Government National Mortgage Association (GNMA) Pass-Through Certificates, Interest Only (IO) Obligation, Principal Only (PO) Obligation, Real Estate Mortgage Investment Conduit (REMIC).*

Moving Average: A sequence of means of a fixed number of consecutive points of data from a time series. The number of data points may be chosen to eliminate seasonal effects or simply to smooth out random short-term fluctuations.

Mule: An apparently innocent domestic currency bond from a highly rated issuer with embedded swaps, options, or forward contracts linking it to a foreign stock, bond, or currency position that an investor could not legally take directly. The name is a reference to the front-line carriers of illegal drugs.

Multi-Asset Option: Any option with a payout dependent on the performance of more than one underlying asset. *See, for example, Alternative Option (diagram), Outperformance Option (diagram), Contingent Payout Option (diagram), Contingent Currency Option, Contingent Exchange Option.*

Multi-Index Option: An outperformance option with a payoff determined by the difference in performance of two or more indexes. *See also Outperformance Option (diagram).*

Multi-Step-Up Callable Bond or Note: A callable step-up note with more than one coupon increase set over the life of the note to "step-up" the pressure on the issuer to refinance and call the note. *See also Callable Step-Up Note.*

Multicurrency Swap Agreement: An exchange of payments covering a series of cash flows among several different currencies to be both paid and received. Analytically, a multicurrency swap agreement can be split into a series of separate bilateral currency swap agreements.

Multifactor Model: One of three types of models that try to explain risk/reward relationships based on two or more factors. Macroeconomic factor models use observable economic time series as measures of the factors correlated with security returns. Fundamental factor models use many of the measurements generated by securities analysts, such as price/earnings ratios, industry membership, company size, book-to-price, financial leverage, dividend yield, etc. Statistical factor models generate statistical constructs that have no necessary fundamental or macroeconomic analogs, but that explain, in the statistical sense, many of the relationships of security returns from the security return data alone. Factor models are used to predict portfolio behavior, and in conjunction with other tools, to construct customized portfolios with certain desired characteristics, such as the ability to track the performance of indexes or other portfolios. *Also called Factor Model. See Arbitrage Pricing Theory (APT), Factor, Eigenvectors, Factor Analysis.*

Multifactor Option: *See Alternative Option (diagram).*

Multilateral Netting: An arrangement among three or more parties in which each party makes payments to an agent or clearing house for net obligations due to other parties, or receives net payments due from other parties. This procedure is used to reduce credit/settlement risk. *See also Multinet.*

Multinet: A currency transaction settlement and netting service operated by International Clearing Systems, Inc., an affiliate of the Options Clearing Corporation. Multinet is designed to prevent Herstatt risk. A recent link with FXNET is designed to increase the scope and flexibility of the overall system. *See also Multilateral Netting, Settlement Risk, Exchange Clearing HOuse (ECHO), Inter-Bank On-Line System (IBOS).*

Multiperiod Option: Any of a variety of option structures whose payout is based on the value of the underlying on several occasions (average rate or price option) or that is really a series or strip of separate options (most caps and floors).

Multiperiod Strike Reset Option (MSRO): *See Cliquet Option (1) (diagram), Coupon-Indexed Note.*

Multiple Listing: *See Dual Listing.*

Multiply Traded Option: Exchange-traded option contracts on the same underlying traded on different exchanges or in different countries. These contracts may or may not be fungible.

Municipal Convertible: A combination of selected features of a zero-coupon bond and a coupon bond, these instruments typically pay no interest in the early years, and become a traditional coupon-paying municipal bond later in life. These bonds trade under a variety of names and acronyms, with stepped tax-exempt appreciation on income realization security (STAIRS) as common as any. *See also Stepped Tax-Exempt Appreciation on Income Realization Security (STAIRS).*

Municipal Derivative: One of a variety of structures designed to accommodate the financing requirements of non-sovereign government units and investors in their debt. The fact that most local government debt is exempt from federal taxation in the U.S. has important implications for this market. Among the more popular structures are INFLOS/SAVRs, or RIBs/SAVRs, created by dividing a fixed-rate payment into coupons for an issue that is half inverse floating-rate notes and half traditional floating-rate notes. *See INverse FLOating Security (INFLOS).*

Municipal Embedded Derivative Security (M-Beddo): A municipal note with an embedded swap, cap, or other structure. The final instrument may be relatively complex.

Municipal Option Put Security (MOPS): A municipal bond with a detachable put. The put allows it to be sold back to the issuer at specified dates prior to stated maturity.

Municipal Over Bond (MOB) Spread: The difference between the yield implicit in the municipal bond futures contract and the yield implicit in the Treasury bond futures contract on the Chicago Board of Trade (CBOT). The spread is sensitive to the shape of the yield curve (the municipal contract components are usually shorter-term bonds) and the perceived credit quality of the municipals.

Mutual Fund: An open-ended investment company. Called a unit trust in the U.K.

Mutual Offset System: A cross-margining system that reduces initial margin requirements on one exchange if a risk-offsetting position is held in a related contract on another exchange. *See also Standard Portfolio Analysis of Risk (SPAN).*

Nakadachi: *See Saitori.*

Naked Option: An option writing (sale) position collateralized by cash or securities other than those on which the option is written. The potential loss on a naked option position can be

The Profit/Loss Patterns of Naked (Short) Options

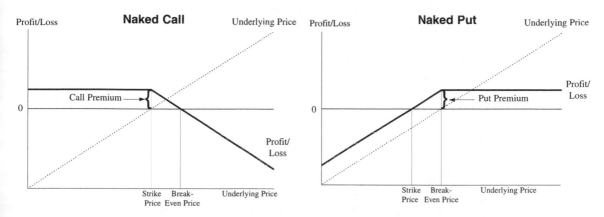

very large—in the case of a naked call on common stock, the possible loss is theoretically unlimited. *See also Covered Call, Option Hedge, Uncovered Writer.*

National (Asset) Risk Premium: The difference between the expected return on an asset in its local currency and its national (local currency) risk-free rate. *See also Dollar Risk Premium.*

National Securities Clearing Corporation (NSCC): The clearing corporation for clearing corporations, NSCC is the securities industry's settlement and account reconciliation organization.

Nationally Recognized Statistical Rating Organization (NRSRO): One of the credit rating agencies whose work is accredited by the SEC for use as a guideline in regulation of portfolio debt quality. *See Bond Ratings—Appendix.*

Natural Currency: The currency used by an issuer to keep its books of account.

Natural Hedge: (1) The shift of production facilities, working capital, or borrowing arrangements to an alternative currency area to offset undesirable cash flow exposures. (2) A condition in which an exposure to a risk factor is offset or partly offset by an opposite exposure to that risk factor.

Natural Logarithm: The power to which the value 2.71828 (e) must be raised to yield a particular number. These logarithms have a special property. The natural logarithm of the quantity, 1 plus a periodic rate of return, equals the continuous rate of return. For example, the natural logarithm of 1.10 equals 9.53%. If one invests $1 at a continuously compounded annual rate of 9.53% for one year, it would grow to $1.10 by the end of the year. *See e.*

Natural Rate of Unemployment: *See Non-Accelerating Inflation Rate of Unemployment (NAIRU).*

N Cap: *See Indexed Strike Cap (diagram).*

Near Month: The next futures or options contract due to expire.

Near Perfect Floating-Rate Note: The investor will have to judge how near. *See Path-Dependent Floating-Rate Note.*

Negative Amortization: In contrast to the traditional planned amortization of mortgage principal with a fixed-rate mortgage, an adjustable-rate mortgage's principal can grow if the market rate (on which the adjustable rate is based) increases.

Negative Carry: The net cost of carrying a position when the cost of funds is greater than the yield on the securities. *See also Positive Carry.*

Negative Convexity: *See Convexity (2).*

Negative Good Will: The excess of book net asset value over market value. *See also Good Will.*

Negative Pledge Clause: A provision of a bond indenture designed to protect the bondholder's position from deterioration as a result of the issuer's actions. For example, unsecured notes may provide that those notes will be secured equally with any secured debt issued in the future. *See also Covenant.*

Negotiability (of a Financial Instrument): Transferability of ownership at will between and among persons (legal).

Net Asset Value (NAV): The amount by which the value of an entity's assets exceeds the value of its liabilities.

Net Commission: In the U.K., a net or principal trade with no commission payable. *See also Net Trade.*

Net Margin Requirement: The margin required after any option premium received by the investor is deducted from the stated option margin requirement.

Net Operating Profit After Tax (NOPAT): The cash earnings a company would generate if its capitalization were unleveraged. *See also Free Cash Flow (FCF), Economic Value Added (EVA).*

Net Present Value (NPV): The expected or certain value of a future cash flow discounted to the present at an appropriate interest (discount) rate.

Net Replacement Value (NRV): The net cost of replacing the net present value of a single contract, of all contracts of a certain type, or of all contracts with a specific counterparty—after allowance for enforceable netting agreements in place. *See also Gross Replacement Value (GRV), Net-to-Gross Ratio (NGR).*

Net Settlement: (1) A procedure for swap payment exchanges in which only one party makes a payment of the net amount due after subtracting the amount owed by the other party. (2) The difference payment from one swap counterparty to the other after their gross obligations to one another are netted against each other.

Net Trade: A principal (dealer) trade on which no commission is charged. *See also Net Commission.*

Net Worth Ratio: Equity capital divided by total capitalization, often expressed as a percentage.

Net Yield: Dividend yield to a foreign investor after deducting a stock's net withholding tax.

Net-to-Gross Ratio (NGR): Typically, the ratio of the current net market value of open positions held between two counterparties to the current gross market value of positions between the same counterparties. The NGR is used to measure the value of netting, and in some capital calculations, to reduce the capital requirements of a financial intermediary to reflect the benefits of enforceable netting. *See also Gross*

Replacement Value (GRV), Net Replacement Value (NRV).

Netting Agreement: Contractual offset of payables against receivables to reduce credit exposure to a counterparty. Netting swap payments in bankruptcy, for example, reduces credit exposure to the net obligation of a counterparty. Netting in bankruptcy or insolvency may not be enforceable in all jurisdictions, but the U.S. federal bankruptcy code and the Financial Institutions Reform, Recovery, and Enforcement Act of 1989 (FIRREA) are designed to permit netting among U.S.-based counterparties. Other sovereign jurisdictions are generally following this example to protect the ability of their financial intermediaries to compete in international markets. *Also called Aggregation, Close-Out Netting, Right of Offset, Right of Setoff. See also Bilateral Netting, Legal Right of Setoff, Offset (2), Payment Netting.*

Netting by Novation: Replacement of all agreements between two parties with a single agreement and a single net payment stream. Formal netting by novation is often a response to financial distress on the part of one counterparty. Also called by various other names, most including the word "netting." *See also Bilateral Netting, Novation.*

Neural Network: An "artificial intelligence" decision-making process modeled on the human nervous system. A neural network searches for patterns in data, "learns" from experience, and develops rules to improve its recognition of patterns. Neural networks are of limited usefulness in some applications because their rules are not subject to traditional analytical evaluation.

Neutral Hedge: A combination of market risk-offsetting positions in related securities or other instruments designed to earn the risk-free interest rate on funds invested whether the underlying goes up or down slightly in price.

Neutral Hedge Ratio: The fraction of a point by which the price of an option contract is expected to change in response to a one-point change in the price of the underlying instrument. Mathematically, the first partial derivative of the option price with respect to the underlying price. If its neutral hedge ratio is 0.5, an option contract should change in price by about $0.50 per underlying unit for each $1 change in the price of the underlying. This relationship is the primary basis of risk management with instruments with option payoff patterns. Of course, higher derivatives, such as gamma and other relationships, must also be monitored and evaluated in an effective risk management program. *Also called Delta (1) (diagrams), Hedge Ratio. See also Delta/Gamma Hedge, Hedge, Stock Equivalent (2).*

New Issue Swap: Swap structures that convert an issuer's lowest relative borrowing cost structure to a structure that fits the issuer's liability management targets. For example, an AA-rated U.S.-based borrower might borrow at relatively lower cost in the fixed-rate dollar market than in the floating-rate sterling market. A lower-rated U.K. borrower might borrow at floating rates in sterling with only a small credit penalty. These borrowers could swap interest payments and/or currencies to their mutual advantage. A medium-term note offering from the AA-rated borrower might be sold with the express design of implementing such a swap.

Newey-West Correction: An extension of the White correction method that simultaneously corrects for heteroskedasticity and serial correlation in ordinary least squares regression analysis. *See White Correction.*

Newton-Raphson Method: A trial and error method for finding the root of an equation. This approach is often used to estimate the implied volatility of an option using the Black-Scholes option equation. Start with a reasonable estimate of volatility and calculate the theoretical option value. Then divide the difference between the theoretical value and the actual option price by the derivative of the Black-Scholes equation with respect to volatility evaluated at the estimated value for volatility, and reduce the prior estimate of volatility by this amount. Proceed in this fashion until the theoretical value and the actual price are sufficiently close.

Next Day Settlement (NDS): The standard for completion of certain securities transactions and fund transfers in which the transaction is completed the day after a trade or the day after agreement on the amount of a payment. Replaced by same day funds settlement (SDFS) for most securities-related funds transfers in the U.S. in early 1996. *See also Same Day Funds Settlement (SDFS).*

Nikkei-Linked Bond (NLB): An equity index-linked bond with the Nikkei 225 stock average as the underlying index.

Ninety-Ten (90-10) Strategy: A multiperiod option purchase plan that avoids large losses in any single investment period by committing 10% of portfolio assets to the purchase of options and investing the balance of the portfolio at interest. Variations from the ninety-ten ratio are common in practice.

No Arbitrage Condition: A boundary condition on option and underlying price relationships that eliminates the possibility of risk-free arbitrage between and among puts, calls, and underlying instruments. *See also Put/Call Parity.*

No Arbitrage Hypothesis: The notion that there is never a situation when the simultaneous purchase and/or sale of assets can result in a riskless profit.

No Cost Option: *See Premium Neutral, Premium Free Option, Zero Premium Option.*

No Cost Risk Reversal or Collar: *See Zero Premium Risk Reversal.*

No Rebate Cash-Out Option: The simplest variant of an up-and-out call or a down-and-out put where the seller's obligation is cancelled if the out strike is breached. Rebate structures are less common than they were in the 1980s.

No Regrets Options: Lookback options. Because lookback calls are always struck at the lowest price during the life of the option, and lookback puts are struck at the highest price, an investor will have no regrets that he might have gotten a more favorable strike. Lookback options carry a higher premium than standard options, so the size of the premium might be a source of regret. *See Lookback Option.*

Noise: A signal or item of market information that looks like news but has no implication for asset prices.

Nominal Quotation: *See Indicative Price (1).*

Non-Accelerating Inflation Rate of Unemployment (NAIRU): Sometimes called the natural rate of unemployment, this is the minimum rate of unemployment attainable without stimulating an increase in the inflation rate.

Non-Amortizing Instrument: A financial instrument with no scheduled reduction in notional principal or no repayment of actual principal before final maturity.

Non-Call Life (NCL) Bonds: Bonds not callable for redemption under any circumstances not specifically noted in the indenture.

Non-Callable Bond Equivalent Yield: *See Option-Adjusted Yield.*

Non-Clearing Member: An exchange member who does not carry positions or clear trades directly with an exchange clearing house. *See also Clearing Broker or Member.*

Non-Cumulative Preferred Stock: A preferred issue that is not entitled to payment of passed dividends before common dividends can be resumed.

Non-Deliverable Forward (NDF): A synthetic foreign currency forward contract on a non-convertible or thinly traded currency. These generally settle in the investor's base currency with terms set against an agreed posted or dealer rate.

Non-Detachable Warrants: Warrants that cannot be separated from their carrier bond and cannot be traded separately.

Non-Par Swap: Any swap with one or both of the equivalent securities underlying the swap payments selling at a discount or premium to parity. *See, for example, Discount Swap, High-Coupon Swap, Low-Coupon Swap.*

Non-Parametric Statistics: Inferential procedures not concerned with population parameters such as mean and standard deviation. The term "non-parametric" is often used to refer to inferential procedures that do not depend on the distribution of the population, although purists refer to the latter procedures as distribution-free statistics. *Also called Distribution-Free Statistics.*

Non-Parametric Test: A reference to any of several techniques used to describe the relationship between or among variables ordinally or by scenarios rather than in terms of statistical parameters. *See Distribution-Free Test.*

Non-Standard Options: *See Exotic Options.*

Non-Sticky Jump (NSJ) Bond: A collateralized mortgage obligation whose principal paydown is changed by the occurrence of one or more "triggering" event(s). Each time the trigger condition is met, the bond changes to its new priority for receiving principal, and it reverts to its old priority for each payment date that the trigger condition is not met.

Non-Systematic Risk: An element of price risk that can be largely eliminated by diversification within an asset class. In factor models estimated by regression analysis, it is equal to the standard error. *Also called Security Specific Risk, Idiosyncratic Risk, Unsystematic Risk. See also Systematic Risk, Diversification.*

Noon Average Rate Contracts (NARCs): Average rate options or forwards in currency markets with the rate calculated, as the name implies, from the average rate prevailing each day at noon in the primary market for the instrument.

Normal Density Function: The integral under the normal distribution function between two points or between one point and infinity. *See Probability Density Function.*

Normal Distribution: A probability distribution that describes the behavior of many natural and

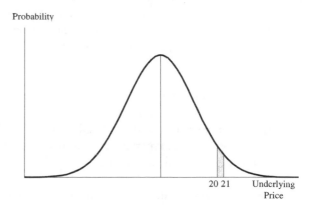

The Normal Density Function Between 20 and 21

manmade phenomena. The normal distribution is particularly useful because it can be described with a relatively simple equation, and analyzed to reveal detailed characteristics of segments of the distribution. For example, about 68% of total observations fall within one standard deviation on either side of the mean of a normal distribution. About 95% fall within two standard deviations, and more than 99% fall within three standard deviations of the mean. If a population distribution is not normal, a sample standard deviation will not have these distribution characteristics, which are often used to estimate the confidence an investigator can have that an observation falls inside or outside the population described by the distribution. *Also called Gaussian Distribution. See also Lognormal Distribution (diagram), Confidence Intervals, Standard Deviation (SD), Sigma (σ), Fat-Tailed Distribution.*

Normal Price of an Option: The option price predicted by an econometric model or any similar technique used to estimate typical underlying price–option price relationships. The normal price is an estimate based on the assumption that relationships that existed in a prior period are still meaningful. Normal price is a prediction of what an option price will be, not necessarily what it should be if fairly valued relative to likely payoffs at expiration. In contrast to a market neutral-hedged position taken at fair value, a position taken at normal price does not necessarily offer an investor the expectation of earning the risk-free rate if the neutral-hedged position is maintained (without frictional costs) through expiration. *Also called Average Price of an Option. See Fair Value of an Option.*

Normative Theory: A theory that describes a norm or standard of behavior that ought to be followed as opposed to one that actually is followed. *See also Positive Theory.*

Northwest Quadrant: The upper left quadrant of a scatter plot depicting combinations of return (vertical axis) and risk (horizontal axis). The points that lie in the northwest quadrant reflect higher than average returns combined with lower than average risk.

Notational: *See Notional Principal Amount.*

Note: A bond, traditionally with a life of more than one year and less than ten years. The terms "bond" and "note" are increasingly interchangeable. *See Bond.*

Note Issuance Facility (NIF): A standby credit agreement with a bank that permits a borrower to obtain financing on specific terms if the borrower does not succeed in selling its medium-term notes to investors. *Also called Issuance Facility, Revolving Underwriting Facility (RUF). See also Swingline, Facility.*

Note Over Bond (NOB) Spread: A yield curve spread created by selling the ten-year U.S. Treasury note futures contract and buying the thirty-year bond contract on the Chicago Board of Trade (CBOT). Alternately, an equivalent position can be created in the cash/repo market. An investor expecting inversion of a flat yield curve would buy the bond contract and sell the note contract in an appropriate ratio. An investor expecting a steepening yield curve would purchase the note contract and sell the bond contract in some proportion.

Notice Day: On many futures exchanges, one or more days on which a notice of intent to deliver may be filed.

Notional Bond: A standardized bond with hypothetical terms (coupon and maturity) that is the basis for a bond futures contract. Each market has its own standard terms and conversion factors for adjusting the terms of actual bonds to the notional standard.

Notional Principal Amount: The nominal value used to calculate swap payments and on which many other risk management contract payments are based. In an interest rate swap agreement, each period's rates are multiplied by the notional principal amount to determine the value of each counterparty's payment. *See also Loan Equivalent.*

Notional Principal Contract: Any swap, forward rate agreement, cap, floor, option, or similar instrument whose value is based on a nominal face amount that is not itself an obligation of one party to the other.

Notionnel: *Fr.* (1) Notional or standardized. (2) The French government bond contract traded on the Marché à Terme International de France (MATIF).

Novation: Replacing one or a series of contracts with a new contract, often with a third party replacing one of the original parties. Novation may be used to cancel agreements that have already been offset with other agreements. It is usually reserved for situations where any risk associated with the creation of a new agreement is offset by the release of capital or credit lines tied up in an unnecessarily complex structure. *See also Netting by Novation.*

Numerical Valuation Model: A pricing or valuation model that uses observed numerical relationships in addition to any theoretical formulas to develop a more complex, but hopefully more realistic, valuation model.

Obligations: *Fr.* Bonds.

Obligations Assimilables du Trésor (OATs): *Fr.* Government bonds underlying the principal French bond futures and options contracts.

Off-Balance Sheet (OBS) Instrument: A notional principal contract that changes an economic unit's risk structure without appearing as an asset or liability on a traditional balance sheet. Swaps, forward rate agreements, and various currency contracts are common OBS instruments. The fact that the balance sheet is not affected does not mean that the instrument is not reported. The size and impact of these instruments in the aggregate is usually summarized in a footnote to financial statements. Financial accounting standards-setting boards in most developed countries and regulators setting capital intermediaries have largely eliminated any disclosure advantage these instruments once had.

Off-Exchange Option Contract: Unlisted option designed to meet specific commercial or investment needs. *Also called Over-The-Counter (OTC) Option.*

Off-Exchange Task Force (OETF): An ad hoc group of Commodity Futures Trading Commission officials who monitor hybrid instruments and other OTC risk management contracts.

Off-Market Coupon Swap: An interest rate or other swap contract with a fixed-rate payment materially different from current coupon rates on bonds or notes of similar term. Ordinarily, this swap has a net present value that requires the counterparties to exchange an extra payment at the beginning or end of the swap tenor. *Also called Adjustment Swap. See High-Coupon Swap, Low-Coupon Swap, Discount Swap.*

Offer Price: The price at which a trader or market maker is willing to sell a security or future.

Office of the Comptroller of the Currency (OCC): The bank regulatory organization with primary responsibility for regulation of the administrative and investment policies of national banks in the U.S. It shares banking regulatory responsibility with a number of agencies, principally the Federal Reserve Board and the Federal Deposit Insurance Corporation.

Offset: (1) A closing transaction in an exchange market that cancels or eliminates an option or futures position. (2) A position with identical but opposite market price or rate responses that cancels some or all of the market risk of an open position but not necessarily the position's credit or settlement risk. *See also Netting Agreement.*

Offsetting Swap: A swap that exactly counters the interest rate or other market risk of a preexisting swap but does not cancel the earlier swap. This structure does not eliminate all risk of the earlier position.

Offsetting Transaction: A trade that creates a new position to offset the market risk characteristics of an old one, or, if the instruments in the new position are fungible with those in the old, cancels or closes out the old position. *See also Fungibility.*

Offshore: A strange and often ill-defined location where investment activity takes place with little or no taxation or regulation. Regulators and tax authorities often have little interest in regulating or taxing these activities because unregulated and untaxed investments can offset some of the market inefficiencies created by mainstream regulation and taxation. *See also Tax Haven.*

Oil Price Derivatives: Any structure available on common stocks, bonds, or indexes with oil as the primary underlying.

Omega ω: (1) The third derivative of the option price with respect to the price of the underlying. The derivative of gamma with respect to underlying price. *Also called Speed.* (2) Currency risk of an option on an instrument denominated in a different currency. *See Omega Risk (1), Quantity Adjusting Option (QUANTO) (1).* (3) One of the less frequently used option sensitivities; specifically, the sensitivity of the percentage change in option value to the percentage change in the underlying price.

Omega Risk: (1) Currency risk associated with an option contract on an underlying instrument priced in a different currency. *See also Quantity Adjusting Option (QUANTO) (1).* (2) Currency risk associated with translating the value of a currency option position in a different currency to a base currency. (3) Currency correlation risk.

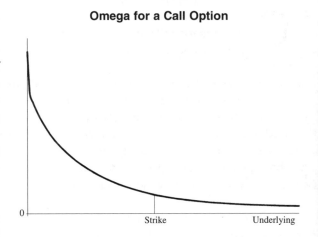

Omega for a Call Option

On the Wire: A reference to a bid or offer from a trader that is firm only if the party on the other side responds immediately. *See Firm Price.*

One Cancels the Other Order (OCO): A contingent order providing that one part of the order is cancelled if the other part is executed. For example, if an investor has limited funds to invest, he might place orders to buy a stock and a bond with the provision that the purchase of the stock cancels the order to buy the bond, and, conversely, that the purchase of the bond cancels the order to buy the stock. *See also Contingent Order.*

One-Off Transaction: (1) An unusual customized contract designed especially to meet a specific requirement, unlikely to be useful in many other risk management situations. (2) A transaction between two parties who do not usually trade with one another.

One-Sided (or -Tailed) Test: An hypothesis test in which the alternative to the null hypothesis maintains that not only is the parameter of interest different from that specified by the null hypothesis, but that this difference has a particular sign. *See also Two-Sided (or -Tailed) Test.*

One-Time Put Bond: A bond with a single opportunity to put it back to the issuer.

One-Touch Option: *See Touch Option.*

One-Way Floater: A floating-rate note with a coupon that can only increase in response to changes in an index rate. The coupon cannot decrease.

Open Interest: The number of listed option contracts of a class or series or the number of identical futures contracts outstanding at a particular time. Open interest figures are available on each listed contract and are often a better indicator than trading volume of public interest in a contract.

Open Order: *See Good 'Til Cancelled (GTC) Order.*

Open Outcry: A method of trading that brings representatives of buyers and sellers together to shout bids and offers. Open outcry provides a high degree of assurance that all contemporary bids and offers have an opportunity to be heard and matched with the most attractive offers and bids from investors on the other side of the market.

Opening: The start of a trading session.

Opening Purchase Transaction: A transaction in which an investor becomes the holder or buyer of an option or futures contract.

Opening Range: The price range at the beginning of a trading session. In some markets, this is simply an opening bid/asked spread; but, in some open outcry markets, there is actually a range of opening transaction prices. Different prices are possible if the market has no formal order matching system. *See also Closing Range.*

Opening Rotation: *See Rotation.*

Opening Sale Transaction: A transaction in which an investor becomes the writer or seller of an option or futures contract. *See also Closing Sale Transaction.*

Operating Free Cash Flow: An estimate of the fundamental underlying earning power of a corporation. *Similar terms include Real Economic Earnings (REE), Sustainable Earnings Level.*

Opportunistic Investment Manager: A portfolio manager who will invest in any market or any asset class that he believes will provide a superior return.

Opportunity Loss or Cost: The value of a lost chance or a potential profit that was not realized because a course of action was taken that did not permit the investor to obtain that profit. The actual or expected cost of following one course of action measured relative to the most attractive alternative. Opportunity loss is not reflected in an accounting statement. An example of an opportunity loss would be the $20 per share profit forgone by a covered call writer who sells a call with a $45 strike price for a $5 premium, only to see the underlying stock jump to $70 in response to a takeover bid.

Opportunity Value: *See Volatility Value.*

Optimal Portfolio: The portfolio that yields the highest level of expected utility. In portfolio theory, it is the portfolio located at the point on the efficient frontier where the investor's indifference curve is tangent to the efficient frontier. *See Indifference Curve (diagram).*

Optimization of a Portfolio: (1) A process that maximizes expected utility as a function of exposure to the component assets, where expected utility is defined as expected return minus the product of risk aversion and variance. (2) Use of a linear or quadratic model to structure a portfolio to maximize or minimize yield, long-term rate sensitivity, etc., or to increase or reduce exposure to certain industries, market sectors, or macroeconomic factors, subject to prespecified constraints. *Also called Portfolio Optimization.*

Optimized Portfolio As Listed Securities (OPALS): Exchange-traded equity instruments based on an optimized equity index tracking portfolio. The optimized stock portfolio is designed to track a single country equity index with fewer issues than the index contains. OPALS may be sold before expiration or settled by physical delivery of the underlying shares. The product is designed for cross-border equity investors who cannot use futures efficiently or for regulatory reasons and who cannot justify their own country-by-country equity operation.

Option: A stipulated privilege of buying or selling a stated property, security, or commodity at a given price (strike price) within a specified time (for an American-style option, at any time prior to or on the expiration date). A securities option is a negotiable contract in which the seller (writer), for a certain sum of money called the option premium, gives the buyer the right to demand within a specified time the purchase (call) or sale (put) by the option seller of a specified number of bonds, currency units, index units, or shares of stock, at a fixed price or rate, called the strike price or rate. Many options are settled for cash equal to the difference between spot value and the aggregate strike price rather than by delivery of the underlying. In the U.S. and many other countries, stock options are written for units of 100 shares. Other units of underlying coverage are standard in other option markets. Options are ordinarily issued for periods of less than one year, but longer-term options are increasingly common. *See Call Option (diagrams), Combination Option, Commodity Option, Expiration Date (1), Premium, Put Option (diagram), Terms of an Option Contract, Option Contract.*

Option Business: *See Premium Business.*

Option Buyer: The investor who buys options to increase leverage, hedge the risks in a portfolio of assets or liabilities, or attain other investment or liability management objectives.

Option Contract: In OTC options, a contract document sets forth the provisions of the option. The terms of a listed option are stated in clearing corporation documents. The buyer's evidence of ownership of an exchange-traded option is his confirmation slip from the executing broker. *See also Option, Terms of an Option Contract.*

Option Hedge: A partially or fully price-hedged position where the investor sells more than one risk-offsetting option against each corresponding underlying unit. The net effect of this position is to maximize the option seller's profit when the underlying sells at the strike price at expiration. The rate of

Option Hedge

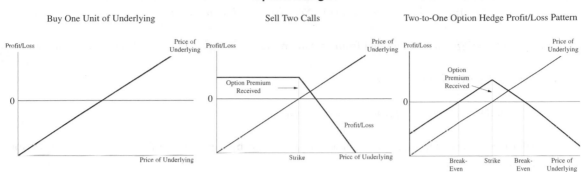

return at expiration declines if the shares sell either above or below the strike price. The writer loses money only if the stock rises or falls beyond a break-even point at expiration. *Also called Ratio Write, Variable Hedge, Hedge. See also Covered Writer, Time Hedge, Reverse Option Hedge, Naked Option.*

Option Income Fund: An investment company following an option writing strategy designed to generate income beyond the normal dividend flow from underlying common stock positions. The risk of this strategy is that the manager will convert an investor's capital into "income."

Option on a Cap: *See Caption (diagram).*

Option on a Floor: *See Floortion.*

Option on a Spread: *See Spread Option (1). Also called Spreadtion.*

Option on a Swap: *See Swaption.*

Option on an Option: *See Compound Option (1) (diagram).*

Option Portfolio: Any portfolio that includes long option positions or collateralized short option positions.

Option Premium: (1) In the U.S., and sometimes other markets, the amount of money an option buyer pays for a conventional put or call or the quoted price of a listed option. (2) The amount by which the price of an option exceeds its intrinsic value. For example, if an option to buy XYZ Corporation at $100 is selling at $9, and the stock is selling at $103, the premium is said to be $6. To avoid confusion between (1) and (2), the term "option price" or "premium" is used to designate the market price of an option, and the term "premium over intrinsic value" is used to designate the amount by which the stock price must rise before the expiration date for the option buyer to break even, neglecting commissions. Premium over intrinsic value is also called time value, volatility value, or opportunity value, with differing degrees of accuracy and usefulness. *See also Premium (4), Time Value, Volatility Value.*

Option Replication: (1) A technique to create an option-like payoff pattern through a series of transactions in the underlying or in related futures contracts as in dynamic hedging and traditional portfolio insurance. *See Replicating Portfolios.* (2) Creating a long-term option out of a sequence of baskets of short-term options. As the price of the underlying moves, there may be a need to trade the replicating options dynamically, but long-term option replication with short-term options generally require fewer portfolio adjustments than option replication with the underlying or with related futures contracts. *Also called Synthetic Option.*

Option Specification Error: The error on a binomial tree that arises from the inability of the binomial lattice to represent the terms of the option accurately. *See also Saw-Toothed Convergence, Quantification Error.*

Option Spread: *See Spread (5).* Distinct from spread option, option-adjusted spread, and option on a spread.

Option Tender Bonds: *See Put Bonds.*

Option to Double: *See Double Option (2), Sinking Fund.*

Option Writer: An investor who sells options collateralized by a portfolio of securities or other performance bonds.

Option-Adjusted Duration: A modified duration calculation that incorporates the expected duration shortening effect of an issuer's embedded call provision. *Also called Adjusted Duration. See also Effective Duration, Modified Duration, Macaulay Duration, Partial Duration.*

Option-Adjusted Internal Rate of Return: An estimate of the internal rate of return adjusted to reflect the expected impact of an embedded option on the investment's cash flows.

Option-Adjusted Net Present Value: An estimate of the net present value of a financial instrument adjusted to reflect the value of an embedded option.

Option-Adjusted Spread (OAS): An alternate way to calculate the call-adjusted yield of callable bonds by comparing the option-adjusted yield to the non-callable bond equivalent yield and its spread versus the Treasury yield curve. *See also Call-Adjusted Yield, Option-Adjusted Yield.*

Option-Adjusted Yield: The expected yield to maturity of a bond or note after adjusting for the probability-weighted impact of an embedded option, usually an issuer's call provision. *See also Call-Adjusted Yield, Option-Adjusted Spread (OAS). Also called Non-Callable Bond Equivalent Yield.*

Option-Dated Forward: A forward foreign exchange contract with an option to select the date of exchange.

Optional Redemption Provision: A clause in some collateralized mortgage obligations (CMOs) that lets the issuer call some or all tranches to refinance them at more favorable rates.

Optioned Asset: The underlying asset to be delivered as specified in an option contract.

Optioned Stock: The underlying stock that is the subject of a stock option contract.

Options Clearing Corporation (OCC): The guarantor of listed security option contracts in the U.S. It is owned proportionately by each of the exchanges trading listed security option contracts. Similar organizations act as contract guarantors in most other option and futures markets. *See Clearing Corporation.*

Options Disclosure Document (ODD): Boilerplate warning distributed to prospective users of U.S. exchange-traded securities options.

Options Exchange: A securities or futures exchange authorized to trade listed options.

Options to Purchase or Sell Specified Mortgage-Backed Securities (OPOSSMS): The name is self-explanatory. One can only be amazed at what people will do to create an acronym.

Order-Driven Market: An auction market like most U.S. securities exchanges and most futures markets worldwide, where bids, offers, and prices are determined principally by the terms of orders arriving at a central marketplace. Specialist or dealer activity is secondary to the impact of public orders. *Compare to Quote-Driven Market.*

Order Flow: The customer purchase and sale inquiries coming to a dealer. A large dealer may be able to offer more competitive terms on a larger fraction of the orders he sees, because heavy order flow helps him judge the state of the market and increases the probability he will find the other side of a transaction soon without incurring large hedging costs.

Ordinary Differential Equation (ODE): A differential equation that contains only simple derivatives from functions with one variable.

Ordinary Least Squares: A technique for calculating the regression equation that minimizes the sum of the squares of the error terms; that is, the differences between the observed values for the dependent variable and the predicted values for the dependent variable. *See also Generalized Least Squares, Least Squares Regression Line (diagram).*

Ordinary Share: Common stock.

Original Issue Discount Bond: A bond issued at a price less than par.

Ornstein-Uhlenbeck Process: *See Mean Reversion.*

Orthogonal: Intersecting or lying at right angles. Uncorrelated variables are orthogonal because when plotted on a graph they form right angles to one of the axes.

Out of the Money: Refers to an option with no intrinsic value because the current underlying price is below the strike price of a call or above the strike price of a put. For example, a put at $100 when stock is selling at $105 is said to be 5 points out of the money. *See also At the Money, In the Money.*

Out Option: An option with an expiration price as well as an expiration date. The option contract expires or pays off (depending on specific contract terms) if the underlying trades at or through the outstrike price. In the case of a down-and-out call, for example, the option expires immediately if the underlying touches the outstrike before the stated expiration date. *Also called Over-and-Out Option, Special Expiration Price Option, Up-And-Away Option (2), Up-And-Out Call, Vanishing Option, Extinguishable or Extinguishing Option, Kick-Out Option, Knockout Option, Down-And-Out Put (diagram), Down-And-Out Call. See also Exploding Option, Path-Dependent Option, Barrier Option, Touch Option.*

Out-of-Sample Data: In modeling, data not used in estimation of a model that is used to test the model. For example, one may develop a model using data from 1970 through 1979. Then the model is tested with data from 1980 through 1989. The data from 1980 through 1989 is out-of-sample data. *See Holdout Period.*

Out-Trade: A transaction that appears on the records of only one of the trading parties. If differences cannot be reconciled, the trade is cancelled. *Also called DK'd Trade.*

Outliers: Extreme observations, usually in the tail(s) of a probability distribution. For some purposes, an analyst may wish to employ a statistical technique that reduces the impact of outliers. For other purposes, the outliers that represent situations of unusual risk or return might deserve increased analytical attention.

Outperformance Option: A call option with a payoff based on the amount by which one of two underlying instruments or indexes outperforms the other. *Also called Dual Option, Exchange Option, Specialty Option, Margrabe Option, Multi-Index Option, Relative Performance Option (RPO), Spread Option. See also Cross-Currency Option or Warrant Bonds. Compare to Alternative Option (diagram), Alternative Currency Option. See Diff or Difference Option, Rainbow Option, Multi-Asset Option.*

The Payout Patterns of an Outperformance Option

Outright Forward Currency Transaction: An isolated forward currency trade that is not part of a swap. *Also called Currency Forward. See also Forward Outright Rate.*

Outstrike: The price at which a down-and-out or up-and-out call or down-and-out or up-and-out put expires or pays off if the price of the underlying touches or trades through it under circumstances meeting the requirements of the contract. Generically, the term outstrike refers to any price at which the terms of a non-standard option change. *Also called Dropout Price.*

Over The Counter (OTC): A security or other instrument that is not traded on an organized exchange or a market that is not part of an organized exchange. OTC instruments can be created with any provisions allowed by law and acceptable to counterparties. OTC markets and instruments are less closely regulated in some ways than exchange markets and instruments. *See also Exchange-Traded Contracts.*

Over-and-Out Call: *See Up-and-Out Call.*

Over-and-Out Option: *See Out Option.*

Over-and-Out Put: *See Up-and-Out Put.*

Over-The-Counter (OTC) Option: *See Off-Exchange Option Contract.*

Over-the-Top Option: An up-and-out option.

Overcollateralization: The practice of posting more than adequate collateral, often to obtain a high debt rating from a credit rating agency or to comfort a creditor.

Overlay Risk Management: An approach to asset risk management that turns over most of the assets of a portfolio to managers selected for their unique skill in particular markets, and assigns an overlay manager responsibility for partial or full asset allocation and/or currency risk management. The overlay manager typically uses options, futures, swaps, and other derivative risk management instruments rather than cash markets to keep execution costs low. *See also Currency Overlay Management, Overlay Strategies.*

Overlay Strategies: Techniques to add risk management of currency or asset allocation on top of the activities of traditional portfolio managers. Call option overwriting, asset allocation, and currency overlays are probably the most common overlay strategies. *See also Overlay Risk Management.*

Overline Situation: A loan participation or other credit extension opportunity that is available because the borrower needs funding that would take him over the credit line that his normal lender can extend.

Overnight Delivery Risk: The risk incurred when one side of a trade settles the day before the other side. This overnight delay exposes one of the counterparties to the risk that the other side will fail to meet its obligations. *Also called Clean Risk (2). See also Daylight Risk Exposure.*

Overriding: *See Overwriting.*

Overwriting: Most frequently, the sale of stock index or common stock call options against a fixed common stock portfolio, with the stated expectation that the options, on average, will expire worthless or be repurchased at a profit. Call overwriting strategies are frequently complex, and may involve repurchasing unprofitable options and selling a larger number of options at a higher strike price in an attempt to turn losses into profits. Investor experience with overwriting strategies has been uneven. In general, overwriting adds modestly to returns in most periods with an occasional dramatic actual or opportunity loss in a bull market. Theory predicts that overwriting will reduce variance rather than enhance return, contrary to the statements of many overwriting advocates. Consequently, overwriters should not expect to improve their long-term risk-adjusted returns unless their strategies rely on finding price anomalies. This conclusion is complicated slightly by the fact that the option seller is selling convexity, and will, consequently, have a different return pattern. *Also called Overriding. See also Dynamic Overwriting.*

Pac Man Defense: A takeover defense pattern named after the video game. The original takeover target attempts to swallow (takeover) the original bidder.

Pack: A package of four consecutive three-month Eurodollar contracts used to create a synthetic one-year Eurodollar strip on the Chicago Mercantile Exchange. *See also Stub (4), Bundle.*

Package Trade: A portfolio trade.

Packaged Equity Trust Securities (PETS): *See Short-Term Equity Participation Units (STEP Units).*

Pairs Trading: Originally, a portfolio management technique based on a classic hedge: a manager looks at stocks in pairs, buying the one he expects to perform best and selling short the one he expects to underperform. The concept has been generalized to accommodate long and short portfolios with different performance expectations. *Also called Long-Short Portfolio. See also Market Neutral Investment Strategy.*

Par: The face value or nominal value of a security. Used more frequently for bonds and other fixed-income securities than for stocks. *See Face Value (1).*

Par Cap: The limit on principal obligations in a mortgage pool. They cannot exceed the unpaid mortgage balance.

Par Value Swap: A reference to the notional value characteristic of a standard swap that involves no initial exchange of principal.

Parallel Loans: A predecessor of the cross-currency swap in which a party in country A made a loan denominated in currency A to a party in country B. The party in country B, in turn, made a loan in currency B to the party in country A. This parallel loan structure has largely been abandoned in favor of notional swaps with netting agreements that expose the parties to substantially less credit risk.

Parallel Shift: A movement of each point on a yield curve up or down by the same distance. Many duration-matching and control strategies assume that any yield curve shifts will be parallel.

Parametric: Description of a relationship by a function. The normal distribution, for example, implicitly assumes the behavior of a random variable is well-modeled by reference to the normal density function.

Parametric Statistics: Inferential procedures that depend on population parameters. T tests and analyses of variance fall into this category.

Pareto Optimality or Efficiency: A desirable characteristic of a transaction or a new regulation in which at least one party is better off as a result of the change and no one is worse off.

Pari Passu: Two securities or obligations that have equal rights to payment are said to rank pari passu.

Parity: (1) The condition in which a bond sells at its nominal or face value. (2) The condition in which an option sells at its intrinsic value. The maximum of zero or spot minus strike for a call and the maximum of zero or strike minus spot for a put. *See also Fair Value of an Option, Intrinsic Value of an Option.*

Parity Graph: A representation of the value of a financial instrument when any premium from the insurance value of an option or the basis of a forward or futures contract has been eliminated by the passage of time—a valuation at expiration or in exercise. The hockey stick diagrams of option payouts at maturity are parity graphs.

Parity Value: *See Conversion Value.*

Parking a Security: (1) An illegal arrangement in which an investor buys shares from another party and holds them for a short period before reselling them to the original holder. The original holder frequently uses this technique in an attempt to create a tax loss. (2) An illegal technique used in corporate takeovers to assure ownership of a substantial block by a friendly money manager. The money manager is indemnified against loss by the party for whom the securities are parked.

Part Contingent Knock-In Option: A knock-in option characterized by a low initial premium and an additional premium paid if the knock-in trigger is activated. The initial premium is lower than the premium on a comparable straight knock-in option, but the total premium, including the contingent component, is greater than the premium on a comparable straight knock-in option.

Partial Collar: Partial collars may be used in asset allocation. A collar covering part of a portfolio might reduce downside exposure in the event of a significant decline, and reduce upside participation if the market for the underlying assets becomes overheated. This is a modest variation on the par-

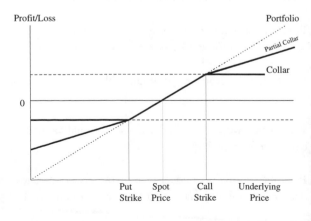

Partial Collar for Asset Allocation

ticipating collar, with both legs of the collar covering less than the value of the entire portfolio. *See Collar (2) (diagram). See also Participating Range Forward.*

Partial Differential Equation (PDE): A differential equation that contains two or more partial derivatives from functions with two or more variables.

Partial Duration: A technique for applying some of the principles of duration analysis to rate changes that affect only part of the yield curve, typically the shorter end of the curve. Partial durations sum to a value that is usually close to the overall effective duration. *Similar concepts are Reshaping Durations, Key Rate Duration. See also Macaulay Duration, Modified Duration, Effective Duration, Option-Adjusted Duration.*

Partial Lookback Warrant or Option: A warrant or option that provides a time window of, say, thirty to ninety days to set or reset the strike price at the most favorable level during that period. After that period, the option is an ordinary American-style option. Because the lookback characteristic covers a limited time, the partial lookback option sells for a price intermediate between a traditional option and a full lookback option. A call warrant of this general type is occasionally called an anti-crash warrant, because the reset allows the holder to obtain a lower strike if a crash occurs during the lookback period. *Also called Anti-Crash Warrant. See also Lookback Currency Option (diagram), Lookback Strike Option (diagram), Reset Option or Warrant (diagram), Step-Down Option or Warrant.*

Partially Protected Equity-Linked Note: A variation on the participating equity-linked note (ELN) in which the investor has full participation on the upside but only partial protection (or partial participation) on the downside.

Participating Account: A separate account at a financial institution used as a synthetic guaranteed investment contract (GIC). A participating account is not subject to claims from the institution's general creditors. *Also called Bank Investment Contract (BIC), Bank Deposit Agreement (BDA). See also Guaranteed Investment Contract (GIC), Synthetic Guaranteed Investment Contract (Synthetic GIC).*

Participating Cap: A partial cap that reduces but does not eliminate exposure to an upward price or rate move. The cap covers a smaller notional amount than the value of the underlying, giving the parties to the cap a participation structure when they average the capped and the uncapped positions.

Participating Capped Floating-Rate Note: A note that behaves like a mixture or an average of an ordinary floating-rate note and a capped floating-rate note. *Also called Participating Note. See also Floating-Rate Note (FRN), Capped Floating-Rate Note.*

Participating Collar: Managers use ordinary collars to confine their equity exposure to a range, to

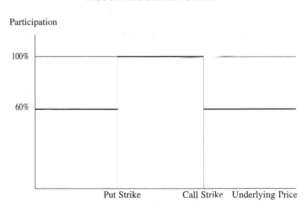

Participation Percentage with Asset Allocation Collar

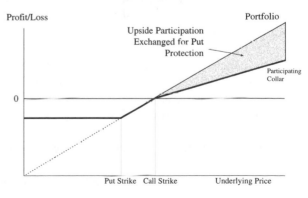

Participating Collar

avoid exposure to extreme movements in any direction. Users of participating collars may seek a firm floor return, combined with reduced participation above a certain level—reflecting the need to give up some upside to pay for downside protection. *See Collar (2) (diagram), Sliding Floor Plan.*

Participating Equity Preferred Stock (PEPS): *See Preference Equity Redemption Cumulative Stock (PERCS) (diagram).*

Participating Forward Contract: A contingent forward contract in which the buyer accepts a floor price below the current forward market in return for a fixed percentage participation in any favorable difference between the spot at expiration and the floor rate. Although used most frequently in currency markets, the participation structure is also used in equity and debt structures. The diagram shows a floor price equal to spot, but the floor could be above spot (but still below the forward price), particularly with a dividend or interest payment on the underlying and a low participation rate. Other things equal, the lower the floor, the higher the participation rate. *Also called Ratio Forward. See also Break Forward (diagram), Participation, Participating Interest Rate Agreement (PIRA) (diagram).*

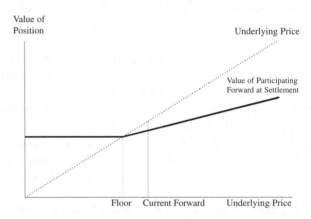

An Illustration of a Participating Forward Contract

Participating Interest Rate Agreement (PIRA): An off-exchange contract designed to meet an investor's or borrower's need to reduce exposure to adverse interest rate changes while continuing fractional participation in favorable interest rate changes. Similar in structure to a participating forward contract. *See also Participation, Participating Forward Contract (diagram).*

Participating Mortgage: A traditional mortgage loan with a supplemental provision that lets the lender share in any increase in the value of the underlying property in return for a lower basic interest rate. *Also called Shared Appreciation Mortgage (SAM).*

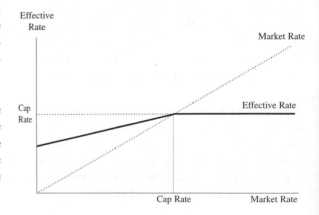

A Participating Interest Rate Agreement That Caps a Borrower's Cost of Funds and Provides Participation in Any Rate Decline

Participating Mortgage Strip: A fixed-rate senior obligation covered by the minimum cash flows due on a pool of participating mortgages. Note that, despite the name, the strip does not participate in cash flows above the minimum—unless a specific instrument carries unusual provisions.

Participating Note: *See Participating Capped Floating-Rate Note.*

Participating Option: Any option that changes the rate of participation in a price or rate movement beyond the strike. The term is usually applied only to options that give some participation below 100% in a price or rate movement beyond the strike. *Also called Profit-Sharing Option.*

Participating Range Forward: A variant of the equity risk reversal, range forward, or forward rate bracket structure with some participation in movement of the underlying below the lower strike or above the upper strike or both, as in the *Partial Collar. Also called Forward Plus.*

Participating Swap: An interest rate swap agreement with a participating interest rate agreement or cap on part of the notional principal modifying the floating-rate payments.

Participation: An option-like structure that typically provides a floor return combined with reduced exposure to a favorable return on the underlying, or a ceiling return combined with reduced exposure to an unfavorable return. The reduction in exposure to favorable events usually pays for the protection of the floor or cap. Intuitively, the most useful way to view a participation is as a combination or an average of an option and a forward or as an average of an option and cash. *See, for example, Participating Forward Contract (diagram), Participating Interest Rate Agreement (PIRA) (diagram). See also Loan Participation, Indexed Notes.*

Participation Agreement: *See Loan Participation.*

Participation Bond: A bond with a minimum required coupon and an additional payment based on the issuer's profitability. In contrast to a convertible bond, which participates in the price action of the underlying common stock, a participation bond has a variable interest rate, some of which is linked to corporate earnings. *Compare to Income Bond.*

Participation Certificate: (1) A security issued by a corporation with a payoff pattern similar to an equity-linked note. (2) A security issued by a corporation to create an additional class of equity shares with a different dividend rate or reduced restrictions on share transfer. *Also called Bearer (Participation) Certificate.*

Partly Paid Bonds: Debt instruments issued in the U.K. with part of the price paid at issuance and the balance paid in one or several installments. Interest is ordinarily paid only on the principal paid in.

Party at Interest: All persons (legal) providing services to an employee benefit plan subject to ERISA regulation. *See also Prohibited Transaction.*

Pass-Through Securities: Securitized mortgages or other debt contracts with interest and principal paid to the investor by the servicing intermediary shortly after interest payments are received from the borrowers. *Also called Pay-Through Securities. See also Securitization, Conduit Tax Treatment.*

Passing the Book: Major financial intermediaries have equity, fixed-income, and currency trading organizations operating in a number of time zones. Currencies, and to a lesser extent, fixed-income and equity positions, are traded in a twenty-four-hour market. Control of the intermediary's risk positions passes from one time zone to another in a procedure known as passing the book.

Passive Management: Most commonly, indexation of a portfolio, giving up the opportunity for superior performance within an asset class in return for protection from inferior performance. *See also Passive Manager.*

Passive Manager: An asset manager who invests assets in index portfolios or unmanaged baskets of securities and other instruments without attempting to select individual securities. Some passive managers, who made little or no effort to outperform an index in the past, now try to improve upon index returns with derivatives and return enhancement strategies, blurring the line between passive and active managers. *Contrast with Active Manager. See also Passive Management.*

Path Dependency: A situation where the terminal value of an option or a dynamic hedging strategy depends on the particular path of the underlying risky asset's price changes. By contrast, a path-independent strategy's terminal value depends only on the terminal value of the underlying risky asset.

Path-Dependent Floating-Rate Note: A floating-rate note with embedded caps or collars that limit the floating-rate adjustment to, for example, 25 basis points from one reset to the next. The rate is path-dependent because the adjustment limit constrains the maximum or minimum rate for later resets as a function of previous rates. *Also called Near Perfect Floating-Rate Note. Compare to Ratchet Swap.*

Path-Dependent Option: While the value of a traditional option depends only on the price of the underlying on the day of exercise or expiration, the value of a path-dependent option depends partly or exclusively on the price pattern the underlying follows in reaching exercise or expiration. Asian (average price or rate) options, lookback options, and barrier options are all examples of path-dependent options. If early exercise could be appropriate for an American option under certain circumstances, that option is also path-dependent in a sense. *See Average Price or Rate Option (APO, ARO) (diagrams), Exploding Option, In Option, Lookback Option, Out Option, Reset Option or Warrant (diagram).*

Pay as You Go Option: *See Installment Option (diagrams).*

Pay Back: *See Break-Even Point.*

Pay Later Option (PLO): Ordinarily, this name refers to a contingent premium option rather than a deferred premium option, but contract terms should be checked. *See also Contingent Premium Option (diagram), Deferred Premium Option.*

Pay on Exercise Option: *See Contingent Premium Option (diagram).*

Pay-In-Kind (PIK) Securities: Bonds, notes, or preferred stocks with interest or dividends paid in securities rather than cash. The securities used are usually identical to the underlying securities, but they occasionally have different terms. Issuance of PIKs usually suggests that the issuer has cash flow problems, but a PIK structure can be selected primarily to relieve an investor of reinvestment risk. A PIK bond with redemption in cash at maturity is the functional equivalent of a zero-coupon bond. *See also Exchangeable Payment-In-Kind (PIK) Preferred Stock.*

Pay-Through Securities: *See Pass-Through Securities.*

Payback Period: The time required to recover cash flows equal to the amount of an investment. *See Break-Even Time.*

Payer's Swaption: A swap option giving the holder the right to pay a fixed rate and receive a floating rate in an interest rate swap. Broadly analogous to a put on a fixed-rate instrument. *Also called Buyer's Right to Pay (BRP) Fixed Swaption, Swaption (diagram), Put Swaption.*

Payment Enhanced Capital Security (Peacs): The Canadian equivalent of *Prescribed Right to Income and*

Maximum Equity (PRIMEs).

Payment Netting: When partially offsetting swap payments are due on the same date, the party owing the most will send a difference check. *See also Netting Agreement.*

Payment Versus Payment (PVP): A simultaneous settlement standard in foreign exchange markets. In terms of safety, the equivalent of delivery versus payment (DVP) in securities settlement.

Payoff: *See Payout.*

Payout: The value of an option at expiration. *Also called Payoff.*

Payout Pattern: A graph of an option's value at expiration over a range of underlying prices.

Payout Protected Option: A put or call with a strike adjustment feature to compensate for periodic cash payouts such as dividends. In the conventional option market, which preceded the introduction of listed stock options in the U.S., put and call strikes were reduced by the amount of cash dividends paid on the stock while the option was outstanding. Today, payout protected options are usually designed to provide protection from unusual payouts, but not from ordinary cash dividends.

Pegging: A form of price stabilization that, through determined bids and/or offers, keeps a security price at a designated level or within a narrow range. Stabilization is legal in most markets only during underwritings and only when approved procedures are followed. *See also Stabilization.*

Penalty Bid: A stabilizing syndicate bid that leads to the loss of selling concession by any syndicate member whose customers hit the bid. *See also Syndicate Bid.*

Penny Stock: Any stock with a low price, usually less than $1 per share in the U.S.

Pension Benefit Guaranty Corporation (PBGC): The U.S. government agency that collects insurance premiums from sponsors of defined benefit pension plans, and assumes the assets and most of the liabilities of failed plans.

Pension Livrée: *Fr.* A financing and securities lending technique used in French markets comparable in structure to a repurchase agreement. *See also Réméré, Repurchase Agreement (Repo), (RP).*

Percent Cap: An interest rate cap contract with a payout that has a variable—often a percentage relationship—to the payout on a normal cap. The payout on a percent cap is usually lower than the payout on a standard cap. A percent cap payout might rise more slowly than a normal cap payout at lower rate levels and at the same rate as the standard cap payout after rates exceed a designated level. Many variations are possible.

PERCS: *See Preference Equity Redemption Cumulative Stock (PERCS).*

Perfect Divisibility: The notion that a quantity can be divided into infinitely small units. The assumption is often necessary for exact hedging. Real world financial instruments are often not perfectly divisible.

Perfect Swap: *See Zero Basis Risk (Zebra) Swap.*

Performance Attribution System: An analytical framework that isolates the effects and measures the return contributions of market allocation, currency management, and security selection decisions. Performance attribution is used to evaluate the quality of the separate asset allocation and selection decisions that create a portfolio.

Performance Bond: (1) A name preferred by some futures exchanges for what is more popularly called margin. *See also Margin.* (2) Any surety for performance used to collateralize a financial contract.

Performance Equity-linked Redemption Quarterly paid Security (PERQS): Synthetic (dealer-issued) preferred equity redemption cumulative stock (PERCS). *Also called Synthetic High-Income Equity-Linked Debenture (SHIELD), Short-Term Appreciation and Investment Return Trust (STAIR). Compare to Equity-LinKed Security (ELKS).*

Performance Fee: *See Incentive Fee.*

Performance Index Paper (PIP): A commercial paper variation on the currency coupon swap. The rate on the paper is denominated and paid in a base currency, but the rate rises or falls depending on the exchange rate with an alternate currency. *See Equity-Linked Note (ELN) (diagrams).*

Performance Plus Shares: Synthetic common stock or stock index instruments issued by a financial intermediary that promises the buyer the total return from the underlying security or index plus an additional return based on a dividend withholding tax credit, a stock loan premium, or some other element of return that the intermediary can obtain more easily than the buyer of these special shares.

Performance-Linked Equity Securities (Perles): Synthetic "shares" in a publicly traded corporation issued by a financial intermediary, often as a mechanism to avoid a tax or regulatory obstacle to cross-border ownership. *See also Qan Macs.*

Peril: A risk or risky event. Used primarily in insurance.

Period Specific: The notion that a particular result depends on the particular period during which it is measured, and that the result is not necessarily characteristic of other past periods or of the future.

Periodic Auction Reset Securities (PARS): A synthetic tax-exempt (municipal) floating-rate note. *See also Auction Rate Note.*

Periodic Cap: A provision of an adjustable-rate mortgage that limits the maximum rate charged for a time interval, typically six to twelve months. *See Step-Up Cap.*

Periodic Reset Swap: A swap with a floating-rate payment based on the average rate on the reference index rate rather than the rate on one day.

Periodic Return: The percentage change in the value of an asset or investment, including reinvestment of income, from the beginning to the end of a period, assuming no contributions or disbursements.

Perpendicular Spread: *See Vertical Bear Spread (diagram), Vertical Bull Spread (diagram).*

Perpetual Floating-Rate Note: A floating-rate note with no fixed maturity. The rate reset mechanism may include a procedure under which the investor could force redemption if the floating rate were no longer attractive. For symmetry, the notes would ordinarily be callable under certain conditions.

Perpetual Preferred Stock (Perp): A fixed-rate equity instrument with no participation in the issuer's profit and no promise of principal repayment. Issued directly or in conversion of other instruments by banks subject to the Basle Capital Adequacy Directive. Perps are counted as Tier I capital. *See also Convertible Capital Note or Security.*

Perpetual Warrant: A warrant granting the right to buy shares of common stock at a fixed price with no expiration date. A perpetual warrant is only exercised if the stock's dividend rate is high enough and safe enough to entice the warrantholder to exercise and claim the forward dividend stream.

Peso Problem: (1) A perennial discount (high money market rate) on a currency officially pegged to the U.S. dollar or some other reference currency. The discount exists because the market perceives a small immediate probability of a large devaluation. (2) Generically, the perception, embedded in a price or rate, of a small probability of a large change.

Petrobond: A debt instrument (usually with a below market interest coupon) with the principal repayment indexed to oil prices.

Phantom Income: Reportable or taxable income without a corresponding contemporary cash flow. An example is the taxable income from a portfolio holding of zero-coupon bonds. A cash flow statement should highlight such problems.

Physical Commodities: Agricultural and industrial products that may underlie commodity futures contracts, as distinguished from financial instruments that may underlie financial futures contracts.

Pick-Up: A gain in yield from the sale of one security and the purchase of another. Used primarily in the bond market. *See Swap (2).*

Pin Risk: The market value risk of an at-the-money option shortly before expiration. A small move in the underlying can have a highly leveraged impact on the value of the option. *Also called Exploding Delta.*

Pink Sheet Stocks: Relatively inactive over-the-counter stocks not included in the Nasdaq daily listing or supplementary listings. Quotations are actually provided on pink sheets of paper, compiled daily, and distributed to dealers, investors, and pricing services.

Pips: Basis points. The term is used primarily in currency markets. *Also called Points (1), Tick.*

Pit: A location on the floor of an exchange where trading in a particular instrument or type of instrument occurs. Pits usually have physical features such as tiers of steps, screens, and electronic equipment to facilitate trading and communication.

Pit Broker: *See Local.*

Plain Vanilla: A reference to a standard financial instrument with few or no bells and whistles.

Plan Assets: A highly technical definition of what instruments an employee benefit plan governed by the Employment Retirement Income Security Act (ERISA) can hold, and what form it can hold them in. Many important "positions" are not defined as plan assets.

Planned Amortization Class (PAC) Bond: A collateralized mortgage obligation that pays principal based upon a predetermined schedule, derived by amortizing the collateral at two different prepayment speeds. These two speeds are the endpoints for the "structuring PAC range." The PAC II range must be tighter than the PAC I range; PAC IIIs are defined as classes with a structuring range narrower than that of the PAC IIs; and so forth. *See also Busted Planned Amortization Class (PAC) Bond, Super Planned Amortization Class (Super PAC) Bond, Very Accurately Defined Maturity (VADM) Bond, Interest Only (IO) Obligation, Principal Only (PO) Obligation.*

Platykurtic Distribution: A distribution that has thin tails and a relatively flat middle. Compared with a normal distribution, a larger fraction of its observations are clustered within two standard deviations of the mean.

Playing the Yield Curve: With a normal yield curve, funding a long-term asset with short-term liabilities. *Also called Rolling Down the Yield Curve.*

Plaza Accord: An agreement reached in 1985 by France, Germany, Japan, the U.S., and the U.K. to drive down the price of the dollar. By 1985, the dollar had reached an all-time high relative to many major currencies, and the U.S. was experiencing a large trade deficit. The coordinated efforts by these countries resulted in a 30% decline in the dollar over the next two years.

Points: (1) Digits added to or subtracted from the fourth decimal place (basis points) to convert a spot exchange rate to a forward rate or to reflect the trading basis in a currency market. *See Pips.* (2) Multiples of the minimum price fluctuation or tick in any market. (3) Payments by a mortgagee to prepay servicing costs and obtain a lower net interest rate.

Poison Pill: A takeover defense in which the target company issues large amounts of a convertible issue with a low exercise price that dilutes any common stock position the hostile acquirer might establish.

Poison Put: (1) A provision of a bond or note that makes the instrument puttable to the issuer following a change of control or a restructuring that reduces the credit quality of the issue. *Also called Event Risk Covenant.* (2) A right distributed to common stockholders that makes some or all of their stock puttable to an acquirer at a very high price in the event of a hostile takeover.

Poisson Jump: The presence of a second distinct return generation process that adds occasional large movements to the random noise movements in a time series. For example, occasional major news events affect securities prices more dramatically than day-to-day noise trading. A price series may have fat tails because of this combination of processes. *See also Jump Process.*

Pollution Futures: Usually a reference to a futures contract based on U.S.-based utilities' transferable rights to emit sulphur dioxide.

Ponzi Scheme: Any investment program that offers impossibly high returns and pays these returns to early investors out of the capital contributed by later investors. Named for Carlo Ponzi, who promoted such a scheme in the 1920s based on a theoretical arbitrage in international postal reply coupons. Sometimes called a pyramid scheme because the structure must be supported by a broader and broader base of gullible investors as time passes. *Also called Pyramid Scheme.*

Pool: *See Reinsurance.*

Pooling of Interests: One of two principal methods of accounting for business combinations through an exchange of common stock. In contrast to the other method, purchase accounting, a pooling of interests is accounted for by adding together the book values of the combined companies. In purchase accounting, good-will is often created that must be amortized against earnings over a forty-year period. Pooling of interests is often preferred, but in the U.S. the companies involved in the pooling must meet clearly defined guidelines for independence for a two-year period prior to the acquisition, and agree to avoid systematic or preplanned changes in ownership of the combined operation. Pooling encounters fewer restrictions outside the U.S. *See also Purchase Accounting.*

Pop-Up Option: An up-and-in option.

Portfolio Approach to Risk Management: Rather than focus on the specific risk characteristics of each position or obligation, an asset or liability manager using a portfolio approach analyzes and aggregates risks by type, trying to achieve an overall balance of risk and return. *See also Global Hedge.*

Portfolio Currency Protection Option (PCPO): *See Equity-Linked Foreign Exchange (Elf-X) Option (diagrams).*

Portfolio Income Note (PIN): *See Equity-Linked Note (ELN) (diagrams).*

Portfolio Insurance: Any of several techniques used to change a portfolio's market exposure systematical-ly in reaction to prior market movements, with the objective of avoiding large losses and securing as much participation as possible in any favorable market move. The most popular forms of portfolio insurance have attempted to create synthetic options with portfolio trades in the cash or futures markets. *See also Dynamic Hedging, Constant Proportion Portfolio Insurance (CPPI), Portfolio Trade, Program Trading.*

Portfolio Optimization: *See Optimization of a Portfolio (2).*

Portfolio System for Institutional Trading (POSIT): An electronic order matching (trading) system for common stocks used primarily by institutional investors.

Portfolio Tilting: The practice of making changes in the industry sector or style weighting in a portfolio in an attempt to improve investment performance.

Portfolio Trade: The purchase or sale of a basket of stocks. By NYSE definition, a portfolio trade (or pro-gram trade) includes more than fifteen different stocks with a total value of $1 million or more entered as a coordinated transaction. Portfolio trades may be undertaken to increase or reduce market exposure in a port-folio or as one side of an EFP or index arbitrage trade. *Also called Basket Trade. See Exchange of Futures for Physicals (EFP), Index Arbitrage, Portfolio Insurance, Program Trading.*

Position Limits: Exchange rules mandated by the SEC that restrict the size of option positions that can be taken by a single investor or a group of investors acting in concert. Generally, CFTC-regulated financial futures options have no meaningful position restrictions. These ill-considered regulations have forced portfo-lio insurers to undertake dynamic hedging of stock positions in the stock or stock index futures markets rather than in the option markets. The contribution of position limits to the impact of portfolio insurance trades on the stock market was largely responsible for the magnitude of the October 1987 stock market break.

Position Trading: An approach to trading and market making in which a trader typically holds meaningful positions for a period of time, rather than attempting to trade out of a position by the end of the day to avoid carrying it overnight.

Positive Carry: The net gain from carrying a position when the cost of funds is less than the yield on the securities held.

Positive Theory: A theory that purports to describe behavior that is actually practiced as opposed to norms or standards that ought to be practiced. *See also Normative Theory.*

Post-Execution Reporting System (PERS): The American Stock Exchange's equivalent of the NYSE SuperDOT electronic order entry and reporting system. *See also SuperDOT.*

Potential Presettlement Exposure: Possible credit exposure that may arise due to favorable market price or rate movement before a contract matures.

Power Bond: (1) A note or bond with a coupon that bears an exponential relationship to a reference rate. One of the most common power bond coupons is a function of LIBOR^2 (squared). *See also LIBOR^2 Swap.* (2) A variant of the reverse floating-rate note with the interest rate set equal to the value of

$$\text{Coupon} = \sqrt{(\text{Fixed Rate})^2 - (\text{Floating Rate})^2}$$

See also Reverse Floating-Rate Note (diagram), Power Warrant.

Power Warrant: A cousin of the power bond, the payout of a power warrant is determined by the square of a rate or spread. There is usually a cap on the payout to insure the solvency of the issuer. *See also Power Bond.*

Praecipuum: A fraction of the management fee of an underwriting calculated on the face amount of the issue and taken by the lead manager(s) for coordinating the issue.

Pratt-Arrow Risk Aversion: A method for comparing the implications of different utility functions for individual decision-making governed by the Von Neumann-Morgenstern axioms of behavior. Pratt-Arrow measures of local risk aversion define risk premia according to one's absolute and relative tolerance for risk.

Precommitment Capital Standard: An approach to capital requirements that literally lets a bank set its own capital requirement for a specific line of business. If an activity subsequently "uses" more capital than the bank set aside (perhaps as a combined result of high volume and unanticipated losses), the regulator imposes penalties. This approach to setting capital requirements developed alongside, and is often linked to, the Internal Model Approach to Capital Management. *See Internal Model Approach to Capital Management.*

Prediction Bias: Analogous to forward rate bias in the currency markets, prediction bias is a reference to the tendency of forward interest rates to forecast higher future spot interest rates than the rates that actually occur. *See also Forward Rate Bias, Yield Curve (diagrams).*

Preference Equity Redemption Cumulative Stock (PERCS): A limited-term, limited participation convertible preferred stock with an enhanced dividend. PERCS shares are convertible at maturity into one share of the underlying common stock if the common stock is selling below the PERCS strike price, and into a fractional share equal in value to the PERCS strike value if the common is selling above the strike. After three years, the PERCS shares are converted to common automatically on these terms, and the dividend drops back to the regular common stock dividend. PERCS were the most successful financial product of 1991, because they provided a relatively high current yield in a declining yield environment. As the illustration indicates, the PERCS is essentially a covered call structure. Synthetic PERCS have been issued by third-party issuers, largely investment banks. *Also called Mandatory Conversion Premium Dividend Preferred Stocks (MCPDPS),*

Stock and PERCS or PERQ Comparison

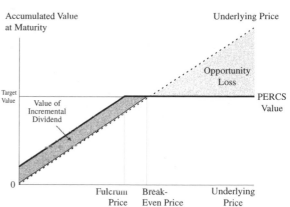

A Comparison of PERCS and Common Stock Values

Participating Equity Preferred Stock (PEPS), Preferred Income Participation Security (PIPS), Equity Redeemable Bond, Common-linked Higher-Income Participation Security (CHIPS), Equity Yield Enhancement Security (EYES), Short-Term Equity Participation Units (STEP Units). See Performance Equity-Linked Redemption Quarterly paid Security (PERQS), Short-Term Appreciation and Investment Return Trust (STAIR), Yield Enhanced Stock (YES), and many other names. See also Americus Trust.

Bond + Short Put = PERCS

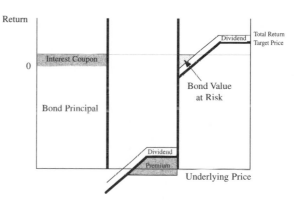

Preferred Habitat Hypothesis: An hypothesis about the term structure of interest rates (the relationship between interest rates and term to maturity) proceeding from the principle that groups of investors prefer to hold bonds within particular maturity ranges to hedge their liabilities or to comply with regulatory requirements. To the extent that the demand for bonds from one group of investors increases relative to the demand from other groups, yields within the maturity range where relative demand has risen will fall relative to the yields within the maturity range where the demand is slack. *Also called Segmented Market Hypothesis.*

Preferred Income Participation Security (PIPS): *See Preference Equity Redemption Cumulative Stock (PERCS).*

Preferred Purchase Unit: *See Mandatory Convertible, Convertible Capital Note or Security.*

Preferred Redeemable Increased Dividend Equity Security (PRIDES): *See Dividend Enhanced Convertible Security (DECS). See also Debt Exchangeable for Common Stock (DECS).*

Preferred Stock: An equity or ownership instrument with certain preferences or priorities over common stock as to dividends and/or distribution of assets upon liquidation.

Premium: (1) In the U.S., and most continental European markets, the amount of money an option buyer pays or an option writer receives for an OTC put or call or the price of an exchange-listed option. *See Option,*

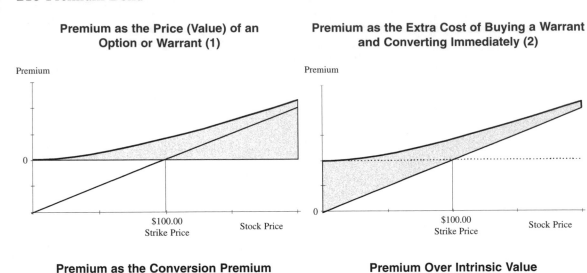

Premium as the Price (Value) of an Option or Warrant (1)

Premium as the Extra Cost of Buying a Warrant and Converting Immediately (2)

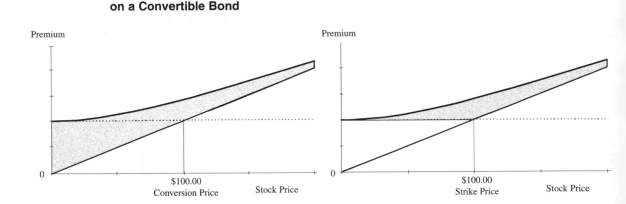

Premium as the Conversion Premium on a Convertible Bond

Premium Over Intrinsic Value

Call Premium. (2) In warrant markets based on the traditions of the U.K., premium is the amount by which the value of an investor's position would decrease if the option or warrant were exercised immediately. *See also All-In Premium, Conversion Premium (on a Convertible Bond) (diagram), Gearing (diagram), Leverage.* (3) In convertible bond markets, the amount by which the value of a position would decrease if the conversion occurred immediately. *See also Conversion Premium (on a Convertible Bond) (diagram), Option Premium (2).* (4) The amount by which the price of an option exceeds its intrinsic value. For example, if an option to buy XYZ Corporation at $100 is selling at $9, and the stock is selling at $103, the premium is often said to be $6. To avoid confusion between (1) and (4), the term "option price" or "premium" is used to designate the market price of an option, and the term "premium over intrinsic value" is used to designate the amount by which the underlying price must move beyond the strike price (for out-of-the-money options) or the current price (for at- or in-the-money options) before expiration for the option buyer to break even, neglecting commissions. *See also Time Value (diagram).* (5) The amount by which a coupon-bearing debt instrument sells over par because its coupon provides an above market yield. (6) The quality or credit yield differential that an issuer must pay above the rate on a government bond with a comparable maturity. (7) The amount by which the price on a futures contract exceeds the price of another contract or the underlying cash instrument. *See also Basis.*

Premium Bond: A bond selling above par because its coupon is higher than current market levels.

Premium Business: In Switzerland, the functional equivalent of a call option contract in the form of a cancellable forward agreement that gives the buyer the right to buy the shares on the due date or to withdraw from the contract. *Also called Option Business. See also Abandonment (1).*

Premium Coupon Synthetic Collateralized Mortgage Obligation: Any combination of discount coupon (below market rate) interest only and principal only strips used to create a synthetic, mortgage-backed instrument with slow prepayment and an above market current yield.

Premium Currency: A currency in which interest rates are lower than rates in the reference (domestic) currency. For many years, the yen and the DM have been premium currencies with respect to many other world currencies. Interest rates in yen and DM were low relative to rates denominated in other currencies. Interest rates and exchange rates are kept in equilibrium by an arbitrage mechanism, but it may be useful to think of premium currencies as belonging to countries with relatively low expected inflation rates. *See also Interest Rate Parity, Discount Currency.*

Premium Free Option: A zero net premium option such as a zero cost collar where the premium is "paid" with the premium from the sale of another option. *Also called No Cost Option, Premium Neutral Option, Zero Premium Option.*

Premium/Gearing Ratio: Premium (3) (U.K. definition) divided by gearing. Often used in the U.K. warrant market as a rough indication of the attractiveness of a warrant. Unfortunately, many of the major determinants of warrant value, such as volatility, interest rates, dividend yields, and even the extent to which the warrant is in or out of the money, are ignored or seriously distorted by this calculation. In the diagram with the definition of gearing, the relationship between the premium (3) line and the gearing line when the warrant is in the money indicates that the premium/gearing ratio is sensitive to the life of the warrant and the level of interest rates. *See also Gearing (diagram).*

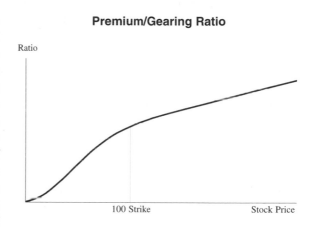

Premium Income: A frequently used term for the proceeds from the sale of an option contract. The term inappropriately refers to the reward side of the transaction with no mention of the possible opportunity loss associated with fulfillment of the option obligation.

Premium Neutral Option: A multiple option position where the net premium exchanged between the two counterparties, or paid and received by one counterparty, is zero. *Also called No Cost Option, Premium Free Option, Zero Premium Option.*

Premium Put Convertible Bond: In addition to the traditional features of a convertible bond, this instrument has an embedded put that permits the investor to redeem it at a premium over parity at some point(s) over the life of the bond. A feature of the liquid yield option note (LYON).

Premium Swap: *See High-Coupon Swap.*

Premium Trigger Option: A variant of the contingent premium option, where the underlying price at which the premium payment is triggered is above the strike price of a call option or below the strike price of a put.

The premium on a premium trigger option is greater than the premium on a corresponding contingent premium option.

Prepackaged Bankruptcy: A Chapter 11 filing characterized by prior consent from all parties to a reorganization plan. The prior consents reduce costs and permit prompt emergence of the reorganized company from bankruptcy.

Prepaid Swap: (1) A (physical) commodity forward contract featuring an upfront payment by the buyer equal to the present value of future commodity deliveries. The commodity deliveries may be priced at spot prices in effect on each delivery date, making the transaction a loan secured by an obligation to deliver the commodity at future market prices. Alternately, the contract may call for delivery of specific quantities on each delivery date, in effect fixing future delivery prices. (2) An annuity-like transaction in which the present value of future payments on one side of a swap is paid up front, and the other (variable) side payments are paid on a traditional swap schedule. The functional equivalent of a variable-rate loan. *See Reverse Zero-Coupon Swap.*

Prepayment: A payment of principal prior to the scheduled or required payment date.

Prepayment Option: (1) A mortgagee's right to prepay a mortgage, sometimes subject to a fee or penalty. The prepayment option may be exercised if the building is sold or if interest rates decline and the mortgage can be refinanced at a lower rate. (2) The embedded call option that allows a bond issuer to retire or refinance a bond prior to its nominal maturity. *See also Callable Securities, Embedded Option, Mortgage Prepayment Cap, Interest Only (IO) Obligation, Refi Rate.*

Prepayment Risk: The opportunity cost associated with early principal repayment of high-yield debt instruments. Common examples include prepayment of mortgage debt and call of high-coupon bonds. *See also Reinvestment Risk.*

Prescribed Right to Income and Maximum Equity (PRIME): PRIMEs, the income component of an Americus Trust unit, were the equivalent of a five-year covered call writer's position at issuance. *See Americus Trust, Special Claim On Residual Equity (SCORE) (diagram), Termination Claim.*

Present Value: The current value of a future cash flow or series of cash flows discounted at an appropriate interest rate or rates.

Presettlement Credit Risk: The risk of a default event prior to the settlement of a transaction. The specific event leading to default can range from disavowal of a transaction, default of a trading counterparty before the credit of a clearing house is substituted for the counterparty's credit, or something akin to Herstatt risk, where one party settles and the other defaults on settlement. *Also called Herstatt Risk. See also Settlement Risk.*

Value of Americus Trust PRIME Termination Claim

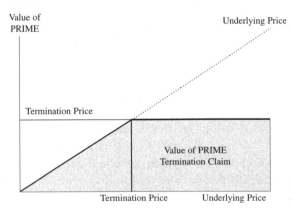

Prêt de Titres: *Fr.* Stock lending.

Price Earnings Ratio: A stock's price per share divided by a reported or forecast figure for annual earnings per share.

Price Jump: An abrupt change in the price of an asset that prevents anyone from trading the asset at an intermediate price. Price jumps reduce the ability of traders to replicate option-like payoffs through dynamic trading strategies. Assets prone to price jumps tend to have leptokurtic (fat-tailed) return distributions. *See Jump Process.*

Price Limits: A system of fixed or variable constraints on some futures price changes in a single trading session. Limits are imposed on most physical commodity futures and some financial futures. The rules of each exchange should be checked to determine how that exchange handles trading when the price goes limit up or limit down. Variable limits may expand price limits during volatile market periods. *See also Limit Up/Limit Down, Trading Limit (2).*

Price Risk: Exposure to loss as a result of a change in the market price of a physical commodity or a financial instrument.

Price Value of a Basis Point (PV 01 or PVBP): *See Value of a Basis Point (PV 01 or PVBP).*

Primary Market: The market where issuers sell newly issued securities to investors, either directly or through financial intermediaries. *See also Secondary Market, Third Market, Fourth Market.*

Prime Rate: A posted or administered rate sometimes used as a base rate for loans to a bank's financially strong borrowers. Market determined rates have replaced the prime rate in many applications.

Principal: (1) Par or face value of a debt instrument or preferred stock. (2) The value of funds invested, the base for a return on investment calculation.

Principal Components Analysis: A relatively simple and mechanical procedure for obtaining statistical measures of factors to use in a multifactor model of security returns. Available in many statistical software packages, principal components analysis operates by constructing one factor that explains the greatest part of historical return variability. It then defines a second factor, unrelated to the first, that explains the next greatest amount of return variability. The third and successive factors are defined similarly.

Principal Exchange Rate-Linked Securities (PERLS): A variation on a dual currency bond that pays both coupon and principal in the base currency, but sets the variable principal payment according to a redemption formula that links it to movements in currency exchange rates between the issue date and maturity. PERLS' principal payments increase as the foreign currency appreciates relative to the base currency, and decrease as the foreign currency declines. Reverse principal exchange rate-linked securities' (Reverse PERLS') principal payments increase as the base currency appreciates relative to the foreign currency, and decrease as the base currency depreciates. *See Reverse Dual Currency Bond. See also Dual Currency Bond, Indexed Currency Option Notes (ICONs).*

Principal Only (PO) Obligation: A special purpose CMO tranche created from a mortgage pool, POs pay holders only from the principal payments made by mortgagees. The value of an early payment PO can increase if interest rates fall and mortgagees exercise their prepayment options at a faster than anticipated rate. Conversely, if rates rise, principal payments may be much slower than anticipated, and the value of early payment POs will decline. Various PO tranches have different characteristics in different environments. *See also Collateralized Mortgage Obligation (CMO), Companion Collateralized Mortgage Obligation, Interest Only (IO) Obligation, Planned Amortization Class (PAC) Bond, Tranche, Mortgage-Backed Securities,*

Stripped Mortgage-Backed Security (SMBS).

Principal Protected Note: Any note that promises—at a minimum—to return the investor's initial or principal investment. The most common type of equity-linked note. *See Guaranteed Bond (2).*

Principal Relationship: In contrast to an agency or broker relationship, a principal or dealer relationship is a relationship of counterparties to a trade. The dealer who buys securities from or sells them to a customer for the dealer's account acts as a principal.

Principal Risk: The risk of losing some of the nominal or face amount or some of the purchase cost of an investment.

Principles and Practices for Wholesale Financial Market Transactions: A derivatives industry document that attempts to define the relationship between derivatives dealers and sophisticated end users. Published in the aftermath of a number of end user derivatives losses.

Prisoner's Dilemma: A situation in game theory in which the best strategy from an individual perspective is the worst strategy from a collective perspective. For example, assume two diamond thieves who have acted in concert are brought in for questioning individually. Each is shown the following matrix:

	Thief No. 1	
Thief No. 2	Confesses	Does Not Confess
Confesses	6, 6	10, 1/2
Does Not Confess	1/2, 10	1, 1

If both thieves confess, they will each be sentenced to six years in prison (upper left). If thief No. 1 does not confess but thief No. 2 does, No. 1 will be sentenced to ten years, and No. 2 will be sentenced to six months (upper right). If they both do not confess, they are each sentenced to one year (lower right). Finally, if No. 1 confesses but No. 2 does not, then No. 1 is sentenced to six months, and No. 2 is sentenced to ten years. Although the best strategy collectively is not to confess—in which case they are each sentenced to one year in prison—the best strategy individually is to confess. If they both confess, however, they are each sentenced to six years. Confessing is the dominant strategy in a prisoner's dilemma.

Private Equity: A reference to the frequently illiquid market for closely held, usually small companies. Transactions are often effected under an exemption from the laws and regulations covering the transfer of publicly traded securities.

Private Market Valuation (PMV): The value of an enterprise in the acquisition market as opposed to the public securities market. A publicly traded company selling for much less than its private market valuation will often be the object of a takeover bid.

Privately Negotiated Derivatives (PND): Another name for OTC derivatives contracts or instruments.

Privatization: The sale or distribution of equity ownership in previously state-owned enterprises to domestic and sometimes international investors. Motives for privatization have been ideological—a result of the political defeat of communist and socialist governments—or simply reactive to the need for government revenue.

Privileges: An archaic name for options. Still used occasionally in the U.K.

Pro Forma Financial Statement: An income statement, balance sheet, or cash flow analysis designed to show what results might have been if an enterprise had been structured in the past as it will be structured in the future, or to indicate what results might be in the future if management's expectations are realized.

Pro Rata Strip (PRS) Bond: A CMO that pays principal in a fixed proportion to the aggregate collateral paydowns.

Probability Density Function: A function that defines the probability distribution of a random variable. By integrating this function between two points, we identify the probability that the random variable will take on a value within the specified interval. *See Normal Density Function (diagram).*

Probability Mass: A technical term that describes the probability of observing a return (or other variable) equal to a certain value. In the context of option analysis it is the probability of observing an option value equal to or greater than the exercise value; i.e., the probability of exercise.

Product Moment Correlation Coefficient: A statistic measuring the degree of linear relationship between two variables that have been measured on interval or ratio scales. It is calculated by multiplying the z scores of the two variables by one another and then calculating the mean of these products.

Profit-Sharing Option: *See Participating Option.*

Program Trading: Originally, trading an entire portfolio in a single coordinated transaction, i.e., "portfolio trading." Program trading has come to encompass index options and futures "arbitrage trading" designed to take advantage of temporary pricing discrepancies between index futures and/or option contracts and the underlying stocks, and "portfolio insurance." The more specific alternative terms "portfolio trading" (*see Basket Trade*), "index arbitrage," and "portfolio insurance" are more descriptive and leave the overused term "program trading" to politicians and polemicists. *See Portfolio Trade, Index Arbitrage, Portfolio Insurance. See also SuperDOT.*

Prohibited Transaction: Any dealing by or on behalf of an ERISA plan with any company or person defined as a "party at interest" with respect to that plan—unless an exemption from the Department of Labor allows such dealing. *See also Party at Interest.*

Projected Benefit Obligation (PBO): The estimated total pension liability of a defined benefit plan sponsor. *See also Accumulated Benefit Obligation (ABO).*

Prospect Theory: The notion that people do not always behave rationally. Prospect theory holds that there are recurring biases driven by psychological factors that influence people's choices under uncertainty. *See also Behavioral Finance.*

Protected Equity Note (PEN): *See Equity-Linked Note (ELN) (diagrams).*

Protected Equity Participation (PEP): (1) Principal guaranteed equity-linked note with upside participation in an individual stock or a basket of stocks and with no cap on return. Identical in structure to a protected index participation (PIP). *See also Equity-Linked Note (ELN) (diagrams), Protected Index Participation (PIP). (2) Another name for Debt Exchangeable for Common Stock (DECS).*

Protected Exchangeable EQuity-linked Securities (PEEQS): An exchange-traded, equity- or index-linked note that can be cashed out substantially earlier than its stated maturity at a value reflecting the interim performance of the underlying. The purpose of the early cash-out privilege is to assure that the non-interest-bearing note does not trade materially below the contemporaneous cash value of the underlying.

Protected Index Participation (PIP): Principal guaranteed equity index-linked notes with upside index participation but with no cap on return. The instrument's rate of participation in the upside movement of the index varies with the dividend rate on the stocks in the index, interest rates, market volatility, yield on the note (if any), and life of the PIP. *See Equity-Linked Note (ELN) (diagrams). See also Protected Equity Participation (PEP) (1).*

Protective Put: A combination of a long put contract and a long position in the underlying. The combination is the risk equivalent of a long call with the same strike price—with some differences in the timing and

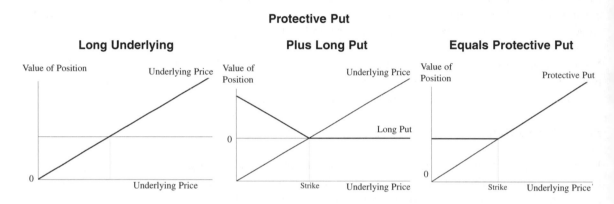

Protective Put

desirability of early exercise if the put is American-style. A protective put sets a downside limit at expiration equal to the strike minus the put premium. *See Married Put.*

Proxy: (1) Written authority to vote stock at a specified stockholders' meeting for the election of directors or for the approval or disapproval of proposals submitted to shareholders. *(2) Agent.*

Proxy Hedging: The use of a price- or rate-correlated financial instrument to hedge a particular risk when a direct hedge for that risk is not available. Common proxy hedges are the use of one currency that moves in concert with another to hedge the risk in the other currency. For example, the more liquid DM market is often used to hedge Swiss franc exposure. Most proxy hedges are subject to some basis risk.

Prudent Expert Rule of ERISA: The Employee Retirement Income Security Act (ERISA) applies a revised and restated version of the prudent man rule to pension and profit-sharing portfolios. ERISA requires that a fiduciary manage a portfolio "with the care, skill, prudence, and diligence, under the circumstances then prevailing, that a prudent man acting in a like capacity and familiar with such matters would use in the conduct of an enterprise of a like character and with like aims." This statement differs from the classic prudent man rule in that familiarity with such matters suggests a higher standard than simple prudence—hence the name, prudent expert rule. Other provisions of the law and U.S. Department of Labor regulations suggest a portfolio approach under which a position imprudent in isolation may be acceptable in a portfolio context. *See also Employee Retirement Income Security Act (ERISA), Prudent Man Rule.*

Prudent Man Rule: A reference to a rule first articulated in the case of *Harvard College versus Amory*. The Supreme Court of Massachusetts stated in 1830 that all that can be required of a trustee is that he conduct himself faithfully, exercise sound discretion, and observe how men of prudence, discretion, and intelligence manage their own affairs—not in regard to speculation, but in regard to the permanent disposition of their funds, considering the probable income as well as the probable safety of the capital to be invested. A standard of prudence in investment policy emphasizes how prudent men invest for "income and safety of principal with a view to the permanent disposition of their funds." Later Court decisions have applied the Prudent Man Rule to individual investments selected by a trustee for the investment of trust funds: good portfolio performance does not excuse a single bad decision. This principle has been modified somewhat by the Prudent Expert Rule of ERISA. *See also Prudent Expert Rule of ERISA.*

Pseudorandom Numbers: Numbers generated by a deterministic process that appear to be random. One such process squares the last four digits of a phone number, extracts the middle four digits of the squared value, squares these digits, and proceeds in like fashion. Although the resulting sequence of four-digit numbers appears random, it is generated deterministically, and may reveal a pattern upon analysis. *See Random Numbers.*

Public Sector Borrowing Requirement (PSBR): The budget deficit in the U.K.

Public Securities Association (PSA): An industry organization best known for its standardized mortgage-backed securities prepayment rate assumptions.

Public Securities Association (PSA) Prepayment Model: Standardized mortgage-backed securities prepayment rate assumptions based on average experience, but which do not take directly into account the current level of interest rates relative to the rate on the mortgages in the pool. *See also Mortgage Prepayment Cap.*

Pundit: An alleged expert on one or more segments of the financial markets. The term is often used sarcastically.

Purchase Accounting: The easiest method of accounting for a business combination. The original or depreciated cost of assets of the acquired company are written up or down to reflect as much as possible of any acquisition premium or discount. Any remaining acquisition premium is accounted for as goodwill, which must be amortized against earnings over a forty-year period. *See Pooling of Interests.*

Purchasing Power Parity (PPP): The principle that, in the long run, currency exchange rates will adjust so that the cost of similar goods and services will tend to be the same in all markets and in all currencies. To preserve purchasing power parity, exchange rate movements tend to reflect relative inflation rates. Unlike interest rate parity, which is enforced by financial arbitrage, purchasing power parity is an influence enforced, in the long run, by goods and services price arbitrage. *See Interest Rate Parity.*

Purgatory and Hell Bond: A heaven and hell bond with a cap on the redemption proceeds.

Put and Call Brokers and Dealers Association (PCBDA): The principal self-regulatory organization for the conventional (unlisted) stock option market in the U.S. through the early years of exchange-traded options. Today it exists largely on paper.

Put Bonds: *Also called Option Tender Bonds. See Early Redemption (Put) Option.*

Put Guarantee Letter: A collateralization mechanism to assure performance by the seller of a put option. A bank issues a guarantee that it holds and is prepared to deliver segregated cash equivalent to the aggregate strike price of the put.

Put Option: The right but not the obligation to sell an underlying at a particular price (strike price) on or before the expiration date of the contract. Alternatively, a short forward position with an upside insurance policy. *See also Option.*

Put Spread: A spread consisting of a long position and a short position in puts on the same underlying. Virtually any call spread structure has an analogous put spread, but put spreads are not commonly used in markets where early exercise is possible. *See specific types of spreads.*

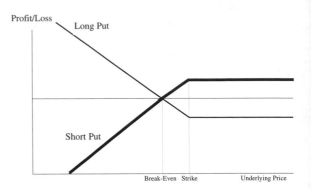

Long and Short Put Positions

Put Swaption: *See Payer's Swaption.*

Put Warrant: A security that, in contrast to a conventional warrant, gives the holder the right to sell the underlying or to receive a cash payment that increases as the value of the underlying declines. Put warrants, like their call warrant counterparts, generally have an initial term of more than one year.

Put/Call Parity: A boundary condition that, subject to transaction costs in the marketplace and the possibility of early exercise, holds relative put and call price relationships within a narrow range. For European options, put/call parity in advance of expiration is subject to the liquidity of the market for the options and the underlying. For American options, an apparent violation of put/call parity often indicates that early exercise is appropriate. *See also Boundary Conditions, No-Arbitrage Condition.*

Put/Call Ratio: The number of puts traded in a market divided by the number of calls traded. Although this ratio is often used as an indication of market sentiment, the necessity for maintenance of approximate put/call parity and the interchangeability of long calls and protective puts for many investors make the put/call ratio's usefulness as a market indicator highly doubtful.

Puttable Bonds: *See Puttable Notes, Early Redemption (Put) Option.*

Puttable Extendible Notes: At the end of each interest period, the issuer may redeem these notes at par or attempt to extend the maturity on terms that he believes the noteholder will accept. The noteholder can put the notes back to the issuer if the new rate is unacceptable. Holders also may have one or more additional put options during the initial interest period. *See also Lender's Option—Borrower's Option (LOBO).*

Puttable Notes: A traditional bond or note with an embedded put that permits the bondholder to sell the notes back to the issuer, usually at par. This put gives the holder some protection from loss of principal due to higher interest rates or credit deterioration of the issuer. *Also called Puttable Bonds, Adjustable Tender Securities. See Early Redemption (Put) Option.*

Puttable Range Floater: An index range note with an embedded put permitting the holder to sell the note back to the issuer at par or at a price based on par as a protection to the holder from a large adverse interest rate move.

Puttable Stock: A unit consisting of common stock and a put giving the buyer of the unit the right to put the stock back to the issuing corporation. In addition, the put feature usually gives the holder the right to obtain more shares at no additional cost if the market price of the shares falls below a stated level, as of a predetermined date or dates. This combination of provisions provides a floor value for each unitholder's position. If the market value of the stock rises above the stated floor value on the valuation date(s), the put has no value. If the market value of the position falls below the floor, the issuer is obligated to issue additional common shares or repurchase the stock. Variations on this basic structure include limitations on the number of shares to be issued, and restrictions on the ability of the issuing corporation to make the unit purchaser whole through the issuance of additional shares or by cash payments, debt, or preferred stock issuance. Puttable stock units enable investors to fully participate in the upside potential of a company with reduced downside risk. Although the structures are very different, the payoff pattern of a puttable stock issue is very similar to that of a convertible bond.

Puttable Swap: A swap agreement in which the fixed-rate receiver has the right to terminate the swap on one or more dates prior to its scheduled maturity. Like a callable swap, this early termination provision protects a party from adverse effects of large changes in fixed rates. In this case, the receiver is protected from a large increase in rates that would reduce the present value of his cash flow from the swap. *See also Callable Swap, Cancellable Swap, Retractable Swap.*

Puttable Warrant: *See Redeemable Warrant.*

Pyramid Scheme: *See Ponzi Scheme.*

Pyramiding: Although the term is often used loosely, pyramiding typically refers to the practice of using the excess margin or "buying power" generated by a successful speculative operation to increase the commitment to that operation. In options, an example might be the naked option writer who writes more options as a favorable move in the price of the underlying frees up margin. A buyer might sell a profitable in-the-money position and invest the proceeds in a larger number of at-the-money options. Pyramiding is probably more common in futures than in options trading, because margin requirements are often lower.

Q Bond: An inverse floating-rate CMO tranche.

Qan Macs: Synthetic Qantas Airways "shares" issued by Macquarie Bank to permit non-Australian investors to participate in Qantas without violating Australian foreign ownership rules. *See also Performance-Linked Equity Securities (Perles).*

Quadrature Method: A numerical method that approximates the area of a region with a curved boundary.

Qualified Covered Call: Covered call writers have a limited exemption from the loss deferral provision of the U.S. tax code's straddle rule if they follow qualified covered call guidelines in selling one or a sequence of calls against a stock position. These guidelines exempt a covered call writer from the straddle rule if he avoids very short-term and most in-the-money call options.

Qualified Financial Contract: Any security contract, commodity contract, forward contract, repurchase agreement, swap agreement, or any similar agreement that the Federal Deposit Insurance Corporation may, by regulation, make subject to safe harbor netting enforcement and collateral rules of the Financial Institutions Reform, Recovery and Enforcement Act of 1989 (FIRREA).

Qualified Investment Buyer (QIB): An investor permitted to purchase securities not offered to the public, with emphasis on instruments offered under Regulation 144a in the U.S. QIBs include insurance companies; licensed small business investment companies; public or private employee benefit plans; business development companies; most corporations, business trusts, partnerships, or charitable organizations; registered investment advisors; dealers acting for their own account or for the accounts of other QIBs (that in the aggregate own and invest on a discretionary basis at least $10 million of securities not affiliated with the dealer); banks or savings and loan associations with an audited net worth of at least $25 million; and registered investment companies that are part of a family of investment companies (that own in the aggregate at least $100 million in securities).

Qualified Opinion: An auditor's opinion letter that highlights limitations on the coverage of the audit, exceptions the auditor takes to the statements, or situations that could materially affect the company's financial condition.

Qualified Professional Asset Manager (QPAM): An investment advisor, registered with the SEC, who represents U.S. pension plans in certain private placement transactions and vets the suitability of those transactions.

Quality Option: The right to deliver any of a set of eligible underlying physical commodities or financial instruments, perhaps at preset quality differentials, in settlement of a futures contract or similar agreement.

Quality Spread: The difference between the interest rate paid for funds of a given maturity by a sovereign issuer and the rate required of a less creditworthy borrower. *Also called Credit Spread (1).*

Quality Spread Differential: The difference in quality spreads at two different maturities. Typically, the quality spread and, hence, the quality spread differential, widen as the term of financing moves farther out on the yield curve. Lenders are more comfortable with their ability to evaluate and accept credit risks in the very short term than over a longer period. The quality spread differential is a consideration in the pricing of interest rate swaps.

Quant Jock: One who specializes in quantitative analysis. This term is sometimes used pejoratively to imply a lack of attention to financial and economic theory.

Quantitative Investment Management: A portfolio management style that applies mathematical and statistical techniques to a single market sector (i.e., equity or debt) or to asset allocation. Quantitative tools vary greatly in sophistication and the underlying variables evaluated may be fundamental or technical. *See also Style Management.*

Quantity Adjusting Option (QUANTO): (1) A fixed exchange rate foreign equity option where the face amount of the currency coverage expands or contracts to cover changes in the foreign currency value of a designated underlying security or package of securities. Quantos are used to adjust the investor's base currency protection on an underlying position that varies in value in the non-base currency. The most common example is a cross-border, equity-linked instrument with currency protection on the value of the foreign equity position in the domestic currency. *Compare with Equity-Linked Foreign Exchange (Elf-X) Option (diagrams). Also called Fixed Exchange Rate Foreign Equity Option. See also Secondary Currency Option, Omega (2), Omega Risk (1), Complex Option, Guaranteed Exchange Rate Warrant, Guaranteed Exchange Rate Option, Quanto Note (diagram).* (2) An option on a percentage change in a currency pair ratio applied to a face amount denominated in a third (base) currency. Double and triple currency QUANTOS combine or offset percentage changes in two or three currency pair ratios, none involving the base currency. One similarity of the equity and currency QUANTOs lies in the difficulty of estimating or hedging the value of the exchange into the base currency. *Also called Currency Quantity Adjusting Option (Currency QUANTO).*

Quantization Error: The error on a binomial tree that arises because the binomial lattice is not continuous. The discreteness of a binomial tree ignores many possible prices, and this coarseness can lead to discrepancies between the theoretical option price and the price calculated from the tree. *See also Option Specification Error, Saw-Toothed Convergence.*

Quanto Note: An equity-linked note in which the percentage change of a foreign equity or equity index is translated into the currency in which the note is denominated (the investor's base currency) for accounting and reporting convenience, and, sometimes, for regulatory necessity. *Also called Fixed Exchange Rate Equity Note. See also Complex Option.*

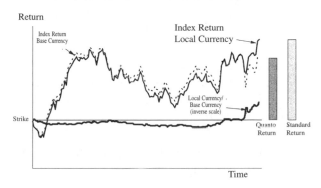

Comparison of Quanto and Standard Equity-Linked Note (ELN) Return

Quanto Swap: Most frequently, an equity swap providing for translation of the percentage equity return in a non-domestic equity or index into the base currency of the equity return receiver to provide currency protection.

QUarterly Income Capital Securities (QUICS): *See Monthly Income Preferred Shares (MIPS).*

QUarterly Income Preferred Securities (QUIPS): *See Monthly Income Preferred Shares (MIPS).*

Quarterly Index Expiration (QIX): A supplementary index option series expiring on the last business day of each calendar quarter to accommodate fiscal period ending requirements.

Quasi-American Option: *Also called Modified American Option. See Deferred Payment American Option. See also American Option, Bermuda Option, European Option, Japanese Option.*

Quick Ratio: (Current Assets – Inventory)/Current Liabilities. *Also called Acid Test Ratio.*

Quote-Driven Market: A dealer market, such as Nasdaq or the London Stock Exchange, with prices determined principally by dealers' bid/offer quotations. *Compare to Order-Driven Market.*

R (Correlation Coefficient): A measure (ranging in value from –1 to 1) of the association between a dependent variable and one or more independent variables. If one variable's values are higher than its average value when another variable's values are higher than its average value, their correlation is positive. By contrast, if one variable's values are lower than its average value when another variable's values are higher than its average value, their correlation is negative. A correlation coefficient is not necessarily a measure of causality, but it does indicate the strength of a relationship. A correlation coefficient of 1 implies that the variables move perfectly in lockstep; a correlation coefficient of –1 implies that the variables move inversely in lockstep; a correlation coefficient of 0 implies that the variables, as calibrated, are uncorrelated. *See Cointegration, Covariance.*

R^2 (Coefficient of Determination): In regression analysis, the fraction of variation in the dependent variable that is explained by variation in the independent variable or variables. R^2 is calculated as the ratio of the sum of the squared differences between the predicted values for the dependent variable, and the average of the observed values for the dependent variable to the sum of the squared differences between the observed values for the dependent variable and the average of those values. R^2 ranges in value from 0 to 1. A high value indicates a strong relationship between the dependent and independent variables, while a low value indicates a weak relationship.

$$R^2 = [\Sigma(\text{Predicted y} - \text{Mean y})^2]/[\Sigma(\text{Observed y} - \text{Mean y})^2]$$

Racketeer Influenced and Corrupt Organization Act (RICO): A U.S. federal law used to prosecute some insider trading and securities fraud cases in the late 1980s. The law provides for triple damages when a pattern of corruption is established.

Radon-Nikodym Derivative: The Radon-Nikodym derivative is a component of the formal adjustment factor that equates the expected outcome of an experiment performed under two different probability measures. The probability adjustment from Girsanov's formula is a function of the Radon-Nikodym derivative. *See Girsanov's Theorem.*

Rainbow Option: An option with a payoff linked to the performance of two or more instruments or indexes. *See Alternative Option (diagram), Outperformance Option (diagram).*

Random Numbers: A sequence of numbers that are independent of each other. Most applications that require random numbers rely on mathematical techniques to generate pseudorandom numbers. These numbers appear random but in fact are generated deterministically. *See Pseudorandom Numbers.*

Random Variable: A variable that takes on a value influenced by chance, such as the toss of a coin or next year's rate of return on the S&P 500 index.

Random Walk Hypothesis: The random walk hypothesis is a variant of the efficient market hypothesis. It holds that stock prices follow a random walk pattern, and, consequently, historic prices are of no value in forecasting future prices. *See also Capital Asset Pricing Model (CAPM) (diagram), Efficient Market.*

Range: (1) The price or rate interval or band that determines an actual or embedded range accumulation option payout. *Also called Band.* (2) The variable payout region of a range forward, collar, or risk reversal.

Range Accrual Note: *See Index Range Note.*

Range Accrual Option: *See Range Accumulation Option or Warrant.*

Range Accumulation Note: *See Index Range Note.*

Range Accumulation Option or Warrant: A series of binary options with each option covering a short period, typically one day or one week. The payoff of the range accumulation option is the sum of the payoffs of the component binary options. The component options, in turn, pay off when the underlying price or rate falls within a designated range. Range accumulation options may be stand-alone instruments, but they are frequently embedded in notes to create index range notes or LIBOR range notes. A dealer usually tries to sell range accumulation options or warrants that pay off over the entire range of possible prices to simplify hedging requirements. *Also called Banking On Overall STability (BOOST), Expected to Accrue Return on Nominal (EARN) Warrant, Range Accrual Option, Hope for A Market STabilization in a givEn Range (HAMSTER), Index Range Note, LIBOR Range Note. Compare with Binary LIBOR Note, Range Warrant (1). See also Binary Swap, Time Trade.*

Range Floater: *See Index Range Note.*

Range Forward Contract: A contingent forward contract with a collar-type payout in a form used primarily in currency markets. The investor can take advantage of favorable price moves to the upper end of the contract range, while remaining protected against moves below the lower end of the contract range. Within the range, the contract settles at the spot rate in effect at maturity. The range is usually chosen so that the customer pays no option premium. As the diagram illustrates, the payoff pattern is identical to an interest rate collar or an equity risk reversal in fixed-income and equity markets, respectively. *Also called Fence or Fence Spread, Cap and Floor, Conversion Spread, Spread Conversion. See also Choke, Equity Risk Reversal (diagram), Interest Rate Collar (diagram), Forward Rate Bracket.*

**An Exchange Rate Range Forward Contract—
Rate Pattern at Settlement**

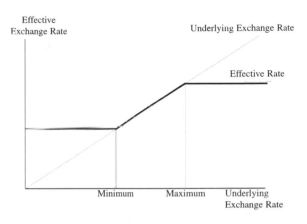

Range Straddle: A combination of a lookback call and a lookback put with the same trade date and expiration date. The payoff of the range straddle is equal to the number of units covered by the option times the range of the underlying price or rate during the life of the option. *See High-Low Option.*

Range Warrant: (1) A multitranche structure that allocates a fixed return on the premium pool collected to range tranches on the basis of the price of the underlying at expiration. One tranche might get the return if the underlying price falls between 0 and 100. The second might get the return if the underlying falls between 101 and 200, and so on. Unsuccessful tranches get a rebate of their premium with a zero return. *Compare with Range Accumulation Option or Warrant. (2) See Trading Range Warrant (diagram).*

Ranking: A credit quality hierarchy within a corporation's debt structure. Subject to specific features of isolated instruments, the following terms designate a typical hierarchy from highest to lowest quality: secured, senior subordinated, junior subordinated.

RAROC 2020: A data set containing financial instrument prices, volatilities, correlations, and a risk measurement methodology sold by Bankers Trust. Unlike its principal rival, J.P. Morgan's RiskMetrics, RAROC 2020 was introduced with option functions.

Ratchet Option: *See Ladder Option or Note (diagram), Cliquet Option (1) (diagram).*

Ratchet Swap: A variant of a modified fixed-for-floating-rate swap in which the fixed rate can be adjusted downward in small increments every reset period if the floating rate drops by more than an agreed amount. A similar ratchet arrangement can be applied to the upside. *Compare to Path-Dependent Floating-Rate Note.*

Rate Differential Swap: An interest rate or other swap with one of the payment rates or returns denominated in a currency different than the currency used to state the notional principal amount. Both rates are calculated against the base currency. *Also called CRoss-Index Basis (CRIB) Swap, Cross-Rate Swap, CUrrency Protected Swap (CUPS), Diff or Difference*

Rate Differential Swap

Swap, Differential Swap, Interest Rate Index Swap, LIBOR Differential Swap. See Swap, Currency Protected Instrument. See also Interest Rate Swap.

Rate Fixing Date: Varies with market custom, but in the U.S. the swap rate fixing date is usually two business days prior to the first date the new rates are effective in a swap or other periodic reset agreement. *Also called Reset Date (1), Roll Date.*

Rating: *See Table of Debt Ratings (Appendix).*

Rating Sensitive Note: *See Credit Sensitive Note.*

Ratio Forward: *See Participating Forward Contract (diagram).*

Ratio Spread: An option spread in which the number of contracts purchased and the number of contracts sold are not equal. *Also called Variable Spread.*

Ratio Write: *See Option Hedge (diagrams).*

Rational Expectations: The notion that market participants form expectations that reflect all available information. The theory of rational expectations holds, for example, that stock prices reflect anticipated changes in relevant factors; hence only unanticipated changes result in stock price movements.

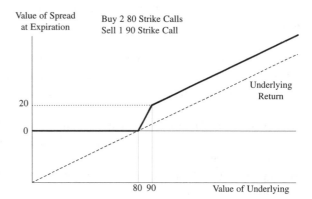

One of Many Possible Ratio Spread Payoff Patterns at Expiration

Ready Market: An active market. Dealers' spreads are relatively narrow and the prices quoted by different dealers are nearly identical.

Real Economic Earnings (REE): An estimate of the fundamental underlying earning power of a corporation. *Similar terms include Operating Free Cash Flow, Sustainable Earnings Level.*

Real Estate Investment Trust (REIT): A vehicle for the securitization of real property and loans on real property.

Real Estate Mortgage Investment Conduit (REMIC): A CMO issued after January 1, 1987, under legislation designed to eliminate certain tax and regulatory problems that limited issuer and investor participation in multiple series (tranche) CMOs. *See also Collateralized Mortgage Obligation (CMO), Stripped Mortgage-Backed Security (SMBS), Mortgage-Backed Securities, Tranche.*

Real Interest Rate: The nominal interest rate less the rate of price inflation. *Also called Real Rate of Return, Real Yield.*

Real Option: (1) An option or choice in the management of real (as opposed to financial) assets or operations, such as the option to accelerate or defer capital expenditures, to change process inputs or outputs, to build or abandon capacity, or to alter the nature or change the scale of a production process. The substantial literature on real options has revolutionized the capital budgeting and real investment process. (2) An option on a physical (as opposed to a financial) asset, such as real property, commodities, etc.

Real Rate of Return: *See Real Interest Rate.*

Real Time Gross Settlement (RTGS): The funds settlement system used on the FEDWIRE and planned for other modern fund transfer systems. Real time means quickly or immediately upon receipt of evidence that the obligation is covered by an account balance, a credit line, or pledged collateral. In some cases, daylight overdrafts are permissible. These transfers are slower than real time in the electronic sense. Gross means that a specific obligation is paid in full, not netted against offsetting obligations. RTGS systems can be integrated with payment netting systems to cut down credit exposure. *See also Designated Time Net Settlement (DTNS).*

Real Yield: *See Real Interest Rate.*

Real Yield Security (REALS): Typically, a floating-rate note with a coupon reset quarterly to the greater of the increase in the consumer price index plus a predetermined real yield spread, or, if the consumer price index should be flat or decline, to the level of the real yield spread. *Also called Inflation-Linked Debt, Inflation Derivative, Inflation Rate Interest-Indexed Bond. See also Indexed-Linked Bonds or Notes, Indexed Notes.*

Realized Yield: The return actually earned on an investment in a security over a period of time, including the return on reinvested interest or dividend payments.

Rebalancing: Periodic revisions to a portfolio necessitated by the effect of the passage of time on asset and liability duration, changes in the constitution of an index, portfolio cash flows, or market-driven departures from a target allocation.

Rebate: A sum repaid to some option buyers if an in option is not activated or an out option is terminated because the underlying hits the outstrike. Rebates provide a payoff pattern intermediate between a traditional option structure, where the position has a minimum value of zero, and a debt-based structure, where the minimum value at expiration might be the value of the initial investment. A structure calling for a rebate may facilitate a dealer's hedging activity. *Examples include Cash-Out Call Option with Rebate, Cash-Out Put Option with Rebate.*

Rebate Strangle Option: A linked pair of knockout options with unusual rebate and payout features. Specifically, the put and call form a strangle, with the strike of each component serving as the knockout trigger for the other. If this trigger is breached, the out-of-the-money option expires immediately, and the strangle seller must refund the entire strangle premium to the buyer. The at- or in-the-money option remains active unless its trigger is touched later. The appeal of this mechanism to the seller is the relatively high strangle premium. If the seller is correct in forecasting that the underlying will stay in the range, his return will be excellent. If the seller is wrong, he loses the cushion provided by the premium and may lose much more if the underlying moves well beyond a strike. *See also Double Barrier Option.*

Receivable Pay-Through Securities: Instruments that give the investor an undivided interest in a pool of securitized receivables.

Receiver's Swaption: A swaption giving the holder the right to receive a fixed rate and pay a floating rate. Broadly analogous to a call on a fixed-rate instrument in terms of its value under different interest rate scenarios. *Also called Call Swaption. See Swaption.*

Recognized Investment Exchange: Any exchange operating legally in the U.K.

Reconstitution: Combining stripped coupon and principal cash flows to reassemble a traditional coupon security.

Reconversion: Most commonly, the process of changing a synthetic call back into a put, typically by selling a position in the underlying. *Also called Reversal (2), Reverse Conversion.*

Recovery Forward Contract: A double barrier (out) option with a rebate provision embedded in a currency forward. With this contract, an end user can sell a non-base currency forward at a premium to the market rate, if the rate does not rise above the contract rate or drop below a lower barrier during the term of the contract. The dealer will rebate part of the contract's premium if the lower barrier is breached.

Red Herring: A preliminary prospectus for a securities offering in the U.S. The red herring usually has full details of the offering except price and, perhaps, size. It has comprehensive financial data on the issuer. The name comes from a required note usually printed in red ink stating that the issue cannot yet be sold because the registration statement is not effective.

Red Noise: A mean reverting stochastic process. *See Mean Reversion. Compare to Blue Noise.*

Redeemable Warrant: A warrant with a cash redemption value as an alternative to traditional exercise. *Also called Puttable Warrant. See Money Back Options or Warrants.*

Reduced Cost Option: Generically, any option with a reduced premium resulting from the implicit or explicit sale of another option, acceptance of a less favorable strike or participation rate, or introduction of a barrier provision.

Reference Asset or Instrument: Usually a sovereign or highly rated debt instrument or an equity index priced to serve as the basis for a market or credit risk contingent payment.

Reference Index: An index underlying and determining some component of the value or the payoff of a financial instrument.

Reference Index Rate: The interest rate serving as the reference index for a contingent instrument. Frequently, a floating rate such as LIBOR.

Refi Rate: The refinancing or runoff rate of a pool of mortgages usually expressed as the annualized conditional prepayment rate (CPR). A high refi rate reduces the value of a high-rate mortgage pool, as mortgagees refinance their debt at lower rates and repay their old mortgages, liquidating the pool. *See Prepayment Option.*

Refunding: Issuance of new debt instruments to replace put, called, or matured debt.

Registered Investment Advisor (RIA): In the U.S., any person (in the legal sense) registered with the SEC, "who, for compensation, engages in the business of advising others, either directly or through publications or writings, as to the value of securities or as to the advisability of investing in, purchasing or selling securities."

Registered Investment Company: A reference to required registration of mutual funds sold in the U.S. with the SEC under the Investment Company Act of 1940. *Compare to Regulated Investment Company (RIC).*

Registered Options Principal (ROP): An employee of a brokerage firm who has passed a test on exchange and SEC rules for handling customer option accounts. A senior registered option principal (SROP) must approve new option accounts, and a compliance registered option principal (CROP) is responsible for the brokerage firm's option compliance program.

Registered Representative (RR): The formal name for a salesperson licensed to sell securities to the public in the U.S. Some firms use their own names for salespersons, such as account executive, investment representative, financial consultant, etc.

Registered Shares: *See Restricted Shares.*

Regular Settlement: The standard settlement period for a securities transaction. In the U.S., the settlement convention ranges from next day for government securities, futures, and options, to three business days for common stocks. Other markets have a variety of settlement conventions, with most markets settling in three business days or less.

Regulated Investment Company (RIC): A reference to income pass-through provisions in the Internal Revenue Code. Apart from SEC registration, an investment company must meet these IRS requirements to avoid taxation at the fund level. *See also Registered Investment Company, Short-Short Rule.*

Regulatory Arbitrage: A financial contract or a series of transactions undertaken, entirely or in part, because the transaction(s) enable(s) one or both of the counterparties to accomplish a financial or operating objective unavailable to them directly because of regulatory obstacles. Recent regulatory arbitrage with customized equity-linked derivative structures has enabled U.S.-based investors to take positions linked to foreign equity indexes when they could not make direct investments in exchange-traded stock index futures contracts. Many structured note transactions are stimulated by regulatory arbitrage opportunities.

Regulatory Risk: *See Legal and Regulatory Risk discussion, pp. 6-7.*

Regulatory Spread: The difference in yield as a result of differences in registration requirements and fees that a borrower encounters in the traditional bond or medium-term note market in the U.S. relative to the yield in the Eurobond market. Simplification in domestic registration procedures has narrowed the regulatory spread substantially since Eurobond trading began.

Reinsurance: The purchase of a second level of insurance by a primary insurance underwriter to reduce exposure to a specific loss or group of losses. Reinsurance is purchased under a treaty that covers broad categories of risks, or under an agreement to reinsure a specific risk. Risk is also spread by allocating risks through underwriting pools, with each pool member receiving a percentage of pool revenue as income and accepting responsibility for a percentage of pool losses.

Reinvestment Rate: The interest rate or yield at which any cash flow from coupon or principal payments can be reinvested.

Reinvestment Risk: Exposure to an unfavorable variation in return as a result of an investor's inability to invest an interest coupon or principal repayment at a rate as favorable as the original return on the instrument generating the cash flow. *Compare to Extension Risk (2). See Bunny Bond, Prepayment Risk.*

Relationship Trade: *See Basis Trade (2).*

Relative Performance Derivatives: A generic term covering spread options and bonds, outperformance options, share ratio contracts, etc.

Relative Performance Option (RPO): *See Outperformance Option (diagram).*

Relative Risk: Volatility or variance of an asset's return measured against the return of a benchmark rather than as the absolute volatility of the asset. *See also Absolute Risk (2).*

Relinking: Entering into an interest rate swap agreement to offset exposure to a floating-rate or reverse floating-rate note that has begun to move against an investor (the note rate is dropping) or an issuer (the note rate is rising).

Remainderman: The person (legal) entitled to the residual assets of a trust after an event has occurred that terminates the trust, such as the death of a life tenant.

Remarketed Preferred Stock: Perpetual preferred stock with a dividend rate that resets at the end of each dividend period to a level determined by a remarketing agent, subject to certain maximums relative to commercial paper rates. Dividend periods and payments may be variable even within a single issue to meet issuer and investor needs. Similar to other adjustable-rate preferred structures except for the rate reset and redistribution mechanism. *See also Adjustable-Rate Preferred Stock (ARPS), Auction Rate Preferred Stock (ARPS).*

Remarketed Reset Notes: Floating-rate notes with an interest rate reset to a rate determined by a remarketing agent, typically a bank or investment bank, that determines what rate will cause the notes to sell at par. If the issuer disagrees with the remarketing agent, the coupon is determined by a formula. Noteholders have a put to protect them from a below market coupon.

Réméré: *Fr.* A collateralized financing technique incorporating transfer of ownership of the collateral as in a repurchase agreement or pension livrée with the distinction that the borrower has an option, not an obligation, to repurchase the collateral. *See also Repurchase Agreement (Repo), (RP), Pension Livrée.*

Rendleman-Bartter Model: A single factor analytic model used to value interest rate dependent claims. The single factor is the short-term interest rate whose changes are represented by geometric Brownian motion.

Renter: *Fr.* Perpetual sovereign bonds. *See also Consols.*

Replicating Portfolios: Combinations of stock, cash, and borrowing that reproduce the return pattern of an option or option-based instrument and form the basis for portfolio insurance and other dynamic hedging strategies or synthetic structures. *See Option Replication (1).*

Repo Rate: The financing rate for government securities sold against repurchase agreements.

Reporting Level: Positions in exchange-traded futures and options must be reported to the exchange when they exceed a mandated reporting size.

Repurchase Agreement (Repo), (RP): A financing arrangement used primarily in the government securities markets whereby a dealer or other holder of government securities sells the securities to a lender and agrees to repurchase them at an agreed future date at an agreed price, which will provide the lender with an extremely low-risk return. Repos are popular because they can virtually eliminate credit problems, but a number of significant losses over the years suggests that lenders in this market have not always checked their collateralization closely enough. Most repo transactions are overnight, but term repos (over thirty days) are common. The repo market is enlarged and enhanced by its use in Federal Reserve Board open market operations in the U.S. Repos operate slightly differently in other markets. *See also Bed and Breakfast, Dollar Roll, Gensaki Rate, Pension Livrée, Réméré, Reverse Repurchase Agreement.*

Request For Proposal (RFP): A public notice or private invitation asking service providers to apply for assignments or mandates. The term is widely used in the financial service industry in connection with manager, custodian, and consultant searches.

Reset Date: (1) The date a swap's periodic payment terms are established. Usually the same as the payment date or two days earlier, depending on local conventions or the agreement of the counterparties. *Also called Roll Date, Rate Fixing Date.* (2) The date on which the strike of a reset or similar option or warrant is determined or modified. *See Reset Option or Warrant (diagram).*

Reset Frequency: The period between reset dates on a swap. Common intervals are three months, six months, and one year.

Reset Note: Any of several varieties of floating-rate note (FRN).

Reset Option or Warrant: Typically, a stock or equity index call option or warrant whose strike price may be reset to a lower strike, or a put whose strike price may be reset to a higher strike, at some point during the life of the instrument if the option is out of the money on the reset date. There may be a limit to the magnitude of the strike price adjustment and the reset may be triggered by a specific price on the underlying rather than set on a specific reset date. *Also called Strike Reset Option or Warrant. See Anti-Crash Warrant, Partial Lookback Warrant or Option, Step-Down Option or Warrant, Barrier Option, Reset Date (2). See also Path-Dependent Option.*

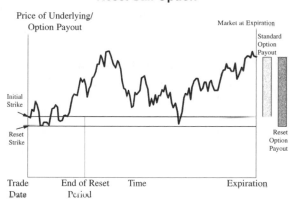

Reset Effect of a Limited Period Reset Call Option

Reset Swap: An interest rate swap agreement with the floating-rate payment based on the reference index rate at the end of the interest period rather than the rate at the start of the period. A floating-rate receiver will prefer a reset swap when a rising yield curve (rising forward rate curve) implies higher rates in the future. *Also called Arrears Swap, Back End Set Swap, LIBOR In Arrears Swap, In-Arrears Swap (diagram).*

Reshaping Duration: *See Partial Duration.*

Residual Interest Bonds (RIBs): Municipal reverse floaters that are paired with select auction variable-rate securities (SAVRs), a direct auction reset floating-rate municipal. The issuer pays a fixed rate on the combined issue, and the fixed rate is divided to pay the floating rate on the SAVRs and the residual on the RIBs. *See Fixed Interest Rate Substitute Transaction (FIRST), Tax-Exempt Enhanced Municipal Security (TEEMS), Bull and Bear Notes, Residual Income Tax-Exempt Security (RITES), Select Auction Variable-Rate Securities (SAVRs).*

Residual Interest Tax-Exempt Security (RITES): A synthetic tax-exempt (municipal) reverse floating-rate note. *See Residual Interest Bonds (RIBs).*

Residual Risk: The component of an asset's risk that cannot be explained by exposure to pervasive factors (the market), common factors (interest rates, industrial production), or by industry affiliation.

Residual Unhedged Risk: Basis or other unmatched risk remaining after the implementation of a hedging position.

Resolution Trust Corporation (RTC): An organization set up under the Financial Institutions Reform, Recovery, and Enforcement Act of 1989 (FIRREA) to dispose of the assets of failed thrift institutions and to maximize possible recovery.

Restricted Shares: Shares that may not be freely transferred in the marketplace because host country law forbids their ownership by foreign investors, prevents their transfer without the approval of the issuer, or restricts their marketability as a matter of investor protection. Restricted, or as they are sometimes called, registered shares, are common in Finland, Switzerland, and in some emerging markets. Sales restrictions based on investor protection legislation are a regulatory issue principally in the U.S. *Also called Registered Shares.*

Restructuring: A major change in the business, and, often, the financial structure of a corporation characterized by writedowns of assets (tangible and intangible), elimination of operations, and reduction in personnel. One of the most common characteristics of restructuring has been the writedown in asset values to assure at least a relative improvement in future earnings.

Retail Price Index (RPI): The principal price index used in the U.K. as a basis for inflation-adjusted gilts, which, in turn, serve as the basis for the largest issues of publicly traded inflation derivatives. *See Inflation Derivative.*

Retractable Note: A debt instrument with an embedded option giving the issuer the right to call it at selected dates. *Compare to Extendible Note (2), Borrower's Option—Lender's Option (BO-LO).*

Retractable Swap: A swap with an embedded option giving one party, usually the fixed-rate payer, the right to cancel the swap under certain conditions. The conditions may be as general as a decline in interest rates or as specific as an issuer's call of the instrument used to generate the fixed-rate payments. *See also Callable Swap, Puttable Swap.*

Return On Assets (ROA): Net income divided by total assets, expressed as a percent.

Return On Equity (ROE): Net income divided by net worth.

Return On Net Capital Employed (RONCE): A return calculation with pretax profit as the numerator and capital committed to the specific operation as the denominator.

Return On Risk-Adjusted Capital (RORAC): Similar to risk-adjusted return on capital (RAROC), except that the rate of return is measured without a risk adjustment, while the capital charge varies depending on the risk associated with the instrument or project. *See Risk-Adjusted Return On Capital (RAROC), Risk-Adjusted Return On Risk-Adjusted Capital (RARORAC).*

Return on Sales: Net income divided by sales.

Return to Hedged Portfolio (RHP): *See Implied Repo Rate.*

Revenue Bond: A municipal bond linked to an income-producing project. The bond pays interest and repays principal only to the extent adequate funds are generated by the project.

Reversal: (1) The termination of a swap through cancellation of the original agreement, or, less frequently, initiation of a partial mirror swap to offset the remaining term of the original swap. (2) *See Conversion (1), Reconversion, Reverse Conversion.* (3) Buying a call to lock in a profit on a short outright forward currency position.

Reverse Annuity Mortgage (RAM): A mortgage that grows over time as a lender makes payments to a homeowner who wants to cover living expenses out of the equity in the house.

Reverse Contingent Premium Option: In contrast to a contingent premium option, the reverse contingent premium option requires payment of a premium if the option is out of the money at maturity. No premium is charged if the option is in the money.

Reverse Conversion: A financing and risk management technique based on put/call parity and an investor's ability to obtain interest on the use of proceeds from a short sale. In a typical transaction, a brokerage firm sells stock short, buys a call, and sells a put (short actual, long synthetic). Depending on borrowing costs for the stock sold short and the relative pricing of puts and calls, a better than money market return might be obtained at very low risk. If the options are American-style, there is some risk that the stock will decline sharply and the short put will be exercised after the long out-of-the-money call has lost nearly all its value. *See Reconversion, Reversal (2).*

Reverse Dual Currency Bond: A bond that pays coupons in a non-base currency (typically the currency of the issuer) and pays principal in the base currency (the currency of the investor). *See also Dual Currency Bond, Indexed Currency Option Notes (ICONs), Principal Exchange Rate-Linked Securities (PERLS), Foreign Interest Payment Security (FIPS).*

Reverse Equity Risk Reversal: Typically, a combination of a short out-of-the-money put, a long out-of-the-money call, and a short futures or cash market position. This combination is the mirror image of the traditional range forward or equity risk reversal structure (see diagram), which is generally used when a simple short swap or futures transaction with unlimited exposure to extreme market movements does not meet risk control objectives. As the diagram illustrates, the value of the investor's position will increase if the value of the underlying declines, and will fall if the value of the underlying increases, with a limit on the downside in the case of a market advance, and on the upside in the case of a market decline. *Also called Reverse Range Forward, Reverse Forward Rate Bracket. See also Bear Spread (diagram).*

Payoff Pattern of a Reverse Equity Risk Reversal

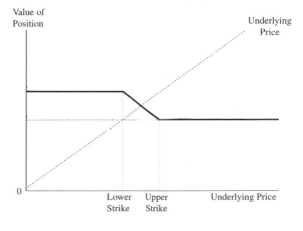

Reverse Floating-Rate Note: A popular floating-rate note structure in which the rate paid increases as market floating rates decline. In a typical case, the rate paid on the note is set by doubling the swap rate (fixed rate) in effect at the time the contract is signed, and subtracting the floating reference index rate for each payment period. If floating rates fall, the result of this calculation is a higher return on the reverse floating-rate note. If floating rates rise, the payment on the reverse floating-rate note declines. *Also called Maximum Rate Notes, Bull Floater, Bull Floating-Rate Note, INverse FLOating Security (INFLOS), Indexed INverse FLOating-Rate Security (Indexed INFLOS), Yield Curve Note, Inverse Floater. See also Bull and Bear Notes, Superfloater Swap, Structured Note, Power Bond, Floating-Rate Note (FRN), Indexed Inverse Floater, Leveraged Reverse Floating-Rate Note. Compare with Bear Floater (diagram).*

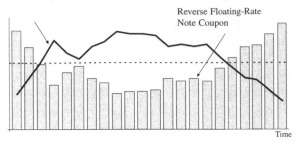

Anatomy of a Five-Year Reverse Floating-Rate Note

Reverse Floating-Rate Swap: A swap structure with a reverse floating-rate payment from one counterparty.

Reverse Forward Rate Bracket: *See Reverse Equity Risk Reversal, Reverse Interest Rate Collar.*

Reverse Interest Rate Collar: A combination of an interest rate collar and a reverse floating-rate note, the reverse interest rate collar provides an interest cost or yield that decreases as rates rise and increases as market rates fall within a range. This structure might appeal to a liability manager who has too much floating-rate exposure, or to an asset manager who is constrained as to allowable portfolio duration but who expects rates to decline. *Also called Reverse Forward-Rate Bracket. See also Reverse Equity Risk Reversal (diagram).*

Reverse Option Hedge: A hedged position in which the investor owns more than one call option for each unit of the underlying he is short. This position becomes profitable as the market price moves away from the

Reverse Option Hedge

Sell One Unit of Underlying Short

Buy Two Calls

Two to One Reverse Option Hedge Profit/Loss Pattern at Expiration

strike price of the options in either direction. *See also Option Hedge, Hedge.*

Reverse Principal Exchange Rate-Linked Securities (Reverse PERLS): *See Principal Exchange Rate-Linked Securities (PERLS).*

Reverse Range Forward: *See Reverse Equity Risk Reversal (diagram).*

Reverse Repurchase Agreement: An overnight or similar-term cash equivalent investment collateralized by transfer of ownership in a Treasury security. The investor side of a repurchase agreement. *See also Repurchase Agreement (Repo), (RP).*

Reverse Stock Split: A change in corporate capitalization that increases the par value per share with a corresponding reduction in the number of shares outstanding and with no change in the common stock account. A reverse stock split is usually instituted when a company has viable operating prospects but so low a stock price as to lead investors to question its viability.

Reverse Swap: A swap agreement with identical terms and opposite counterparties to an existing swap. A reverse swap eliminates net obligations under the original swap, but is used only if tax or accounting reasons make simple cancellation of the original swap unattractive to one of the counterparties.

Reverse Zero-Coupon Swap: The zero-coupon payment is made upfront, and interest rate and principal payments are paid by the counterparty over time. Like a zero-coupon swap, this is the functional equivalent of a loan. *See Prepaid Swap (2). See also Zero-Coupon Swap.*

Reversible Swap: A combination of an interest rate swap agreement and a swaption on twice the notional principal of that swap. The swaption permits one of the counterparties to reverse the swap, e.g., switch from paying fixed to receiving fixed.

Reversion: Removal of assets from an overfunded defined benefit pension plan by the plan sponsor. Increasing tax and regulatory obstacles have made reversion uncommon.

Revolving Underwriting Facility (RUF): *See Note Insurance Facility (NIF).*

Rho ρ: (1) The dollar change in an option price in response to a percentage point change in the risk-free interest rate. *See also Delta-Gamma-Kappa-Rho Hedge.* (2) Greek letter often used to denote the correlation coefficient.

Right: An in-the-money option, usually with a very short life, distributed to a firm's shareholders and giving them the opportunity to purchase a new issue of securities below current or expected market prices. Rights may be sold or exercised, or, on rare occasions, allowed to expire. Because rights are in the money at issuance, expiration is more often a result of error or inattention than of the rights having lost all value. *Also called Stock Right, Subscription Warrant.*

Right of Offset: *See Netting Agreement.*

Right of Setoff: *See Netting Agreement.*

Rising Star: A bond whose rating has been increased by a rating agency as a result of improvement in the credit quality of the issuer. *See also Fallen Angel, Junk Bond.*

Risk: Exposure to uncertain change. In popular

Rho for a Call Option

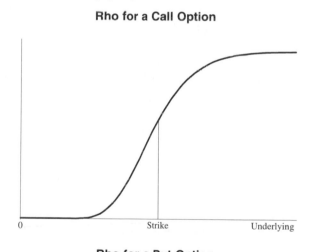

Rho for a Put Option

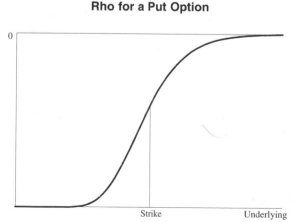

usage, adverse change is appropriately emphasized. Annualized standard deviation of return is the generic measurement of risk in most markets, but both asset and liability managers increasingly add other statistical measures, such as skewness and kurtosis, to a risk profile, or, even better, look at the entire probability distribution of returns and the maximum cost of adverse developments. *See Kurtosis, Skewness, Standard Deviation (SD, σ), Volatility, and specific types or causes of risk.*

Risk Analysis Program (RAP): A computer graphics and/or spreadsheet program used to measure the static market exposure of a portfolio and/or to analyze the portfolio's performance under a series of rate or price scenarios.

Risk Arbitrage: *See Arbitrage.*

Risk Assessment Matrix (Ram): A tabular organization and quantification of risk types, levels, and locations in an operation or organization. The Ram is an intermediate step in some systems for risk measurement and control.

Risk Averse: An attitude toward risk that causes an investor to prefer an investment with a certain outcome to an investment with the same expected value but an uncertain outcome.

Risk Aversion Coefficient: The marginal rate at which an investor is willing to sacrifice expected return in order to lower variance by one unit.

Risk Equivalent Unit (REU): The delta of an option times the aggregate underlying position covered by an option contract. *See, for example, Stock Equivalent (2).*

Risk Management: The application of financial analysis and diverse financial instruments to the control and, typically, the reduction of selected types of risk. *Also called Exposure Management. See Risk Management discussion, pp. 3-4.*

Risk Measurement: Typically, a reference to the oversight activities performed for the top management of a corporate or fund management organization. The risk measurement staff evaluates and oversees the risk management activities of others, including traders and first-line management. *See also Capital Adequacy Directive.*

Risk Measurement Systems: *See RiskMetrics, RAROC 2020.*

Risk Measurement Units (RMUs): Currency-denominated risk ratings assigned to specific financial instruments. RMUs extend the probability techniques applied through value at risk to take into account average correlation relationships among financial instruments used by an enterprise. In this sense, they are roughly additive (or subtractive, if negative) in measuring the total currency-denominated financial risk exposure to which the enterprise is subject.

Risk Neutral: An attitude toward risk that leads an investor to be indifferent between an investment with a certain outcome and a risky investment with the same expected value but an uncertain outcome. A risk neutral investor's indifference curve is flat in dimensions of expected return and risk. *See also Indifference Curve.*

Risk Pool: A term used in insurance to designate a collection of risks associated with a specific set of contingent obligations and usually financed by a specific agreement among underwriters.

Risk Premium: (1) An additional required rate of return due to extra risk incurred from investing in an asset. (2) The difference between the expected total return from a risky investment and the risk-free rate.

Risk Reversal: *See Equity Risk Reversal.*

Risk Seeking: An attitude toward risk that causes an investor to prefer an investment with the same expected value but an uncertain outcome to an investment with a certain outcome.

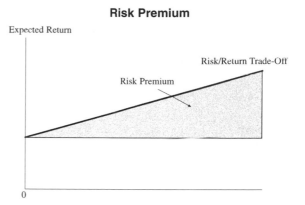

Risk Transfer: The use of a security or contract to change the pattern of cash flows in a portfolio of assets or liabilities.

Risk-Adjusted Return On Capital (RAROC): A technique for risk analysis and project evaluation that requires a higher net return for a riskier project than for a less risky project. The risk adjustment is performed by reducing the risky return at the project or instrument return level, rather than by adjusting the capital charge. *See also Return On Risk-Adjusted Capital (RORAC), Risk-Adjusted Return On Risk-Adjusted Capital (RARORAC), RAROC 2020.*

Risk-Adjusted Return On Risk-Adjusted Capital (RARORAC): A combination of risk-adjusted return on capital (RAROC) and return on risk-adjusted capital (RORAC), in which specific risk adjustments are made to the return stream and the capital charge is varied to reflect different expectations of risk in different businesses. While this may seem like double-counting, the adjustments on each side of the process usually cover different risks. *See Return On Risk-Adjusted Capital (RORAC), Risk-Adjusted Return On Capital (RAROC).*

Risk-Controlled Arbitrage: A complex risk management strategy practiced by some savings institutions. The bank buys mortgages financed with short-term borrowings, swaps the mortgage cash flows, and uses collars to reduce various components of interest rate and prepayment risk. Many thrifts who used these techniques found their position was neither risk-controlled nor an arbitrage.

Risk-Free Rate: Modern portfolio theory postulates the existence of at least one risky asset and one risk-free asset, usually taken to be Treasury bills or comparable short-term sovereign debt. The risk-free rate is the rate of return on the risk-free asset. This risk-free rate is lower than the expected return on the risky asset, because issuers have to offer a risk-averse investor the expectation of a higher return to induce him to abandon the risk-free asset for an investment with uncertain returns or, say, credit risk.

RiskMetrics: A data set containing financial instrument prices, volatilities, and correlations distributed without charge by J.P. Morgan. Its early availability, its "price," and an excellent job of explanation by J.P. Morgan have made it the principal basis of comparison for all subsequent risk management databases.

Risk Neutral Valuation: A valuation process based on the ability to establish a perfect hedge either dynamically or through a buy and hold strategy. Although this valuation assumes that the expected growth rate is equal to the risk-free rate, because risk neutral investors do not demand a risk premium, the solution applies to all investors regardless of risk preference.

Robust Statistic: A statistic that retains its usefulness even when one or more of its assumptions is violated.

Rocket Scientist: The popular press' designation for the creators of risk management products and services and for the managers of risk management programs. Frequently used as a pejorative.

Roll Date: *See Reset Date (1), Rate Fixing Date.*

Roll Down: To close an option position and replace it with a new position with a lower strike price.

Roll Forward: To close an option or futures position and replace it with a new position with a more distant expiration date. *Also called Switch.*

Roll-Geske-Whaley Model: An application of Geske's compound option pricing formula that yields an exact formula for the value of an American call option on a discrete dividend-paying asset.

Roll Risk: *See Rollover Risk.*

Roll Up: To close an option position and replace it with a new position with a higher strike price.

Roll-Down Call: A call option with a special provision that provides for reset of the strike to a lower level if the underlying falls far enough to hit the trigger price—which is usually the same as the reset strike. The option then becomes a down-and-out call struck at the lower level with an outstrike at an even lower level. If the underlying price continues to decline and hits the outstrike prior to maturity, the call is cancelled and expires worthless, regardless of what happens to the asset price after that time. *See also Roll-Up Put (diagrams). Compare with Strike-Step Option.*

Roll-Up Put: A put option with a special provision that provides for reset of the strike to a higher level if the price of the underlying rises enough to hit the trigger price—which is usually the same as the reset strike. The rolled-up put then becomes an up-an-out put, with an outstrike at an even higher price on the underlying. If the underlying asset price hits the outstrike prior to maturity, the put is cancelled and expires worthless regardless of what happens to the asset price after that time. *See also Roll-Down Call. Compare with Strike-Step Option.*

Rollercoaster Swap: An interest rate swap agreement with a notional principal amount that fluctuates periodically or in response to a change initiated by one of the counterparties, usually to accommodate the seasonal or other periodic

Comparison of Roll-Up and Standard Put Option Payouts Under Three Price Scenarios

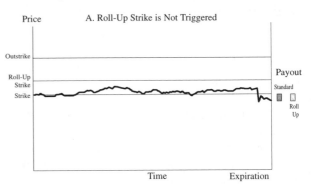

A. Roll-Up Strike is Not Triggered

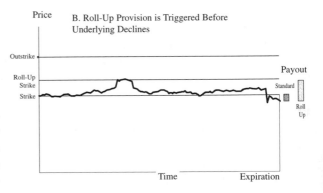

B. Roll-Up Provision is Triggered Before Underlying Declines

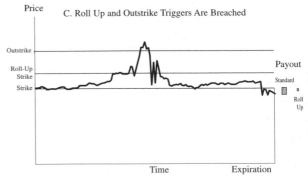

C. Roll Up and Outstrike Triggers Are Breached

financing requirements of that counterparty. *Also called Concertina Swap.*

Rolling Down the Yield Curve: *See Playing the Yield Curve.*

Rolling Hedge: Using the relatively high liquidity in exchange-traded futures and option contracts to maintain a continuous (relatively short-term) risk-offsetting position by closing contracts as they approach maturity and opening more distant positions.

Rolling Over: (1) The process by which an investor closes an option or futures contract with a near-term expiration and opens a contract on the same side of the market (long or short) with a more distant expiration. (2) More generally, substituting a position with a different expiration date and/or a different strike price for a previously established position. The process is called rolling up when substituting an option with a higher strike price, rolling down when substituting an option with a lower strike price, and rolling forward when substituting an option or futures contract with a more distant expiration.

Rolling Spot Currency Contract: A currency contract introduced by the Chicago Mercantile Exchange to permit currency futures trading without the problems usually associated with spot/futures basis. A daily adjustment at the spot/next (day) swap rate creates a futures contract that has essentially no carry cost or benefit.

Rollover Replication: Any method of replicating or hedging a long-term option position with a series of shorter-term option positions.

Rollover Risk: Exposure to actual or opportunity loss from mispricing of an option or futures contract at the time an old position must be closed and a new position opened. *Also called Roll Risk. See also Execution Risk, Unwinding Risk.*

Rotation: In some markets, notably listed stock and stock index option markets, market makers may go through an opening rotation in which all the option series in a particular underlying are opened in turn using a call auction procedure. A similar reopening rotation may be followed if trading is interrupted due to a major development during the course of a trading day. A closing rotation may be followed to determine appropriate closing prices or quotes, particularly on inactive issues. Increasing reliance on automatic quotation devices encourages option specialists to open all series at once.

Round Trip: A purchase followed by a sale or a sale followed by a purchase of a cash instrument or a derivative security.

Round Turn: An opening trade in a futures market followed by a closing trade. Futures commissions are often charged on a round turn rather than on a single transaction.

Rubinstein-Dupire-Derman Models: *See Dupire-Derman-Rubinstein Models.*

Rule of Seventy-Two: A close approximation of the time it takes for money invested at a particular interest rate to double. Money invested at 6% will double in approximately twelve years.

$$\frac{72}{6} = 12$$

Rule 144A: An SEC rule issued in 1990 that modified a two-year holding period requirement on privately placed securities by permitting large institutions to trade these positions among themselves.

Rung: A threshold or minimum payout level in a ladder option or note. *Also called Value Lock Level, Threshold Level.*

Russian Option: A perpetual lookback option that is either American or Bermudian in style.

S

Safe Harbor: A set of conditions specified by a regulatory body describing the circumstances under which an activity may be conducted without regulatory risk or interference.

Safe Return Certificate: An equity-linked note (ELN) with a guaranteed return of principal. *See Equity-Linked Note (ELN) (diagrams).*

Safety First Objective Function: An objective function that has as a primary consideration the attainment of a minimum target and as a secondary consideration the attainment of a more ambitious target. Maximization of expected return subject to 95% confidence of a positive return is an example of a safety first objective function.

Saitori: Special members of the Tokyo Stock Exchange who match buy and sell orders in stock, futures, and options markets. In contrast to specialists in some U.S. markets and market makers in most world equity markets, Saitori do not take positions for their own account. They do assume responsibility for maintaining orderly and, to the extent possible, continuous markets. A trade that adversely affects market stability is often delayed by the saitori to see if an order on the other side of the market will arrive. Individuals filling a similar role on the Osaka stock exchange are called *nakadachi* members. *Compare to Specialist.*

Same Day Funds Settlement (SDFS): A payment and funds transfer system introduced in the U.S. in early 1996 to increase payment and settlement efficiency and reduce transaction-related risks by adopting a new same day payment standard to replace next day (overnight) settlement (NDS). *See also Next Day Settlement (NDS).*

Same Day Securities Settlement (SDSS): A proposed system to clear and settle securities transactions on the day of the trade.

Same Day Settlement: *See Cash Settlement (3).*

Samurai Bond: A yen-denominated bond issued by a non-Japanese company in Japan. Analogous to Yankee bonds in the U.S. and Bulldog bonds in the U.K. *See Shibosai Bond.*

Samurai Warrants: European-style capped calls convertible into non-voting equity. The non-voting feature is usually linked to restrictions on foreign ownership or control.

Sandwich Spread: *See Alligator Spread, Butterfly Spread (diagram).*

Saturday Night Special: A surprise takeover attempt launched over a weekend.

Saw-Toothed Convergence: A phenomenon associated with using numerical methods to price options. The approximation to the analytical value improves with the number of periods, then gets worse, then again improves, and then worsens, repeating this pattern as it approaches the analytical value. This problem occurs when using a binomial tree to price barrier options, and is caused by option specification error. *See Option Specification Error, Quantization Error.*

Scale Order: Instructions to buy or sell part of the order at each price as the market rises (scale up) or declines (scale down). The order may give precise instructions on how much is to be bought or sold at a given price, or some discretion may be left with the broker.

Scaling Factor: (1) A multiplier or divisor used to bring a raw index number or other quantity into a desired range for trading purposes or for comparison with other figures. (2) A multiplier, originally set at 3, used to increase a bank value at risk calculation to arrive at a capital requirement.

Scatter Plot: A graph consisting of a collection of points meant to show the relationship between one variable plotted on the vertical or Y axis, and another plotted on the horizontal or X axis.

Scenario Analysis: A risk measurement technique that revalues a position or portfolio at several distinct values of the underlying asset(s) within a specified interval, typically the current price plus or minus 2 or 3 standard deviations of daily or monthly moves. The emphasis is on estimating the profit or loss under specific circumstances, especially under unfavorable circumstances. *See also Simulation Analysis.*

Scheduled (SCH) Bond: A collateralized mortgage obligation that pays principal based on a schedule, but does not fit the definition of a planned amortization class (PAC) bond or a targeted amortization class (TAC) bond.

Scorched Earth Policy: A takeover defense strategy that jettisons assets and takes on liabilities to render the target company unattractive if the acquirer proceeds.

Screen Trading: A reference to a trading system that involves the display of firm bids and offers on a computer monitor. The underlying trading system may permit completion of trades with orders entered at a terminal (Globex, DTB), or larger trades may be completed only after the parties exchange a telephone call (Nasdaq).

Scrip: A temporary document used as a money substitute or as evidence of a right to receive a security or a fractional unit of a security.

Seagull: A long at- or near-the-money call financed by the sale of an out-of-the-money call and an out-of-the-money put. A high-cost bird. *See Stair Step Option Strategy.*

Seasonal Swap: A variable notional principal swap designed to accommodate the financing or currency needs of a seasonal business. *See Tailored Swap.*

Seasoned Security: (1) A stock, bond, or other security that has been trading long enough to shake off any effects of its public offering on its price behavior. (2) A security that has been outstanding for at least forty days after a Euromarket offering has been completed. Seasoning must precede any sale of a Euromarket security to certain U.S. investors.

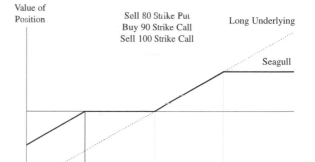

Payoff Pattern of a Seagull

Value of Position

Sell 80 Strike Put
Buy 90 Strike Call
Sell 100 Strike Call

Long Underlying

Seagull

Short Put Strike 80   Long Call Strike 90   Short Call Strike 100   Value of Underlying

Second Generation Duration: A measure of duration in which the relevant cash flows are discounted not by the yield to maturity of the instrument in question, but rather by the yields associated with zero-coupon bonds that mature simultaneously with each cash flow.

Secondary Currency Option: An option contract or an equity or debt instrument with a payoff in a different currency than the underlying's trading currency. *See, for example, Guaranteed Exchange Rate Warrant, Quantity Adjusting Option (QUANTO), Currency Option.*

Secondary Market: In contrast to the primary market, where new security issues are sold to investors, the secondary market is the traditional exchange or over-the-counter market where previously issued securities are bought and sold by individual and institutional holders with brokers and dealers as intermediaries. *Also called After-Market. See also Primary Market, Third Market, Fourth Market.*

Secondary Warrants: A warrant with another warrant or a warrant fund as the underlying. A kind of compound warrant.

Section 20 Subsidiary: A highly regulated investment banking subsidiary/affiliate of a commercial bank that is eligible to conduct a narrow or broad range of investment banking activities in the U.S. under specific powers granted by the Federal Reserve Board.

Sector Rotation: An equity management style that attempts to produce superior returns by exploiting changes in the relative attractiveness of industry sectors, or, less frequently, investment concepts (i.e., information superhighway) or valuation factors (i.e., interest rates).

Secure Principal Energy Receipt (SPER): A unit consisting of interests in natural gas or oil-producing properties and zero-coupon Treasury obligations. The oil and gas interests provide a high initial cash flow and tax credits or depletion allowances to investors. The zero-coupon Treasuries assure the return of the investors' nominal principal at maturity.

Secured Investor Trust: A pool of collateralized mortgage obligations that provide the cash flow for kitchen sink bonds. The high credit ratings of these trusts may not reflect all the investment risks in the bonds. *See Kitchen Sink Bond.*

Secured Lease Obligation Bond (SLOB): As the name implies, a securitized lease asset-backed vehicle.

Securities Act of 1933: Original U.S. securities legislation requiring full disclosure of material facts in a registration statement preceding the offering of securities and prohibiting false representations and other fraudulent activities.

Securities and Exchange Commission (SEC): The regulatory agency charged with regulation of securities and securities options markets in the U.S.

Securities and Investment Board (SIB): The regulatory agency charged with regulation of securities and derivatives markets in the U.K.

Securities Exchange Act of 1934: Expanded the registration and anti-fraud provisions of the Securities Act of 1933. Regulates insider trading, proxy solicitation, and secondary trading of securities. Established the SEC.

Securities Investor Protection Corporation (SIPC): An agency that provides insurance for customer accounts carried by U.S. brokerage firms. The accounts are insured against certain losses due to failure of the firm.

Securities Lending: A carefully collateralized process of loaning portfolio positions to custodians, dealers, and short sellers who must make physical delivery of fungible positions. Securities lending can reduce custodial costs or enhance annual returns by a full percentage point or more in some markets at some times. Improvements in securities settlement procedures and systems to facilitate securities lending tend to reduce lending premiums over time. *See also Stock Loan Contracts.*

Securities Lending Credit: A special cost reduction or return enhancement component built into a financial instrument. The credit exists because the issuer of the instrument obtains a benefit from lending out a securities position. Competitive market forces push this credit on to the buyer, embedding it in the instrument. *Also called Embedded Securities Lending Credit.*

Securities Market Line: *See Market Line.*

Securitization: A process by which a loan (originally made by a bank or other financial intermediary) or some other non-traded instrument is converted into a security to increase its liquidity as a financial instrument and to reduce the financial intermediary's capital requirements (disintermediation). Securitization may involve the sale of loans (with or without recourse to the originating lender) or issuance of stand-by letters of credit and loan commitments. While securitization increases the liquidity of relatively standardized loans, it may increase the intermediary's role as a depository or holder of last resort for illiquid and relatively risky loans. *Also called Liquid Asset-Backed Securities (LABS), Securitized Receivables. See Structured Financial Transaction (1). See also Disintermediation, Pass-Through Securities.*

Securitized Options: Packaged stock or stock index options combined with another security such as a note. *See Equity-Linked Note (ELN) (diagrams).*

Securitized Receivables: *See Securitization.*

Security Specific Risk: *See Non-Systematic Risk.*

Segmented Market Hypothesis: (1) *See Preferred Habitat Hypothesis.* (2) The notion that some markets are artificially compartmentalized. One variation of this hypothesis notes that investors display a home bias in their choice of assets. Even though a more efficient portfolio is obtainable through optimal international diversification, investors sacrifice portfolio efficiency and overweight assets in their own countries.

Seigniorage: The profit made by a sovereign in issuing currency.

Select Auction Variable-Rate Securities (SAVRs): A direct auction reset municipal floating-rate note paired with residual interest bonds (RIBs) so that the municipal issuer pays a fixed rate on the combined tranches. *See Bull and Bear Notes, FLOating Auction Tax Exempts (FLOATS), Residual Interest Bonds (RIBs). See also Tax Exempt Enhanced Municipal Security (TEEMS).*

Self-Regulatory Organization (SRO): In the U.S., the front-line market regulators, such as exchanges, the National Association of Securities Dealers (NASD), and the Municipal Securities Rule Making Board (MSRB). The Investment Management Regulatory Organization (IMRO) and the Securities and Futures Authority (SFA) are important SROs in the U.K. Decisions by an SRO can be reversed by regulatory agencies and the courts.

Seller's Option: (1) A put option. (2) A securities transaction settlement arrangement by which delivery and payment can be arranged at a time of the seller's choosing (within limits).

Semi-American Option: *See Bermuda Option, Japanese Option.*

Semi-Fixed Swap: A variant on the fixed-for-floating interest rate swap with the "fixed" rate for each payment period set above or below the market swap rate dependent on the level of a designated index on the reset date. For example, with the swap rate at 6.00%, a semi-fixed swap's "fixed" rate payment might be 5.50% if the designated index is below the agreed trigger level; the rate might be 7.25% if the index is above the trigger. Trigger indexes can be any financial or economic variable chosen by the parties to the semi-fixed swap.

Semistrong Form: *See Efficient Market.*

Semivariance: A measure of downside risk computed as the average of the squared deviations below the mean return. $\dfrac{\sum\limits_{i=1}^{n}(x_j - \mu)^2}{n}$ for all $x_i \le \mu$, zero otherwise. *See also Lower Partial Moment.*

Sensitivity: A measurement, description, or graph of the relationship between or among two or more of the variables determining option value or option value derivatives.

Separately Traded Registered Interest and Principal Securities (STRIPS): *See STRIPS, Stripped Treasury Securities.*

Separation of Variables Technique: A procedure for solving differential equations.

Separation Theorem: The idea, proposed by James Tobin, that the investment process can be separated into two distinct steps: (1) the construction of an efficient portfolio, which is a mathematical result that is invariant to preference, as described by Markowitz; and (2) the decision to combine this efficient portfolio with a riskless investment. The optimal allocation between the efficient portfolio and the riskless asset depends on investor preference. This separation plays a major role in construction of the capital market line and in the development of the Capital Asset Pricing Model.

Sequence: An electronic trading and market data system proposed by the London Stock Exchange for U.K. and international equities.

Sequential Pay (SEQ) Bond: A CMO that starts to pay principal when classes with an earlier priority have paid to zero. The SEQ bond receives uninterrupted payment of principal until paid to zero balance. A SEQ may share principal paydown on a pro rata basis with another class.

Serial Bond: One of a group of debt instruments from a single issuer with a common issue date and tranches with different maturities, and, usually, different coupons.

Serial Dependence: The association between successive observations (first order) or between observations and more distant prior values. Positive first order serial dependence indicates the presence of trends, while negative first order serial dependence indicates the presence of reversals.

Serialized Mortgage-Backed Security: *See Collateralized Mortgage Obligation (CMO).*

Series of Options: All listed option contracts of the same class having the same exercise price and expiration date, i.e., all General Motors July $40 calls.

Setoff: In case of default, the right of the non-defaulting party to reduce its debt to the defaulting party by the amount owed it. Rights of setoff, to the extent they exist in a specific situation, are a function of law in the appropriate jurisdiction, the nature of the respective obligations, and the agreement between the parties.

Settlement: (1) The process by which a trade is entered onto the books and records of all the parties to the transaction, including brokers or dealers, a clearing house, and any other financial institution with a stake in the trade. *See Improving Settlements discussion, p. 8.* (2) Completion of any required payment between two parties to discharge an obligation.

Settlement Date: The date on which the exchange of cash, securities, and paperwork involved in a transaction is completed.

Settlement Price: (1) A price, typically the exact or approximate opening or closing price, on which any maintenance or variation margin payment or cash exercise settlement is based. (2) The final delivery price used to evaluate contracts held to maturity. *Also called Delivery Price, Exchange Delivery Settlement Price (EDSP).*

Settlement Risk: Related to credit risk but not identical, settlement risk is the risk that an expected settlement payment on an obligation will not be made on time. A common example involves bilateral obligations in which one party makes a required settlement payment and the counterparty does not. Settlement risk provides an important motivation to develop netting arrangements and other safeguards. *Also called Delivery Risk, Herstatt Risk. See also Cross-Currency Settlement Risk, Daylight Risk Exposure, Fail, Multinet, Presettlement Credit Risk.*

Severability: The right to separate a hybrid instrument into components such as a bond and a warrant. In the U.S., certain customized instruments may not be severable without jeopardizing a regulatory exemption.

Shad-Johnson Agreement: An accord reached by the chairmen of the SEC and the CFTC to divide jurisdiction over options and futures on financial instruments in the U.S. This agreement was ratified by legislation in 1982. *Also called Johnson-Shad Agreement.*

Shapiro-Wilk Test: A statistical test used to determine if a set of data conforms to the normal distribution.

Share Ratio Contract: A relative performance contract introduced by the Australian Stock Exchange to compete with the Sydney Futures Exchange's single stock futures. The contract pays an amount based on the difference between the performance of a stock and the performance of a market index.

Shared Appreciation Mortgage (SAM): *See Participating Mortgage.*

Shared Currency Option Under Tender (SCOUT): *See Contingent Currency Risk.*

Shark Repellent: Any of a variety of devices designed to deter or defeat a hostile takeover. Examples include staggered multiyear terms for directors, supermajority voting requirements on some corporate actions, and golden parachute severance arrangements.

Sharpe Ratio: A risk-adjusted measure of return that divides a portfolio's return in excess of the riskless return by the portfolio's standard deviation. Because it adjusts return for total portfolio risk, an implicit assumption of the Sharpe ratio is that the portfolio will not be combined with other risky portfolios. It is relevant for performance evaluation when comparing mutually exclusive portfolios. *Compare to Treynor Measure.*

Shelf Registration: A procedure for keeping a perennially up-to-date filing with the SEC to permit an issuer to offer securities quickly when capital is needed or the market is receptive.

Shibosai Bond: A privately placed Samurai bond. *See also Samurai Bond.*

Shogun Bond: A dollar-denominated bond issued by a non-Japanese company and sold in Japan. *Also called Geisha Bond.*

Short: (1) A position whereby an investor incurs rights and obligations that mirror the risk/return characteristics of another investor's asset position, and, consequently, change in value in opposite directions to that asset position. (2) An investment position that benefits from a decline in price. (3) An investor whose position benefits from a decline in the market. *See also Short Sale.*

Short Against the Box: A short sale of securities when an identical long position is owned in the account but will not be delivered against the sale until a later date. In the U.S., selling short against the box has been used to eliminate price risk while deferring taxes on profits. Legislation has been proposed that would eliminate the tax-deferral opportunity.

Short Hedge: A risk-offsetting position that protects an investment or a liability against the adverse effects of a price decline.

Short Interest: The number of shares of an individual stock or of all the stocks listed on an exchange sold short and not yet repurchased.

Short Position: (1) A position that appreciates in value when the underlying market price decreases. Examples include selling a stock short, selling a future, buying a put, or selling a call. (2) The position of the stock or futures short seller or of the writer or seller of an option contract. Note the anomalous position of the short put that benefits from an increase in the price of the underlying.

Short Proceeds: The cash received from the short sale of a security. The interest return from investment of the short proceeds is usually divided between the short seller, who gets partial "use of proceeds," and the securities lender.

Short Sale: The sale of a security or other financial instrument not previously owned by the seller in the expectation that it will be possible to repurchase that instrument at a lower price some time in the future. The term "short sale" is ordinarily applied only to the sale of securities, but an equivalent synthetic short position can be attained through the sale of an uncovered call option and the purchase of a put or by selling a forward or a future. *See also Short (3).*

Short Sale Rule: A mildly controversial requirement imposed by the SEC requiring that short sales can only be made on a plus tick or zero plus tick. Supporters of this rule argue that it prevents bear raiders from selling short to drive a stock down.

Short Squeeze: An upward movement in the price of an instrument stimulated by shorts rushing to cover their positions in response to a fundamental or technical development or in response to a request from a lender for the return of borrowed stock.

Short Tendering: The practice of tendering more shares in response to a tender offer than an investor owns outright and has not covered with short in-the-money call positions. Most short tendering has been illegal in the U.S. since 1985.

Short-Dated Swap: An alternative to futures contracts used to adjust the effective maturity of commercial paper or similar borrowings.

Short-Short Rule: A provision of the tax code that disqualifies a mutual fund from income pass-through treatment as a regulated investment company if more than 30% of its gross income before deduction of losses is from gains on positions held less than three months. The purpose of this rule is to discourage active trading by mutual funds. *Also called 30% Rule. See also Full Investment Note (FIN), Regulated Investment Company.*

Short-Term Appreciation and Investment Return Trust (STAIR): A synthetic PERCS-type structure consisting of long positions in Treasury securities and short in-the-money puts on a portfolio. STAIRs have a payout pattern equivalent to PERCS and short-term equity participation units (STEP units). *Also called Performance Equity-Linked Redemption Quarterly Paid Security (PERQS). See Trust for Income Participation from Stocks (TIPS). See also Preference Equity Redemption Cumulative Stock (PERCS) (diagram).*

Short-Term Auction Rate (STAR): *See Auction Rate Preferred Stock (ARPS).*

Short-Term Equity Participation Units (STEP Units): A synthetic PERCS structure using a portfolio or index rather than a single stock. The basic structure features a higher yield than the underlying instrument(s) and full participation in the value of the underlying up to the capped price. The proceeds from the sale of a cap (call) are invested in an annuity to pay the higher dividend yield. A minor tax feature defers tax on the incremental yield until maturity, typically three years. At expiration of the trust, large unitholders can elect to receive stock; otherwise, shares will be sold and proceeds distributed. Unlike PERCS, these synthetics raise no new capital for issuers. *Also called Packaged Equity Trust Securities (PETS). See Trust for Income Participation from Stocks (TIPS). See also Preference Equity Redemption Cumulative Stock (PERCS) (diagrams).*

Short-Term Instruments Linked to Treasuries (STILTs): A principal protected note with a variable coupon linked to the absolute or relative performance of one or more Treasury instruments or index rates.

Short the Basis: A hedged position usually consisting of a long futures or forward contract and a short cash or actual. The opposite position would be long the basis. *See also Basis.*

Shortfall Constraint: An approach to risk management that places primary emphasis on the undesirability of an asset shortfall, i.e., of having more liabilities than assets when the liabilities come due. This approach is beginning to supplant the traditional emphasis on standard deviation as the measure of risk for many pension plan sponsors.

Shout Option: (1) An option contract with the strike set at—or relative to—the spot price of the underlying at the time the optionholder "shouts" to fix the strike. *See Deferred Strike or Strike Price Option.* (2) Less frequently, an option contract with the settlement price set at the spot price in effect at the time the optionholder "shouts" to fix the settlement price. The settlement is not made until the scheduled expiration date. *See Deferred Payment American Option.* (3) A variation of a ladder option in which the holder has one opportunity to lock in a minimum payout during the life of the option. When the owner contacts the seller and "shouts" to lock in the intrinsic value of the option at a minimum, the investor retains further potential to benefit from favorable moves, but is assured of a minimum payout. *See also Ladder Option or Note (diagram).*

Side-by-Side Trading: Trading a security and its options on the same exchange within a space where non-electronic communication is possible between markets.

Siegel's Paradox: The observation that if two investors from different countries have the same expectation of the probable distribution of future exchange rates, the expected returns of the two currencies are not offsetting. If the current exchange rate of U.S. dollars per pound equals 1.5, and a U.S. investor and a U.K. investor both expect it to change to 1.6, the expected return of the dollar from the U.K. investor's perspective equals –6.25%, while the expected return of the pound from the U.S. investor's perspective equals 6.67%.

Sigma σ: The standard deviation or volatility of the price or rate of an instrument, frequently the instrument underlying an option. *See Standard Deviation (SD, σ), Normal Distribution.*

Signal Analysis: Interpretative techniques that see financial decisions as diverse as dividend declarations, stock repurchase announcements, debt versus equity financing choices, and changes in cash balances as indications of management's confidence or intentions. The signals attributed to management are treated as probabilistic indications of attitudes and convictions. In some cases, management may be sending an intentional signal; other signals may be inadvertent or even incorrect interpretations of management's position.

Simulation: A technique used to illustrate what might have happened if a particular investment program had been followed during a past period or in a hypothetical random price or yield environment. Simulations may be useful at times, but they are often based on subtly unrealistic assumptions, particularly when options are involved.

Simulation Analysis: A risk measurement technique based on ranges of historical price changes and/or Monte Carlo methods. Typically, the position or portfolio is revalued at each price or set of prices generated by the price generation mechanism. Either the largest absolute loss or a conservative percentile of losses reflecting a confidence interval analysis is selected as the appropriate measure of the "worst case" position or portfolio risk. *See Worst Case, Scenario Analysis.*

Single Issue Options: Low strike price options traded in Finland to provide investors with most features of stock ownership when actual ownership of registered shares cannot be transferred. *See also Low Exercise Price Options (LEPOs).*

Single Monthly Mortality (SMM): A method of measuring the prepayment rate of a mortgage pool. Specifically, the single monthly mortality is equal to the unscheduled prepayments during a month divided by the scheduled balance for the end of the month expressed as a percentage. *See also Conditional Prepayment Rate (CPR).*

Single Point Adjustable-Rate Stock (SPARS): A floating-rate preferred stock with a dividend reset every forty-nine days at a specified relationship to high-grade commercial paper. *See Adjustable-Rate Preferred Stock (ARPS).*

Sinking Fund: A provision of a bond indenture that commits an issuer to call bonds prior to maturity or to purchase them in the open market. Option theory has been applied to evaluate a sinking fund provision to determine how best to meet the sinking fund obligation when the issuer has some flexibility. *See also Double Option (2).*

Skew: A reference to a graph or table of the at- and out-of-the-money strike implied volatilities structure of put and call options with a common underlying and common maturity. Less frequently, a reference to the term structure of volatility. *See also Implied Distribution, Smile, Term Structure of Volatility.*

Skew Measure: The change in volatility (standard deviation) for a 1% change in option strike or exercise price ($\Delta\sigma/\Delta E$). *Sometimes called Iota (I).*

Skewness: A measure of the non-symmetry of a distribution. Symmetrical distributions have a skewness value of zero. A distribution with negative skewness has more observations in the left tail (left of the peak or mode), and a distribution with positive skewness has more observations in the right tail. *See also Risk.*

Sleeping Beauty: A potential takeover target that has not yet attracted the attention of suitors.

Sleeping Point: An investment policy linked to the saying that an investor should sell down to the sleeping point—the point at which he or she is no longer losing sleep over the risk of the position.

Sliding Floor Plan: A price protection strategy that calls for a commodity producer to pay for a strip of put options on his expected production volume by granting lookback calls on part of the expected production. *A variation on a Participating Collar (diagram).*

Small-Cap Investment Manager: An equity portfolio manager who specializes in smaller companies. In the U.S., for example, his benchmark might be the Russell 2000 Index or the Standard & Poor's 600 Small Cap Index.

Smile: A reference to the common shape of a graph of at- or out-of-the-money put and call implied volatilities for options with a common expiration date. The name comes from the fact that the furthest out-of-the-money options generally have the highest implied volatilities, causing the ends of the graph to turn up. Oftentimes, the implied volatilities do not curve upward for strike prices above the market price, resembling more of a smirk than a smile. *See also Dupire-Derman-Rubinstein Models, Implied Distribution, Implied Binomial Tree, Skew, Term Structure of Volatility.*

Smithsonian Agreement: A currency exchange rate plan that replaced the fixed exchange rates and gold convertibility of the dollar under Bretton Woods with a major currency realignment and broader intervention ranges. A prelude to the subsequent floating exchange rate mechanism.

Society for Worldwide Interbank Financial Telecommunications (SWIFT): A bank-owned support organization and network for international message transfer and securities and currency trade processing. The sponsor of the SWIFT codes for currency designation. Corporations have limited access to the SWIFT network through sponsorship by their member bank.

Soft Call Protection: A limited premium to parity that an issuer must pay to call a bond after any period of hard call protection has passed. Non-convertible bonds can usually be called at a premium that declines gradually as the bond approaches maturity. A typical soft call provision might require a 50-basis point per year premium for an early call. *See also Call Protection, Hard Call Protection.*

Solvency: Ability to meet financial obligations on an ongoing basis. Some financial organizations (insurance companies and banks, for example) are subject to specific solvency tests imposed by regulators.

Sovereign Risk: *See Country Risk.*

Span: A state space is spanned if there exists a security or combination of securities that pays off in every possible state. If markets are complete, a portfolio of Arrow-Debreu securities will completely span the state space. In a complete market, all outcomes can be replicated with elemental securities, thereby rendering derivative instruments redundant. *See also Arrow-Debreu Security.*

Spearman Rank Correlation Coefficient: The correlation between the data of two series that have been transformed from their original units into their respective rankings.

Special Claim On Residual Equity (SCORE): The warrant-like component of an Americus Trust Unit. *See also Americus Trust, Prescribed Right to Income and Maximum Equity (PRIME) (diagram), Termination Claim.*

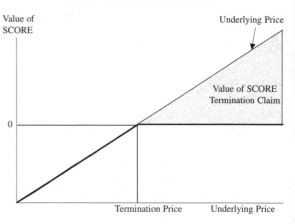

Valuation of Americus Trust SCORE Termination Claim

Special Drawing Rights (SDR): Reserve assets that serve as a substitute for gold and convertible currencies. Special drawing rights, which are allocated by the International Monetary Fund to its member countries, are backed by the full faith and credit of the governments of the members.

Special Equity Claim Security (Specs): The Canadian equivalent of an Americus Trust *Special Claim On Residual Equity (SCORE).*

Special Expiration Price Option: *See Barrier Option, Down-and-Out Call, Down-and-Out Put, Out Option, Up-and-Out Call, Up-and-Out Put.*

Special Miscellaneous Account (SMA): An account defined in Regulation T that is used to accumulate the value of a brokerage customer's excess margin and buying power. The workings of a special miscellaneous account often enable an investor to borrow somewhat more than Regulation T requirements appear on the surface to permit.

Special Purpose Vehicle (SPV): *See Bankruptcy Remote Entity, Derivatives Product Company (DPC).*

Special Quotation (SQ): The special opening settlement price that determines the value of a Japanese stock index futures or options contract at expiration. Similar settlement prices are computed in other markets.

Special Repo Rate: A below market overnight or term lending rate on a loan collateralized by a "special" on-the-run Treasury security that is in short supply and that dealers need to borrow. The spread between the general repo rate on securities not in much demand and the special repo rate on a specific bond or note is that issue's loan premium. *See also Repurchase Agreement (Repo), (RP).*

Specialist: A floor member of an exchange who accepts primary responsibility for making a fair and orderly market in a security at all times the exchange is open for business. In general, a specialist will make a two-sided market and provide limited liquidity to other market participants. *Compare to Saitori.*

Specialty Management: Any of a variety of limited scope investment management styles or techniques offered by managers not attempting to provide a full range of investment management products and services. Specialty managers are often, but not always, small firms.

Specialty Option: *See, for example, Alternative Option (diagram), Collar (2) (diagram), Outperformance Option (diagram). Often called Exotic Options.*

Specie: Metal money. Use of the term is often confined to gold and silver coins—as distinct from the base metal coins in widespread use today.

Specific Risk: *See Non-Systematic Risk.*

Speculation: (1) A term of opprobrium applied to any financial instrument or transaction of which the speaker or writer disapproves. (2) A financial transaction characterized by the acceptance of greater exposure to price change than might be usual or appropriate for the individual or entity taking the position. (3) A technical term characterizing certain transactions on a futures or commodity exchange in which the entity taking the position is increasing rather than reducing exposure to a specific category of price risk. (4) A position taken because it offers the prospect of capital gain. (5) Purposeful ownership of a less than fully diversified portfolio in pursuit of a superior risk-adjusted return. See "Exactly What Do You Mean by Speculation?" by Martin S. Fridson, *The Journal of Portfolio Management*, Fall 1993, pp. 29-39, for illustrations of the difficulties of defining speculation adequately.

Speed: An option derivative or sensitivity calculation that measures the change in gamma in response to the change in the price of the underlying, *ceteris paribus*: $\Delta\gamma/\Delta x$. The third derivative of option price with respect to the underlying price. *Also called Omega (1) (diagram).*

Spin-Off: Usually a reference to a corporation that was a wholly owned subsidiary of another corporation until the parent distributed some or all of the subsidiary's shares by sale or by dividend.

Spline Smoothing: In data analysis, a technique used to fit a smooth curve to an otherwise irregular scatter plot of points on a graph. The technique involves fitting a polynomial function to ranges of the data in such a way that the fitted curves join as the curve passes from one range to the next and have the same slopes and second derivatives at such points.

Split Cylinder or Split Risk Reversal: The classic equity risk reversal or collar structure with one modification: different expiration dates on the put and call (cap and floor).

Split-Fee Option: A compound option, usually a long call on a long put, used in mortgage markets to offset the risk of interest rate fluctuations between the time a mortgage commitment is made and the date the mortgages are scheduled to be delivered. *See also Compound Option (1) (diagram).*

Spot Deferred Contract: A forward contract that gives the seller the option to roll the contract forward rather than make delivery on a specific date. Often used by gold producers to hedge gold price exposure. *Also called Undated Forward.*

Spot Exchange Rate: The exchange rate at which one currency can be exchanged for another at the present time as opposed to a future date. Settlement of spot transactions usually occurs within two days.

Spot Market: The market for a cash or current (as opposed to forward) commodity or financial instrument taking the form of (1) an organized, self-regulated central market; (2) a decentralized over-the-counter market; or (3) a local organization that provides a market for a small region.

Spot Month: The shortest available futures contract.

Spot Price: The current market price. For example, the current price of a stock, bond, or currency for normal delivery or of a cash commodity for prompt delivery.

Spot Start: A financial contract whose effective life begins at the time the agreement is reached. *Contrast with Forward Start Agreement.*

Spot versus Forward Delta Hedge: An adjustment in the size of a hedging position to allow for the effect of cost of carry on the forward price. The adjustment can be made on the delta of the position or on the forward price or rate. If the adjustment is made on the delta, the spot delta is multiplied by 1 + basis (with basis expressed as a rate or decimal fraction of the underlying), and the resulting forward delta is used to compute the size of the position to be taken in the forward or futures market.

Spot and Forward

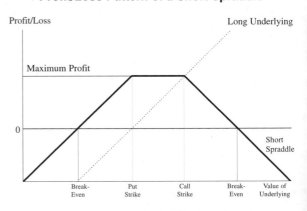

Spraddle: A combination option similar to a straddle in which the put side and the call side have the same expiration date but different strike prices. The put strike price is below the call strike price, leaving a range of prices on the expiration date at which both options will expire worthless. *Often called a Strangle or a Surf and Turf. See also Spread (7). See Combination Option.*

Profit/Loss Pattern of a Short Spraddle

Spread: (1) The difference between the bid and the asked price in any market. (2) The difference between the yields or prices of two financial instruments. (3) The price or rate difference between two delivery months in a futures market. (4) A transaction designed to profit from a narrowing or widening of a price or yield spread. *Also called Spread Position, Spread Warrant.* (5) For listed options: The purchase of one option and the sale of another of the same type on the same security or index. The investor setting up the spread hopes to profit from a favorable change in the difference between the prices of the two options. If the number of options purchased is not equal to the number sold, the position may be called a ratio spread or a variable spread. *Also called Spread Position, Option Spread. See Hedge.* (6) The difference between the price investors pay an underwriter for a new securities offering and the proceeds of the financing paid to the issuer. (7) In the old conventional stock option market (largely pre-1973): A straddle-like position in which the put side and the call side were struck at different prices. Typically, the put strike was below and the call strike was above the market price of the stock at the time the spread was established. In the listed option market, this position is called a *Spraddle* or a *Strangle. See Combination Option.*

Spread Conversion: *Also called Conversion Spread. See Equity Risk Reversal (diagram), Forward Rate Bracket, Interest Rate Collar (diagram), Range Forward Contract (diagram).*

Spread Hedge: An arbitrage or an operator's risk management position in a commodity complex. Examples include trades designed to lock in or profit from an expected change in the oil refiner's margin (the crack spread) or the soybean processor's margin (the crush spread).

Spread Option: (1) Usually, an option to lock an interest rate spread into the terms of a financial instrument. The rates may be denominated in different currencies, and the spread option may be embedded in a note or bond. *Also called Option on a Spread, Spreadtion. See Cross-Currency Cap or Floor. See also Diff or Difference Option, International Spread Option, Warrant or Note.* (2) *See Outperformance Option (diagram).*

Spread Position: *See Spread (4), (5).*

Spread Put Bond: A bond puttable to the issuer or to an underwriter at a spread measured in basis points over the yield of a comparable maturity Treasury issue. The purpose behind a spread put provision is to protect the bond buyer from an adverse change in the issuer's credit rating.

Spread Risk: A generalized measure of exposure to changing spreads, usually between government and non-government yields. Spread risk is typically measured by simulating a 50-basis point (0.5%) move in all non-government yields while government yields are fixed. *See also Absolute Risk, Curve Risk, Loss Limit.*

Spread Warrant: *See International Spread Option, Warrant, or Note, Spread (4).*

Spread-Lock Agreement: (1) A contract to buy or issue a debt instrument at a preset spread to the yield on a specific bond or note at a specified future date. A forward contract on a yield spread. (2) A contract that guarantees an investor's cost of rolling futures contracts from one expiration to the next, relative to a calculated fair value basis. The cost of a futures roll spread-lock is primarily a function of the liquidity of the market and the extent to which a rollover spread premium and/or discount is typically available.

Spread-Lock Option: (1) An option to enter into a spread-lock agreement on a yield spread. (2) An option to roll one or a sequence of futures contracts forward to more distant months at an absolute spread or a specific spread relative to the fair value basis.

Spread-Lock Swap: (1) An interest rate swap agreement with an option to fix the floating-rate payment at a fixed spread over a benchmark Treasury at some date or during some period in the future. *See Swap Spread Lock.* (2) An interest rate swap agreement with one payment stream referenced at a fixed spread over a benchmark rate, usually a non-standard benchmark rate.

Spreadtion: *See Spread Option (1), Option on a Spread.*

Springing Warrants: *See Debt with Springing Warrants.*

Square Mile: *See City (of London).*

Square Root Law: The principle that the standard deviation of a Markov process usually increases proportionately to the square root of time. This relationship is often used to estimate an annualized volatility from a short-term volatility measurement or estimate. For example, a monthly volatility (standard deviation) can be converted to an annualized number by multiplying it by $\sqrt{12}$. *See also Markov Process.*

Square Root of Three ($\sqrt{3}$) Rule: The observation that the effective volatility of the underlying used in pricing an average rate or average strike option is equal to the actual volatility (standard deviation) divided by $\sqrt{3}$: σ $\sqrt{3}$).

Square Root Process: A characteristic of a stochastic volatility model that holds that variance increases proportionately with the quantity: time divided by the square root of the underlying asset price. *Compare Constant Elasticity of Variance (CEV) Model.*

Squeeze: Pressure (usually upward) on a price resulting from a temporary shortage of supply. An extreme shortage might lead to a corner. *See Corner.*

St. Petersburg Paradox: The paradox that the expected value equals infinity for a game in which a player's winnings keep doubling for consecutive tosses of a fair coin that continues to come up heads, but that no reasonable person would be willing to pay more than a few dollars to participate in this game. If the first toss of the coin has a 50% chance of returning $1.00, that opportunity has an expected value of $0.50. There is a 1/4 chance of two consecutive heads, thus the second toss has a 25% chance of returning $2.00, which corresponds to an expected value of $0.50. The third toss has a 1/8 chance of returning $4.00, and again an expected value of $0.50. Therefore, the expected value of participating in this game is the sum of an infinite sequence of $0.50 values. For investors who have a log wealth utility function, however, the expected utility of this game is only $2.68, which is the limit of the following sequence:

$$1/2 \times ln(1) + 1/4 \times ln(2) + 1/8 \text{ x } ln(4) + 1/16 \times ln(8) + ... = 2.68$$

Stabilization: Entry of a series of bids and offers designed to keep a security price or rate within a narrow band for a period of time. *See also Pegging.*

Stabilized Mortgage Reduction Term (SMRT) Bond: A CMO tranche with principal payments matched to the sinking fund schedule of a corporate bond unless the prepayment rate on the mortgage bond falls outside a designated range.

Stack and Roll: *See Stack Hedge.*

Stack Hedge: A risk-offsetting position in which a long-term cash market commitment is hedged with a rolling sequence of risk-offsetting contracts expiring on dates appropriate to the risk being hedged. Compared to a strip hedge, the stack hedge usually has more near-term contracts. *Also called Stack and Roll. See also Strip Hedge.*

Staged Drawdown Swap: *See Accreting Principal Swap (APS).*

Stair Step Option Strategy: A position created with options and/or the underlying instrument that has a profit loss profile similar to two stair steps when profit and loss is graphed against the price of the underlying. *See Seagull (diagram).*

Stakeholder: A reference to any individual or organization with a "stake" in the fortunes of an enterprise. Connotes the viewpoint that corporate management has responsibilities to employees, suppliers, communities, and others, as well as to shareholders.

Stamp Tax: (1) A tax imposed on the issuance of new securities. (2) Often used to designate the securities transfer tax in the U.K. *See also Transfer Tax.*

Standard & Poor's 500 Depositary Receipts (SPDRs, pronounced "spiders"): A warehouse receipt structure, similar to the Toronto Exchange's TIPs, that provides the investor with an interest in the holdings of a trust designed to track the return of the S&P 500 index. SPDRs were introduced by the American Stock Exchange as a replacement for their ill-fated index participations. They have become one of the fastest growing fund products in history. *See also Frozen Index Fund, EXchange TRAded (EXTRA) Funds.*

Standard & Poor's Index Notes (SPINs): (1) Originally, a fixed coupon note with a below market yield and the principal payment linked to the value of the S&P 500 stock index. *Also called Stock Performance Exchange-Linked Bonds (SPELBonds).* (2) A zero-coupon equity-linked note with an American-style early exercise and settlement feature available when the index is above the embedded strike. *See Equity-Linked Note (ELN) (diagrams).*

Standard & Poor's (S&P) "r" Symbol: A lower case "r" added to S&P's ratings of certain derivatives and hybrid instruments to alert investors to the possibility of high volatility or dramatic fluctuations in expected returns.

Standard Deviation (SD, σ): The square root of the mean of the squared deviations of members of a population from their mean. The most widely used measurement of variation about a mean, and, for many purposes, a proxy for risk. The standard deviation of normally distributed random variables has many useful characteristics that, unfortunately, do not usually apply to distributions truncated or skewed by option payoff patterns. *See Sigma σ. See also Normal Distribution, Risk.*

$$\sigma = \sqrt{\frac{\sum_{i=1}^{n}(x_i - \mu)^2}{n}}$$

where σ = standard deviation of population, n = number of observations, Σ = summation sign, x_i = the value of each observation, and μ = mean of population. Note that the standard deviation for a sample is calculated by substituting $n - 1$ for n in the denominator.

Standard Error of the Mean: Standard deviation of the distribution of sample means. The word "error" refers to the sampling error, and the standard error of the mean is a measure in standard deviation terms of how close the sample mean is likely to be to the population mean.

Standard Option: A plain vanilla European- or American-style option with no bells or whistles to complicate its evaluation.

Standard Portfolio Analysis of Risk (SPAN): A margin calculation technique for a portfolio of futures and futures option positions. Originally developed for the Chicago Mercantile Exchange, it is now used by a growing number of futures and futures option markets as a mechanism for calculating margin requirements. *See also Mutual Offset System.*

Standard Prepayment Assumptions: Standard monthly and annualized mortgage principal prepayment rates published by the Public Securities Association (PSA). While the PSA rates usually bear little resemblance to actual prepayment rates, they do provide a basis for comparison and discussion. Actual rates are often described as a percentage of the PSA rate.

Standardization: A characteristic of exchange-traded derivatives instruments and publicly traded corporate offerings that makes it possible for buyers and sellers to learn the pertinent characteristics of an instrument based on a few words of description or a security identification number or symbol.

Standstill Agreement: A commitment not to purchase a target company's equity securities for a specific time period without the company's permission.

Start Date: The date—spot or forward—when some feature of a financial contract becomes effective or when interest payments or returns begin to be calculated. *Also called Effective Date.*

State Contingent Claim: *See Arrow-Debreu Security.*

STated Rate Auction Preferred Stock (STRAPS): A floating-rate preferred with an initial fixed dividend period of several years. After the fixed dividend period, the issuer resets the rate every forty-nine days by Dutch auction. *See also Auction Rate Preferred Stock (ARPS), Dutch Auction Interest and Dividend Reset.*

Statement of Financial Accounting Standards (SFAS): *See Financial Accounting Standards (FAS), Statement of Position (SOP).*

Statement of Position (SOP): An authoritative policy statement issued by the FASB mandating an accounting standard for enterprises subject to its authority. *Also called Statement of Financial Accounting Standards (SFAS). See also Financial Accounting Standards Board (FASB), Exposure Draft (ED), Financial Accounting Standard (FAS).*

Statement Of Recommended Practice (SORP): Accounting guidance for U.K. entities. SORPs are developed by industry bodies, subject to a statement from the Accounting Standards Board (ASB) that they are not inconsistent with U.K. accounting standards. Roughly equivalent to a *Financial Accounting Standard (FAS)* in the U.S.

Statute of Frauds: A law enacted in most jurisdictions requiring certain contracts to be in writing and signed by any party charged with failing to fulfill obligations under the contract. Contracts required to be in writing cannot be enforced unless they meet the requirements of the statute.

'steenth: One-sixteenth.

Step Premium Option: A variant on the contingent premium option that shares the feature that the buyer pays no upfront premium. However, at designated price levels, as the option moves toward and through the strike, some premium is paid. The premium is greater than the premium on a standard option if the option is in the money at expiration, but the total premium is less than the premium on a contingent premium option.

Step-Down Coupon Note: A debt instrument with a high coupon in earlier payment periods and a lower coupon in later payment periods. This structure is usually motivated by a low short-term rate environment, regulatory, or tax considerations. *See also Step-Up Coupon Note.*

Step-Down Option or Warrant: A stock or equity index call warrant with a downward strike price reset during a limited period, at a specific future date, and/or as a consequence of a drop in the underlying to a predetermined level. Specific terms vary with the issue. *See also Anti-Crash Warrant, Complex Option, Partial Lookback Warrant or Option, Reset Option or Warrant (diagram).*

Step-Down Swap: (1) An interest rate swap agreement with a decrease in the fixed payment rate over the life of the swap. (2) A variety of amortizing swap with a small number of reductions in the notional principal amount.

Step-Lock Option or Note: *See Ladder Option or Note (diagram).*

Step-Up Bond: *See Callable Step-Up Note.*

Step-Up Cap: A cap structure, typically embedded in a floating-rate note, that limits an interest coupon increase to a certain amount (called the jump) at each reset date. For example, a note with a step-up cap may pay 5.0% at first. With a twenty-five-basis point jump, subsequent rates will be set at the lower of (1) the reference index rate plus the agreed spread, or (2) the previous period's rate plus 0.25%. *Also called Periodic Cap. See also Jump, Lookback Step-Up Cap, Ladder Cap, Path-Dependent Floating-Rate Note.*

Step-Up Capped Floating-Rate Note: A capped floating-rate note with a cap strike that increases periodically.

Step-Up Coupon Note: A debt instrument with a low initial coupon and a higher coupon in later payment periods. *Also called Callable Step-Up Note. See also Step-Down Coupon Note.*

Step-Up Income Redeemable Equity Note (SIREN): A variation on the traditional convertible bond with a coupon rate that rises to a higher level—typically on the bond's first call date. The appeal of SIRENs lies in their ability to provide higher income in an environment where, because of rising rates, the underlying equity may not have risen enough to give the conversion feature appreciable value. In return for the higher coupon, the issuer gets easier call terms to permit refinancing if market rates drop.

Step-Up Option or Warrant: A call option with one or more scheduled increases in the strike price. Most common in the common stock warrant market, these instruments are usually designed to be held to expiration, barring a large increase in the underlying stock's dividend. Analytically, the value is rarely much greater than the value of a single strike option or warrant struck at the last (highest) strike. *See Complex Option.*

Step-Up Recovery Floater (SURF): A variation on a floating-rate note that typically pays one-half a constant maturity Treasury rate plus a spread and is subject to a floor. *A Deleveraged Instrument.*

Step-Up Swap: (1) An interest rate swap agreement with an increase in the fixed rate at one or more dates over the life of the swap. (2) A variety of accreting swap with a small number of increases in the notional principal amount. *See Accreting Principal Swap (APS).*

Stepped Tax-exempt Appreciation on Income Realization Security (STAIRS): A municipal zero-coupon bond converted to an interest-bearing security at a designated time after issuance. *See Municipal Convertible.*

Sterling At Risk (SAR): Value at risk denominated in sterling.

Sterling Transferable Accruing Government Securities (STAGS): Stripped U.K. gilts, comparable to *Separately Traded Registered Interest and Principal Securities (STRIPS), Certificate of Accrual on Treasury Securities (CATS), and Treasury Investment Growth Receipts (TIGRs)* in the U.S.

Sticky Jump (SJ) Bond: A CMO whose principal paydown is changed by the occurrence of one or more triggering event(s). The first time a trigger condition is met, the bond changes to its new priority for receiving principal and remains in its new priority for the life of the bond.

Sticky Prices: In monetary theory, the notion that goods prices react more slowly than asset prices to monetary shocks. According to the "Sticky Price Monetary Model" posited by Rudiger Dornbusch, this discrepancy causes exchange rates to overshoot their equilibrium values as measured by purchasing power parity. *See also Purchasing Power Parity.*

Stillhalters: *Swiss.* Covered calls.

Stochastic Dominance: A strategy that produces a result at least as good as the result of an alternative strategy in all states, and better than the alternative strategy in one or more states, is said to stochastically dominate the alternative strategy.

Stochastic Process: A mathematical model tracking the occurrence, at each moment after the initial time, of a random phenomenon. Brownian motion, often used to describe security price changes, is a stochastic process. In finance, stochastic processes are mechanisms for describing future prices or rates based on a combination of spot rates or prices and a random variable. Developers of option models attempt to select the random variable generating process that best matches the empirical pattern. A calculus of stochastic processes forms the basis of many option valuation models. *Also called Diffusion Process. See also Brownian Motion, Markov Process, Martingale Process, Wiener Process.*

Stochastic Volatility: A condition in which the volatility of a random variable changes randomly as the value of the random variable changes.

Stock Appreciation Income-Linked Securities (SAILS): *See Dividend Enhanced Convertible Security (DECS), Debt Exchangeable for Common Stock (DECS).*

Stock Appreciation Right: A form of incentive compensation that ties part of the income of a firm's employees to the performance of the corporation's stock. In contrast to employee stock options, stock appreciation rights pay the appreciation to the employee in cash, or in shares of the stock whose value determines the value of the appreciation rights. Accounting and tax treatment of stock appreciation rights is quite different from the treatment of employee stock options. For example, with stock appreciation rights, strong stock performance increases the corporation's compensation costs and reduces its tax payments and reported earnings. The entire payment is taxable to the employee at ordinary income rates upon receipt.

Stock Equivalent: (1) A simple or complex option position that changes in value as if it were a position in the shares of the underlying stock as the price of the underlying stock changes. The option position has risk characteristics similar or identical to the number of shares it imitates. Note that an option position does not behave as a fixed stock equivalent position at all possible prices of the underlying. (2) The share equivalent of a single option position is approximately equal to the instantaneous neutral hedge ratio at the spot price times the contract multiplier. *Also called Underlying Equivalent. See also Risk Equivalent Unit (REU), Synthetic Stock, Neutral Hedge Ratio.*

Stock Index Contingent Option: A put or call on a stock index that has value only if it is in the money and if an additional condition, usually an interest rate level, is satisfied. An example might be a call on the CAC 40 index, conditional on a six-month PIBOR rate below 6% at the option's expiration (exercise) date. *See Contingent Payout Option (diagram).*

Stock Index Futures Contract: With one exception (the failed Osaka Stock Futures 50), a cash settled futures contract with a stock average or index as the underlying. These contracts have been among the most popular and useful futures contracts wherever they have been introduced.

Stock Index Growth Notes (SIGNs): *See Equity-Linked Note (ELN) (diagrams).*

Stock Index Insured Account: An equity-linked certificate of deposit with the payoff contingent on the performance of an average rate option. Usually the minimum payoff is equal to the initial investment. *See Equity-Linked Note (ELN) (diagrams).*

Stock Index Return Security (SIRS): *See Equity-Linked Note (ELN) (diagrams).*

Stock Lending: *See Securities Lending.*

Stock Loan Contracts: Exchange-traded contracts facilitating the lending of securities traded on the OM in Sweden. *See also Securities Lending.*

Stock Market Annual Reset Term (SMART) Note: A variable-rate note with the periodic coupon dependent on the performance of a stock market index rather than on an interest rate or rate spread. *Generically, a Coupon-Indexed Note. See also Cliquet Option (1) (diagram).*

Stock Option: A put or call option with an individual stock issue as the underlying. Traded on a number of exchanges worldwide and over the counter. *Also called Equity Option.*

Stock Performance Exchange-Linked Bonds (SPELBonds): *See Standard & Poor's Index Notes (SPINs), Equity-Linked Note (ELN) (diagrams).*

Stock Purchase Warrant: *See Warrant.*

Stock Right: *See Right.*

Stock Upside Note Security (SUNS): An annual reset or cliquet-type note with the annual coupon linked to the annual appreciation percentage of a designated instrument or index less a fixed percentage to pay for the option component of the return. The index is reset each year relative to the year-end level, making it possible to achieve a greater return than the cumulative return of the underlying instrument or index. 100% of principal is returned at maturity. *See also Cliquet Option (1) (diagram).*

Stock Warrant Off-Balance Sheet Research and Development (SWORD) Financing: A financing technique used principally in the biotechnology industry in which a separate corporation or partnership owns the property rights to certain research and development results. The financial statements of the separate organization are designed to have no impact on the sponsoring "parent," and the financing comes from a public offering of units in the R&D venture. Each unit has one share of the venture's common stock that can be called by the sponsoring parent and one warrant to purchase a share of the common stock of the parent that permits the investor to maintain a position in the results of the venture.

Stock-Over-Bond (SOB) Warrant: An outperformance warrant with a payoff based on the performance of a stock index less the return on a bond index. These instruments are issued on a variety of fixed-income and equity indexes. *Compare Bond-Over-Stock (BOS) Warrant.*

Stop Limit Order: A variation of a stop order in which a sale must be executed at or above the limit price designated in the order. A buy must be executed at or below the limit price. Usually the stop price and the limit price are the same, but occasionally the limit price is different from the stop price to provide some margin of flexibility to a floor broker, while protecting the investor who placed the stop limit order from the adverse effect of a major price move beyond the limit.

Stop Loss Order: *See Stop Order.*

Stop Order: A stop order to buy or sell becomes a market order when the market reaches the price specified in the order or trades through that price. For example, a stop order to buy becomes a market order when the instrument trades or is bid at or above the stop price. A stop order to sell becomes a market order when the instrument trades or is offered at or below the stop price. A sell stop order is placed below the prevailing market price and a buy stop order is placed above the market. *Also called Stop Loss Order.*

Stopped Stock: A purchase or sale agreement entered into on the floor of an exchange in which the specialist guarantees to purchase or sell to another broker at either the price of the next sale or at a stopped price—whichever is more advantageous to the broker's customer.

Stoption: *See Barrier Option.*

Straddle: A combination option consisting of one put and one call, both short or both long. Either option is exercisable or salable separately and the strike prices are identical. *See Combination Option.*

Straddle Rule: A U.S. tax provision enacted in 1986 that defers the realization of losses on some transactions associated with other positions that have unrealized gains.

Strangle: A combination of a short put and a short call or a long put and a long call on the same underlying security, usually with the same expiration date and different strike prices. If both options are out of the money, the position is often called a *Surf and Turf.* If both options are in the money, an alternate name is mambo combo. *See Combination Option, Mambo Combo (diagram), Spraddle (diagram), Spread (7).*

Strap: A combination option consisting of two calls and one put, all short or all long. *See Combination Option.*

Strategic Asset Allocation (SAA): A value or expected return-oriented portfolio management technique that, in contrast to portfolio insurance (or dynamic asset allocation), tends to increase exposure to a market when recent market performance has been poor, and to reduce exposure when recent market performance has been good. *See Asset Allocation, Tactical Asset Allocation (TAA).*

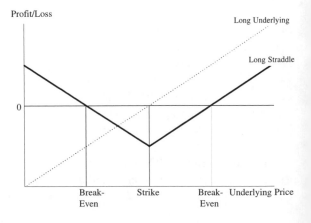

Strategic Business Unit (SBU): A relatively independent business with a coherent set of products, strategies, objectives, and competitors. Many large corporations consist of a number of SBUs.

Strategic Risks: Risk exposures that are part of an economic unit's natural environment and can have a significant effect on its revenues, earnings, market share, product offerings, etc. Strategic risks are usually the primary risk management focus.

Street Name: A reference to securities registered in the name of a broker or a nominee such as a clearing house instead of in the name of the beneficial owner. Street name registration facilitates transfer and is growing in popularity since the move to three-business day settlement for stocks. *See also Direct Registration of Securities (DRS).*

Stress Testing: Any of several techniques, often based on Monte Carlo simulations, that examine the response of an asset or liability portfolio (or both) to a variety of types of financial distress. The purpose of the stress test is to evaluate how the organization whose portfolio is being tested would fare under a specific set of adverse market conditions. *See also Cash Flow Sensitivity Analysis.*

Strike Bonus Option: The value added to a standard option by a lookback or strike reset feature. The value of a lookback option is equal to the value of the corresponding standard option, plus the expected value of the cash flows necessary to exchange the initial option position for options with successively more favorable strikes. The expected value of these cash flows is called the strike bonus option. *See also Lookback Option.*

Strike Level of a Swaption: The terms of a nominal fixed-rate obligation underlying the subject swap contract.

Strike Premium: The premium paid for the second option in a compound option at the time the first option is exercised. *See also Compound Option (1) (diagram).*

Strike Reset Option or Warrant: *See Reset Option or Warrant.*

Strike, Strike Price, Strike Interest Rate, or Strike Rate: The price or rate at which an option begins to have a settlement value at expiration. While the strike price or rate is usually set at the time the option contract originates, some strike prices are subject to adjustment under certain circumstances. *See Exotic Options, Adjusted Strike Price or Adjusted Exercise Price.*

Strike-Step Option: A strike-step option is a barrier option characterized by a change in the strike when a barrier or trigger price or rate is touched or breached. Specifically, a strike-step put option provides for an increase in the put strike corresponding, at least in part, to an increase in the underlying price or rate. The

Strike-Step Put Option

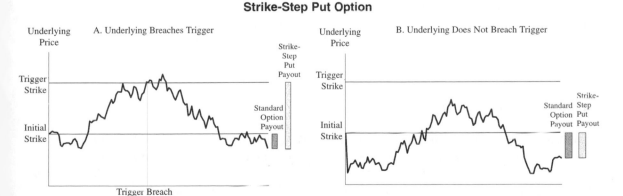

strike-step put provides protection based on a higher strike of the put if the underlying rises through the higher strike without payment of an additional option premium. A strike-step call provides similar protection with a lower strike for a call if the underlying drops to or through the lower strike. The restruck options are standard options that contrast with the roll-up put and roll-down call that convert standard options into knockout options. *See also Barrier Option, Roll-Up Put (diagrams), Roll-Down Call.*

Strip: (1) A sequence of options of the same type, usually covering non-overlapping time periods. *Also called Tandem Options.* (2) A combination option consisting of two puts and one call, all short or all long. (3) A series of forward rate agreements. *See also Average Price or Rate Option (APO, ARO) (diagrams), Combination Option.*

Strip Hedge: A risk-offsetting position that uses a strip of risk management forward or option contracts expiring on dates appropriate to the risk being hedged. *See also Stack Hedge.*

Strippability: The combination of characteristics of a bond that makes it suitable for coupon stripping.

Stripped Mortgage-Backed Security (SMBS): (1) As in the government strips market, CMOs are decomposed to create a variety of specialized instruments, such as "interest only" or "principal only" obligations and a variety of other MBS structures. (2) Any segment of the mortgage payment stream underlying a CMO or a real estate mortgage investment conduit (REMIC) that has been divided into a series of tranches, usually based on the nominal coupons of the mortgages or the classification of payments as interest or principal. *See Collateralized Mortgage Obligation (CMO), Interest Only (IO) Obligation, Principal Only (PO) Obligation, Real Estate Mortgage Investment Certificate (REMIC).*

Stripped Municipals (M-CATS): Principal and interest components of municipals, as with stripped Treasuries. All gains on these zero-coupon instruments are tax-exempt unless the total yield exceeds the YTM of the whole bond when it was issued.

Stripped Treasury Securities: *Also referred to as Coupon Stripping, Separately Traded Registered Interest and Principal Securities (STRIPS), Treasury Investment Growth Receipts (TIGRs), Certificate of Government Receipts (COUGRs), Certificate of Accrual on Treasury Securities (CATS).*

Stripping: The act of creating stripped Treasury securities from suitable bonds or notes.

STRIPS: An acronym for Separately Traded Registered Interest and Principal Securities. Zero-coupon notes and bonds are created by trading note and bond coupon and principal payments stripped from Treasury securities. *Also called Certificate of Accrual on Treasury Securities (CATS), Certificate of Government Receipts (COUGRs), Treasury Investment Growth Receipts (TIGRs), Treasury STRIPS, Treasury Receipts (TRs). Comparable to Zero-Coupon Eurosterling Bearer or Registered Accruing (ZEBRA) Certificate. Other acronyms have included LION, COUGRs, DOGs, GATORs, EAGLEs, STARs.*

Strong Form: *See Efficient Market.*

Structure: *See Structured Product.*

Structured Early Intervention and Resolution (SEIR): A set of procedures for regulatory interaction with a troubled bank. The procedures attempt to duplicate what would happen in the absence of the inappropriate incentives created by deposit insurance and the "too big to fail" doctrine. Ultimately, a declining bank would be recapitalized or closed. *See also Garn-St. Germain Act (1982), Too Big to Fail.*

Structured Enhanced Returns Trust (STEER): A mechanism designed to permit an institutional investor to enter into a swap indirectly or to obtain indirect participation in an instrument that it might not be able to acquire directly. An intermediary organization (the "Trust") purchases an instrument to serve as the basis for a swap, and the return on that instrument is swapped with a third party to provide the exposure the investor seeks. The STEER structure is more cumbersome and generally more costly than the simple purchase of a structured note with appropriate embedded return characteristics.

Structured Financial Transaction: (1) A security backed by financial assets such as loans or lower-quality bonds or notes. The security may trade on a limited basis or be the subject of a public offering. *See Securitization.* (2) A combination of a conventional security and an embedded derivative. *See also Hybrid Security.* (3) A packaged guaranteed series of payments issued by an insurance company in settlement of litigation, an insurance closing, or a long-term lottery payout. The nominal value of the settlement is usually much greater than the present value of the scheduled payments. *Also called Structured Settlement.*

Structured Note: A debt obligation, usually in the form of a medium-term note or bank certificate of deposit, with one or more embedded risk/return modification components (swaps, forwards, options, caps, floors, etc.) that change its return pattern. A corporation or government agency that issues a structured note usually buys the risk/return modification components from a financial intermediary, but the issuer remains ultimately responsible for all payments to the holder of the note. *Also called Hybrid Debt. For examples, see Convertible Money Market Units (CMMUs) (diagram), Equity-Linked Note (ELN) (diagrams), Reverse Floating-Rate Note (diagram).*

Structured Product: An over-the-counter (OTC) financial instrument created specifically to meet the needs of one or a small number of investors. The instrument may consist of a warrant, an option, or a forward embedded in a note or any of a wide variety of debt, equity, and/or currency combinations. *Also called Structure.*

Structured Settlement: *See Structured Financial Transaction (3).*

Structured Upside Participating Equity Receipt (SUPER): *See Equity-Linked Note (ELN) (diagrams).*

STRuctured Yield Product Exchangeable for Stock (STRYPES): A specialized form of debt exchangeable for common stock (DECS) used to facilitate the public sale of a low-dividend stock by increasing the yield for a few years at a sacrifice in upside price participation.

Structurer: An unpretentious rocket scientist or financial engineer.

Stub: (1) The highly leveraged common stock remaining after a leveraged buyout or other recapitalization. The stub's value is affected by the issuance of debt to replace much of the original common stock. The stub is difficult to evaluate except as an option on the firm. (2) An interim period at the beginning or end of a swap or other periodic reset agreement that is of non-standard length. For example, a two-month stub at the end of a quarterly reset swap. *Also called Back Stub Period, Front Stub Period.* (3) The ex-warrant bond originally issued with a detachable warrant. (4) A package of three consecutive one-month LIBOR contracts used to create a synthetic three-month Eurodollar position on the Chicago Mercantile Exchange. *See also Pack, Bundle.*

Style Drift: Any tendency of an investment manager offering a specific investment style to change that style over time. Style drift can occur as a manager responds, consciously or not, to changing investment fashions or because a manager does not respond to changes in the style characteristics of his holdings.

Style Management: An investment management technique that emphasizes a particular market sector or divides the market in a specific way. Style management is most common in equity markets, but is found in fixed-income markets with increasing frequency. *See, for example, Value Management, Growth Management, Market Neutral Investment Strategy, Quantitative Investment Management, etc.*

Style of Exercise: *See American Option, Bermuda Option, Deferred Payment American Option, European Option, Japanese Option, etc.*

Subdiversification: The ownership of a mixed bag or idiosyncratic collection of assets other than a fully diversified, market-weighted portfolio.

Subject Bid or Offer: A tentative or indicative bid or offer for an inactive security. *See Indicative Price (2).*

Submartingale Process: A martingale process with a positive drift. *See Martingale Process.*

Subordinated Obligation: A debt or preferred issue with claims on the cash flows and assets of an issuer that rank behind otherwise similar fixed obligations.

Subrogation: Substitution of another person (legal) in the place of a creditor. This person succeeds to all rights of the original creditor.

Subscription Warrant: *See Right.*

Subsidiary Corporation: A corporation controlled by another corporation through partial or full stock ownership or some other financial or legal connection.

Suitability Risk: A reference to the possibility that a judge or regulator might set aside a risk management contract or void an instrument on the grounds that a counterparty was not capable of understanding its terms or that the contract was inappropriate to the counterparty's stated objectives. *See Suitability Risk discussion, p. 7.*

Suitability Rules: Principles required by the SEC and enforced by securities exchanges that attempt to ensure that securities salespeople do not solicit inappropriate business from individuals unable to make informed decisions about risk. Individuals who may be qualified to engage in certain transactions may not be encouraged to engage in other types or numbers of transactions that may not be suitable given their capacity to accept risk, their net worth, and other aspects of their personal and financial situation.

Sunset Provision: A provision in a statute, regulation, or contract that terminates the statute, regulation, or contract on a specific date. One of the best-known sunset provisions in finance terminates the existence of the CFTC in the event that the Commodity Exchange Act (CEA) is not renewed periodically by Congress.

Super Planned Amortization Class (Super PAC) Bond: A PAC with a narrowly defined prepayment schedule and relatively little prepayment or extension risk. *See also Planned Amortization Class (PAC) Bond, Very Accurately Defined Maturity (VADM) Bond.*

Super Upside Note (SUN): A leveraged equity-linked position with little or no downside protection from a stock or index decline. SUNs use the present value of expected dividends to provide the holder with leveraged exposure to price appreciation. The expected dividend, in effect, is used to buy call options on the underlying.

SuperDOT: The NYSE's name for its electronic order entry and reporting system. Although designed for small order entry, SuperDOT has played a major role in portfolio or basket trading. *See Post Execution Reporting System (PERS), Program Trading.*

Superfloater Swap: A fixed-for-floating-rate swap with a reverse risk reversal (or reverse collar) on the floating-rate payment. *See also Reverse Equity Risk Reversal (diagram).*

SuperLYONS: *See Synthetic Zero-Coupon Convertible Bond.*

Supermartingale Process: A martingale process with a negative drift. *See Martingale Process.*

Supershare: The instrument at the end of a complex series of trusts and funds sponsored by Leland O'Brien, Rubinstein Associates' Supershares Service Corporation. Supershares are designed to come in a number of flavors that decompose the returns in an S&P 500 index fund and a money market fund into elements that resemble PRIMEs (covered calls), SCOREs (call warrants), and option spreads (risk reversals and reverse risk reversals). The drawbacks of the Supershare structure are its complexity and inherently high cost.

Supershare Option: Not to be confused with any of the Supershare components, the supershare option is a mechanism for breaking down security returns into a very large number of components to enhance the completeness of the market. Basically, a series of binary options covering the full range of possible returns. *See Arrow-Debreu Security.*

Supervisory Analyst: A financial analyst who has passed an NYSE exam testing the analyst's qualifications to approve research reports for public distribution.

Support (SUP) Bond: A collateralized mortgage obligation (CMO) tranche that receives principal payments after scheduled payments have been made to some or all of the planned amortization class (PAC), targeted amortization class (TAC), and/or scheduled (SCH) bonds for each payment date. *See also Companion Collateralized Mortgage Obligation.*

Support Collateralized Mortgage Obligation: *See Support Bond, Companion Collateralized Mortgage Obligation.*

Surf and Turf: *See Spraddle (diagram).*

Survivorship Bias: A flaw in some databases that eliminates unsuccessful cases, distorting some time series studies such as equity risk premium and mutual fund performance analysis. *See also Equity Premium Puzzle.*

Sushi Bond: A Eurobond issued by a Japanese issuer that does not count against a Japanese institution's limits on holdings of foreign securities.

Sustainable Earnings Level: An estimate of the fundamental underlying earning power of a corporation over a period of years. *See Operating Free Cash Flow, Real Economic Earnings (REE).*

Swap: (1) A contractual agreement to exchange a stream of periodic payments with a counterparty. Swaps are available in and between all active financial markets. The traditional interest rate swap agreement is an exchange of fixed interest payments for floating-rate payments. A generic currency swap is an agreement to exchange one currency for another at a forward exchange rate or at a sequence of forward rates. While an equity index swap might involve the exchange of one index return for another, a more common structure is the exchange of an equity index return for a floating interest rate. "Official" definitions of swaps and swap-related terminology and standard swap provisions are provided in the International Swap and Derivatives Association publication, *Definitions. See LIBOR Index Principal Swap (LIPS), LIBOR In-Arrears Swap. See also Accreting Principal Swap (APS), Commodity Swap, Asset Swap, Constant Maturity Swap, Interest Rate Swap, Rate Differential Swap (diagram).* (2) The practice of exchanging one bond for another to improve yield, change credit exposure, reflect an interest rate view, or register a tax loss. This type of swap is very different from an interest rate, currency, or index swap, but the term "swap" has been in use longer in this context. The different uses occasionally confuse new users of cash flow swaps. *See also Pick-Up.* (3) Futures price minus spot: basis (uncommon).

Swap Arranger: A third party who brings two swap counterparties together. The role of a swap arranger contrasts with the role of a market maker or dealer who warehouses swaps, acting as a principal.

Swap Buyer: *See Fixed-Rate Payer.*

Swap Curve: A yield curve illustrating the relationship of swap rates at various maturities. Based on the zero-coupon yield curve.

Swap de Taux d'Intérêt: *Fr. See Interest Rate Swap.*

Swap Market Maker: A financial intermediary who runs an unmatched swap book and stands ready to quote terms for a variety of swaps that he hedges with offsetting swaps or with positions taken in other financial markets.

Swap Offset Agreement: A contract providing for a netting of payments between counterparties to an individual swap and for termination and netting of all swaps between two counterparties in the event of default on any swap. The purpose of a swap offset agreement is to reduce credit risk exposure.

Swap Option: *See Swaption.*

Swap Rate: (1) The market interest rate on the fixed-rate side of a swap. At the time the swap is initiated, the swap rate is typically the same as the fixed-rate payment (adjusted for any negotiated premium or discount). As rates move, the swap rate may differ materially from the fixed rate exchanged under a specific swap agreement. (2) Forward points on a currency rate. Adjustments to the spot exchange rate to compensate for interest rate parity differences across the two currencies.

Swap Rate Differential: The difference between a bond or note yield and the swap rate for the same maturity.

Swap Rate Lock: An agreement that sets the absolute swap rate level for a swap with a future start date.

Swap Replacement Cost: The cost incurred to replace a defaulted or cancelled in-the-money swap with a comparable instrument.

Swap Rules: Regulations adopted by the Commodities Futures Trading Commission (CFTC) exempting certain swap agreements from regulation by the Commission. To qualify, a swap agreement (1) must be made between eligible swap participants, (2) cannot be part of a fungible or standardized class of agreements, (3) must consider credit, though collateralization and credit enhancement are permitted, and (4) cannot be traded on a multilateral transaction execution facility (exchange). *See also Eligible Swap Participant.*

Swap Seller: *See Floating-Rate Payer (1).*

Swap Spread: (1) The negotiated interest rate differential reflecting supply and demand and counterparty credit ratings that is added to or subtracted from the (fixed) swap rate. (2) The interest rate differential between the swap rate and the comparable government borrowing rate in the applicable currency. Adding (1) and (2) will give the spread between the rate on a specific swap and the comparable maturity default-free rate. The total swap spread is usually expressed as a market maker's spread (bid/asked) over a specific U.S. Treasury rate.

Swap Spread Lock: An agreement that gives a would-be fixed-rate payer (receiver) a guaranteed maximum (minimum) spread over a specific Treasury rate in a swap agreement starting on a fixed future date. *See Spread-Lock Swap (1).*

Swap Yield Curve: The term structure of swap rates in a specific currency. *See also Yield Curve.*

Swap-Driven Primary Issuance: It is often relatively cheaper for a U.S.-based borrower to use the U.S. dollar bond market, but the borrower's liability management objective may be to borrow DMs and pay floating rates. The U.S.-based borrower may find it expedient to issue U.S. dollar bonds and swap with a relatively more efficient DM floating-rate borrower. The choice of markets for the primary issuance is driven by the combination of swap opportunities and that market's relative cost to the borrower.

Swap-In-Arrears (SIA): *See In-Arrears Swap (diagram).*

Swaps with Option Payoffs: The most common swap with an option payoff is a fixed-for-floating-rate swap with the floating rate subject to a collar.

Swaps with Timing Mismatches: An uncommon type of swap in which one party is paying on a more frequent interval than the other, so that opportunities for offsetting or netting flows are limited. This type of swap has inherently higher credit/settlement risk than a standard swap.

Swaption: An option to enter into a swap contract, either as an opening transaction or as an offsetting swap, that cancels an existing swap position. A payer's swaption is the right to be a fixed-rate payer and a receiver's swaption is the right to be a fixed-rate receiver. The settlement of a swaption is entry into the nominal exchange called for under the swap agreement. The strike is a specific (fixed) swap rate. Alternatively, a swaption can be described as an option on a portfolio of forward rates. *Also called Interest Rate Swaption, Swap Option. See Contingent Swap, Payer's Swaption, Receiver's Swaption, Option on a Swap. See also Contingent Swap.*

Sweep Account: An account that serves as a temporary collection point for cash balances collected

Swaption—Effects of Rate Changes

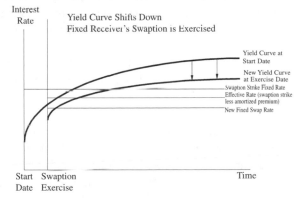

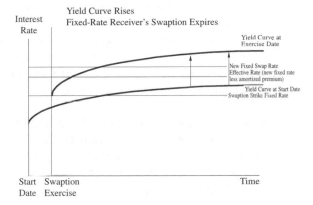

from other accounts and destined for deposit in a money market fund or for purchase of a money market instrument.

Sweetener: *See Kicker.*

Swingline: A short-term note issuance facility (NIF) designed to accommodate a borrower's needs between the time the notes are offered and the funds are received. *See also Note Issuance Facility (NIF).*

Swiss Market Index Liberte Emission (SMILE): An equity index-linked note with a low coupon and a redemption payment linked to the Swiss Market Index.

Switch: *See Roll Forward.*

Switchback Option or Warrant: A complex instrument combining a capped call and an up-and-in put or a floored put and a down-and-in call. To describe the former structure in more detail, the capped call has an early exercise trigger that provides a maximum payoff to the holder when the underlying rises through the cap. Typically, the instrike of the put is identical to the cap/trigger price of the call, creating a standard put and offering a profit opportunity on the downside for the remaining life of the option. *See also As-You-Like Warrant.*

Symmetric Distribution: A distribution without skewness—with the opposing sides symmetric about the mean and median.

Symmetric Payoff: A pattern of changes in value that moves continuously and proportionally up or down in response to price movements of an underlying security or other instrument. Traditional securities, futures, and forwards tend to have symmetric payoffs. Options and instruments with option components typically have asymmetric payoff patterns over some price ranges. *See Asymmetric Payoff (diagrams).*

Syndicate Bid: A stabilizing bid posted by an underwriting syndicate to ensure that the price of a security being offered is not available more cheaply in the open market than from a member of the syndicate. *See also Penalty Bid.*

Syndicate Department: The group or organization within a securities dealer responsible for managing the firm's relationships with other investment banks in the underwriting of new issues of securities. The syndicate department also provides marketing information to the sales force—often with some assistance from securities analysts. *See also Underwriting of Securities.*

Synthetic: As the definitions of specific synthetic instruments on these pages suggest, but do not always state explicitly, any instrument described or prefaced by the word "synthetic" is, as the root of the word implies, made from something else or from components. In most cases, a financial intermediary or dealer is the active entity in the creation of synthetic financial instruments. A synthetic instrument may consist of a single contract, security, etc., or it may be a separable collection of instruments whose combined features are comparable to the instrument it replicates.

Synthetic Agreement for Foreign Exchange (SAFE): A type of forward currency exchange rate agreement designed to provide a currency hedge over a specific forward period. A notional principal agreement, like an FRA, a SAFE provides risk control usually linked but not attached to another position or transaction. A SAFE is equivalent to a forward period currency swap without a principal exchange. *See also Exchange Rate Agreement (ERA).*

Synthetic Asset: A package of risks and returns created by combining other instruments to approximate very closely the package of risks and returns available in a traditional security. A position that behaves like a put, call, or some other standard instrument but has been created using different positions or dynamic trading techniques. For example, portfolio insurers create synthetic puts, equity portfolio managers often create synthetic stock or synthetic calls, index arbitrageurs may create synthetic Treasury bills, and bond futures traders may create synthetic bonds.

Synthetic Bond: A combination of financial instruments or components designed to behave like long-term bonds. Examples might include money market instruments plus bond futures, a long bond call combined with a short bond put and a money market position, or any of a variety of other risk equivalent combinations.

Synthetic Call Option: Typically, a combination of a long put and a long position in the underlying. The put strike is the strike of the synthetic call.

Synthetic Convertible Debt: (1) A debt and warrant package structured to resemble a traditional convertible debt issue. The components of the package may be separable, unlike traditional convertibles, or they may be in the form of an equity-linked note. (2) An equity-linked note issued by an entity other than the issuer of the underlying equity instrument. *See also Equity-Linked Note (ELN) (diagrams), Hybrid Debt.*

Synthetic Equity: A derivatives instrument with the essential risk/reward characteristics of a direct investment in a stock, a specific basket of stocks, or an appropriately weighted basket of stocks equivalent to a stock index.

Synthetic Foreign Bond: A domestic currency-denominated bond with all payments marked to the market in terms of a foreign currency. All coupons are computed against the principal denominated in the foreign currency value at the issue date, and converted into the domestic currency at the spot exchange rate on the coupon payment date. Repayment of principal is converted into the domestic currency at the spot rate at maturity. In short, the only difference between this instrument and a true foreign bond is that the issuer is responsible for conversion of all payments into the investor's domestic currency.

Synthetic Forward: A combination of a long European call and a short European put with the same expiration date and strike price. This combination provides the functional equivalent of a forward contract on the underlying. *Also called Synthetic Futures Contract.*

Synthetic Futures Contract: *See Synthetic Forward.*

Synthetic Guaranteed Investment Contract (Synthetic GIC): A guaranteed account secured by a pool of assets owned by the investor (the assets are segregated to protect them from claims by the financial institution's general creditors) with a separate guarantee issued by the institution. *See Guaranteed Investment Contract (GIC), Participating Account.*

Synthetic High-Income Equity-Linked Debenture (SHIELD): Comparable in structure to preference equity redemption cumulative stock (PERCS), but issued by an entity other than the issuer of the underlying stock. *Also called Convertible Money Market Units (CMMUs), Performance Equity-Linked Redemption Quarterly Paid Security (PERQS). See Common-linked High-Income Participation Security (CHIPS), Synthetic PERCS.*

Synthetic Long: A combination of a long call and a short put plus a money market position. (The money market position is sometimes omitted from the definition or ignored, but it is necessary for full comparability.)

Synthetic Option: *See Option Replication (2).*

Synthetic PERCS: *See Equity-LinKed Security (ELKS). Also called Yield Enhanced Equity-Linked Debt Security (YEELDS), Common-linked Higher Income Participation Security (CHIPS), Synthetic High-Income Equity-Linked Debenture (SHIELD).*

Synthetic Put Option: A combination of a short position in the underlying asset, instrument, or index and a long position in a call option, or a long position in the underlying and a short call.

Synthetic Short: A combination of a long put and a short call plus a loan. (The loan is sometimes omitted from the definition.)

Synthetic Stock: (1) A combination of a long call and a short put, or a short call and a long put, on the same stock with the same strike and expiration date. A separate cash equivalent position necessary to replicate the stock return fully may or may not be incorporated. (2) A single stock swap. Other techniques that only approximate the risk/reward characteristics of long or short stock positions with options or swaps are usually called stock equivalents. *See also Box Spread (2), Jellyroll, Time Box.*

Synthetic Warrants: *See Covered Warrants.*

Synthetic Zero-Coupon Convertible Bond: A combination of a zero-coupon note and a detachable warrant with an equal term to expiration. The notes are usable to exercise the warrants and the issuer may enjoy an advantage in interest deductibility over other issuers of zero-coupon convertibles. *Also called Super-LYONS. See also Liquid Yield Option Note (LYON).*

Systematic Risk: Risk associated with the movement of a market or market segment as opposed to distinct elements of risk associated with a specific security. Systematic risk cannot be diversified away; it can only be hedged. Within the context of the Capital Asset Pricing Model (CAPM), exposure to systematic risk is measured by beta. *See also Diversification, Non-Systematic Risk.*

Systemic Risk: Risk associated with the general health or structure of the financial system. Almost invariably discussed in terms of the system's inability to handle large quantities of market, credit, or (most likely) settlement risk.

T Test: A test of significance that assumes the sample standard deviation is different from the population standard deviation. The level of confidence that a particular value is different from the null hypothesis value is derived from a t distribution rather than a normal distribution. The t distribution is wider than the normal distribution to correct for the difference between the observed sample standard deviation and the unobserved normal distribution. As the size of the sample increases, the t distribution approaches the shape of the normal distribution.

Table Top: An option combination consisting of a bullish call spread with an additional short call at a higher strike. *Also called Christmas Tree. See Ladder Trade (diagram).*

Tactical Asset Allocation (TAA): As usually described, TAA is indistinguishable from strategic asset allocation (SAA). Some TAA practitioners emphasize shorter-term adjustments, but there is no widely accepted distinction. *See Asset Allocation, Strategic Asset Allocation (SAA).*

Tail: (1) A reference to the ends of a probability distribution where the chances of an occurrence get relatively small. Some distributions, however, have fat tails, i.e., provide a relatively greater chance of a large price or rate movement and a smaller chance of a moderate movement than a standard normal distribution. (2) The residual of a risk pool as in the tail of remaining obligations out of a series of long-term liabilities under an insurance policy. (3) The change in the number of futures contracts needed to hedge a position because of variation margin flows. *See Tail Hedging.* (4) The number of excess futures contracts in a basis trade. (5) The difference between the average price and the lowest bid price in a Treasury auction.

Tail Hedging: Adjusting the number of futures contracts in a hedge position so that the present market exposure of the hedge offsets the underlying exposure. The need for tail hedging stems from the costs and benefits of interest expense or earnings associated with variation margin flows. *See Tail (3).*

Tailored Swap: Any of a variety of changing notional principal swaps designed to meet the financing or currency needs of a business with seasonal, growing, or declining interest rate or currency risk management requirements. *See, for example, Accreting Principal Swap (APS), Amortizing Swap, Seasonal Swap.*

Take: A call option.

Takeout Loan: Permanent mortgage financing that replaces construction loans on a real estate project or bridge financing on a takeover.

Takeover: The acquisition of control of a business enterprise.

Talon: The last portion of a bond after all coupons have been removed.

Tandem Options: A sequence of options of the same type (call or put, cap or floor) usually covering non-overlapping time periods and often with variable strikes. *See Strip (1).*

Target: Expected time to exercise of an American option. *Also called Fugit.*

Target Company: A company that is the object of a takeover attempt.

Target Price: The price at which the holder of a capped instrument such as a preference equity redemption cumulative stock (PERCS) stops participating in further price appreciation.

Target Return: (1) The minimum return acceptable to an investor. *See Downside Probability, Average Downside Magnitude.* (2) The maximum return available to the holder of a capped instrument such as a preference equity redemption cumulative stock (PERCS).

Target Stock: A special class of common or preferred shares with dividends and/or earnings participation linked to a specific segment of the issuer's business. *Also called Alphabet Stock, Letter Stock (2), Tracking Stock.*

Targeted Amortization Class (TAC) Bond: A collateralized mortgage obligation (CMO) tranche that pays principal based upon a predetermined schedule, derived by amortizing the collateral at a single prepayment rate.

Tau τ: The sensitivity of the value of an option to changes in the volatility variable. Usually expressed as the dollar change in the value or price of an option for a percentage point change in the standard deviation of the underlying. Also commonly known as vega. Although vega is not a Greek letter, it starts with a "v" and sounds acceptable to most market participants. *See also Kappa (κ).*

Taux Annuel Monétaire (TAM): *Fr.* A French floating benchmark rate calculated by annualizing the latest twelve monthly overnight average rates. TAM is widely used as a benchmark floating rate and as an alternative to LIBOR. *See also Monthly OverNight Average (MONA) Swap.*

Tax Arbitrage: The creation of instruments or transactions that can be priced attractively to both counterparties because their joint tax bill is reduced. The most common examples involve cross-border equity positions, municipal securities, or semiperpetual debt. Taxes may be avoided directly or reduced by changing the character of a cash flow.

Tax Efficiency: A characteristic of a financial instrument that permits a dealer or an end user to establish or modify a position in a way that requires lower tax payments from either or both parties to the transactions than an alternate similar position or instrument. Mutual funds are frequently evaluated on the basis of their ability to defer tax for their shareholders.

Tax Haven: A country or designated zone where investments or investors are nominally domiciled to avoid some tax obligations, and, often, some regulatory oversight. *See also Offshore.*

Tax Risk: Usually a reference to a tax provision that, by accident or design, frustrates a reasonable business or economic transaction by making the economics unattractive after taxes or by injecting significant tax uncertainty. *See Tax Risk discussion, p. 7.*

Tax Straddle: A reference to any of a variety of low market risk tax reduction techniques. These techniques frequently use options and futures to create an advantageous tax position with deductions available early and income deferred. Alternately, non-deductible capital losses may be converted to ordinary losses that can be deducted against ordinary income. Opportunities for tax straddles were sharply reduced in the U.S. by the 1986 tax reform act.

Tax-Exempt Enhanced Municipal Security (TEEMS): A synthetic reverse floating-rate note created when a municipal issuer enters into an interest rate swap agreement that permits it to enjoy fixed interest costs over the life of the instrument but to pay investors an inverse floating rate for the life of the swap. Alternately, the fixed-rate issue can be divided into two tranches: a floating-rate note and a reverse floating-rate note. The fixed-rate payment is apportioned between the tranches to create the necessary cash flows. *See also Residual Interest Bonds (RIBs), Select Auction Variable-Rate Securities (SAVRs).*

Tax-Exempt Swap: An interest rate swap agreement with one or both payments based on municipal securities yields.

Taylor Series Approximation: A mathematical technique that approximates a function that has finite, continuous derivatives with a polynomial function. The technique takes higher and higher order derivatives of the function at a chosen point and uses the information to estimate the value of the function at another point.

Technical Analysis: An effort to forecast prices, rates, or returns in financial markets largely by analyzing data internal to the market, such as price or volume numbers.

Teeny: A reference to the smallest tick size in a market or to one-sixteenth (the smallest tick in most equity and options markets in the U.S.).

Tender: (1) Part of the process by which a company's shares change hands in a leveraged buyout or other recapitalization. *See Tender Offer.* (2) The notice from a futures contract seller to the clearing house that she intends to deliver securities or commodities in settlement of the contract.

Tender Bond: A municipal bond or note, with an embedded forward sale price linked to the market rate on a specific Treasury bond or note or a constant maturity Treasury (CMT) rate. The underlying municipal is sold at par plus an enhanced yield if the Treasury-linked rate is below a designated level. It is sold at a discount to par as the linked rate rises materially above current rates. Discounts to par of 30%-40% are possible if rates rise sharply. Some of these bonds were involved in significant reported losses in early 1994.

Tender Offer: An offer (by the issuer of securities or by a third party desirous of acquiring a larger interest in or control of the issuer) to purchase some or all of a designated class of securities under terms spelled out in a document filed with regulatory authorities. The legal document sets forth the terms of the offer and the conditions under which shares may be accepted or rejected. *See Tender (1).*

Tenor: The term or life of a contract or instrument.

Term Sheet: A written summary of the characteristics of a financial instrument, usually prepared by an underwriter in the case of a public offering, or by the issuing dealer in the case of an OTC derivatives instrument. While term sheets are not usually technically binding on offerings for which a prospectus or other offering circular is prepared, they are frequently incorporated into the contractual terms of an OTC instrument.

Term Stock Right (TSR): *See Warrant.*

Term Structure of Interest Rates: The pattern, usually represented graphically as a yield curve, of interest rates on sovereign or other consistent quality debt of various maturities. Where sovereign debt is not actively traded at appropriate maturities, the swap curve may be the best indicator of the term structure of interest rates in a specific currency. The term structure also sets relationships for arbitrage-free debt instrument option models. *See Yield Curve (diagrams), Forward Yield Curve. See also Yield Curve Option.*

Term Structure of Volatility: A curve, broadly analogous in purpose to an interest rate yield curve, that illustrates the relationship of yield or price volatility to maturity or duration. Much like the term structure of interest rates, the curve illustrates the pattern of implied volatilities of representative (usually at-the-money) options as option maturities extend forward. A term structure can be calculated or estimated for any strike, spot, or forward. *Compare with Smile (diagram), Skew. See also Dupire-Derman-Rubinstein Models, Volatility Cone.*

Term to Maturity: The life of a financial instrument. The period until an instrument is to be exercised or converted into cash or an underlying position.

Termination: Cancellation of an agreement or instrument with settlement based on previously agreed terms.

Termination Claim: The exercise value of an Americus Trust PRIME or SCORE. With the exception of a small fee, the aggregate termination claims of the PRIMEs plus the aggregate termination claims of the SCOREs are equal in value to the underlying stocks deposited in the trust. *See Americus Trust, Special Claim On Residual Equity (SCORE) (diagram), Prescribed Right to Income and Maximum Equity (PRIME) (diagram).*

Termination Date: The effective date of termination of a swap or other agreement, often as a result of a default.

Termination Price: The strike price used to calculate Americus Trust termination claims.

Termination Rating: A credit rating given by Standard & Poor's to a derivatives products company that is designed to protect counterparties by closing out derivatives contracts in response to a trigger event like default or bankruptcy. The S&P ratings of these companies carry the suffix "t," as in AAt.

Terms of an Option Contract: The terms of an option contract are defined by the conventions of the market in which the option is traded and the specifications of the contract. A securities option is defined by (1) exercise or strike price, (2) expiration date, (3) instrument on which the option is written, (4) dividend or interest adjustment, if any, (5) adjustment for splits and other capital changes, if any, and (6) quantity of the underlying security that makes up the unit of trading. Non-standard or exotic options may have additional specifications. *See Call Option, Option, Option Contract.*

Tesobono: A Mexican government bond denominated in pesos, with coupons and principal indexed to U.S. dollars at the spot rate in effect at issuance.

Texas Hedge: A transaction that increases risk. Alternately, two or more related positions whose risk is additive rather than offsetting. An example might be buying calls to "hedge" a long position in the underlying.

Theoretical Distribution: The distribution of parameter estimates that can be expected purely by chance if the null hypothesis is true. This distribution is used in hypothesis testing, where one seeks to examine whether a sample estimate is extreme relative to the value specified by the null hypothesis.

Theoretical Intermarket Margin System (TIMS): The method used by the Options Clearing Corporation (OCC) to determine option clearing firm margin requirements.

Theoretical Value: The value of an option as determined by a specific option model based on the model's input parameters. Another name for fair value. The term is occasionally used disparagingly to suggest a lack of substance to option value calculations. Disparagement may be appropriate if the option evaluator's assumptions or model specifications are unsound.

Theta θ: The sensitivity of an option's price to the passage of time with the price of the underlying and implied volatility unchanged. A measurement of the "wasting asset" characteristic of an option, i.e., its rate of time decay (Δp/Δt).

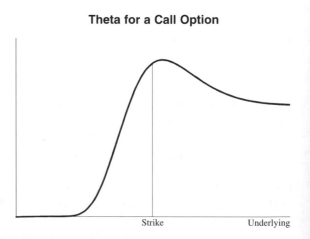

Theta for a Call Option

Third Market: Off-exchange trading of exchange-listed stocks by institutions using a broker as an intermediary. *See also Primary Market, Secondary Market, Fourth Market.*

Third-Party Pledge System: A more flexible option collateralization technique than the escrow receipts used in early option trading to collateralize short option positions. The securities serving as collateral are pledged by a third party (usually a bank) for the benefit of the clearing corporation, the clearing member carrying the account, and the customer on the other side of the trade.

Third-Party Warrants: *Another name for Covered Warrants.*

30% Rule: *See Short-Short Rule.*

Threshold Level: A value on an underlying price or rate that sets or resets the minimum payment on a ladder option or note. *Also called Rung, Value Lock Level.*

Tick: The minimum price fluctuation available in a marketplace—expressed in terms of points or fractions of a point of the price or rate. *Also called Minimum Price Fluctuation. See Pips.*

Tier I Capital: The permanent equity capital of a bank, consisting of equity capital and disclosed reserves. Equity capital includes cumulative preferred stock, non-cumulative perpetual preferred stock, and other instruments that cannot be redeemed at the option of the holder.

Tier II Capital: Secondary bank capital consisting of undisclosed reserves, evaluation reserves, general provisions, and general loan loss reserves. Certain hybrid debt/equity instruments and subordinated term debt may be included in the computation of Tier II capital.

Tiered Interest Bonds (TIBs): A collateralized mortgage obligation (CMO) tranche created at the same time as a capped floater and an inverse floater from the cash flows of a fixed coupon CMO class, a TIB combines some of the characteristics of a high fixed coupon note and an inverse floater. When the interest rate index (typically LIBOR or COFI) that determines the TIB rate is below a level called the lower strike, the TIB coupon is fixed at a relatively high level called the TIB cap. As the index moves above the lower strike, the TIB becomes a leveraged inverse floater with a rate that drops to zero at an upper strike rate. The upper strike is usually a few percentage points above the lower strike.

Time Bargains: Options and/or futures.

Time Box: Offsetting synthetic stock positions with different expirations and, often, different strike prices. *See Box Spread (2), Jellyroll, Synthetic Stock (2).*

Time Decay: The loss in value of an option or an instrument with an embedded option as the expiration date approaches.

Time Discount Option: A variation on the contingent premium option with no premium paid until expiration. The premium paid at expiration equals the number of days the option was in the money, divided by the number of days in the life of the option, all times an agreed premium level. If the option was never in the money, there will be no premium. The premium used in the calculations will be much greater than the premium on a comparable standard option.

Time Diversification: The notion that above average returns tend to offset below average returns over long time horizons. It does not necessarily follow, however, that time diversification reduces risk. Paul Samuelson and others have shown that, although the likelihood of a loss given investment in a risky asset decreases with time, the potential magnitude of a loss increases with time if risky asset returns are random, suggesting that exposure to risky assets should be invariant to one's horizon. If risky asset returns mean revert, however, investors with a utility function that is more risk averse than a logwealth utility function should be willing to allocate a larger fraction of their wealth to risky assets given a long horizon, than they would given a short horizon.

Time Hedge: Another name for a short option hedge. The name comes from the tendency of this position to improve with time if the underlying security is not volatile. *See Option Hedge (diagrams).*

Time Series Data: Values for a variable measured at regular intervals, such as daily, monthly, quarterly, etc. Time series data are analyzed for trends and cyclical behavior and often used as indicators of future developments.

Time Spread: *See Calendar Spread (diagram).*

Time Trade: *See Range Accumulation Option or Warrant.*

Time Value: Commonly a reference to the difference between an option's price and its parity or intrinsic value. Unfortunately, the term is misleading because it fails to distinguish its two most important constituents: basis value and volatility value. A series of simple word equations should help clarify some of these relationships. Time value is in quotation marks in these equations to reflect its common but confusing usage.

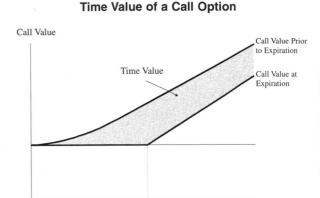

Time Value of a Call Option

Option Price = Intrinsic Value + "Time Value" = Premium (1)
              = Parity + Basis (1) + Insurance

"Time Value" = Basis (1) + Volatility Value
              = Basis (1) + Insurance
              = Premium (2)

For out-of-the-money options:

"Time Value" = Volatility Value = Opportunity Value

See also Option Premium (2), Premium (4) (diagrams), Volatility Value.

Time-Weighted Return: The geometric (compounded) return measured on the basis of periodic market valuations of assets. An alternative to the dollar-weighted return measure, it abstracts from cash flows; however, in principle, it requires valuations to be made on the occasion of each cash flow. Approximations to this measure can be obtained by prorating cash flows to successive valuation points or by computing internal rates of return between valuation points and linking them. If there are no interim cash flows, the time-weighted return, compounded annually, determines the ending value of an investment. *See also Dollar-Weighted Return.*

Times Interest Earned: (Income before taxes plus interest expense)/interest expense.

Timing Option: A provision of some futures contracts that permits the short to make delivery at a time he chooses within the delivery month. Ordinarily, the short must give notice of intention to deliver in advance.

To-Arrive Contract: (1) An early grain futures contract. (2) A grain forward contract, often cash settled.

To Be Announced (TBA) Trading: In the mortgage-backed securities market, most trades take place on a to-be-announced basis, which means that the purchaser does not know the actual pools being delivered to back the specific securities purchase until just prior to settlement. The buyer only knows that the pools meet

Public Securities Association good delivery requirements. Trades made on a TBA basis are generally priced lower, i.e., to yield higher returns, than trades based on specific pools with known characteristics.

Tobin's Q: The ratio of the value of a firm (or the weighted average firm in the financial markets) to the net replacement cost of firm assets. A measure of valuation that may help predict the likelihood of market appreciation or decline, takeover activity versus capital expenditures, etc.

Tombstone Advertisement: A starkly simple advertisement run by an underwriting syndicate or investment banker to claim credit for a role in the completion of a financial transaction.

Too Big to Fail Policy: The theory followed by U.S. bank regulators prior to 1991 that certain depository institutions were too big to fail. The FDIC, in effect, insured all depositors of most large banks. In 1991, the FDIC changed its policy to protect individual and business depositors only up to the insured maximum of $100,000 for each insured account. *See also Conjectural Guarantee.*

Toronto Index Participations (TIPs): Warehouse receipt-based instruments designed to track the Toronto-35 index. Comparable in structure to the AMEX's SPDRs (Standard & Poor's 500 depositary receipts).

Total Coverage Period: The life, from start date to final settlement determination, of a financial instrument.

Total Return: Usually expressed as income plus any principal gain or minus any principal loss during a measurement period divided by principal (investment) and expressed as a percent.

Total Return Options: In contrast to most security options that pay off on a change in price, the payoff of these options includes (in the case of a call) or is reduced by (in the case of a put) any dividend or interest income attributed to the underlying during the life of the option.

Total Return Swap: Any swap in which the non-floating-rate side is based on the total return of an equity or fixed-income instrument with a life longer than the swap. Total return swaps are most common in equity or physical commodity markets, but they can be used in fixed-income markets where the non-domestic holder of a fixed-income security is subject to a withholding tax, but where the withholding tax may be avoided if the debt instrument is held by a domestic investor who pays the total return to a foreign investor by way of a total return swap. Total return swaps are also used to transfer credit exposure.

Touch Option: Any of several variations of barrier options that become in, out, or explode at an early exercise trigger when the instrike, outstrike, or early exercise price is touched once, twice, or some other number of times, or when the underlying trades at or through the barrier. *Also called One Touch Option. See Baseball Option, Exploding Option, In Option, Out Option.*

Touch-Up or Touch-Down Option: A binary option with a fixed payout at expiration if the underlying price touches an instrike above or below the spot price prior to expiration.

Toxic Waste: Securities with unusual risks and limited marketability that few investors and market makers want to touch. These securities are often highly illiquid and pricing may be quoted subject or indicative only. The term is most often applied to unpopular mortgage-backed instruments and high-yield bonds.

Tracking Error: An unplanned divergence between the price behavior of an underlying position or portfolio and the price behavior of a hedging position or benchmark. Tracking error can create a windfall profit or loss. Usually expressed (ex ante) as an expected 1-standard deviation percentage variation from the return of a benchmark portfolio or index. *See Basis Risk (3), Correlation Risk, Index Tracking, Maverick Risk.*

Tracking Stock: *See Target Stock.*

Tractable Integral: An integral expression that has an analytic solution.

Trade Date: The date on which all the terms and methods for resolving any remaining contingencies in a financial instrument are agreed upon.

Trade or Fade Rule: A rule adopted by U.S. options exchanges to facilitate multiple exchange option trading without customer orders appearing to trade through better bids or offers that are not real quotes where a trade can be done. If the market maker at an exchange receiving a customer order is not willing to match another exchange's posted better bid or offer, the receiving market maker may offer to trade with the market maker who is posting the better price. The market maker with the better quote must trade at that price or change his quote to prevent the appearance of a trade through. *Compare with Trade or Send Rule.*

Trade or Send Rule: A proposed rule to facilitate multiple exchange option trading without permitting customer orders to trade through better bids or offers. If the market maker at an exchange receiving a customer order sees a better bid or offer at another exchange listing the option, he must trade at the better price or send the order to that market. This rule has not been implemented partly because it would require an expanded electronic linkage among the exchanges. *Compare with Trade or Fade Rule.*

Trade Through: A transaction executed at a less favorable price than the best bid or offer posted at the time of the trade. Trade-throughs occur because a market's rules or its systems do not prevent them.

Trading Book: A financial institution's proprietary portfolio of instruments purchased or sold (as principal) to facilitate trading with customers, to profit from spreads between buying and selling prices, to arbitrage valuation disparities, or to hedge other trading positions. A firm may have separate trading books oriented toward different markets and underlying instruments and toward different objectives.

Trading Derivative: A distinction made in some Financial Accounting Standards Board (FASB) statements. A free-standing derivative held by an accounting entity for trading or inventory purposes. The changes in value of a trading derivative are marked to the market in the earnings account during each accounting period. *See also Free-Standing Derivative, Held for Risk Management (HRM) Derivative.*

Trading Limit: (1) The maximum number of futures contracts a trader may buy or sell in one trading session. (2) The maximum price change permitted in a trading session. *See Limit Up/Limit Down, Price Limits.*

Trading on the Equity: Using borrowed money to obtain leverage in taking an enlarged investment position.

Trading Range Warrant: An instrument that provides a relatively high return if the underlying sells within a specified trading range at expiration and a declining return if the underlying trades out-

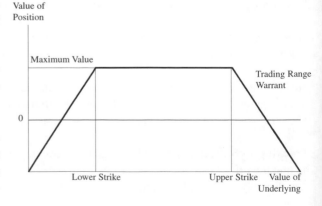

Profit/Loss Pattern of a Trading Range Warrant

side the trading range. As the diagram shows, the payoff pattern is much like that of a short spraddle or strangle. *Compare with Range Warrant.*

Tranche: One of a related series of security issues—each with different cash flows, strike prices, expiration dates, and/or return patterns—created to meet differing investor or issuer requirements or to carve up the returns from a set of underlying cash flows in a marketable way. Mortgage-backed securities, equity-linked notes, and range warrants are often created in tranches. *For example, see Collateralized Bond Obligation (CBO). See also Principal Only (PO) Obligation, Real Estate Mortgage Investment Conduit (REMIC), Interest Only (IO) Obligation.*

Transaction Cost: The cost of buying or selling a financial instrument measured in the context of its impact on the portfolio, including, at a minimum, any purchase or sale commission charged by the brokerage firm executing the trade and part of the spread between the bid and the asked prices. More sophisticated transaction cost measurement systems add the market impact of large trades and the opportunity cost of unexecuted trades. The most useful measurements of transaction costs include commissions and fees, market makers' spreads, and opportunity costs associated with not transacting when a trade is not executed. *See also Execution Cost, Market Impact.*

Transaction Risk: Currency exchange rate risk for the period between the date a contract is signed and the date of payment. Can be hedged with a variety of currency instruments.

Transfer Accounting Lodgment for Investor Stock MANagement for principals (TALISMAN): An obsolete London Stock Exchange clearance and settlement system being replaced by CREST. *See CREST.*

Transfer Pricing: The valuation of purchases and sales of goods and services between the divisions of an enterprise, frequently across international boundaries. Transfer prices are frequently the subject of tax litigation. *See also Advance Pricing Agreement.*

Transfer Tax: A tax levied on the seller or buyer of a security in a secondary market. Although different from a stamp tax levied on new security issues, a transfer tax is occasionally called a stamp tax. Ordinarily, exchange-traded and OTC options and other derivatives contracts are exempt from transfer taxes or are taxed at a lower rate. *See also Stamp Tax (2).*

Transition Probability: In a binomial model, the probability that the price will move from one node to the next along a specific path.

Transitional Density Function: The probability density function associated with a particular transitional probability distribution. *See Transitional Probability.*

Transitional Probability: The probability that a particular state variable will finish in a particular state at a specific time conditioned on the current time and space coordinates.

Translation Risk: Currency exchange rate risk that affects the valuation of balance sheet assets and liabilities between financial reporting dates. Can be hedged with a variety of currency instruments.

Transparent Market: A trading system characterized by prompt availability of accurate price and volume information that gives participants comfort that the market is fair.

Treadway Commission: The popular name for the National Commission on Fraudulent Financial

Reporting, named after its first chairman, former SEC Commissioner James C. Treadway. The Commission has issued a number of recommendations for the prevention of fraud in financial reports.

Treasury Investment Growth Receipts (TIGRs): *See Stripped Treasury Securities, STRIPS, Treasury Receipts (TRs).*

Treasury Rate Index Principal Swap (TRIPS): An index principal swap based on the Treasury bill auction rate, typically the three-month bill, rather than on LIBOR. A variation is the LIBOR index principal swap (LIPS).

Treasury Receipts (TRs): Stripped coupons and principal repayments from Treasury bonds and notes. Usually traded as zero-coupon instruments. *See STRIPS, Treasury Investment Growth Receipts (TIGRs).*

Treasury STRIPS: *See STRIPS.*

Treasury/EuroDollar (TED) Spread: The yield differential between Treasury bill and Eurodollar futures contracts expiring at the same time. Because the Treasury rate is considered default-free, while the Eurodollar rate reflects the credit standing of corporate borrowers, a wide spread suggests investors/lenders have a strong preference for safety. *See Basis Rate Swap, Credit Risk (4). See also Bundle, Treasury/EuroDollar (TED) Spread Swap.*

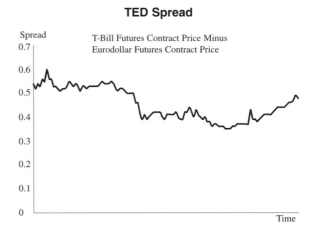

TED Spread

T-Bill Futures Contract Price Minus
Eurodollar Futures Contract Price

Treasury/EuroDollar (TED) Spread Swap: A basis swap with the respective floating-rate cash flows referenced to LIBOR and the similar-term Treasury Bill rate. *See also Treasury/EuroDollar (TED) Spread.*

Trend Option: A variation on an average rate option where preexpiration price behavior is time-weighted according to a formula agreed upon by the parties prior to initiation of the trade.

Treuhand Bond: A direct debt obligation of the Federal Republic of Germany on a par with bunds, bobls, and other German sovereign debt.

Treynor Measure: A risk-adjusted measure of return that divides a portfolio's return in excess of the riskless return by its beta. Because it adjusts return based on systematic risk, it is relevant for performance measurement when evaluating portfolios separately or in combination with other portfolios. *Compare to Sharpe Ratio.*

Trigger Forward: *See Break-Forward (diagram).*

Trigger Note: A structured note that matures if the trigger rate—usually a short-term floating rate—rises above or falls below a preset level.

Trigger Option: *See Barrier Option, Early Exercise Price Trigger.*

Triggering Event: A specified event, such as achievement of a particular price or rate relationship, a credit downgrade, a formal acquisition offer, etc., that requires a specific action, such as a deposit of collateral, cancellation of a swap, repayment of principal, or exercise of an option.

Trimmed Standard Deviation: The standard deviation computed so as to exclude extreme values or outliers.

Trinomial Model: Similar to a binomial model, but with three possible branches at each node rather than two. The trinomial branches reconverge (up-down equals down-up) to keep computations manageable. *See also Lattice.*

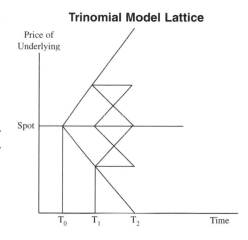

Trinomial Model Lattice

Triple Witching Hour: During a period in the mid-1980s, the triple congruence of stock option, index option, and index futures expirations at the stock market close on the third Friday of March, June, September, and December led to brief flurries of extraordinary trading activity, and, occasionally, extraordinary volatility. A series of changes in market structure, changes in the timing of expiration and settlement, and, most importantly, broader dissemination of information have largely diffused this phenomenon since late 1986.

Truncated Distribution: Typically arising in the context of options analysis, a distribution (for example, the terminal value of the option) that obtains when some underlying distribution (price of the underlying asset) is transformed in such a way that values beyond a particular point (the exercise price) are replaced by values that occur precisely at that point. In the case of a put option, the tail of the distribution of price is replaced by a "spike" at the exercise price.

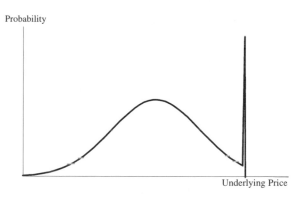

A Truncated Probability Distribution

Trust for Income Participation from Stocks (TIPS): A synthetic PERCS structure renamed package equity trust securities (PETS) before issuance because of a name conflict with the Toronto Stock Exchange's index deposit receipt product. *See Preference Equity Redemption Cumulative Stock (PERCS) (diagram), Short-Term Appreciation and Investment Return Trust (STAIR), Short-Term Equity Participation Units (STEP Units).*

Trust Originated PReferred Securities (TOPRS): *See Monthly Income Preferred Shares (MIPS).*

Tunnel Option: A set of collars with constant strike prices or rates, or centered on corresponding forward prices or rates, covering non-overlapping periods forward from the trade date. *See also Equity Risk Reversal (diagram).*

Turbo Option or Warrant: Typically, a combination of two call options on the same side of the market with different strikes. The net effect is to increase the holder of the options' exposure to the underlying as the options move into the money. For example, if the strikes of the component call options in a turbo warrant were 100 and 105, the investor might have 100% exposure to price movements of the underlying between

100 and 105, and 200% exposure to movement of the underlying above 105. A comparable put structure would have similar relationships on the downside.

Turbo Swap: *See LIBOR² Swap.*

Turbos: *See Long Bond Yield Decrease Warrants (Turbos).*

Turnover: (1) In the U.K., volume. (2) In a portfolio, usually calculated as (Purchases + Sales)/(Beginning Value + Ending Value). If a portfolio has an average turnover of 50% by this measure, approximately half the securities (in a portfolio with modest contributions and withdrawals) are replaced with new positions each year.

12b-1 Fund: A mutual fund taking advantage of SEC Rule 12b-1 that allows the fund to take out up to 1.25% of average daily fund assets each year to cover the costs of marketing its shares.

Two Dollar Broker: An independent floor broker on the floor of a U.S. stock exchange who executes orders for other exchange members for a fee—at one time $2 for 100 shares of stock.

Two-Factor Option Pricing Model: While the traditional Black-Scholes model allows for one stochastic variable (volatility), a two-factor model used to evaluate a traditional equity option or, perhaps, an option embedded in a bond, provides for a second stochastic variable—usually an interest rate. The final value of the security is a function of both variables as well as the other inputs in the option valuation mechanism.

Two-Sided (or -Tailed) Test: An hypothesis test where the alternative to the maintained or null hypothesis states simply that the parameter of interest is different in value from that specified under the null hypothesis. It is easier to reject a particular null hypothesis if the test is not two-sided, because the critical value of the appropriate statistic is lower for a one-sided test. A one-sided test incorporates the additional information that deviations from the null hypothesis parameter value can only occur in one direction. *See also One-Sided (or -Tailed) Test.*

Two-Tiered Index (or Interest) Bonds (TTIBs): *See Tiered Interest Bonds (TIBs).*

Type of Option: The classification of an option as a put, a call, a combination option, or a specialized option such as a cap, floor, or swaption.

Type I Error: In hypothesis testing, rejecting the proposition when it is true. *See also Hypothesis Testing.*

Type II Error: In hypothesis testing, failure to reject the proposition when it is false. *See also Hypothesis Testing.*

Ultra Vires Act: An act performed without any legal authority to act. An action beyond the scope of the powers of a corporation, state, province, or municipality. *See also Capacity, Capacity to Trade, Legal Risk, Hammersmith and Fulham, London Borough of.*

Unbiased Estimators: Estimators of underlying parameters constructed so that, in repeated experiments, the average or expected value of the estimator would equal the true or underlying parameter value.

Unbundled Stock Units (USUs): A proposed division of common stock returns into three components: a thirty-year bond with a yield equal to the stock's current dividend, a preferred issue that would pay dividends equal to any increase in the common stock dividend, and a thirty-year warrant on the common. This proposed structure encountered investor disinterest and regulatory opposition.

Uncovered Interest Arbitrage: The notion that the forward exchange rate is an unbiased estimate of the future spot rate. Uncovered interest arbitrage assumes that, on average, an investor who borrows in a low interest rate country, converts the funds to the currency of a high interest rate country, and lends in that country will not realize a profit or suffer a loss. It follows from uncovered interest arbitrage that the expected return of a forward contract equals 0%. *See also Forward Rate Bias.*

Uncovered Writer: A call option writer who does not own or a put option writer who is not short the underlying instrument that is the subject of an option. *See Covered Writer, Naked Option.*

Undated Forward: *See Spot Deferred Contract.*

Underlying: The security, cash commodity, forward, futures, swap, or other contract or instrument that is the subject of a derivatives contract or instrument.

Underlying Equivalent: *See Stock Equivalent.*

Underlying Tenor Period: The applicable term of the reference index rate. For example, LIBOR is regularly quoted for one-month, three-month, and six-month terms. The term chosen has a significant effect on the magnitude of swap or other interest payments.

Undertaking for Collective Investment in Transferable Securities (UCITS): A proposal and program for harmonizing requirements for distribution and management of unit trusts (mutual funds) and other collective investment vehicles in the European Union (EU).

Underwriter: (1) An investment banker who purchases securities for his own account with the express intention of reselling them in the open market. *See Bought Deal (1), Underwriting of Securities.* (2) An insurer who undertakes to furnish an insurance contract in exchange for a premium.

Underwriting of Securities: The process by which an underwriting syndicate of securities firms, or less frequently, a single security firm, guarantees the sale of an issue of securities by purchasing it at a stated price from the issuing enterprise for resale to public customers at a slightly higher price. *See Underwriter (1). See also Syndicate Department.*

Uniform Acts: A series of model statutes recommended for implementation by all states in the U.S. to provide a consistent legal framework for business and individuals. Examples include the Uniform Commercial Code, the Uniform Consumer Credit Code, the Uniform Gift to Minors Act, the Uniform Limited Partnership Act, etc.

Uniform Distribution: A distribution where there is an equal probability of experiencing each possible outcome.

Unilateral Margin Agreement: A collateralization arrangement in which the least creditworthy of two counterparties is required to post initial and/or variation margin to assure performance on a contract.

Unit: (1) Often a derivative security is combined with a conventional security at the time of initial issue to create a unit. This unit structure can be broken up and the derivative and conventional components traded separately. (2) The combination of a PRIME and a SCORE in an Americus Trust unit.

Unit Trust: (1) An investment company or mutual fund, especially in the U.K. *Also called Authorized Unit Trust.* (2) A limited life, special purpose regulated investment company in the U.S.

United Currency Options Market (UCOM): An OCC collateralized currency option (flex) system introduced by the Philadelphia Stock Exchange.

Universal Hedge: An approach to portfolio currency risk management developed by Fischer Black. Black argued that some currency hedging is appropriate and that one "universal" hedging ratio applies to all investors. One difficulty in applying this technique is that the universal hedge ratio is sensitive to changes in a number of unstable variables.

Unlisted: *See Over The Counter (OTC).*

Unlisted Trading Privileges: A provision of many U.S. securities exchanges' rules that allow a security to be traded upon the request of one or more members as distinguished from a listing application from the issuer. These privileges may be granted only with permission of the SEC.

Unmargined Spread: An option spread in which, for one or more of the following reasons, the short option is margined as a "naked" option rather than as part of a spread: (1) The long option expires before the short option. (2) The price relationships in certain vertical or diagonal spreads may be such that the margin requirements for a naked option are more favorable than those for spread margin treatment. (3) One or both of the options are unlisted.

Unmatched Swap: A swap agreement not linked to a specific asset or liability of either party. Examples include swaps undertaken as part of a global or overall risk management strategy or as parts of a warehousing or market making strategy by a swap dealer.

Unrealized Loss: An economic loss not yet recognized for tax and/or reporting purposes. *Also called Embedded Loss.*

Unrelated Business Income Tax (UBIT): A tax imposed on otherwise tax-exempt entities in the U.S. to prevent their non-charitable or non-investment activities from enjoying a competitive advantage over tax-paying participants in similar businesses. Until 1992, there was some question of the applicability of this tax to swaps and other notional principal contracts. An IRS ruling has clarified the exemption of these contracts.

Unsystematic Risk: *See Non-Systematic Risk.*

Unwinding Risk: The risk that reversing or closing out a risk management position will be difficult or costly. *See also Execution Risk, Rollover Risk.*

Up-and-Away Option: (1) *See Exploding Option.* (2) *See Out Option, Up-and-Out Call, Up-and-Out Put.*

Up-and-In Option: *See Barrier Option.*

Up-and-Out Call: A call option that expires if an outstrike is breached, or a call spread that pays off early if an early exercise price trigger is tripped. An example would be exchange-traded CAPS. *Also called Over-and-Out Call, Cash-Out Call Option with Rebate, Up-and-Away Option (2), Special Expiration Price*

Option. See also Exploding Option, Out Option.

Up-and-Out Put: A put option that expires worthless (or provides a rebate of a portion of the option premium) if the market price of the underlying rises above a predetermined expiration price. *Also called Over-and-Out Put, Up-and-Away Option (2), Special Expiration Price Option.*

Up-Tick Rule: In the U.S., securities listed on a national securities exchange may not be sold short unless the last trade prior to the short sale at a different price was at a price lower than the price at which the short sale is executed. *See Zero Plus Tick.*

Upfront Payment: A payment on the contract or trade date of a swap or other agreement to cover a fee or a dealer's spread or the current value of the right to pay or receive the fixed rate called for in the swap.

Upside Call: An out-of-the-money call option.

Upside Capture: In a portfolio insurance strategy, the fraction of the risky asset's terminal value (not return) that is captured by the overall strategy. Ex ante, upside capture equals the starting value of the portfolio minus the price of a shadow put option, all divided by the starting value of the portfolio.

U.S. Person: A (legal) person who is considered a resident of the United States for purposes of specific securities regulations.

Useable Security: A bond or, rarely, a preferred stock that may be valued at par and used as a substitute for cash in the exercise of a warrant. *See also Host Bond.*

Usury: Lending money at a rate of interest in excess of the maximum rate fixed by law for a specific type of loan or transaction.

Utility: A measure of satisfaction or happiness usually described as a function of wealth or return. This concept was introduced by Daniel Bernoulli, who argued that, for the typical person, utility increased with wealth but at a decreasing rate.

Utility Theory: A set of principles held to lie behind every economic transaction and most non-economic transactions. In general, utility theory holds that rational individuals attempt to maximize their expected utility. Subsidiary principles include risk aversion (risk is undesirable), and diminishing marginal utility (more is better than less, but more is worth progressively less per unit).

V-Rating: A formal grading of collateralized mortgage obligation (CMO) tranches according to their expected volatility. Published by Fitch Investors Service.

Valeurs: *Fr.* Securities.

Value Added Tax (VAT): A tax levied on the value added at each stage of production, in contrast to a sales tax or consumption tax levied only on the final selling price.

Value At Risk (VAR): (1) A currency-denominated measurement of the loss a dealer or an end user of financial instruments would experience in the event of, say, a two-standard deviation adverse move in reference prices or rates in the course of a day or other standardized period. Non-dealers, especially those who mark their portfolios to the market less frequently than daily, may use longer periods. While value at risk is increasingly the dominant risk measurement technique, users must be alert to the implicit assumptions that historic price or rate volatility is an appropriate "gauge" of likely future volatility, and that the distribution is approximately normal. VAR should always be supplemented by a stress test or other technique designed to test the sensitivity of the results to the underlying assumptions. A one-day VAR calculation is often called daily earnings at risk (DEaR). (2) Value at risk is sometimes defined as the daily calculation for value at risk multiplied by the square root of the time required to close out a position. A careful study of the way some value at risk calculations change with time

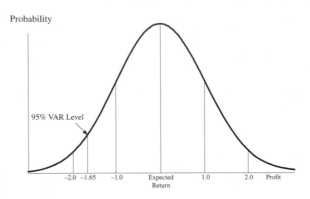

A Value At Risk (Daily Earnings at Risk) Diagram

suggests that this square root of time calculation probably understates the risk, particularly of some illiquid positions. Careful attention to the assumptions and algorithms in any VAR calculation is essential. *See also Add-On, Capital at Risk, Daily Earnings at Risk (DEaR), Cash Flow Sensitivity Analysis.*

Value Date: The date on which parties to a financial instrument calculate and exchange payments to settle their respective obligations.

Value Lock Level: A minimum payout level on a ladder option or note. *Also called Rung, Threshold Level.*

Value Management: An equity management style that emphasizes the inherent earning power or asset value of a company, and, especially, the value of its equity securities. Value managers often look for low ratios of book value to market value, low price/earnings ratios, or other indications that a stock is undervalued. *See Style Management.*

Value of a Basis Point (PV 01 or PVBP): A measure of a bond's price/yield relationship that specifies the dollar value of a basis point change in yield. Also called value of an "01," and abbreviated PV 01 or DV 01. *Also called Dollar Value of a Basis Point (DV 01), Price Value of a Basis Point (PV 01 or PVBP).*

Vanishing Option: A down-and-out call, an up-and-out put, or any other option with an expiration price. *See Exploding Option, Out Option.*

Variable Annuity: An annuity contract in which the value of periodic income payments may fluctuate as a result of changes in securities market values, a cost of living index, or some other designated index.

Variable Common Rights (VCR): A limited term average price call option issued to shareholders of an acquired company. The VCR pays the selling shareholders additional common shares if the acquiring company's stock sells above a specified average price during a preset pricing interval.

Variable Coupon Renewable Notes: Floating-rate notes with a coupon set weekly at a fixed spread over the ninety-one-day T-bill rate. Generally, these instruments are puttable to the issuer to protect holders against credit deterioration.

Variable Cumulative Preferred Stock: A floating-rate preferred with an issuer option to select between a Dutch auction reset and a remarketing reset arrangement at the end of each dividend period. *See Adjustable-Rate Preferred Stock (ARPS).*

Variable Hedge: *See Option Hedge (diagrams).*

Variable Maturity Option: A put or call that matures substantially sooner than its nominal final expiration date if the underlying has moved significantly prior to an early maturity date stated in the contract. The early maturity may be effective if the underlying price moves by a set amount in either direction or only in the favorable direction. With rare exceptions, the premium on an early maturity option is significantly less than the premium on a standard option.

Variable Redemption Bonds: Bonds with both fixed and variable components of principal redemption. The variable portion is linked to an index or rate. Examples include "heaven and hell" and other currency-linked bonds. *See Heaven and Hell Bond, Dual Currency Bond.*

Variable Spread: Partially offsetting long and short positions are taken in two options of the same type and class but with different strike prices and/or expiration dates. The number of contracts short will be different from the number of contracts long in a variable spread. *Also called Ratio Spread.*

Variable-Rate Mortgage: *See Adjustable-Rate Mortgage (ARM).*

Variable-Rate Renewable Notes: Floating-rate notes with a coupon rate set monthly at a fixed spread over the one-month commercial paper rate. Each quarter, the maturity automatically extends an additional quarter unless the investor elects to terminate the extension and put the notes back to the issuer.

Variance: The mean of the squared deviations of each observation from the mean. The square of the standard deviation.

$$\frac{\sum\limits_{i=1}^{n}(x_i - \mu)^2}{n}$$

Variance Drain: The difference between mean return and compound return over a period of time (usually a number of years) due to the variance (or variability) of periodic returns. The greater the variance of periodic returns, the more the compound return will fall below the mean return. In general, the compound return falls below the mean return by about one-half the variance. *See also Covariance Assets, Diversification, Geometric Return.*

Variance Ratio: A measure of the randomness of a return series. Variance ratio is computed by dividing the variance of returns estimated from longer intervals by the variance of returns estimated from shorter intervals (for the same measurement period), and then normalizing this value to 1 by dividing it by the ratio of the longer interval to the shorter interval. A variance ratio greater than 1 suggests that the returns series is positively serially correlated or that the shorter-interval returns trend within the duration of the longer interval. A variance ratio less than 1 suggests that the return series is negatively serially correlated or that the shorter-interval returns tend toward mean reversion within the duration of the longer interval.

Variation Call: *See Variation Margin.*

Variation Margin: The cash transfer that takes place after each trading day (and sometimes intraday) in most futures markets to mark long and short positions to the market. Unlike a forward contract that settles only when the contract matures, most futures contracts are settled daily by the payment of variation margin from the party who has lost money that day to the party who has made money. If each point in the price of a contract is worth $1,000, and the futures price goes up by 1/2 point during a session, the short will pay the long $500 per contract in variation margin. Holders and sellers of futures options do not exchange variation margin under current margin procedures, but the ability to capture accumulated variation margin payments through exercise affects the value of an American-style futures option. *See also Maintenance Margin, Margin.*

Vasicek Model: A single-factor analytic model used to value interest rate dependent claims. The single factor is the short-term interest rate. Although this model was the first to incorporate mean reversion, the interest rate dynamics underlying it permit negative interest rates.

Vega: Although not a Greek letter, a common designation for the dollar change in option price in response to a percentage point change in volatility, when volatility is measured in percentage terms. *Also called by the Greek letters Kappa (κ), Tau (τ), Lambda(Λ), and Zeta (ζ).*

Velocity: (1) The rate at which money circulates through the economy. (2) Volatility, usually expressed as a percent change of an index. Generally equal to the standard deviation percentage change times the beta of the position.

Venture Capital: Money advanced by aggressive investors who seek substantially above average returns (often in illiquid positions), and who are willing to accept correspondingly high risks. Often associated with corporate start-ups.

Vertical Bear Spread: Regardless of whether two puts or two calls are used to create this option spread, the option purchased has a higher strike than the option sold. The number of contracts purchased equals the number sold, and both options expire on the same date. *Also called Perpendicular Spread, Money Spread.*

Vertical Bull Spread: Regardless of whether two puts or two calls are used to create this option spread, the option purchased has a lower strike than the option sold. The number of contracts purchased equals the number sold, and both options expire on the same date. *Also called Perpendicular Spread, Money Spread.*

Vertical Cap: (1) The upper cap on a corridor interest rate cap structure. (2) The entire corridor structure.

Very Accurately Defined Maturity (VADM) Bond: A class of collateralized mortgage obligations (CMOs) with relatively little prepayment or extension risk. *See Planned Amortization Class (PAC) Bond, Super Planned Amortization Class (Super PAC) Bond.*

Vigorish (Vig): The profit, often implicitly above average, expected from a transaction or a type of transaction.

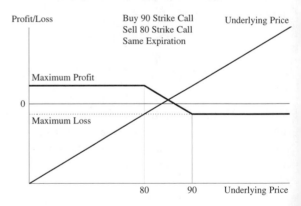

Profit/Loss Pattern of a Vertical Bear Spread at Expiration

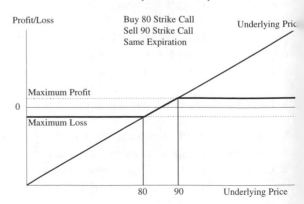

Profit/Loss Pattern of a Vertical Bull Spread at Expiration

Virtual Currency Option: An option that pays out as a function of a currency exchange rate and is denominated and settled in the investor's base currency, making it unnecessary to actually hold or take delivery of the foreign currency.

Volatility: A statistical measure of the tendency of a market price or yield to vary over time. Volatility, usually measured by the variance or annualized standard deviation of the price, rate, or return, is said to be high if the price, yield, or return typically changes dramatically in a short period of time. Volatility is one of the most important elements in evaluating an option, because it is usually the only valuation variable not known with certainty in advance. *See also Risk.*

Volatility AutoRegressive Integrated Moving Average (VARIMA) Model: A mean reverting model for volatility estimation. *See AutoRegressive Moving Average (ARMA) Models, Mean Reversion.*

Volatility Cone: A technique for visualizing current option implied volatility relative to historic volatilities at different maturity ranges. This technique, developed by Galen Burghardt, uses the range of historic volatilities for each option's maturity from, say, one month to two years or longer, depending on the maturities of instruments available in the market. An historic volatility series is calculated for each period and 25% and 75% confidence intervals on either side of the mean historic volatility line are added. When the current implied volatility term structure is drawn on this diagram, the investor is able to determine how current option premiums compare to historic premium levels at various maturities.

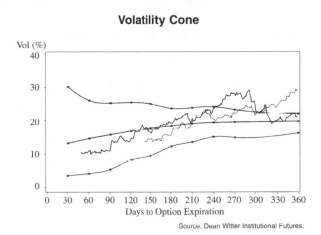

Volatility Effect: A reference to the fact that a higher volatility reduces the sensitivity of delta (gamma) to differences in maturity (time).

Volatility Event: An occurrence such as a news report, economic development, or even a seemingly exogenous market movement that causes a temporary change in actual or implied price or rate volatility.

Volatility Option: A proposed option contract with a payoff linked to the level of volatility in a market.

Volatility Point (Vol Point): 1% of annualized standard deviation. Over-the-counter options often trade on the basis of bid/asked spreads expressed in vol points.

Volatility Risk: The risk that the holder or seller of a standard or embedded option incurs if actual volatility or the market's expectations for future volatility change. Other things equal, an optionholder benefits from an increase in actual or expected volatility and suffers from increased price or rate stability. An option seller is hurt by an increase in volatility and helped by a decrease. Some compound, barrier, and average rate options can provide protection from various types of volatility risk.

Volatility Skewness: (1) A measure of the relationship between the implied volatility of options and the strike prices of those options. According to the Black-Scholes option pricing model and its underlying assumption of costless trading, implied volatility should not vary with the strike prices of options.

Empirically, however, implied volatilities of options on stocks and stock indexes tend to increase on out-of-the-money options. *See Smile and Skew.* (2) The tendency of the volatility of an underlying stock or stock index to be inversely correlated with stock price or the tendency of interest rate volatilities to be inversely correlated with the level of interest rates.

Volatility Swap: A reference to a transaction in which a fixed payment or series of fixed or indexed payments is exchanged for a payoff or a series of payoffs from volatility-based transactions such as straddles, strangles, or range options. Many such transactions can be described more usefully as option purchases or sales, perhaps with an unusual premium determination process.

Volatility Value: The entire value of an out-of-the-money (forward) option. With basis value added, the sum is the premium over intrinsic value for an in-the-money option. *Also called Opportunity Value. See also Insurance (2), Option Premium (2), Time Value. See Call Option (diagram).*

Volume: The number of shares, bonds, notes, or contracts traded in a market. Along with units outstanding and open interest, volume is one of the few measures of the liquidity in a market available to an outside observer.

Vulnerable Black-Scholes Option Pricing Model: A variation of the original Black-Scholes option pricing model that incorporates default risk into the pricing equation.

Vulnerable Option: An option subject to writer default risk. Many OTC options are vulnerable because they are subject to material credit risk.

Vulture Fund: A pooled account, created by public or private subscription, that specializes in distressed investments such as high-yield bonds in or near default, fallen angels, or highly leveraged equities.

W

Walkaway Clause: *See Limited Two-Way Payment (LTP) Clause.*

Walrasian Market: *See Call Market.*

Warehouse: A reference to a swaps market maker's practice of running a book of unmatched swaps, managing the book as a whole rather than as pairs of matched deals.

Warehouse Receipt: Originally, a receipt for goods stored in a warehouse. The warehouse company agreed to be responsible for the safe custody and release of the goods upon presentation of the receipt for the indicated goods. Increasingly, in financial markets, the term refers to an instrument issued by a custodian as evidence of deposit of the securities. The SPDRs traded on the American Stock Exchange are, in effect, warehouse receipts that, when reaggregated, can be used to redeem shares deposited with a custodian. *See Standard & Poor's 500 Depositary Receipts (SPDRs).*

Warrant: An option to purchase or sell the underlying at a given price and time or at a series of prices and times outlined in the warrant agreement. A warrant differs from a put or call option in that it is ordinarily issued for a period in excess of one year. Warrants are issued alone or in connection with the sale of other securities, as part of a merger or recapitalization agreement, and, occasionally, to facilitate divestiture of the securities of another corporation. Ordinarily, exercise of a common stock warrant sold by the issuer of the underlying increases the number of shares of stock outstanding, while a call or a covered warrant is an option on shares already outstanding. Index warrants and many put warrants are cash settled. *Also called Stock Purchase Warrant, Term Stock Right (TSR). See also Call Option, Covered Warrant, Dilution, Equity Warrant.*

Warrant Dilution: Covered warrants and exchange-traded or OTC options do not result in dilution of the interest of common shareholders because the shares underlying these instruments are outstanding shares: no new shares need be issued upon their exercise or settlement. Warrants issued by a corporation as part of its capitalization can dilute the interest of prior shareholders. The best way to estimate this dilution is to divide the market value of the warrants by the market value of the corporation's common shareholders' equity plus the market value of other convertible securities—in the simplest case, the market value of the warrants. The resulting fraction expressed as a percent will give a good measure of the dilution attributable to the warrants. If a warrant dilutes the interest of the shareholders, the value of the warrant itself is reduced. *See Dilution.*

Warrant-Driven Swap: A swap with an "attached" warrant allowing a counterparty affected by a bond warrant exercise to increase the size of the swap. This structure makes the impact/value of the warrant a factor in pricing the swap.

Wash Sale: Under U.S. tax law, wash sales occur when substantially identical stock or other securities are bought within thirty days before or after a sale. Losses realized on wash sales are added to the basis of the reacquired securities, and are not immediately deductible for tax purposes. *See also Bed and Breakfast.*

Wasting Asset: (1) A long option position that declines in value, other things equal, with the passage of time. (2) Exhaustible natural resources such as mineral deposits, oil and gas, etc.

Weak Form: *See Efficient Market.*

Wealth Relative: A value equal to 1 plus the periodic rate of return. This value is used to link returns in computing the geometric average, and its logarithm is equal to the periodic return's corresponding continuous return.

Wedding Band Swap: (1) A swap variation with a relatively low floating-rate payment if an index rate stays within a preset range over a designated observation interval. If the rate touches or exceeds the limits of the range during the observation interval, the floating rate will rise, often by a leverage factor for the next reset period or for the remaining life of the swap. (2) A corridor swap or its complement, depending on a counterparty's position. One counterparty makes a binary payment if an index rate, typically LIBOR, is outside the designated range at a settlement date.

Weekend Effect: (1) A tendency for implied volatilities (calculated on the basis of calendar days to option expiration) to rise from Friday to Monday. (2) A mild tendency for the U.S. stock market to rise slightly on Friday and to decline on Monday.

Weighted Average Cost of Capital (WACC): The sum of the implied or required market returns of each component of a corporate capitalization, weighted by that component's share of the total capitalization. *See also Economic Value Added (EVA).*

Weighted Average Coupon (WAC): The coupon of each position in a mortgage pool (or other debt instrument portfolio) weighted by the size of the position to compute an average coupon for the pool. Ordinarily, a detailed schedule of coupons is more useful in predicting prepayment rates than a weighted average.

Weighted Average Life (WAL): The time-weighted average of expected principal repayments on a fixed-income security. Used as a measure of portfolio tenor.

Weighted Average Loan Age (WALA): The dollar-weighted average age of the mortgage loans in a mortgage pool.

Weighted Average Maturity (WAM): The maturity of each position in a mortgage pool (or other debt instrument portfolio) weighted by the dollar value of the position to compute an average maturity for the pool.

Weighted Average Months Remaining to Maturity (WARM): The dollar-weighted average number of months remaining to maturity in a pool of mortgages, or the weighted average maturity taken at some point well into the life of a mortgage pool or other debt instrument portfolio, otherwise analogous to weighted average maturity (WAM).

Weighted Average Rate/Price Option (WARO): Similar to an average rate option except that the weighting of each daily, weekly, or monthly price or rate varies depending upon the agreement of the parties. The weighted average rate option may be used when the timing and magnitude of cash flows is known but price or rate is uncertain. *See also Average Price or Rate Option (APO, ARO) (diagrams).*

Weighted Collar: A collar or equity risk reversal with an imbalance between the quantities covered by the cap and the floor.

When-Issued Option: An option on the next Treasury bond or note to be issued with a specific maturity.

Whipsaw: A sharp price movement followed quickly by a sharp reversal.

White Correction: A method for correcting for heteroskedasticity in ordinary least squares regression analysis. *See also Newey-West Correction.*

White Knight: A friendly acquirer whose interest in a takeover target is welcome after a hostile takeover bid has been launched.

White Noise: A random process that is invariant to time and space because all of the elements are uncorrelated.

Wholesale Uninsured Financial Institution (WUFI): A proposed regulatory framework for a multipurpose financial intermediary that can engage in any banking transaction except taking insured deposits.

Wiener or Wiener/Bachelier Process: A Gaussian stochastic process with independent increments, a vanishing mean, and the property that, considered as a Gaussian random variable, the increment of the process during any given time period has a variance proportional to the time period. A Wiener process is automatically a Markov process as well as a martingale process. It arises as a limit of random walks of the following type: during every unit of time a particle moves on a line at a fixed distance either to the left or to the right with equal probability. Sample paths are nowhere differentiable, and the usual chain rule from calculus does not apply to operations involving these paths. A special chain rule known as Ito's Lemma is used instead. *See Ito's Lemma.*

Wild Card: Provisions in several futures contracts whereby the investor who is short the contract can deliver any of a number of securities or commodities in settlement of the delivery obligation, can choose the instruments to be delivered at the last moment, and/or can deliver anytime within a prescribed period. The option to change the item delivered or the time of delivery enhances the flexibility of the short's position, and occasionally exacerbates price volatility in the underlying near expiration.

Winding-Up Risk: The risk of not being able to close out a position quickly and/or at reasonable cost.

Window Warrants: Warrants that can be exercised only during limited intervals in the life of a host bond.

Windsor Declaration: An agreement by market regulators from sixteen nations meeting in Windsor, England in 1995 to improve international information sharing, protection of customer assets, default procedures, and emergency cooperation among regulators. The conclusions were greatly influenced by the Barings collapse. *See Barings Collapse.*

Wing Nuts: Deep out-of-the-money options.

Withholding Tax: Of pertinence to global risk management transactions, most governments impose a withholding tax ranging from 15% to 30% on some interest payments and nearly all dividends paid on securities owned by foreign investors. Reciprocal withholding tax treaties usually reduce the withholding tax among the major industrial countries to 15%.

Withholding Tax Agreement: One of a number of bilateral treaties that reduces non-resident dividend withholding taxes for stockholders in the signatory countries.

Workout Market: A market in which any quote a dealer furnishes is subject to his ability to find the other side of the trade. Frequently, these markets are thin, and the dealer is not willing to commit his own capital except at a prohibitive markup. Prices quoted (or, more accurately, estimated) by different dealers may vary greatly in a workout market. *See also Indicative Price (2).*

World Equity Benchmark Shares (WEBS): A family of exchange-traded (EXTRA) single country funds. Each fund is designed to approximate the return pattern of a designated Morgan Stanley Capital International (MSCI) country benchmark index.

Worst Case: A relatively unlikely and relatively adverse scenario, but rarely the worst possible outcome. In most applications this would be a 95 or 99 percentile outcome. *See Simulation Analysis. See also Loss Limit, Capital at Risk.*

Worst-Of-Two-Assets Option: *See Alternative Option (diagram), Better-Of-Two-Assets Option.*

Wrap Account: An account that pays a brokerage firm a flat annual fee to cover the cost of money management services and trading commissions.

Writer: *See Option Writer.*

Yankee Bond: A dollar-denominated bond issued by a non-U.S. company in the U.S.

Yankee Certificate of Deposit (YCD): A negotiable certificate of deposit issued and payable in dollars to the bearer in the U.S. by the branch office of a foreign bank.

Yield: A percentage rate of return. *See also Current Yield, Yield to Maturity.*

Yield Curve: A graph illustrating the level of interest rates as a function of time—obtained by plotting the yields of all default-free coupon bonds in a given currency against maturity, or, occasionally, duration. Yields on debt instruments of lower quality are expressed in terms of a spread relative to the default-free yield

Normal Yield Curve and Forward Curve

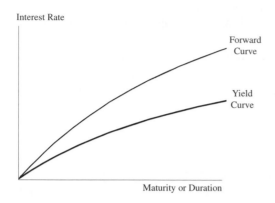

Inverted Yield Curve and Forward Curve

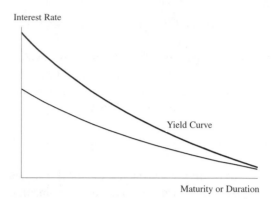

curve. In the diagrams, a normal yield curve on the top features short-term yields lower than long-term yields. The inverted yield curve on the bottom illustrates short-term rates in excess of long-term rates and characterizes periods when the central bank is attempting to restrict growth in the money supply and, hence, the level of economic activity. Forward curves derived from each yield curve are also illustrated. *See also Expectations Hypothesis. See Term Structure of Interest Rates, Forward Yield Curve, Implied Forward Interest Rate, Zero-Coupon Yield Curve, Prediction Bias.*

Yield Curve Flattening Warrants: An option with a payoff contingent on the yield spread between two debt instruments on opposite ends of the yield curve. For the maximum risk of a premium, the holder can participate in a narrowing of the yield spread relative to the strike spread. *See also Yield Curve Option.*

Yield Curve Note: *See Reverse Floating-Rate Note (diagram).*

Yield Curve Option: An option on the spread between two rates at different maturities on a yield curve. Depending on the specific terms selected, the option will pay off on flattening or steepening of the yield curve. A yield curve option costs less than separate put and call options on the representative issues used to construct the yield curve because the yield curve option pays off only on the change in the spread, while one of a pair of separate options might be in the money as a result of a parallel shift in the yield curve. *See also Term Structure of Interest Rates, Yield Curve Flattening Warrants.*

Yield Curve Swap Agreement: A swap with interest payments reflecting floating rates at two different points on the swap yield curve. Typically, a constant maturity swap (CMS) agreement.

Yield Curve Twist: An interest rate shift characterized by a change in the spread between two interest rates at different maturity points along the yield curve. Yield curve twists can cause problems if an investor or risk manager uses tools that rely on all interest rate changes being characterized by parallel yield curve shifts.

Yield Decrease Warrant: An interest rate warrant that increases in value as long bond yields decline, and, conversely, declines in value when yields rise. Similar to a call on a bond, but the strike and the payment are based on yield changes.

Yield Differential Warrant: Contract in which the payoff, if any, is a function of a yield differential in two markets, such as a short-term and a long-term rate in a particular country or a rate of the same maturity in two countries. *Also called Yield Spread Option or Warrant. See, for example, BOATs, Diff or Difference Option (2).*

Yield Enhanced Equity-Linked Debt Security (YEELDS): *See Equity-LinKed Security (ELKS), Synthetic PERCS.*

Yield Enhanced Stock (YES): A synthetic PERCS issue. *See Equity Yield Enhancement Security (EYES), Preference Equity Redemption Cumulative Stock (PERCS) (diagram), Dividend Enhanced Convertible Stock (DECS).*

Yield Enhancement: Any of a variety of strategies used to increase the actual or apparent yield of a debt instrument. Frequently these strategies are based on continuous option selling programs that may increase apparent yields during most periods, but can substantially reduce returns from time to time and in the long run. Occasionally, yield enhancement strategies are based on arbitrage-type transactions, where the probability of return enhancement is quite high during any period the position is in place.

Yield Spread Option or Warrant: *See Yield Differential Warrant.*

Yield to Maturity: The compound rate of return obtained by holding a bond to maturity under certain assumptions. The yield to maturity calculation assumes that any coupon payments received before maturity can be reinvested at this yield.*See Dollar-Weighted Return. See also Yield.*

Yield to Worst: The yield to maturity under the least desirable bond repayment pattern assuming that market yields are unchanged. If market yields are higher than the coupon, the yield to worst would assume no prepayment. If market yields are below the coupon, yield to worst would assume prepayment at the earliest call date.

You Choose Warrant: *See As-You-Like Warrant.*

Z Bond: An accrual tranche of a collateralized mortgage obligation (CMO)—usually one of the last segments to be paid off in cash. *Also called Accrual Bond, Z Tranche. See also Collateralized Mortgage Obligation (CMO).*

Z Score Analysis: A company failure or bankruptcy prediction model based on multiple discriminatory analysis developed by Prof. Edward Altman of New York University. Typically, a company's Z score is a positive function of five factors:

- (net working capital)/(total assets)
- (retained earnings)/(total assets)
- (EBIT)/(total assets)
- (market value of common and preferred)/(book value of debt)
- (sales)/(total assets)

Although the factor weights are not equal, the higher each ratio, the higher the Z score, and the lower the probability of bankruptcy. *Also called Zeta (ζ).*

Z Tranche: *See Z Bond.*

Zaitech: *Jap.* Financial engineering.

Zero Basis Risk (Zebra) Swap: A swap between a municipality that pays a fixed rate and a financial intermediary that pays a floating rate exactly equal to the floating-rate requirement on the municipality's floating-rate debt. Receiving the exact floating rate called for under the terms of the municipal debt issue prevents problems with federal regulations that prohibit arbitrage transactions on municipal debt. *Also called Perfect Swap, Actual Rate Swap. See also Arbitrage Bond.*

Zero Cost Collar: An equity risk reversal with equal premiums on the cap and floor. *See Equity Risk Reversal (diagram).*

Zero Cost Hedge: *See Zero Cost Option, Equity Risk Reversal (diagram).*

Zero Cost Option: A slightly misleading description of a situation in which the premium from an option sold pays the premium of an option purchased. *Also called Zero Cost Hedge. See Equity Risk Reversal (diagram).*

Zero Plus Tick: A price unchanged from the last price at which a security sale took place. The last different price was lower than the current price, qualifying a transaction at this price for execution of a short sale on U.S. exchanges. *See Up-Tick Rule.*

Zero Premium Option: Any combination option or a combination of an option, a note, and a participation that provides an asymmetric return pattern characteristic of option payoffs without the explicit payment or receipt of a net premium by either party to the contract. Examples include zero premium collars and equity risk reversals and many equity-linked notes. *Also called No Cost Option, Premium Free Option, Premium Neutral Option.*

Zero Premium Risk Reversal: Reflecting the reluctance of many investors to pay a premium for an option, the premium taken from the sale of the call (cap) is designed to exactly match the cost of the put (floor) purchased. Typically, an investor designates one strike price and expiration date, and the provider of the risk reversal determines the other strike price. *Also called No Cost Risk Reversal or Collar.*

Zero Strike Price Options: Options with an exercise price of zero, or very close to zero, traded on options exchanges in countries where there is a transfer tax, ownership restriction, or other obstacle to the transfer of securities, especially stock. Zero strike price options are frequently cash settled so that no transaction in the underlying occurs. The holder of the option has full participation in the underlying price, as if he held a long position in the stock, and the seller has full offsetting participation in the stock price, as if he had taken a short or short against-the-box position. *See also Low Exercise Price Options (LEPOs).*

Zero Sum Market: A reference to the fact that derivatives markets reallocate uncertain cash flows among market participants without enhancing aggregate cash flow in any way, actually reducing the cash flow by the amount of transaction costs in the market. This viewpoint neglects the reallocation of utility among market participants. It also ignores the opportunity that market participants have to transact at lower costs than they might be able to obtain in traditional markets. Derivatives markets also offer the opportunity to implement forecasts that might not be expressed readily in traditional securities positions.

Zero-Coupon Accrual Note: A variant of the range accumulation note with an initial price below par, a negligible or zero-coupon rate, and a supplementary interest accrual determined by an embedded range accumulation option feature. Typically, the total redemption payment is capped at par with automatic maturity and principal redemption. The more accurate the range forecast, the higher the return and the earlier the opportunity to reinvest in a new forecast.

Zero-Coupon Bond: A debt instrument sold at a discount to its face value. The bond makes no payments until maturity, at which time it is redeemed at face value. *See Discount Instrument (1).*

Zero-Coupon Convertible Debt: Convertible bonds that are typically puttable to the issuer during the early years of their lives and convertible into the issuer's common stock on terms calculated to provide a return somewhat less than the return on common stock with significantly reduced risk. In the U.S., the issuer has been able to deduct an implied interest payment even if the instrument is converted and no interest is actually paid. *See Liquid Yield Option Note (LYON).*

Zero-Coupon Bond

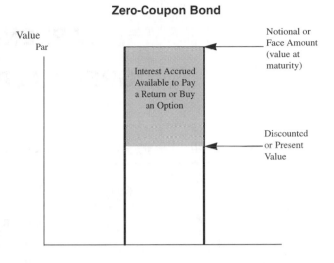

Zero-Coupon Currency Swap: A long-term currency forward exchange agreement (FXA) in the form of a swap agreement with a single cash exchange at maturity. *See also Forward Exchange Agreement (FXA).*

Zero-Coupon Eurosterling Bearer or Registered Accruing (ZEBRA) Certificate: Stripped Eurosterling notes. *Comparable to STRIPS.*

Zero-Coupon Swap: An interest rate swap agreement with the fixed-rate side based on a zero-coupon bond. With agreement of the counterparty, the swap agreement may call for a single fixed payment at maturity by the holder of the zero. The payments on the other side may follow typical swap interim payment schedules. Because of the payment mismatch, a zero-coupon swap exposes one of the counterparties to significant credit risk and is the functional equivalent of a loan. *See also Reverse Zero-Coupon Swap.*

Zero-Coupon Yield Curve: A graph of the term structure of default-free zero-coupon rates. *See Implied Forward Interest Rate. See also Yield Curve (diagrams), Forward Yield Curve, Implied Zero-Coupon Swap Curve.*

Zeta (ζ): *See Kappa (κ), Vega, Z Score Analysis.*

Zillmerising: An adjustment in the actuarial value of a long-term insurance policy to spread the cost of acquiring new business over a period of time.

Zombie Bond: A highly speculative bond, once mistaken for dead, that shows new signs of life.

APPENDIX

GREEK ALPHABET

Greek Letter		Greek Name	English Equivalent
A	α	Alpha	a
B	β	Beta	b
Γ	γ	Gamma	g
Δ	δ	Delta	d
E	ε	Epsilon	e (as in "led")
Z	ζ	Zeta	z
H	η	Eta	e (as in "need")
Θ	θ	Theta	t
I	ι	Iota	I
K	κ	Kappa	k
Λ	λ	Lambda	l
M	μ	Mu	m
N	ν	Nu	n
Ξ	ξ	Xi	x
O	o	Omicron	o (as in "nod")
Π	π	Pi	p
P	ρ	Rho	r
Σ	σ	Sigma	s
T	τ	Tau	t
Y	υ	Upsilon	u
Φ	φ	Phi	ph
X	χ	Chi	ch
Ψ	ψ	Psi	ps
Ω	ω	Omega	o (as in "load")

SELECTED CURRENCY SYMBOLS

Society for Worldwide Interbank Financial Telecommunication (SWIFT) codes and Chicago Mercantile Exchange (CME) symbols for currencies.

Currency	SWIFT Code	CME Symbol
Austrian Shilling	ATS	
Australian Dollar	AUD	AD
Belgian Franc	BEF	
Brazilian Real	BRL	BR
Canadian Dollar	CAD	CD
Swiss Franc	CHF	SF
Deutsche Mark	DEM	DM
Danish Krone	DKK	
Spanish Peseta	ESP	
Finnish Markka	FIM	
French Franc	FRF	FR
British Pound Sterling	GBP	BP
Hong Kong Dollar	HKD	
Israeli Shekel	ILS	
Indian Rupee	INR	
Italian Lira	ITL	
Japanese Yen	JPY	JY
Korean Won	KRW	
Mexican Nuevo Peso	MXN	MP
Malaysian Ringgit	MYR	
Netherlands Guilder	NLG	
Norwegian Krone	NOK	
New Zealand Dollar	NZD	
Peruvian Nuevo Sol	PEN	
Philippine Peso	PHP	
Pakistan Rupee	PKR	
Polish Zloty	PLZ	
Russian Ruble	RUR	
Saudi Riyal	SAR	
Swedish Krona	SEK	
Singapore Dollar	SGD	
Thailand Baht	THB	
Turkish Lira	TRL	
U.S. Dollar	USD	
Venezuelan Bolivar	VEB	
South African Rand	ZAR	

DEBT RATINGS

Rating agencies usually have separate ratings for short-term instruments, but long-term ratings are the measure of credit quality emphasized by most risk managers.

Rating Agency						Description of Rating*
S&P	IBCA	Moody's	Duff & Phelps	Fitch	Thomson Bankwatch	
AAA	AAA	Aaa	AAA	AAA	AAA	Highest credit quality. The risk factors are negligible, being only slightly more than for risk-free U.S. Treasury debt.
AA	AA	Aa	AA	AA	AA	High credit quality. Protection factors are strong. Risk is modest but may vary slightly from time to time because of economic conditions.
A	A	A	A	A	A	Protection factors are average but adequate. However, risk factors are more variable and greater in periods of economic stress.
BBB	BBB	Baa	BBB	BBB	BBB	Below average protection factors but still considered sufficient for prudent investment. Considerable variability in risk during economic cycles.
BB	BB	Ba	BB	BB	BB	Below investment-grade but deemed likely to meet obligations when due. Present or prospective financial protection factors fluctuate according to industry conditions or company fortunes. Overall quality may move up or down frequently within this category.
B	B	B	B	B	B	Below investment-grade and possessing risk that obligations will not be met when due. Financial protection factors will fluctuate widely according to economic cycles, industry conditions, and/or company fortunes. Potential exists for frequent changes in the rating within this category or into a higher or lower rating grade.
CCC	CCC	Caa	CCC	CCC	CCC	Well below investment-grade securities. Con-

Rating Agency						Description of Rating[*]
S&P	IBCA	Moody's	Duff & Phelps	Fitch	Thomson Bankwatch	
CC C	CC	Ca C		CC C	CC	siderable uncertainty exists as to timely payment of principal, interest, or preferred dividends. Protection factors are narrow, and risk can be substantial with unfavorable economic/industry conditions, and/or with unfavorable company developments.
D	C		DD	DDD, DD, D	D	Defaulted debt obligations. Issuer failed to meet scheduled principal and/or interest payments.
+ −	+ −	1 2 3	+ −	+ −	+ −	Symbols used to provide more detailed gradation of quality.
AA–CCC	AAA–C	Aa–B	AA–B	AA–C	AAA–D	Range of ratings for which quality gradations are provided.

[*]Duff & Phelps descriptions are used because they tend to be the most concise. The rating agencies try to use similar definitions even if they do not always agree on an individual issuer's rating.

Sierra System

Sierra System is available either in a full implementation, or on a desk-by-desk basis. FNX uses a modular approach, which allows FNX products to be used as stand-alone front or back office systems, or integrated in any combination to suit particular trading operations.

SYSTEM FEATURES

FRONT OFFICE

- Pricing
- Deal Capture
- User Defined Instruments
- On-Line Analytic Blotters
- On-Line Position & P/L Blotters
- Real-Time Data Feeds

MIDDLE OFFICE

- Value at Risk
- Position Maintenance
- On-line Credit Limit Monitoring
- Detailed P/L Analysis
- Regulatory Reporting

BACK OFFICE

- Full Confirmation Capabilities
- S.W.I.F.T. Confirmations
- Nostro/Vostro Accounts
- Full Security & Audit Trail Reporting
- Cash Slip Processor
- General Ledger

PRODUCT COVERAGE

INTEREST RATE

- Bonds
- Swaps
- Money Markets
- FRAs
- Repos
- Futures
- Exchange Traded Options
- Options on Cash Bonds
- Swaptions

FOREIGN EXCHANGE

- Foreign Exchange Options
- Foreign Exchange Cash

COMMODITY TRADING

- Precious Metals Options & Physicals
- Energy Derivatives
- Base Metals

FNX Limited was founded in 1992. Since its inception, the company has expanded worldwide, opening sales and support offices in New York, London, Tokyo, Singapore, and Melbourne, with the headquarters located in Philadelphia, and a client base of the most prestigious financial institutions. FNX's clients include global and multiple installations at AIG, Australia & New Zealand Banking Group Ltd., Bear Stearns, Citibank, Credit Suisse, Deutsche Bank, Norinchukin, Nippon Credit Bank, Prudential Securities, Sakura Bank Ltd. and Union Bank of Switzerland. FNX currently employs over 90 specialists to provide the highest level of service to its clients worldwide.

On-Line Position & P/L Blotters, such as the Precious Metals Physicals Trading Blotter, allow traders to enter their spot, forward, and future trades while viewing their real-time profit and loss by individual trade, commodity, or for the entire portfolio. Numerous trade details can be selected for display, as well as various P/L calculations, including Spot, Contango, and Mark-to-Market P/L.

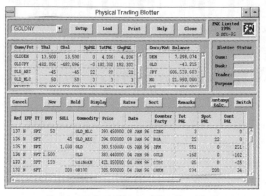

Precious Metals Physical Trading Blotter

F r o n t   t o   B a c k ...

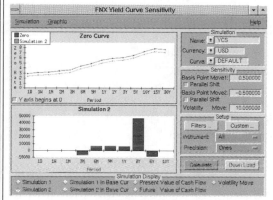

Yield Curve Sensitivity

Portfolio Risk Management is provided by the Yield Curve Sensitivity on-screen analytic, which displays how user-defined parallel and nonparallel shifts in the yield curve effect a portfolio of interest rate sensitive instruments, including bonds, money markets, swaps, and caps/collars/floors, as well as the interest rate risk embedded in foreign exchange instruments such as options and futures.

... S o l u t i o n s

The Cash Slip Processor allows back office users to consolidate and approve money transfers for outgoing as well as incoming funds. With various filtering capabilities, for Nostro, ID, Counterparty, Transaction Date, Settlement Date, and Verification Date, the user has the flexibility to select transactions that need to be processed at a certain date. The Processor also offers a sophisticated netting function that allows the user to assign an unlimited number of payments/receipts to be netted" against each other or subsequently generate a single payment or receipt order.

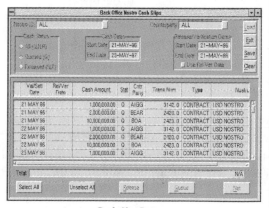

Cash Slip Processor

For more information, please contact any FNX sales office, or visit our web site at http://www.fnx.com

FNX LIMITED
Global Trading & Risk Management Systems

NEW YORK	LONDON	TOKYO	SINGAPORE	MELBOURNE
(212) 764 3691	(44) 171 600 4101	(81) 3 3432 0393	(65) 734 4284	(61) 39 273 3750

Get on the Leader Board.

Why use a putter in a sand trap?

With GAT Decision™, even the longest shots get legs. Callable corporates? Birdie. Floating rate notes? Eagle. Swaptions? Hole in one. Analyzing re-REMICs is a chip shot. Because of our extensive database of everything from treasuries to asset-backed securities, you don't need extra strokes to analyze your entire portfolio.

With Decision, you'll drive farther off the tee than you ever thought possible. Analyze portfolio risk using OAS duration and convexity. Perform scenario analysis with your viewpoint on rates, spreads and volatilities. Structure portfolios using immunization, enhanced index strategies, cash flow analysis. Windows-based analytics make it easy, so you'll produce down the stretch like a seasoned pro.

Don't risk slicing or hooking with inferior models. GAT's research is rigorous, consistent and accurate. We have an ongoing effort to examine, refine and enhance our work. Whether it's interest rate lattice generation, term structure modeling, path sampling, prepayment modeling, advanced risk measures like Key Rate Durations, or performance attribution, you'll always be pin high.

GAT's technology allows you to shape your shots to the circumstances. Integrate Decision with your own database and run it on your own hardware; it's ODBC-compliant and runs on multiple platforms. The flexible architecture of our object-oriented design ensures that you'll keep pace with the financial markets as new innovations appear. With our commitment to leading edge technology, you'll never find yourself facing an unplayable lie.

Fixed Income Books Published By Frank J. Fabozzi

Bond Portfoilo Management, Frank J. Fabozzi, 1996, $65
TOC: Introduction; Investment Objectives of Institutional Investors; Bonds; Mortgage-Backed Securities and Asset-Backed Securities; Interest Rate Derivative Instruments; General Principles of Fixed Income Valuation; Valuation Methodologies; Valuation of Derivative Instruments; Tax Considerations; Total Return Framework; Measuring Interest Rate Risk; Historical Return Performance and Bond Indexes; Active Strategies; Structured Portfolio Strategies; Use of Derivatives in Portfolio Strategies; International Bond Portfolio Strategies; Measuring and Evaluating Performance

Valuation of Fixed Income Securities and Derivatives, Frank J. Fabozzi, 1995, $50
TOC: Fundamental Valuation Principles; Spot Rates and Their Role In Valuation; Forward Rates and Term Structure Theories; Measuring Price Sensitivity to Interest Rate Changes; Overview of the Valuation of Bonds With Embedded Options; Binomial Method; Monte Carlo Method; Valuation of Inverse Floaters; Valuation of Convertible Securities; Valuation of Interest Rate Future Contracts; Valuation of Interest Rate Options; Valuation of Interest Rate Swaps.

Measuring and Controlling Interest Rate Risk, Frank J. Fabozzi, 1996, $55
TOC:Overview of Measurement and Control of Interest Rate Risk; Valuation; Measuring Level Risk: Duration and Convexity; Measuring Yield Curve Risk; Probability Distributions and Their Properties; Measuring and Forecasting Yield Volatility from Historical Data; Correlation Analysis and Regression Analysis; Futures; Swaps; Exchange-Traded Options; OTC Options and Related Products; Controlling Interest Rate Risk with Derivatives; Controlling Interest Rate Risk in an MBS Derivative Portfolio.

Corporate Bonds: Structures & Analysis, Richard S. Wilson and Frank J. Fabozzi, 1996, $65
TOC: Overview of U.S. Corporate Bonds; Bond Indentures; Maturity; Interest Payments; Debt Retirement; Convertible Bonds; Speculative-Grade Bonds; Corporate Debt Ratings; Bond Pricing and Yield Measures; Principles of Valuing Corporate Bonds; Valuing Callable Corporate Bonds; Valuation of Putable Bonds, Structured Notes, Floaters, and Convertibles; and Managing Corporate Bond Portfolios.

Collateralized Mortgage Obligations: Structures & Analysis (2nd Ed), Frank J. Fabozzi, Chuck Ramsey, and Frank R. Ramirez, 1994, $50TOC: Introduction; Collateral for CMOs; Prepayment Conventions and Factors Affecting Prepayments; Sequential-Pay CMOs; Floater, Inverse Floater, PO, and IO Bond Classes; Planned Amortization Class Bonds; TAC Bonds, VADM Bonds, and Support Bonds; Whole-Loan CMOs; Static Cash Flow Yield Analysis; Total Return Framework; Analysis of Inverse Floaters; Accounting for CMO Investments; and Regulatory Considerations.

Asset-Backed Securities, Anand K. Bhattacharya and Frank J. Fabozzi (Eds.), 1996, $75
TOC: The Expanding Frontiers of Asset Securitization; Securitization in Europe; Credit-Card Receivables; Collateralized Automobile Loans; Manufactured Housing Securities; Analysis of Manufactured Housing-Backed Securities; Introduction to the B&C Home-Equity Loan Market; Evolution of the B&C Home-Equity Loan Securities Market; Equipment-Lease Backed Securities; SBA Loan-Backed Securities; The Securitization of Health-Care Receivables; The Commercial Property Market and Underwriting Criteria for Commercial Mortgages; CMBS Structures and Relative Value Analysis; Investing in Interest-Only Commercial Mortgage Backed Securities; Credit Enhancement in ABS Structures; Early Amortization Triggers; Home-Equity Loan Floaters; Dynamics of Cleanup Calls in ABS; ABS B-Pieces; Prepayment Nomenclature in the ABS Market; Prepayments on ABSs; Z-Spreads; Introduction to ABS Accounting

CMO Portfolio Management, Fabozzi (Ed.), 1994, $50
TOC: Overview; The Challenges of CMO Portfolio Management; CMO Collateral Analysis; CMO Structure Analysis; New Challenges in MBS Prepayment Simulation: Issues and Methods; Valuation of CMOs; Advanced Techniques for the Valuation of CMOs; Forward Rates and CMO Portfolio Management; Valuation of PAC Bonds without Complex Models; A Portfolio Manager's Perspective of Inverse and Inverse IOs; Investment Opportunities in Mortgage Residuals; Total Return Analysis in CMO Portfolio Management; Market Neutral trading Strategies; Rule-Based Analysis of CMO Securities and Its Application; and Yield Curve Risk of CMO Bonds.

The Handbook of Commercial Mortgage-Backed Securities, Frank J. Fabozzi and David P. Jacob (Eds.), 1996, $95 TOC: A Property Market Framework for Bond Investors; The Commercial Mortgage Market; Commercial Mortgage Prepayments; The Commercial Mortgage-Backed Securities Market; The Role of the Servicer; Structural Considerations Impacting CMBS; The Effects of Prepayment Restrictions on the Bond Structures of CMBS; An Investor's Perspective on Commercial Mortgage-Backed Coupon Strips; How CMBS Structuring Impacts the Performance of the Bond Classes; Rating of Commercial Mortgage-Backed Securities; Defaults on Commercial Mortgages; Assessing Credit Risk of CMBS; A Framework for Risk and Relative Value Analysis of CMBS: Theory; A Framework for Risk and Relative Value Analysis of CMBS: Practice; Investing in Subordinate CMBS Bonds; High Yield CMBS; An Option-Based Approach to Valuing Default and Prepayment Risk in CMBS; Performing Financial Due Diligence Associated with Commercial Mortgage Securitizations; Legal Perspectives on Disclosure Issues for CMBS Investors; Evolving Generally Accepted Accounting Principles for Issuers of and Investors in CMBS; Federal Income Taxation of REMICs and CMBS

Valuation of Interest-Sensitive Financial Instruments, David F. Babbel and Craig B. Merrill, 1996, $55 TOC: Spot Interest Rates, Forward Interest Rates, Short Rates, and Yield-to-Maturity; An Introduction to Valuation of Fixed-Interest-Sensitive Cash Flows; Discrete-Time One-Factor Models; Continuous-Time One-Factor Models; Solution Approaches to Single-Factor Models; Multi-Factor Continuous-Time Models; Multi-Factor Discrete-Time Models; Simulation Approaches.

Dictionary of Financial Risk Management, Gary L. Gastineau and Mark P. Kritzman, 1996, $45 Risk management terminology comes by many markets – cash, forwards/futures, swaps, options – and from many disciplines – economics, probability and statistics, tax and financial accounting, and the law. The vocabulary of the risk manager continues to expand with the creation of new products and new concepts. All these words and phrases are carefully defined and illustrated in this comprehensive dictionary.

BOOK ORDER FORM

Name: _____

Company: _____

Address: _____

City: _____ State: _____ Zip: _____

Phone: _____ FAX: _____

Books Published by Frank J. Fabozzi:

Book	Price:	Quantity:	Sub-Total:
Bond Portfolio Management Fabozzi, 1996	$65		
Valuation of Fixed Income Securities and Derivatives Fabozzi, 1995	$50		
Measuring and Controlling Interest Rate Risk Fabozzi, 1996	$55		
Corporate Bonds: Structures & Analysis Wilson and Fabozzi, 1996	$65		
Collateralized Mortgage Obligations: Structures & Analysis Fabozzi, Ramsey, and Ramirez, 1994 2nd Ed.	$50		
Asset-Backed Securities Bhattacharya and Fabozzi (Eds.), 1996	$75		
The Handbook of Commercial Mortgage-Backed Securities Fabozzi and Jacob (Eds), 1996	$95		
Valuation of Interest-Sensitive Financial Instruments Babbel and Merrill, 1996	$55		
Dictionary of Financial Risk Management Gastineau and Kritzman, 1996	$45		
CMO Portfolio Management Fabozzi (Ed.), 1994	$50		

Books Distributed by Frank J. Fabozzi:

Book	Price:	Quantity:	Sub-Total:
Fixed Income Mathematics Fabozzi, (Irwin, 1996) 3rd Ed.	$60		
The Handbook of Mortgage-Backed Securities Fabozzi (Ed.), (Irwin, 1995) 4th Ed.	$85		
The Handbook of Fixed Income Securities Fabozzi and Fabozzi (Eds.), (Irwin, 1994) 4th Ed.	$90		
Advanced Fixed Income Portfolio Management Fabozzi and Fong, (Probus, 1994)	$65		
Active Total Return Management of Fixed Income Portfolios Hattatreya and Fabozzi, (Irwin, 1995)	$65		
Municipal Bond Portfolio Management Fabozzi, Fabozzi, and Feldstein, (Irwin, 1994)	$80		
Handbook of Fixed Income Options Fabozzi, (Probus, 1995) Rev. Ed.	$65		
Handbook of Asset/Liability Management Fabozzi and Konishi (Eds.), (Irwin, 1996) Rev. Ed	$75		

SHIPPING: ($4.00 for first book, $1.00 each additional)*

*International or bulk orders please call for shipping estimate (215) 598-8930

TOTAL: [_____]

Make check payable to Frank J. Fabozzi

Mail order form along with check to:
Frank J. Fabozzi
858 Tower View Circle
New Hope, PA 18938

Forthcoming Books From Frank J. Fabozzi Associates:
Call for information

Fabozzi, *Fixed Income Securities*
Fabozzi (Ed.), *Securities Lending and Repurchase Agreements*
Fabozzi/Ramsey/Ramirez/Marz (Eds.), *Investing In Nonagency Mortgage-Backed Securities*
Fabozzi, *Advances in Fixed Income Valuation Modeling and Risk Control*
Fabozzi/Wickard, *Credit Union Investment Management*

TREPP RISK MANAGEMENT, INC.

Specialists in Risk Management

A Member of THE TREPP GROUP
Focused on Providing

- Asset/Liability Management Services
- Risk Management Consulting
- Derivatives Valuation and Risk Assessment
- Software Selection and Implementation
- Data Warehouse Implementation Assistance

NEW YORK • BOSTON • DENVER

477 Madison Avenue - New York, NY 10022

TEL: 212.754.1010   FAX: 212.832.6738   INTERNET: www.trepp.com

TREPP RISK MANAGEMENT, INC.
a Member of The Trepp Group

DERIVATIVE VALUATION AND MODEL VALIDATION

TREPP PROVIDES AN INDEPENDENT SOURCE OF FAIR VALUE ESTIMATES
FOR A WIDE RANGE OF COMPLEX INVESTMENTS AND OFF-BALANCE
SHEET DERIVATIVES. OUR ANALYSIS SUPPORTS INTERNAL RISK
MANAGEMENT EVALUATIONS, PUBLISHED FINANCIAL STATEMENTS,
OR INTERNAL AUDIT REVIEW OF VALUATIONS.

UNPARALLELED EXPERTISE. We are a long standing national expert with years of experience in structured finance and derivative contracts.

STRESS TEST EVALUATIONS. Valuations can be provided for various stress test conditions as specified by each client.

RISK PARAMETERS. Trepp provides clients with risk parameters (e.g., duration, convexity, etc.) on a customized basis as selected by each organization to support its risk management activities.

CUSTOMIZED VALUATIONS. Every assignment is tailored to the specific requirements of each client, and is based on detailed instrument by instrument analysis.

COMPREHENSIVE REPORTS. Comprehensive, customized reports are provided showing fair value estimates, stress test results, and risk parameters requested by clients.

COUNTERPARTY CREDIT EXPOSURE. Reports can be prepared to your specifications that present counterparty credit exposure.

NEW YORK • BOSTON • DENVER

477 MADISON AVE. - NEW YORK, NY   212.754.1010
22 PITTSBURGH ST. - BOSTON, MA   617.856.1206

T

TREPP RISK MANAGEMENT, INC.
a Member of The Trepp Group

ASSET/LIABILITY MANAGEMENT SERVICES
TREPP CAN HELP YOU FINE TUNE YOUR ALM PRACTICES WITH COMPREHENSIVE OR NARROWLY FOCUSED ENGAGEMENTS THAT ADDRESS A WIDE RANGE OF IMPORTANT ISSUES.

SOFTWARE SELECTION. Select and implement ALM, transfer pricing, profitability reporting, data warehouse investment and derivatives software systems.

DATA EXTRACTION. Extract data from legacy systems and populate data warehouses or ALM systems.

INTEREST RATE RISK MEASUREMENT. Assess the exposure of earnings and market values to changes in economic and interest rate environments.

PERFORMANCE IMPROVEMENT STRATEGIES. Develop balance sheet strategies to increase earnings and more effectively manage risk. Strategies may include investments, loans, deposits, non-deposit funding, and derivatives.

INVESTMENT PORTFOLIO STRATEGIES. Assist in the development of investment strategies (including CMOs, MBS and structured notes) to optimize total balance sheet performance.

PREPAYMENT MODELING. Assist in measuring your historic prepayment experience and developing models to project future activity.

NON-MATURITY DEPOSIT STUDIES. Estimate the interest rate risk characteristics of savings, NOW and demand deposit accounts.

ALM AND INVESTMENT COMPLIANCE. Conduct comprehensive reviews of ALM practices for compliance with current and prospective regulatory requirements.

NEW YORK • BOSTON • DENVER

477 MADISON AVE. - NEW YORK, NY   212.754.1010
22 PITTSBURGH ST. - BOSTON, MA   617.856.1206